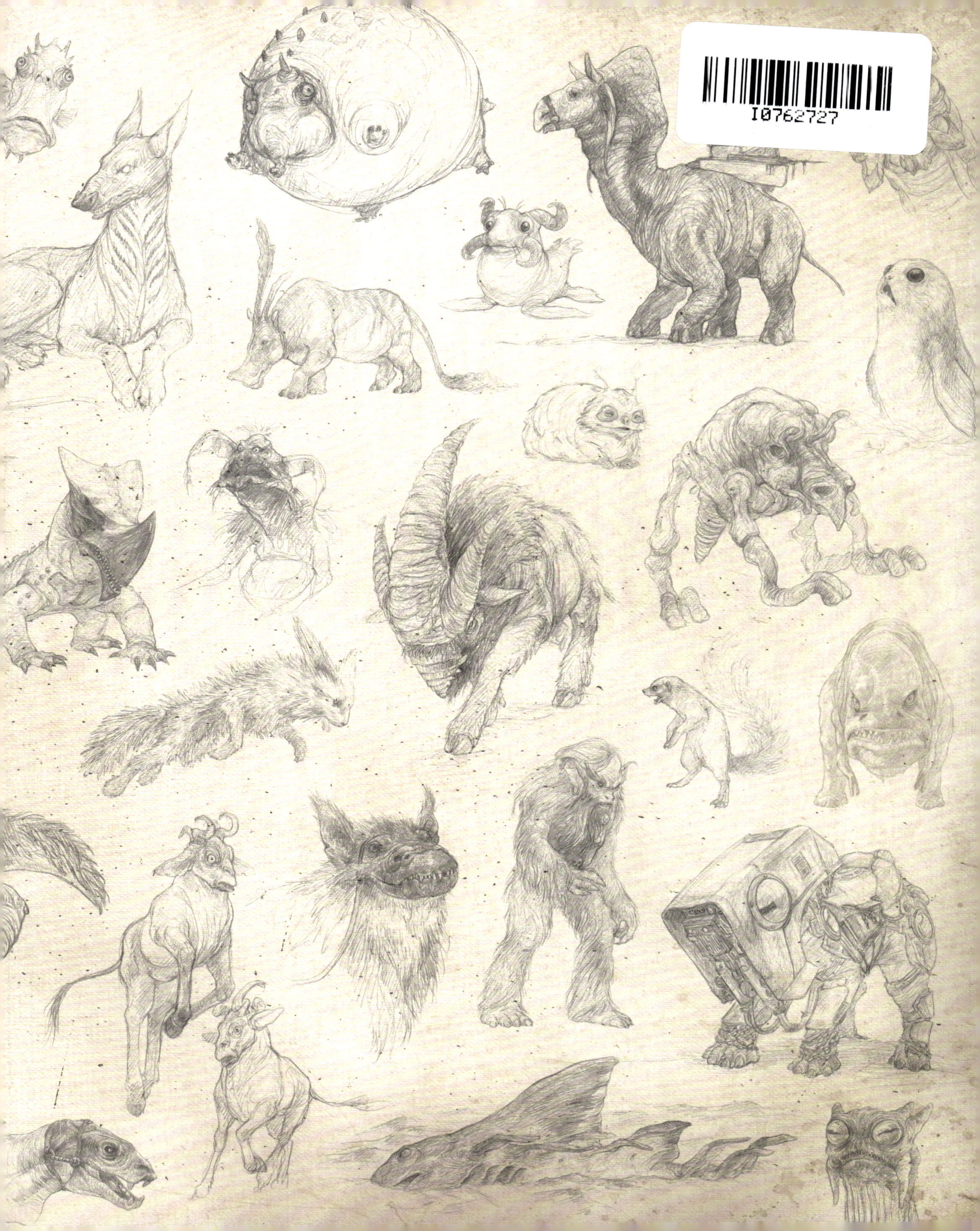

STAR WARS™
BESTIARY
VOL. I

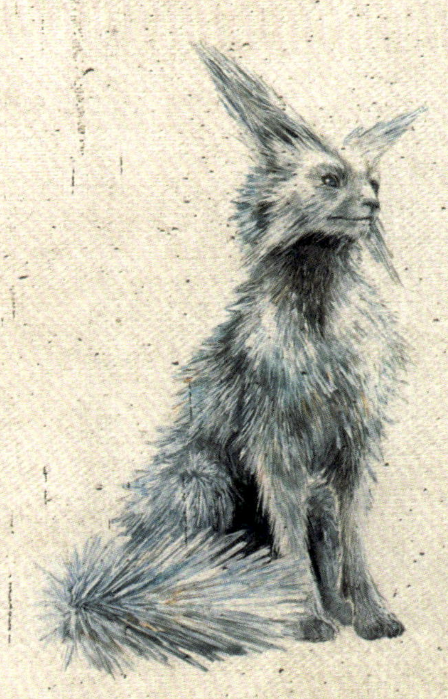

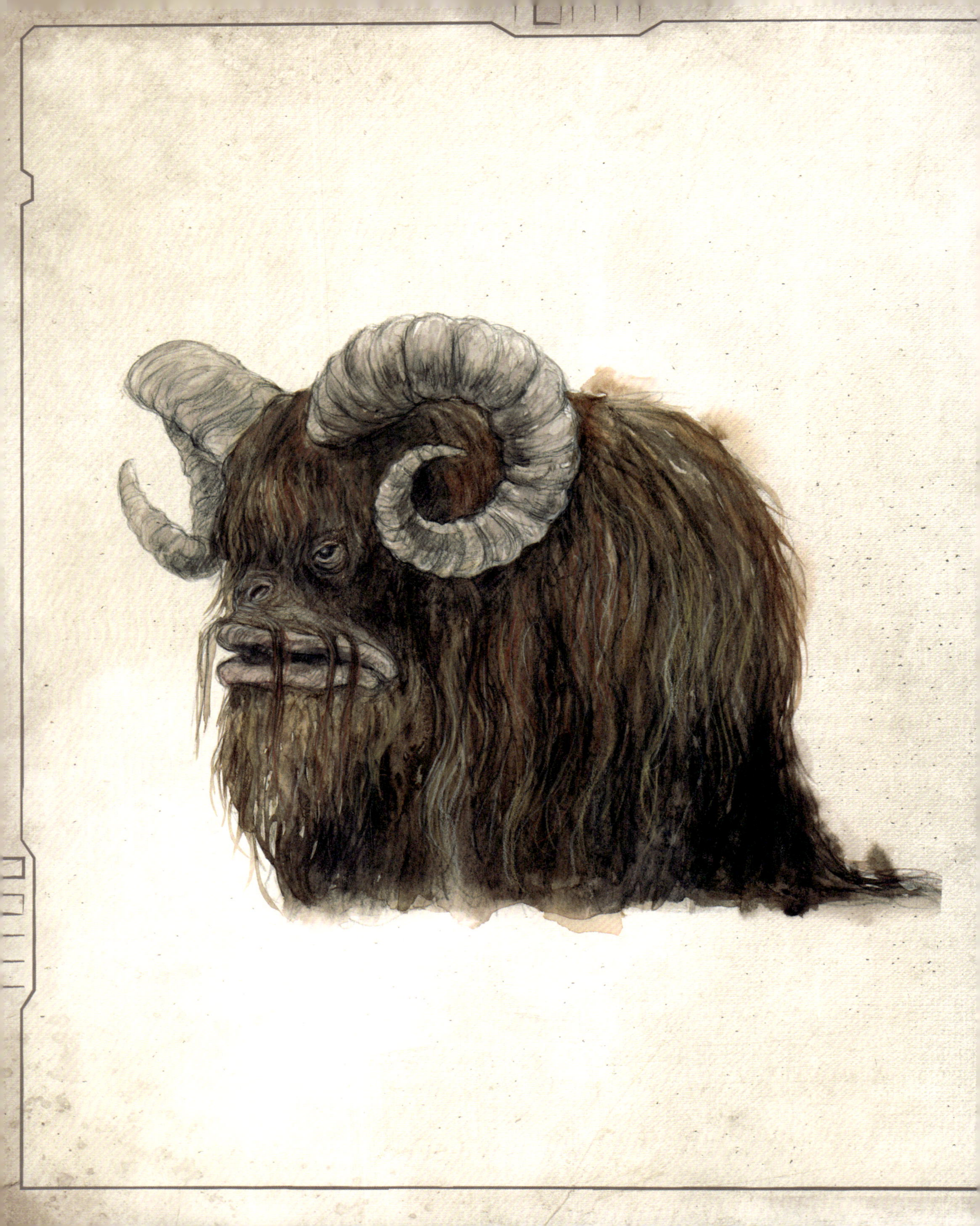

STAR WARS BESTIARY

VOL. I

Creatures of the Galaxy

Written by S.T. BENDE

Illustrations by IRIS COMPIET

SAN RAFAEL • LOS ANGELES • LONDON

CONTENTS

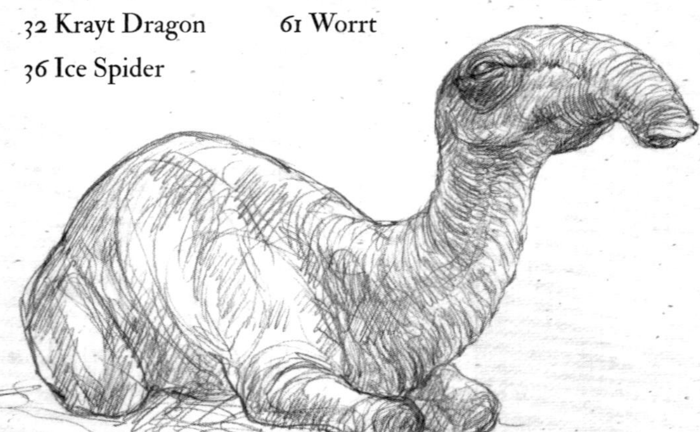

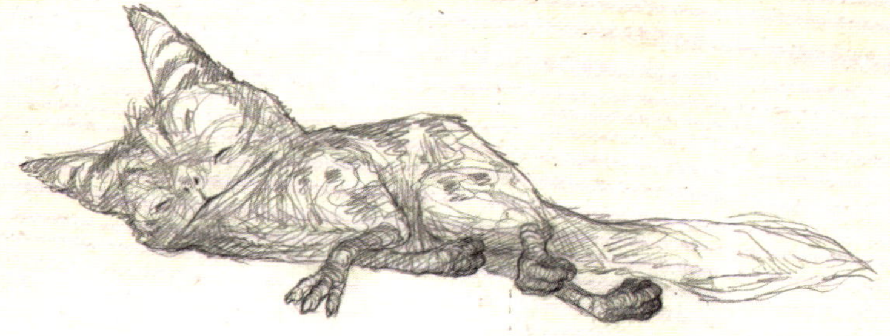

74 GRASSLAND CREATURES

92 ICE AND SNOW CREATURES

108 MOUNTAINS, ROCKY PLAINS, AND VOLCANIC CREATURES

118 URBAN CREATURES

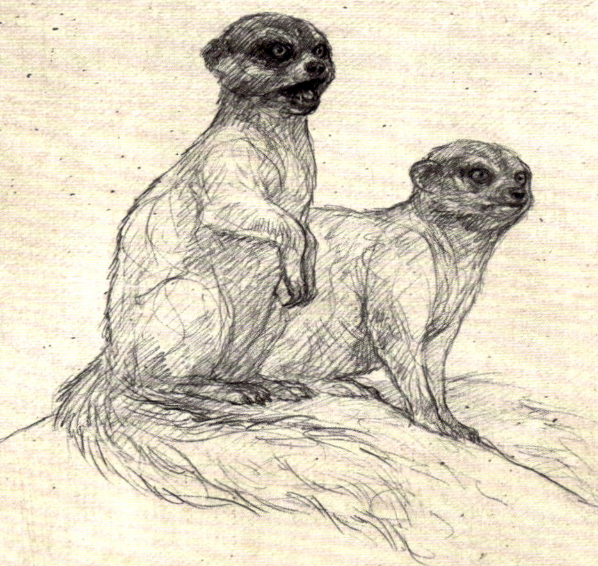

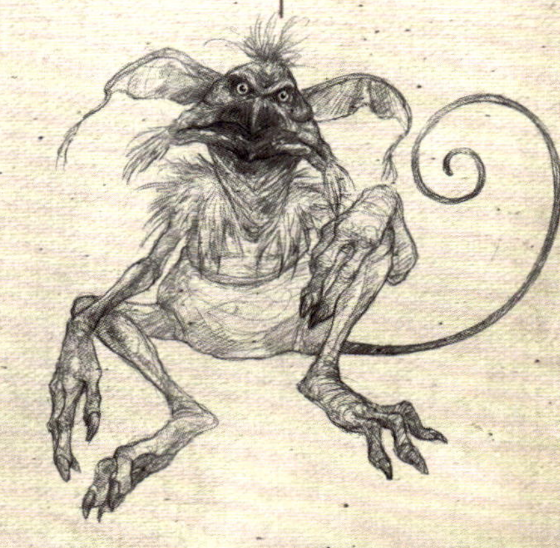

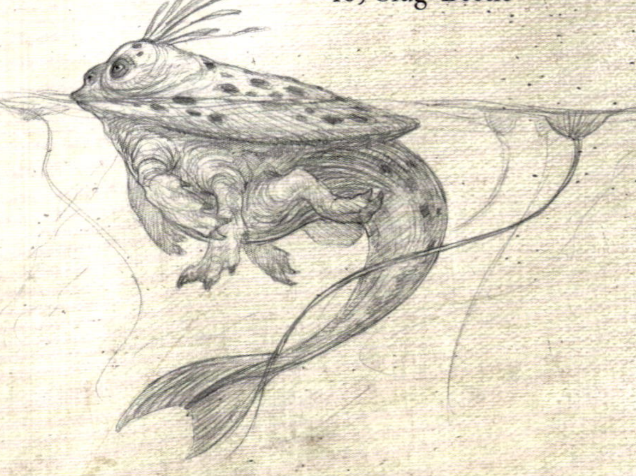

173 AIR AND SPACE ENVIRONMENTS

174 AIR CREATURES

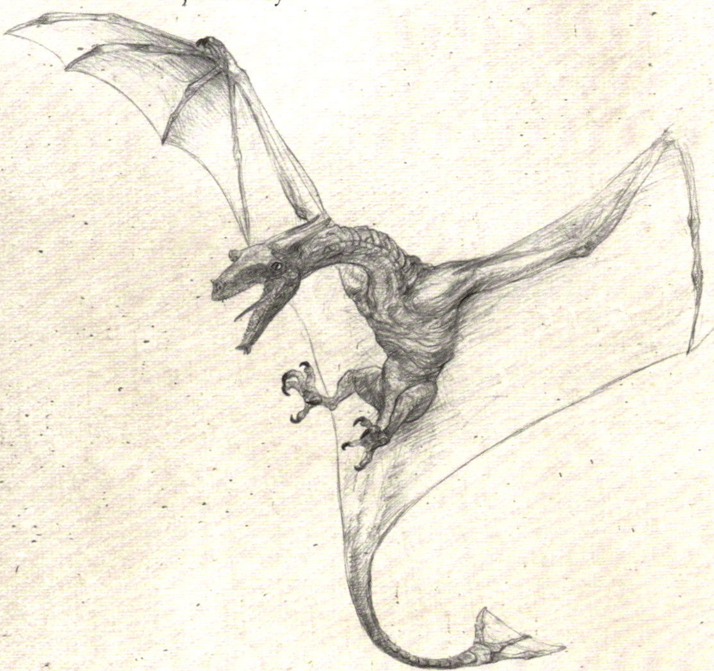

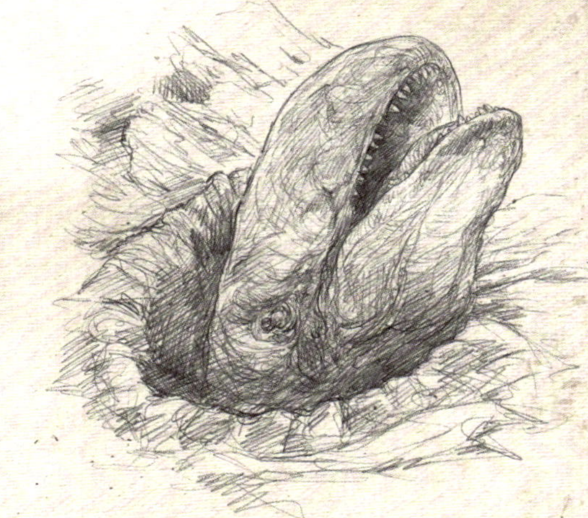

192 SPACE CREATURES

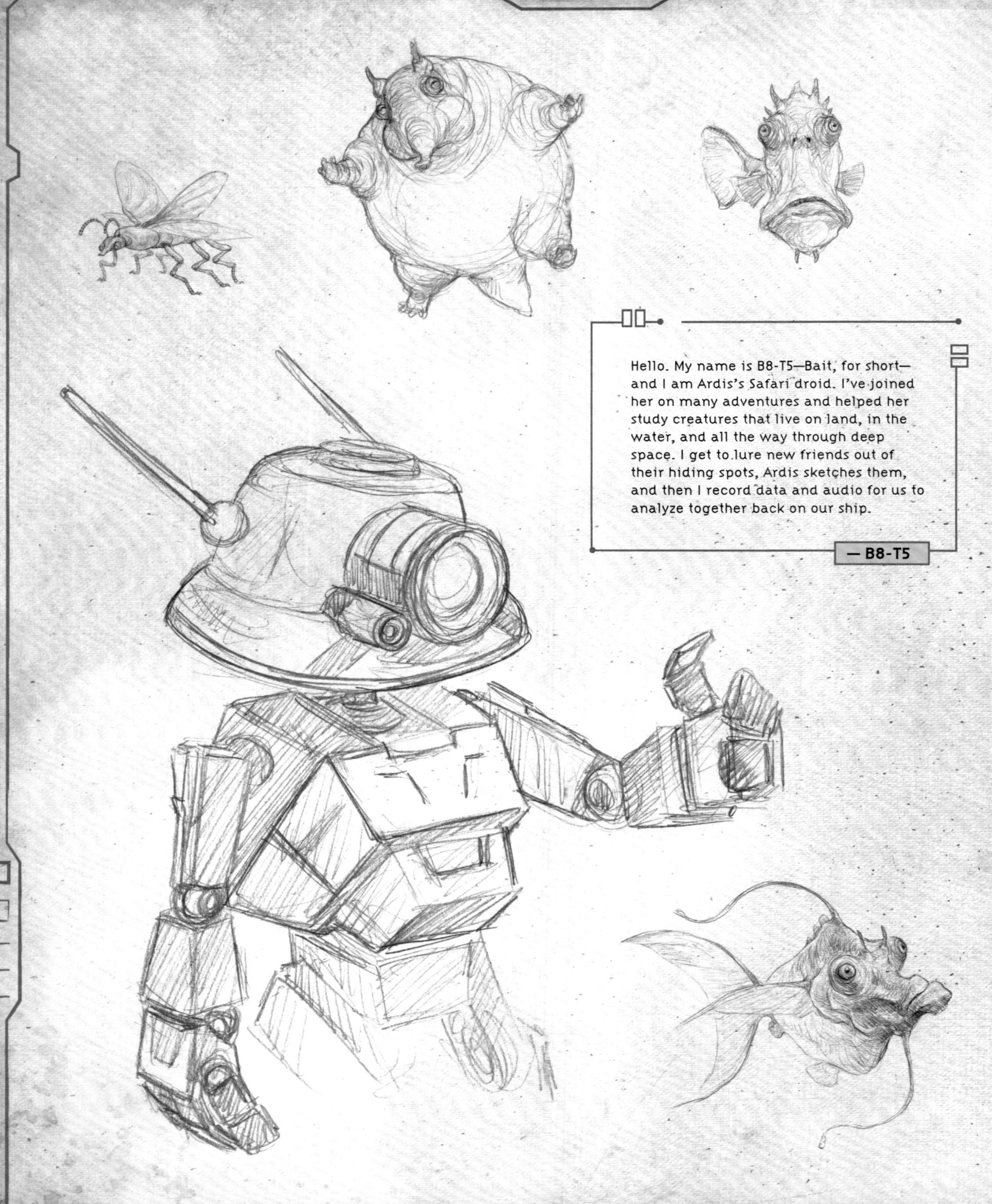
Hello. My name is B8-T5—Bait, for short—and I am Ardis's Safari droid. I've joined her on many adventures and helped her study creatures that live on land, in the water, and all the way through deep space. I get to lure new friends out of their hiding spots, Ardis sketches them, and then I record data and audio for us to analyze together back on our ship.
— B8-T5

INTRODUCTION

During the era of the High Republic, the Galactic Society of Creature Enthusiasts (GSCE) was established for the purpose of furthering our understanding of the galaxy's nonsentient beings. As we sentients expanded our trade routes and territories, the habitats, ecological systems, and migration routes of many creatures were impacted by our ever-growing footprint. Over time, it became apparent that many of these populations had dwindled to worryingly low numbers . . . and, unfortunately, that some of them might eventually disappear. By the time I joined the organization, after the defeat of the clone Emperor, a fair number of creatures had landed on the GSCE's list of Rare and Endangered Species. I sought to draw attention to their plight, working my way up the Society's ranks until I found myself in a position to effect change. These days, I study and chart the galaxy's multitude of beasts, from tooka cats to tauntauns, as the GSCE's Chief Creature Cartographer—a position borne of my passion for the natural world and my rather unique upbringing.

My love of wildlife developed at a young age. As a child, I traveled with my family across the galaxy, continuing the San Tekka clan's legacy of locating and mapping out hyperspace lanes. While my parents worked, I'd sneak off to explore whatever planet we'd landed on, searching for new-to-me creatures. I sketched my discoveries in my trusty datapad and noted any defining characteristics I managed to identify, creating a *very* rudimentary form of this accounting. When it came time for me to join the family business, my hyperspace charting career was blessedly brief. After a short stint, I followed my heart to the GCSE. I took a position cataloguing data in the Youngling Care Space Station and attended zoology classes in the evenings. After I completed my degree, I joined the Creature Husbandry Team, where I devised care and release plans for the creatures under my watch. However, I soon realized that my background in hyperspace exploration uniquely positioned me to take on a role in a very special department.

Because I'd spent so much time traveling (and mapping) the galaxy, I set my sights on joining the Creature Cartography Division, a department whose mission is to catalog creatures across the various worlds and deep space regions and then to disseminate this data for the purpose of educating galactic citizens about the natural world. In the process, my department has also interacted with local residents, enabling us to learn about the cultures, traits, and habits of the many sentient beings whose ecosystems depend on these creatures. I now lead a division of scientists who travel the galaxy charting creatures as they exist in their homeworld habitats. Of course, I've also made my own journeys alongside my trusty Safari droid, B8-T5—whom I simply call "Bait" because of his propensity to attract curious (and often predatory!) specimens.

The following pages are the culmination of our many adventures documenting the nonsentient creatures we have been fortunate enough to encounter in our travels. I hope to see still more one day, but for now, I am thrilled to share the multitude of species that have crossed my path to date. I hope these pages lead to a greater understanding of these magnificent creatures and inspire in you the same sense of awe for our galaxy—and its varied inhabitants—that I have felt since my childhood travels through hyperspace. May your appreciation of our natural world grow through better understanding the majesty of its many ecosystems, environments, and inhabitants—even the arachnids.

Ardis San Tekka

Director of Creature Cartography,
Galactic Society of Creature Enthusiasts

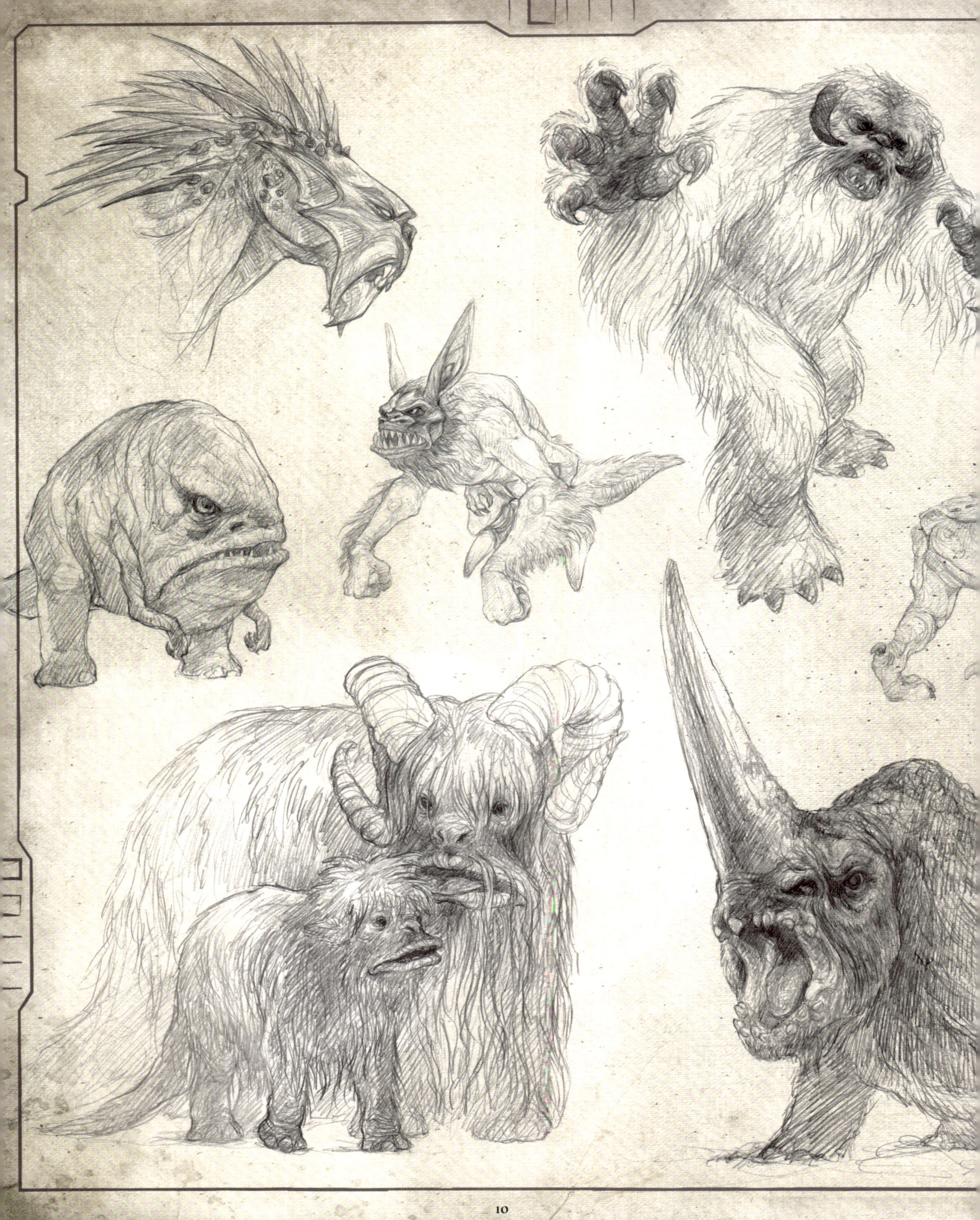

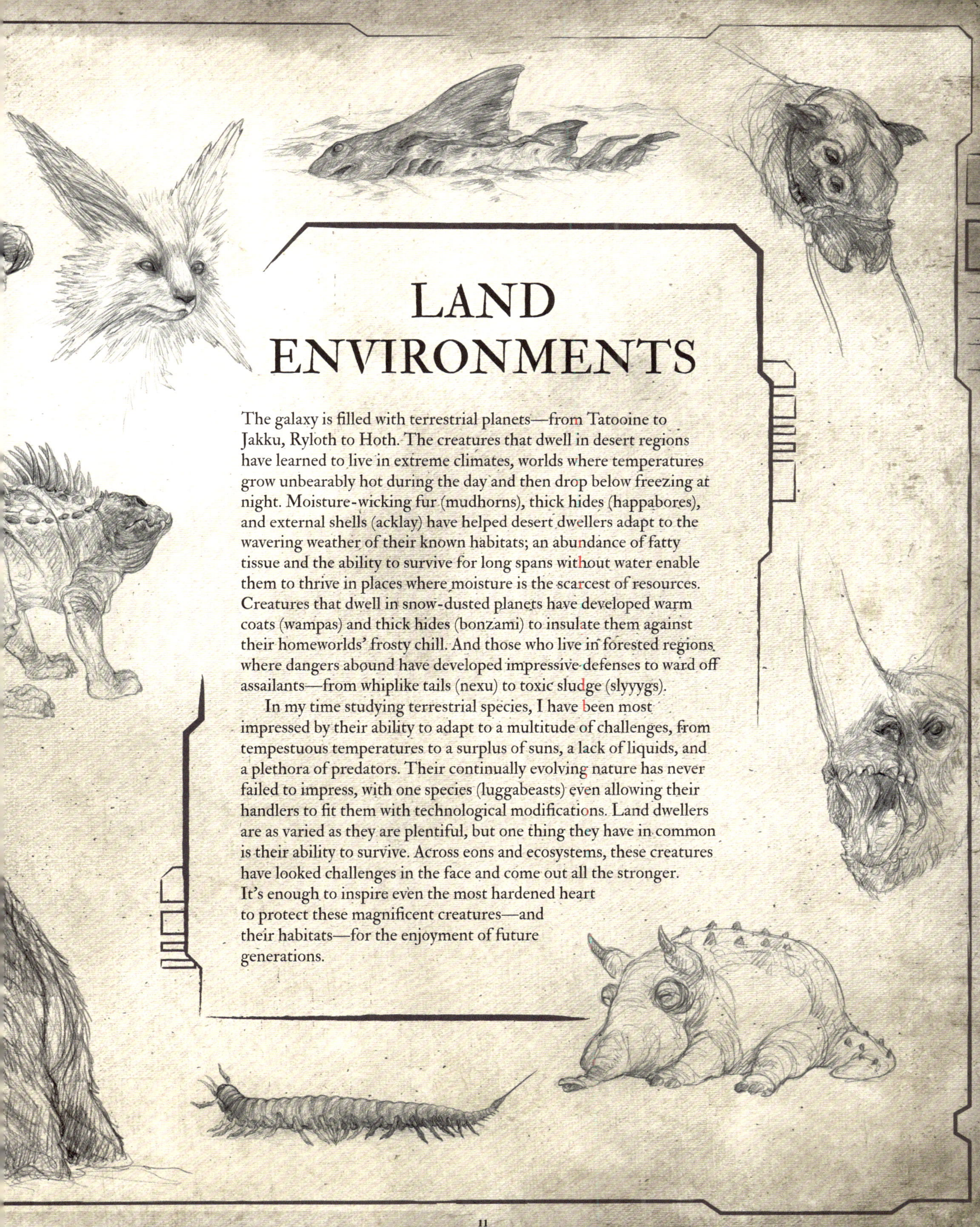

LAND ENVIRONMENTS

The galaxy is filled with terrestrial planets—from Tatooine to Jakku, Ryloth to Hoth. The creatures that dwell in desert regions have learned to live in extreme climates, worlds where temperatures grow unbearably hot during the day and then drop below freezing at night. Moisture-wicking fur (mudhorns), thick hides (happabores), and external shells (acklay) have helped desert dwellers adapt to the wavering weather of their known habitats; an abundance of fatty tissue and the ability to survive for long spans without water enable them to thrive in places where moisture is the scarcest of resources. Creatures that dwell in snow-dusted planets have developed warm coats (wampas) and thick hides (bonzami) to insulate them against their homeworlds' frosty chill. And those who live in forested regions where dangers abound have developed impressive defenses to ward off assailants—from whiplike tails (nexu) to toxic sludge (slyyygs).

In my time studying terrestrial species, I have been most impressed by their ability to adapt to a multitude of challenges, from tempestuous temperatures to a surplus of suns, a lack of liquids, and a plethora of predators. Their continually evolving nature has never failed to impress, with one species (luggabeasts) even allowing their handlers to fit them with technological modifications. Land dwellers are as varied as they are plentiful, but one thing they have in common is their ability to survive. Across eons and ecosystems, these creatures have looked challenges in the face and come out all the stronger. It's enough to inspire even the most hardened heart to protect these magnificent creatures—and their habitats—for the enjoyment of future generations.

DESERT CREATURES

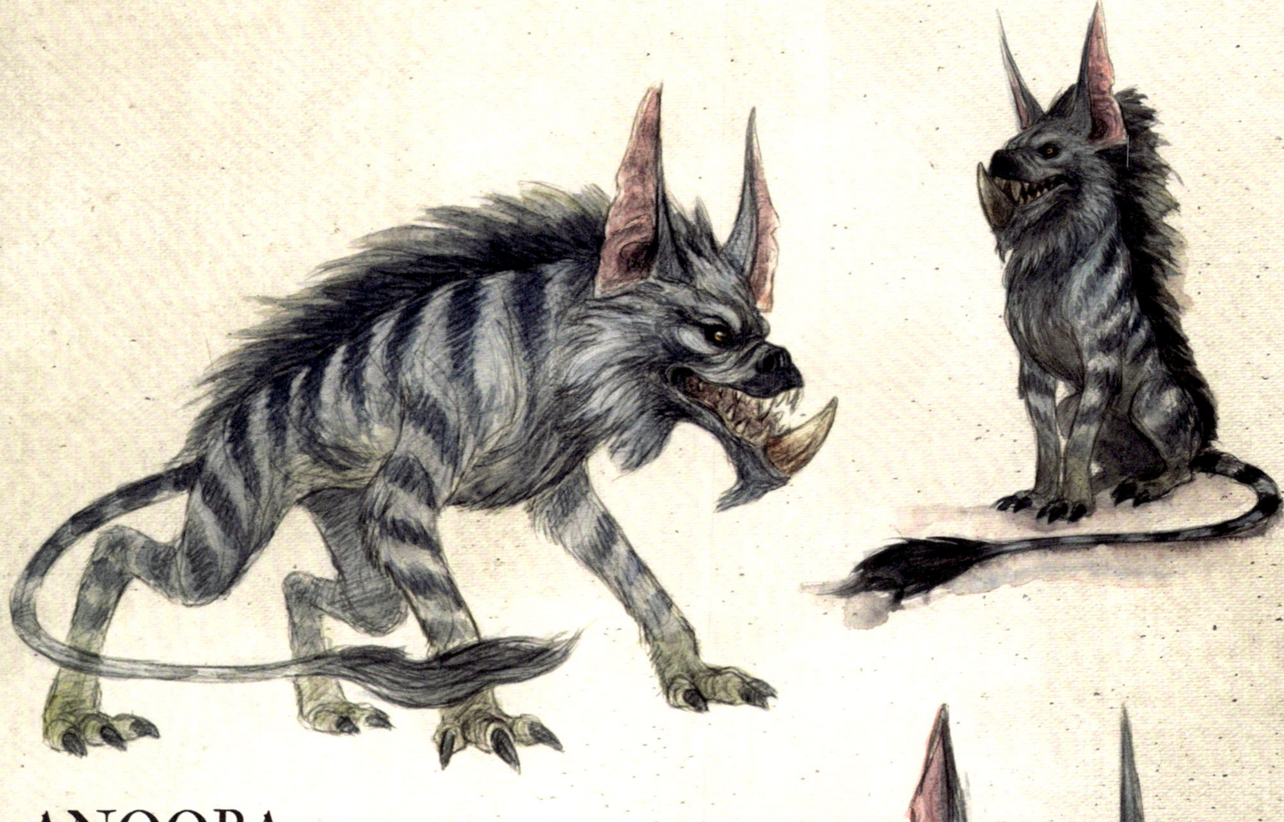

ANOOBA

With horn-shaped ears and sharp, pointed claws, these carnivorous, caninelike anoobas spark fear across their homeworld. Traveling in packs of ten to twelve, they corner their prey and then stab the creature with their massive chin tusks before shredding it with their fangs and claws. Smaller anoobas lack a chin tusk, but they can be every bit as vicious as their larger counterparts. The creatures act as both predators and scavengers, often working as a pack to take down larger species such as rontos or eopies.

Measuring 2.7 meters in length, a fully grown anooba boasts thick, furry patches along its spine, giving the creature the appearance of additional height. Its strong jaw and ferocious teeth enable it to easily crush bones, and a long tail aids in keeping its balance during its fierce sprints while chasing down prey.

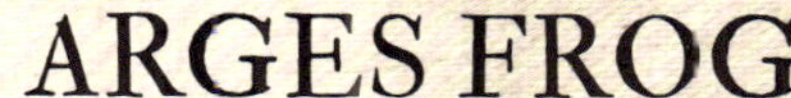

ARGES FROG

The one-eyed, high-leaping arges frog makes its home in the deserts and forests of several planets, although Arges is believed to be its planet of origin. Whether by accident or by design, the frogs managed to make their way across the galaxy and eventually turned up on Nevarro, Ossus, and Arvala-7. Nonpoisonous and highly populous, the frogs have been known to quickly overtake any pond or waterway. Their slippery skin and camouflage color patterns make them difficult to capture. Once in hand, however, their gentle nature makes them an amenable playmate for a curious child. The creatures come in a variety of colors, from a muddied yellow-green to a brilliant blue.

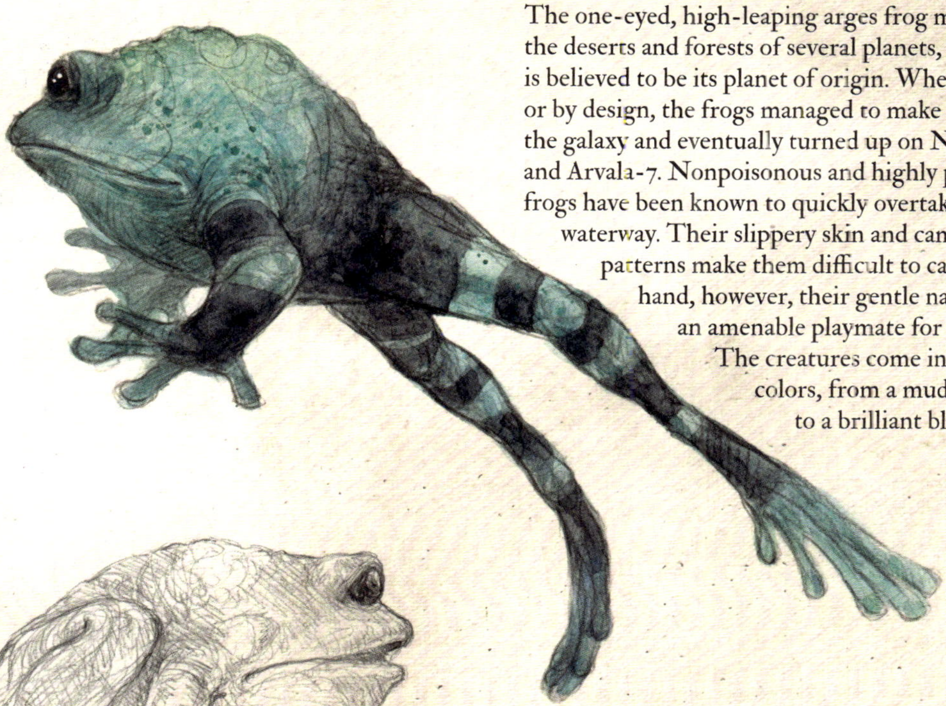

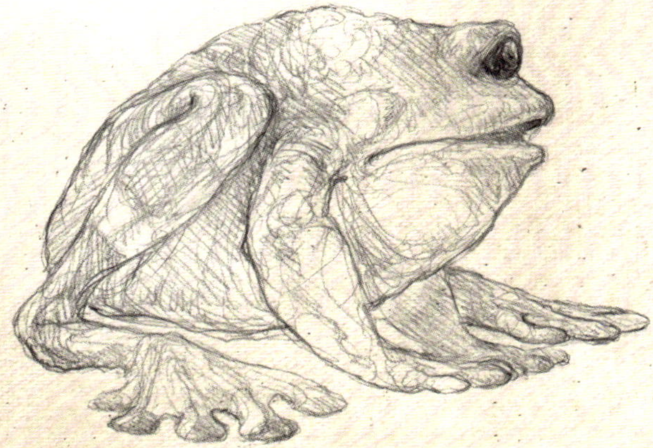

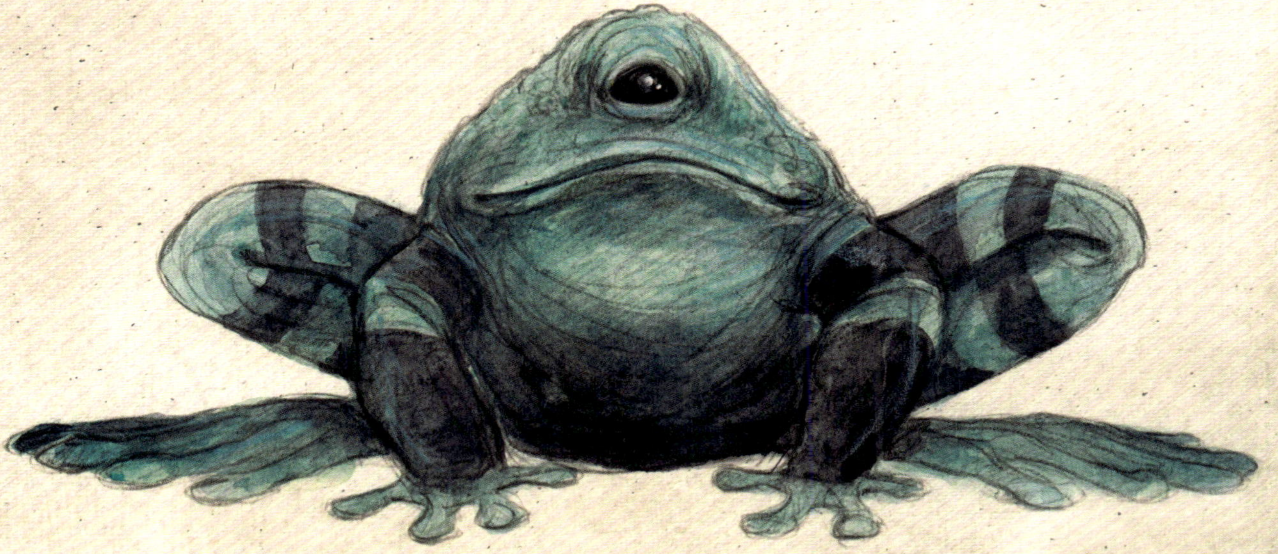

BANTHA

Weighing an astounding four thousand kilograms and measuring two-and-a-half meters in height, Tatooine's beloved banthas roam the desert in herds. Spiraled horns sprout from both male and female skulls at the rate of one knob per year, marking the creatures' age in clearly measurable nodules. These segments offer a glimpse into a bantha's well-being: Thicker segments designate years in which food was plentiful, and thinner, cracked sections point to famine or drought. The males' segments are wider than their female counterparts; additionally, males' horns complete two spirals over the course of a lifetime, whereas females' horns complete only one. Dark, shaggy fur protects the bantha from Tatooine's twin suns, and their long tail is useful in swatting unwanted pests. The creatures' four-toed feet spread wide across the sand, dispersing heat across their rough, padded surfaces.

Banthas are omnivorous mammals. Domesticated specimens feed on vegetation found in the wild, as well as scraps doled out by their handlers. Strong, dexterous tongues contain olfactory glands for detecting scents and can also carry heavy objects and communicate with the herd. In addition to the common bantha, two other species are known to exist: the diminutive dwarf bantha, which dwells in the canyons and cliffs of Tatooine's outermost deserts, and the less furry dune bantha, which is capable of surviving in the heat (and severe drought!) of the equatorial zone. Although they are native to Tatooine, banthas are utilized across the galaxy for labor, food, and goods. In addition to serving as benign beasts of burden, they produce a distinctly blue milk that can be consumed directly or used as an ingredient in foods like butter, yogurt, or ice cream. Bantha meat can be cooked into burgers or steaks, or dried and cut into an easily transportable jerky. Bantha dung can be burned as fuel, and tanned bantha hides are used to create clothing and furniture.

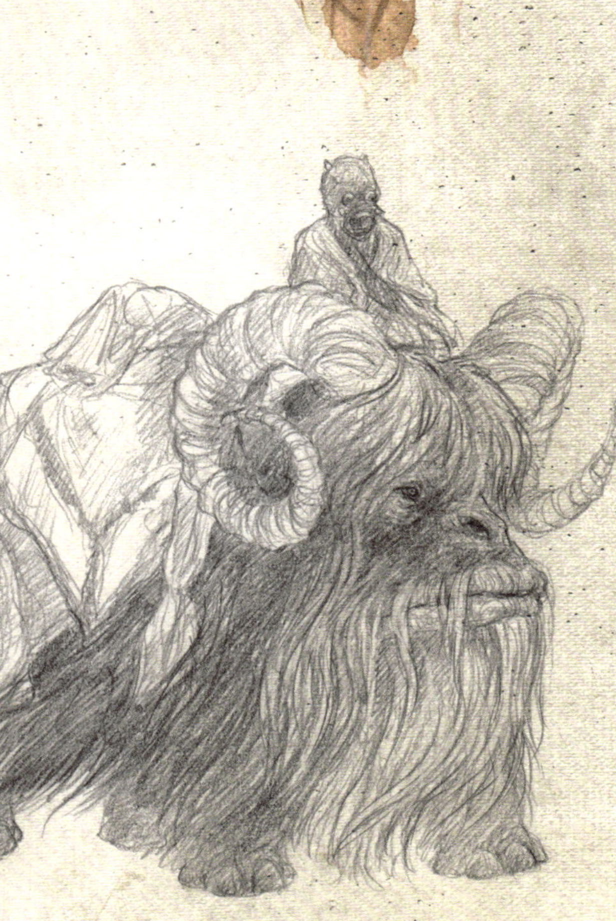

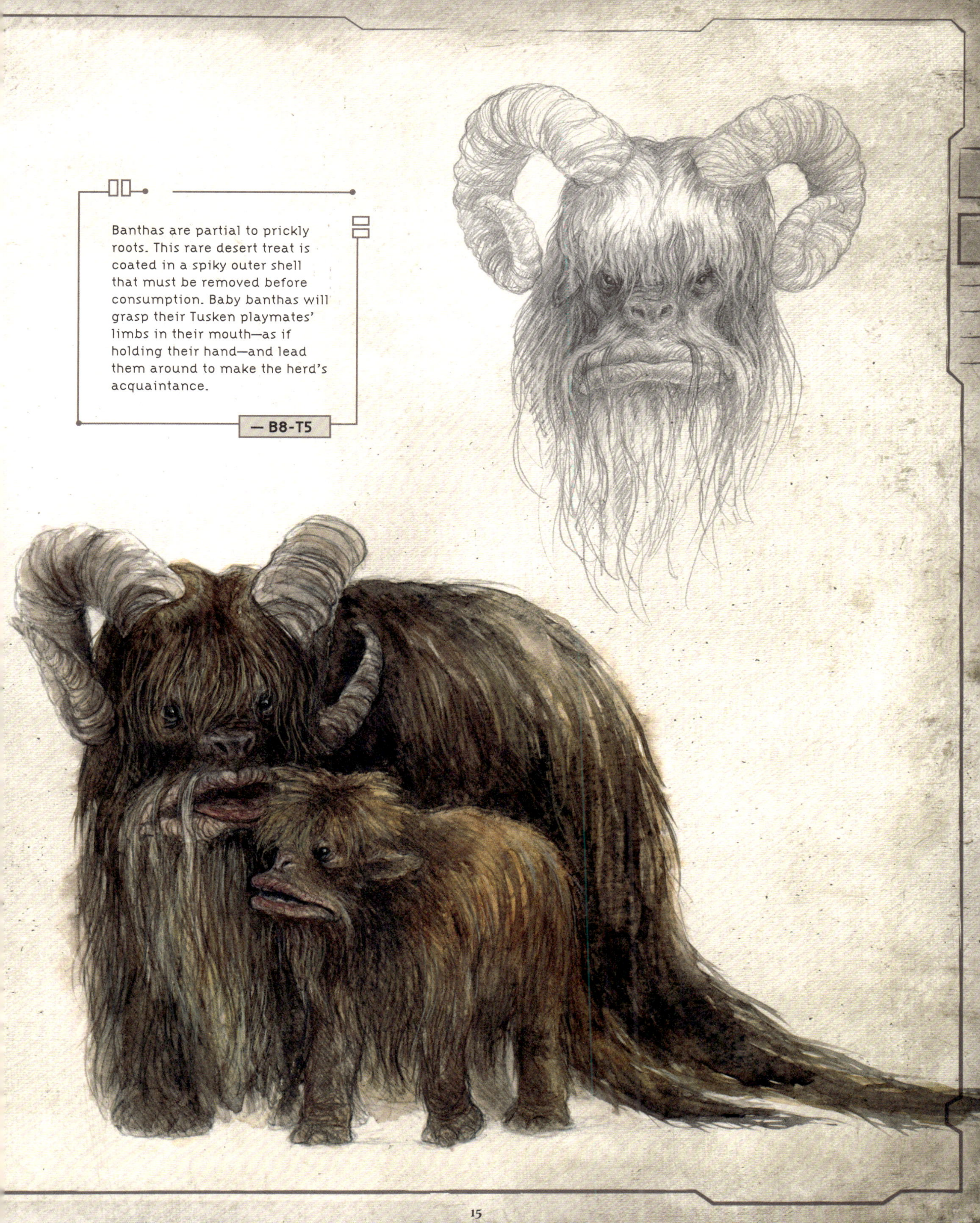

Banthas are partial to prickly roots. This rare desert treat is coated in a spiky outer shell that must be removed before consumption. Baby banthas will grasp their Tusken playmates' limbs in their mouth—as if holding their hand—and lead them around to make the herd's acquaintance.

— B8-T5

Banthas are highly intelligent, relying on a well-established social structure to manage herds of up to twenty-five members. Their matriarchal society defers power to the oldest, strongest female, who trains her watchful eyes on the herd to oversee squabbles and protect against predators, particularly anoobas and krayt dragons. When a matriarch ages out of her role, she passes her duties to the most capable candidate. Herds that grow too large split themselves in two, with the second-strongest aging female taking control of the new group. When a member dies, the herd gathers its bones in a graveyard of sorts, clinging to the remains in a seemingly ritualistic display.

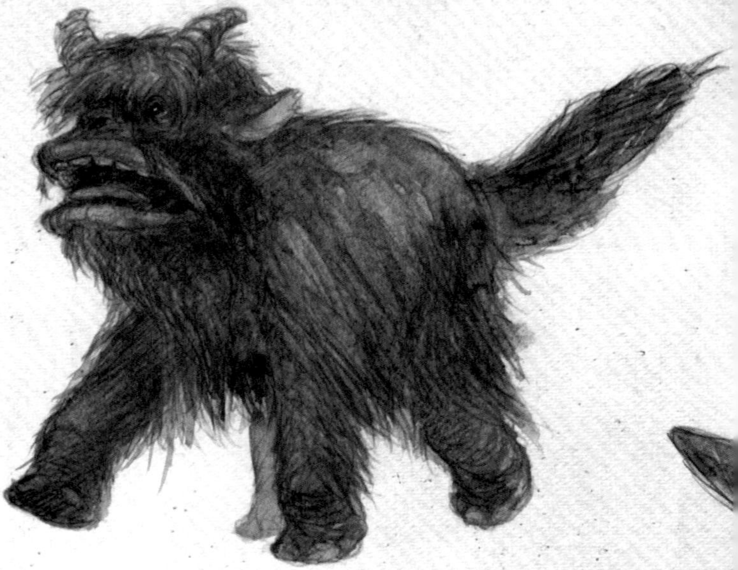

Often accompanied by Tuskens, whose domestication of the gentle creatures has resulted in a sweetly symbiotic relationship, banthas are capable of hauling heavy loads and a multitude of passengers. Tuskens revere their bantha brethren; respect for the creatures serves as a cornerstone of the Tuskens' cultural identity. At the age of seven, a Tusken youth is matched with a similarly gendered bantha calf in a ceremony that seals the pair for life. When the bantha reaches the age of maturity, it accompanies its Tusken counterpart into the desert, where the duo jointly undertakes initiation rites. When Tuskens marry, their banthas likewise become mates, forging bonds across the species that cannot be broken. With banthas living between eighty and one hundred years, pairs have been known to live parallel lives. The death of its bonded Tusken can cause a bantha to fall into a deep depression or even die soon afterward. When a member of the herd dies, Tuskens collect the creature's bones and repurpose them as tools and tent supports. Thus, the two species maintain their relationship even after death.

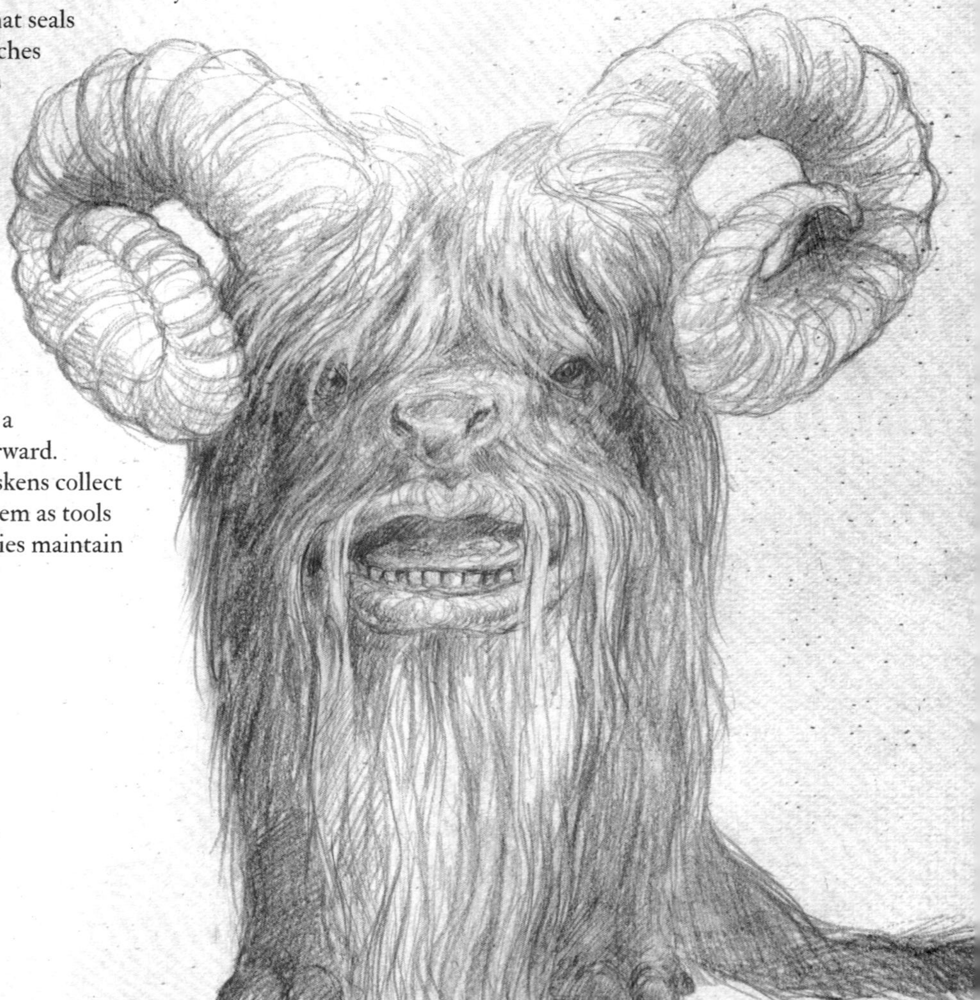

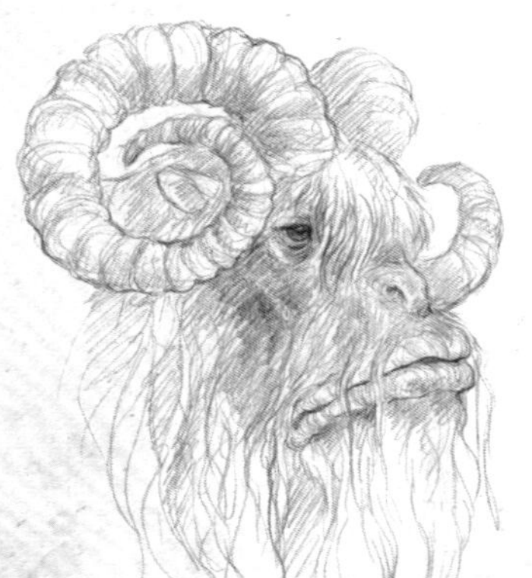

BLURRG

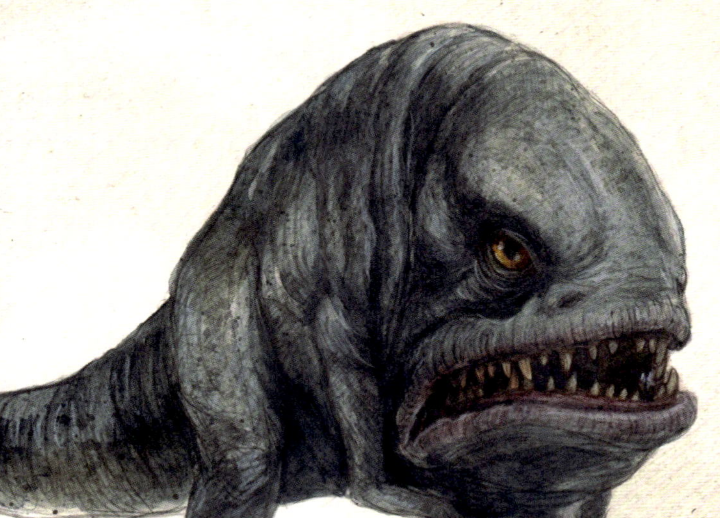

These bipedal reptilian beasts stand up to two meters tall and are four meters long, which includes the creature's muscular tail that it uses for both defense and balance. Blurrgs are native to Arvala-7, Endor, and Ryloth, where domesticated specimens are often employed as mounts. Large mouths and sharp teeth enable them to consume a varied diet, consisting of grass, weeds, small creatures, and even members of their own species. To procure vegetation, blurrgs use their short, clawed arms to scrape edible flora from rocks and dirt. Their green, gray, or black-and-brown coloring helps them blend into their environment, although some blurrgs have brighter color patterns—occasionally, specimens reveal orange or white markings. Blurrgs are capable of running at speeds that exceed seventy-five kilometers per hour, and their strong musculature has made them a valuable beast of burden; they are used for agricultural purposes and also serve as mounts in battle. Blurrgs possess a low level of intelligence and tend to grow hostile when agitated. After mating, females have been known to consume their partners.

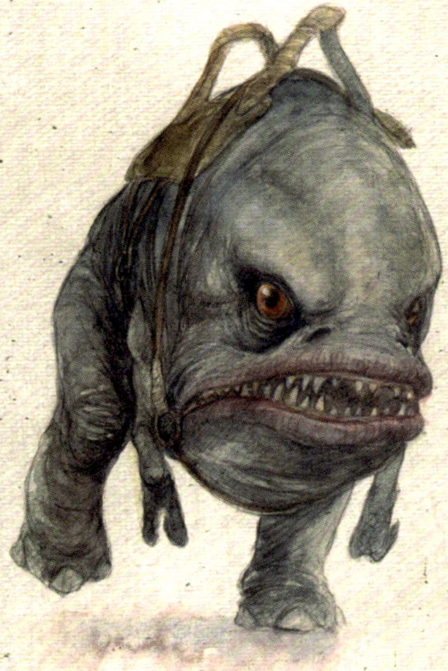

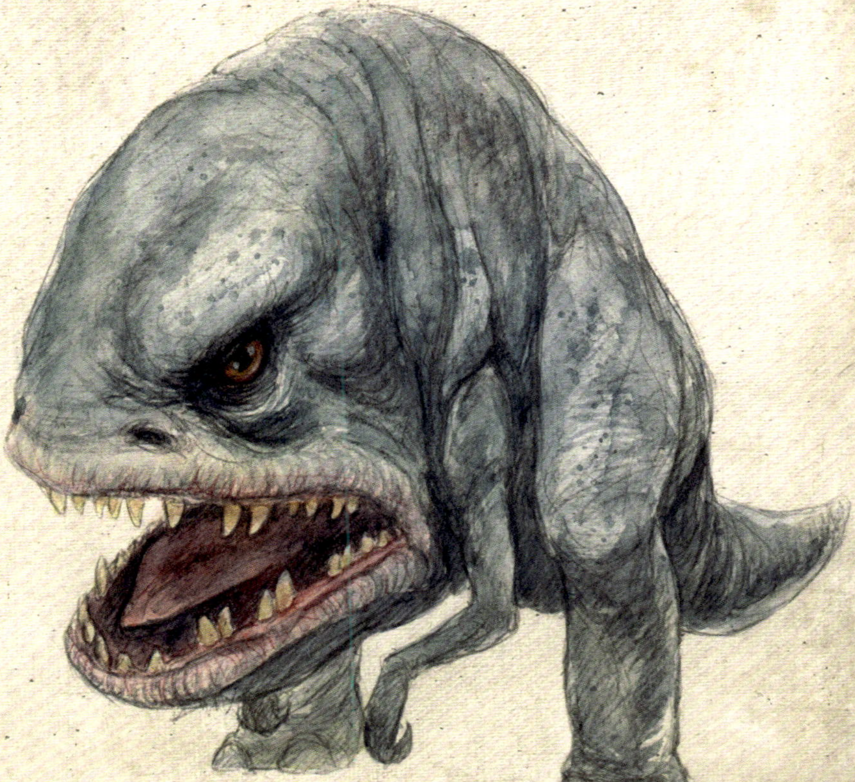

DEWBACK

The sturdy, reptilian dewback is named for its habit of licking the dew from the backs of fellow herd members. These creatures are known for their thick hides, which preserve bodily fluids while simultaneously offering protection against Tatooine's blazing suns. Cold-blooded dewbacks huddle together for warmth when temperatures drop. They generally move slowly but can occasionally run at speeds of up to fifty kilometers per hour across short distances.

Dewbacks are among the galaxy's prized "big game" animals, and their trophies are proudly displayed at notable hunting lodges. These omnivores dine on small prey, along with tubers, sage, and other desert vegetation. They communicate using a series of low grunts that are similar to the call of a bantha.

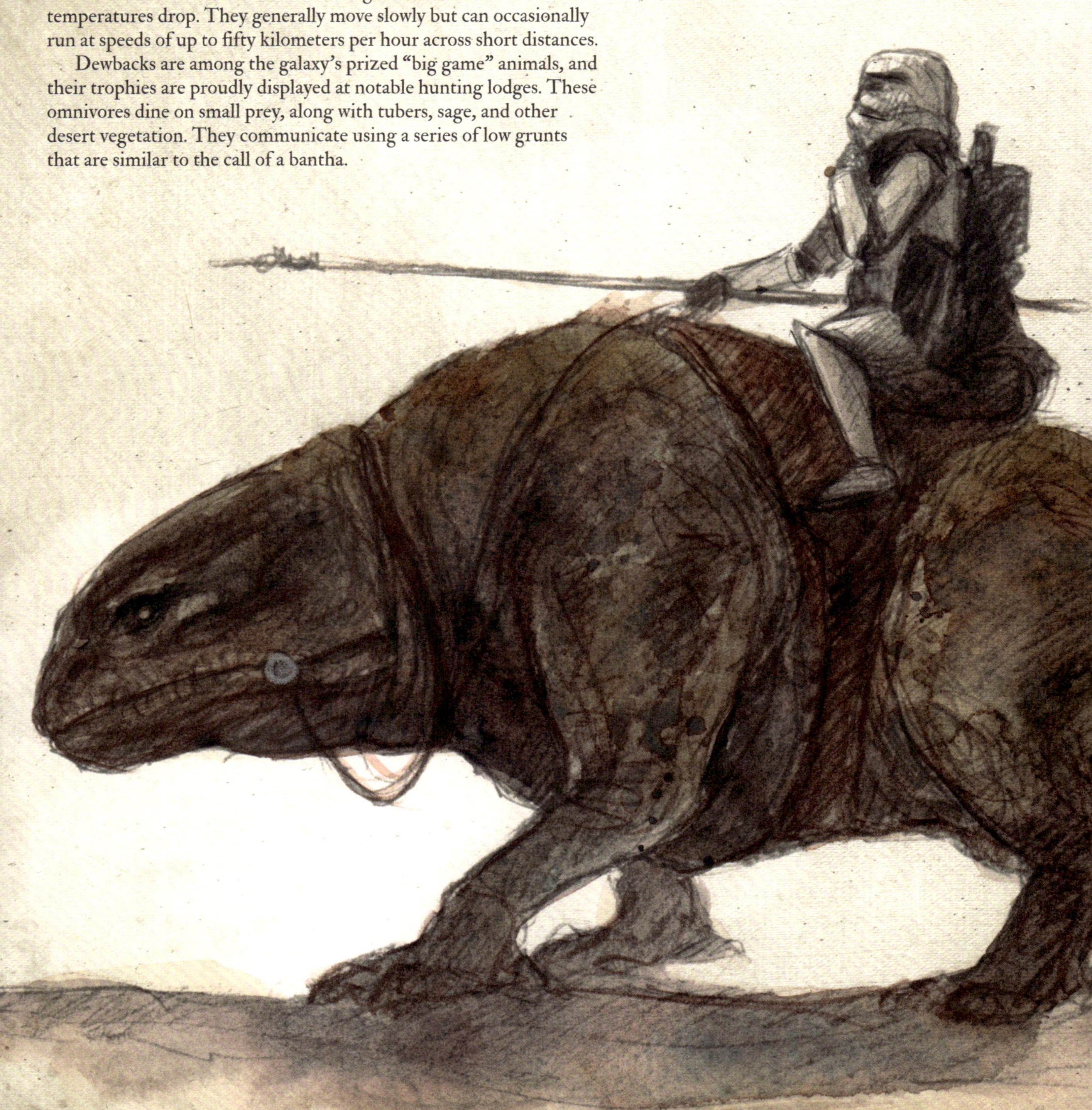

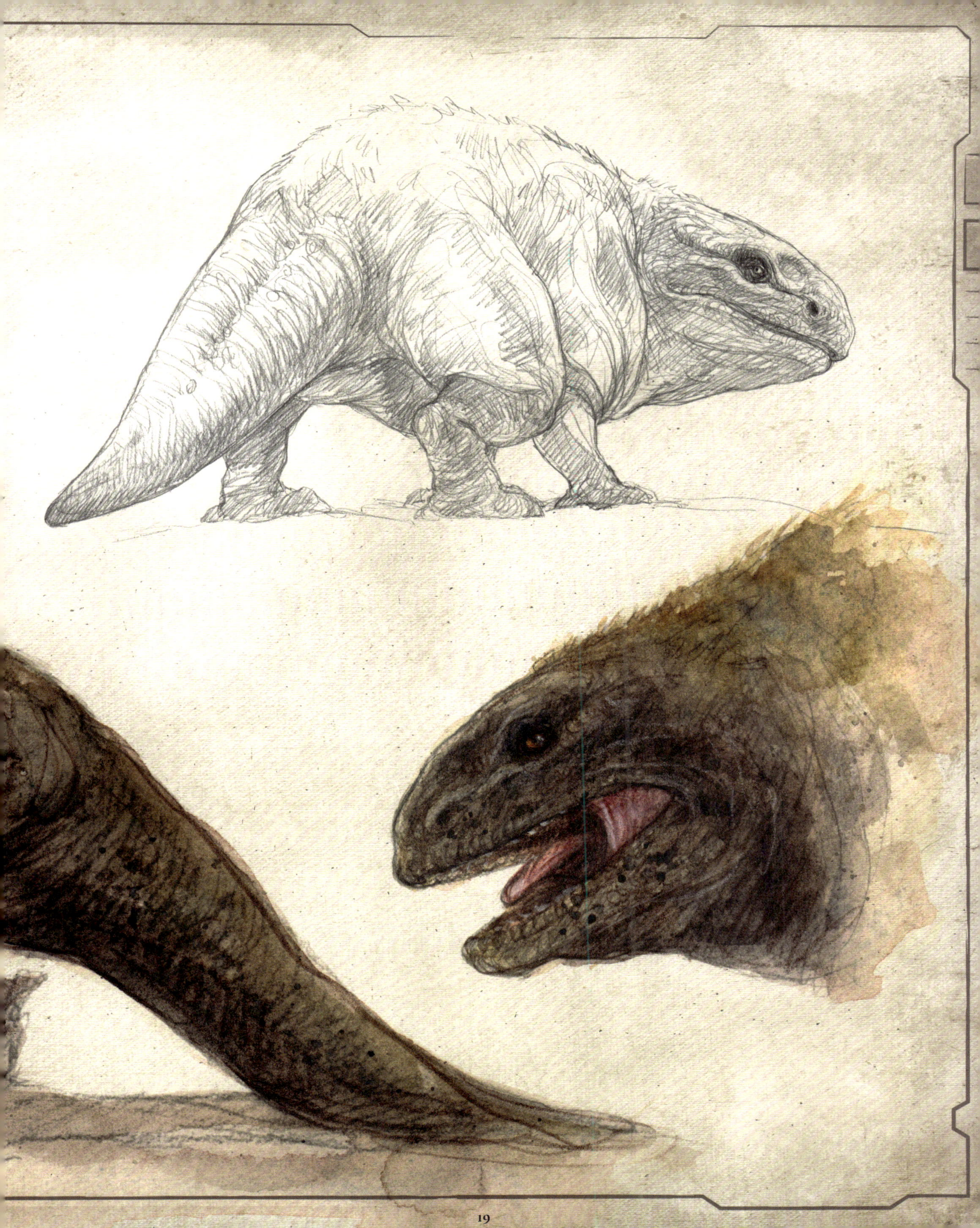

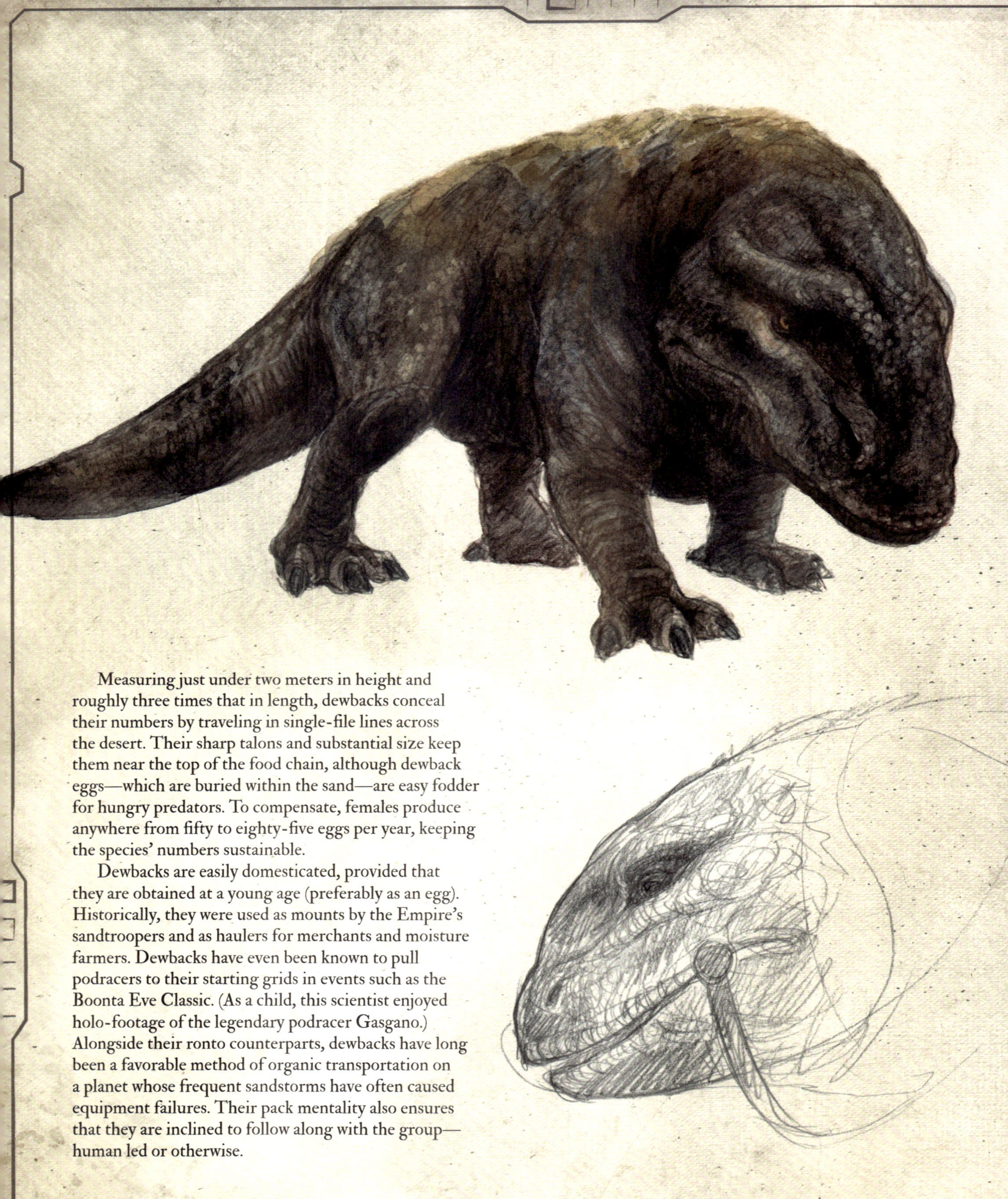

Measuring just under two meters in height and roughly three times that in length, dewbacks conceal their numbers by traveling in single-file lines across the desert. Their sharp talons and substantial size keep them near the top of the food chain, although dewback eggs—which are buried within the sand—are easy fodder for hungry predators. To compensate, females produce anywhere from fifty to eighty-five eggs per year, keeping the species' numbers sustainable.

Dewbacks are easily domesticated, provided that they are obtained at a young age (preferably as an egg). Historically, they were used as mounts by the Empire's sandtroopers and as haulers for merchants and moisture farmers. Dewbacks have even been known to pull podracers to their starting grids in events such as the Boonta Eve Classic. (As a child, this scientist enjoyed holo-footage of the legendary podracer Gasgano.) Alongside their ronto counterparts, dewbacks have long been a favorable method of organic transportation on a planet whose frequent sandstorms have often caused equipment failures. Their pack mentality also ensures that they are inclined to follow along with the group—human led or otherwise.

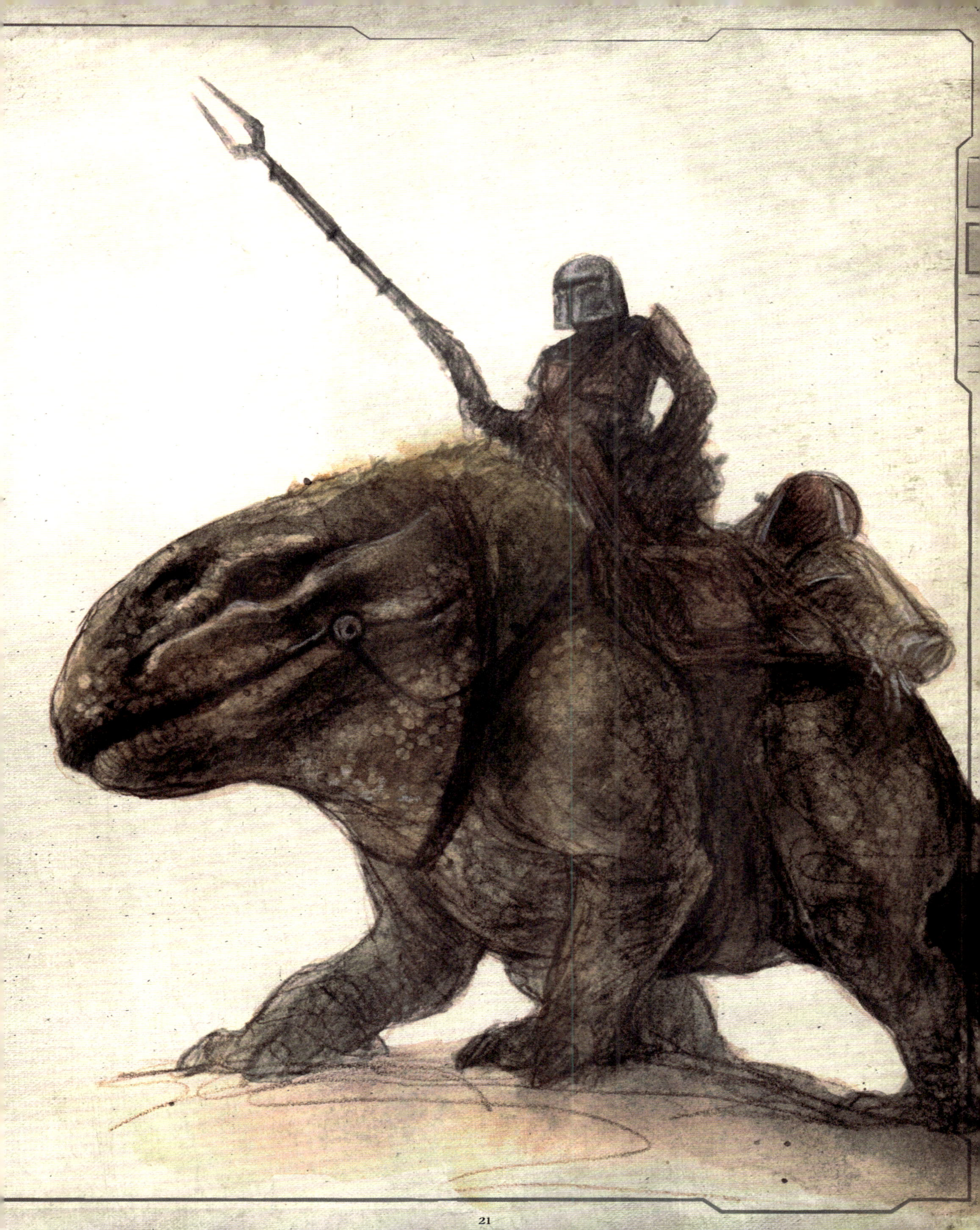

EOPIE

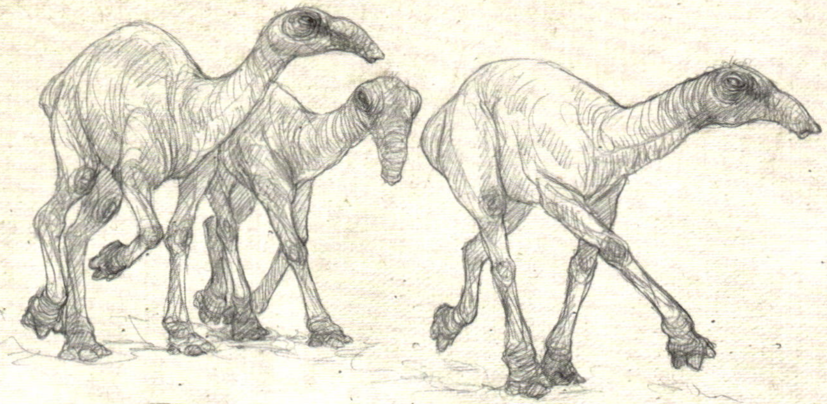

These mammalian herbivores are among my favorite of the desert species. Standing at 1.75 meters tall, these herd-dwelling quadrupeds have long been domesticated and used as mounts by residents of Tatooine. An eopie's rough skin protects the creature from the planet's twin suns, and its three-toed hooves are well adapted to climbing rocky surfaces and cliffs. Eopies spit glands secrete an adhesive that the creature layers over its eyes—as well as the eyes of its young—to protect against sandstorms. Eopies are known to be protective; while traveling, they shield their offspring with their own shadow, to prevent overheating. Although the gentle herbivores are capable of consuming meat without harm to their digestive system, their preferred diet consists largely of the vegetation native to the desert. In fact, eopies receive much of their moisture from tubers and desert lichens. They are native to Tatooine, but eopie have been found across the galaxy, including on Saleucami, on Zardossa Stix, and even among ancient ruins on the outskirts of Black Spire Outpost on Batuu.

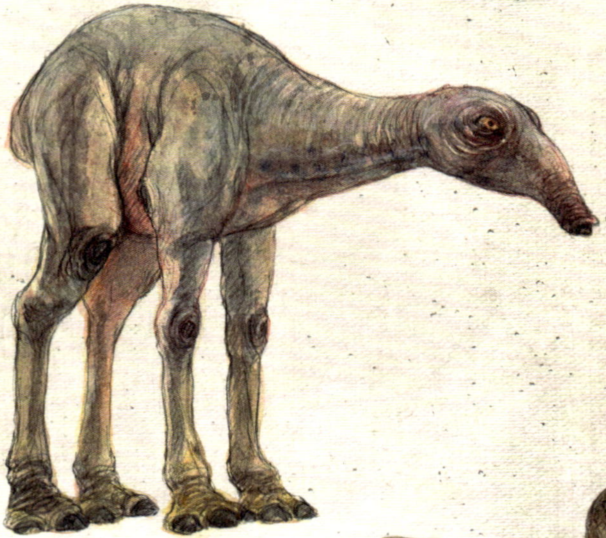

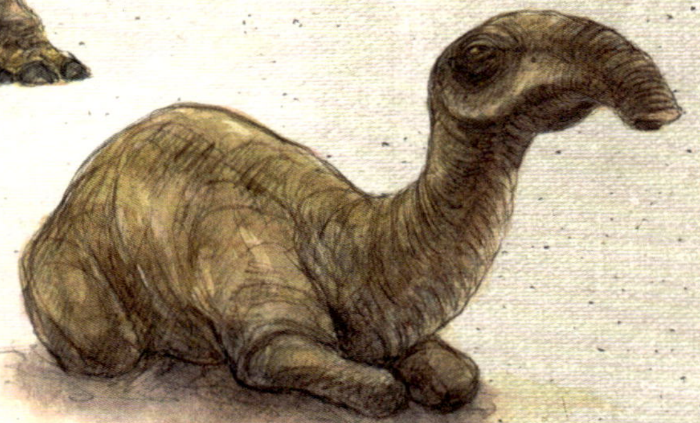

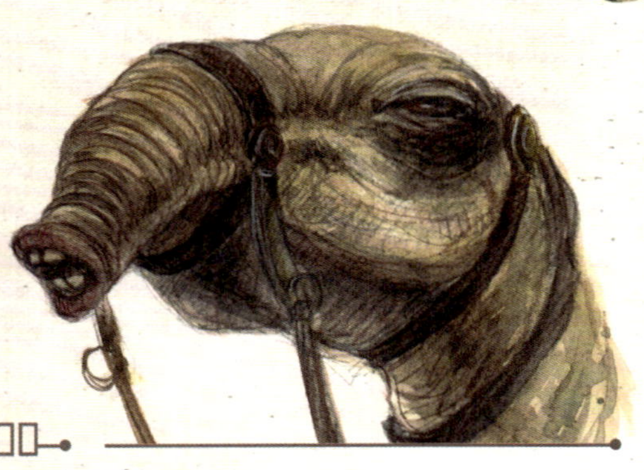

To thrive in the hot climates of their homeworld, eopies consume vast quantities of water, which they store in fatty tissues along their backs. Batuu also boasts a droid depot, an establishment where ronto meat is cooked over a podracer engine, and a renowned cantina that employs a droid DJ who once worked with the galactic travel agency Star Tours.

— B8-T5

Eopies have long been employed as both transport and haul animals. However, their stubborn nature and ill temper have earned them the reputation of being difficult (a trait this scientist finds rather endearing). When overburdened, they are known to exhibit fetid flatulence, leading many travelers to request a spot in the *front* of an eopie caravan. Furthermore, an enraged eopie may spit undigested stomach acid at whoever has caused its irritation—a painful experience, by all accounts. Eopies quickly grow fond of their handlers, however; when they become too old to work, they are often kept on as family pets, with younger members of the household taking on the duties of care.

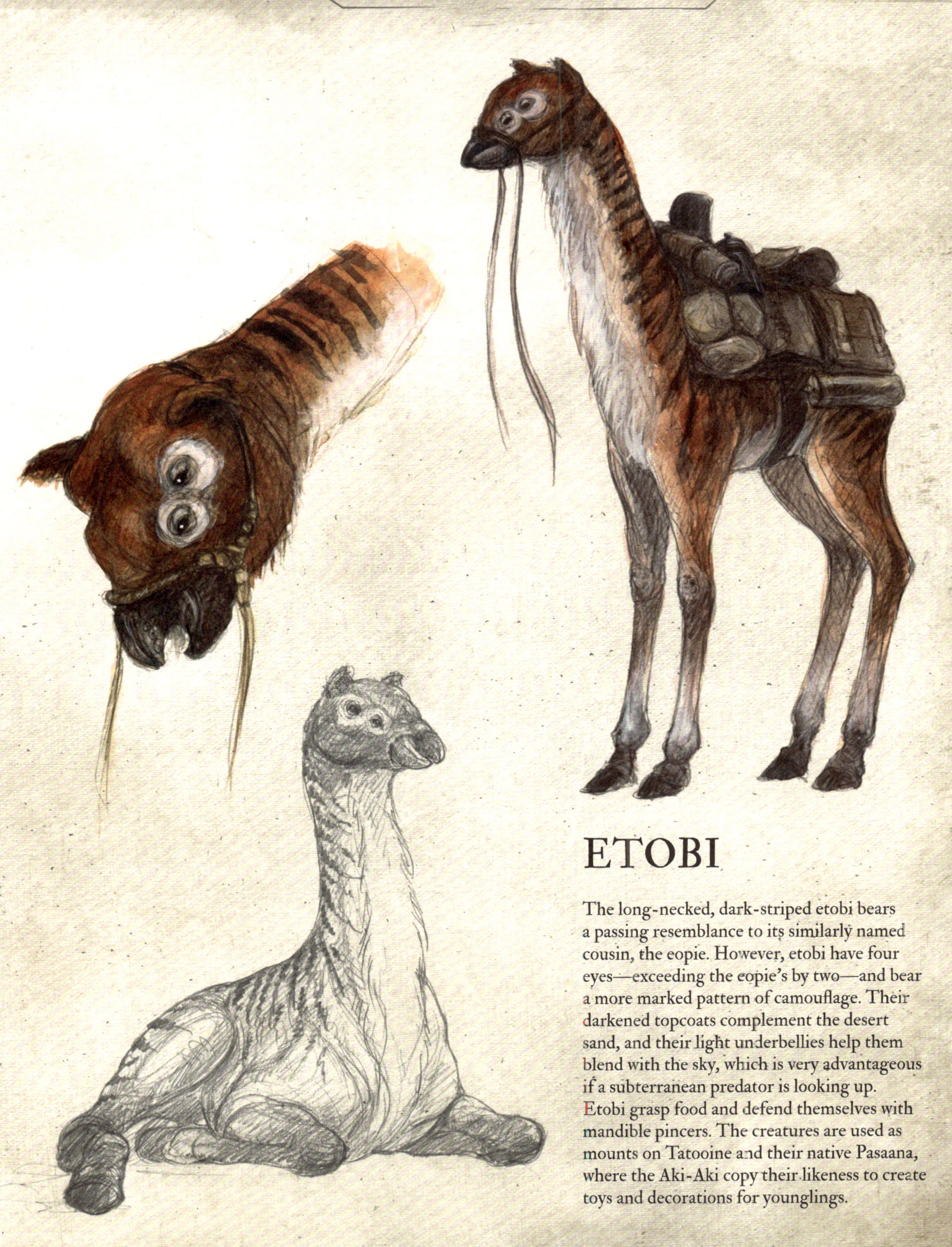

ETOBI

The long-necked, dark-striped etobi bears a passing resemblance to its similarly named cousin, the eopie. However, etobi have four eyes—exceeding the eopie's by two—and bear a more marked pattern of camouflage. Their darkened topcoats complement the desert sand, and their light underbellies help them blend with the sky, which is very advantageous if a subterranean predator is looking up. Etobi grasp food and defend themselves with mandible pincers. The creatures are used as mounts on Tatooine and their native Pasaana, where the Aki-Aki copy their likeness to create toys and decorations for younglings.

GUNDARK

Vanqor's fierce, carnivorous creatures are feared across the galaxy. The gundark's reputation as a lethal predator is well deserved: It stands at 3.7 meters tall and possesses no fewer than sixteen bladelike claws—along with a mouth filled with equally sharp teeth! Crimson-hued skin helps the creature blend into its desert environment, and long ears and a strong sense of hearing ensure that it remains at the top of the food chain. Gundarks are fiercely protective of their young and have been known to slaughter any creature that dares to approach its nest.

Gundark pelts—and parts—are highly prized, partly because of the species' reputation as being voraciously vicious. Hunting guilds stalk gundarks, skinning their kill and proudly displaying the hides. Gundark bones have been set decoratively within weapons: At least one gang leader possesses a rifle with a gundark bone for its grip. Citizens across the galaxy also wear a range of gundark hide accessories, from belts to gloves—melding fashion and function in a uniquely artistic way.

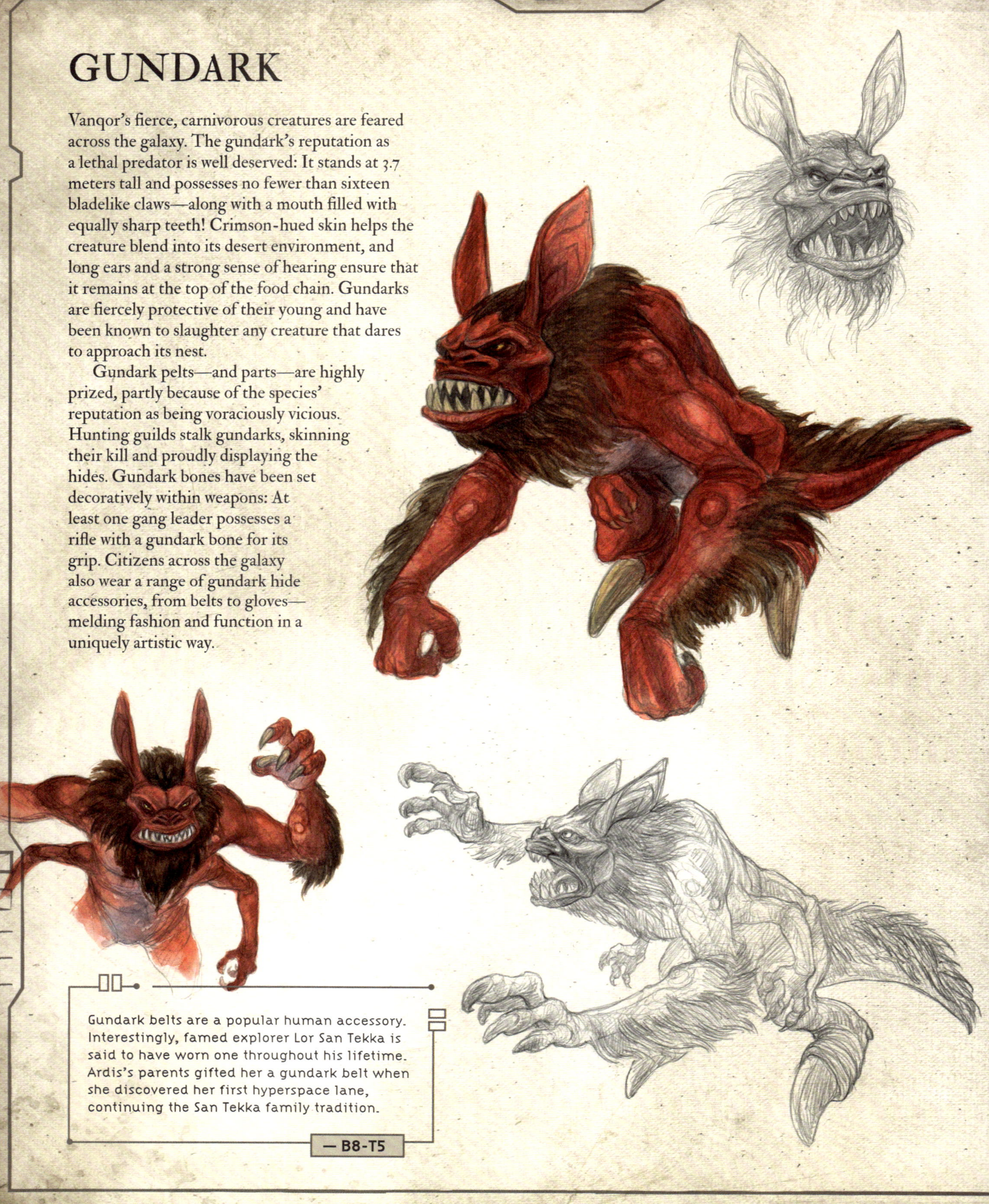

Gundark belts are a popular human accessory. Interestingly, famed explorer Lor San Tekka is said to have worn one throughout his lifetime. Ardis's parents gifted her a gundark belt when she discovered her first hyperspace lane, continuing the San Tekka family tradition.

— B8-T5

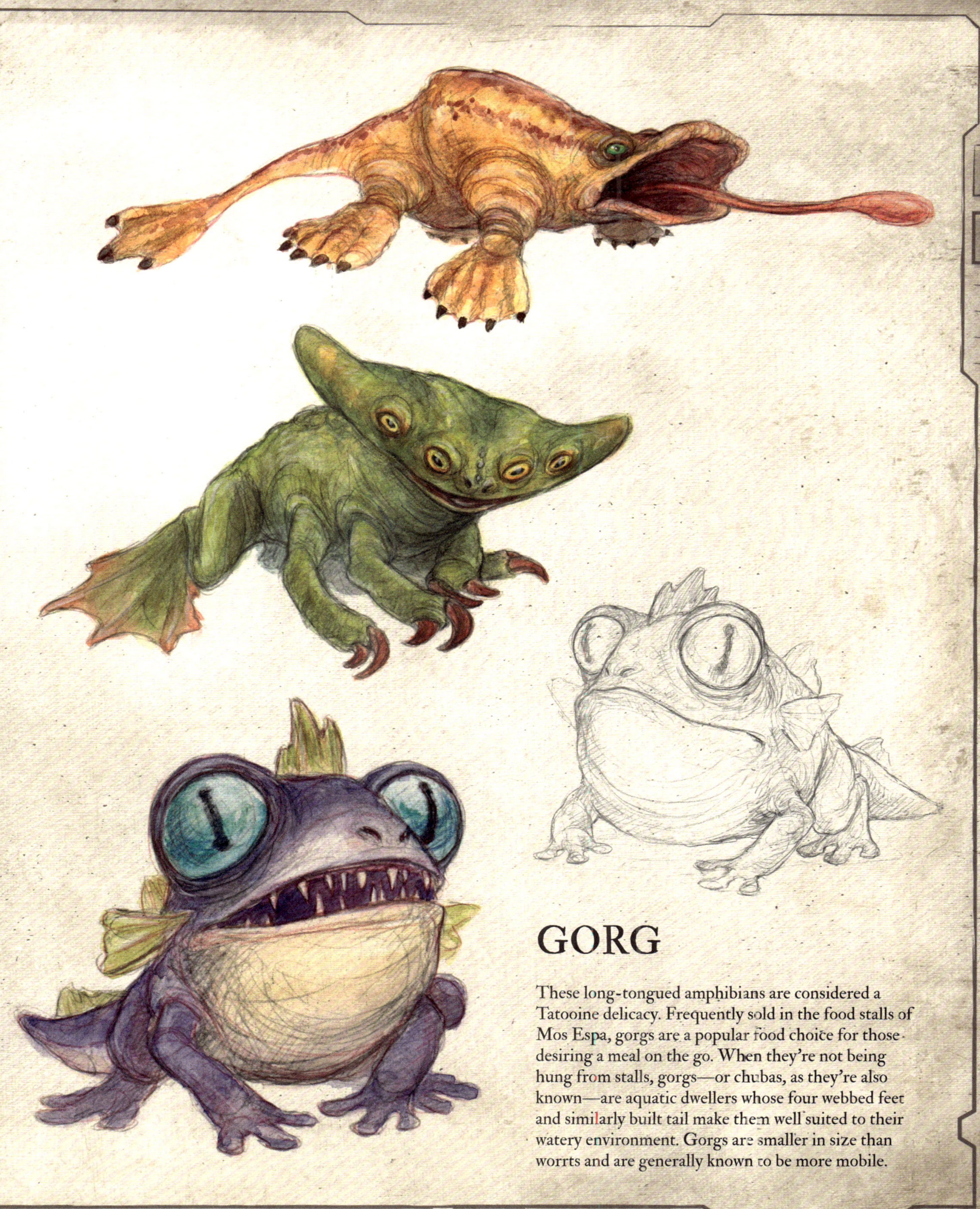

GORG

These long-tongued amphibians are considered a Tatooine delicacy. Frequently sold in the food stalls of Mos Espa, gorgs are a popular food choice for those desiring a meal on the go. When they're not being hung from stalls, gorgs—or chubas, as they're also known—are aquatic dwellers whose four webbed feet and similarly built tail make them well suited to their watery environment. Gorgs are smaller in size than worrts and are generally known to be more mobile.

MASSIFF

The aggressive, imposing massiff is a deadly hunter that makes its home in the desert planet of Tatooine. Also residing on Geonosis and Florrum, the massiff boasts an armored hide with spiky spines that appear along the bridge of its back. The breadth of these spikes serves as an indicator of the animal's age as spikes continue to grow. In addition to their prickly protections, massiffs possess large eyes that are well suited to night vision. Their mouths are filled with sharp teeth, and their jaws are capable of an expansive—and powerful—bite, making the creatures formidable opponents.

These (almost) meter-tall reptiles have long been domesticated, and with proper training, they can serve their masters as loyal guard animals. They are frequently employed by Weequay pirates and clone troopers as both sentries and trackers, but they are perhaps most well known for their relationship with Tuskens, who live alongside massiffs and treat the creatures as pets. Because of the massiff's vicious nature, certain planets have statutes that require any domesticated massiff to be walked on a leash. This is perhaps wise, as the creatures are fiercely loyal pack animals who will stop at nothing to neutralize perceived threats to those they consider family.

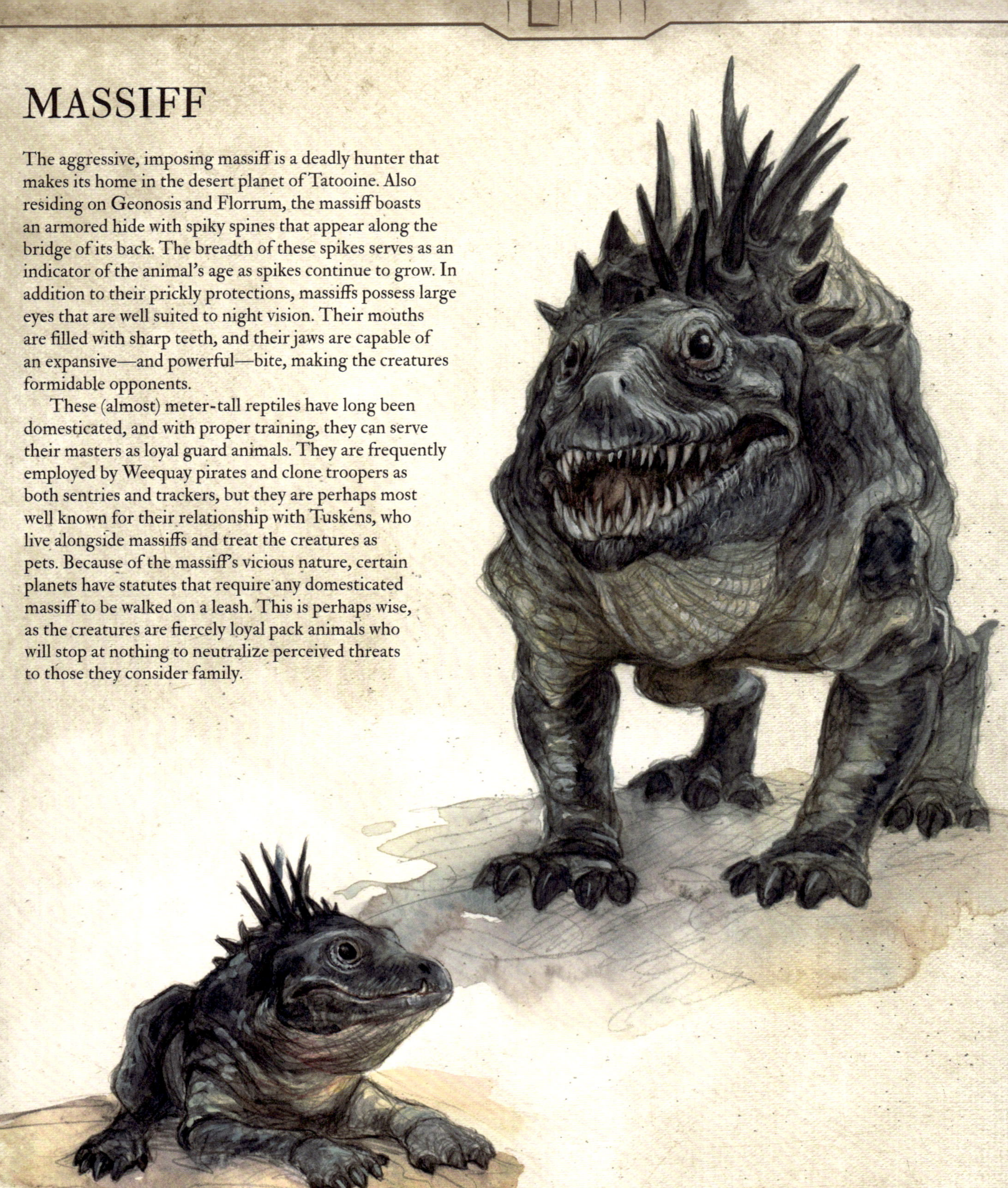

MUDHORN

Among the creatures I was most nervous to witness is the merciless mudhorn, a staunch defender of its territory. This behavioral trait makes it a rare find—at least, among explorers who value their limbs! Its most distinguishing feature is an enormous pointed horn. Sitting atop its nostrils and spanning the width of a large tree trunk, this horn serves as the creature's primary means of defense. With considerable strength and a propensity to charge, a raging mudhorn is feared in just about any habitat.

The oviparous quadruped is found on the desert planet of Arvala-7, where it makes its home in the caves that line the desert's rocky ranges. Here it builds its nest and tends to its young. Females of the species bear only a single egg at a time. Mudhorns stand an impressive five meters tall and ten meters long. They are covered in long woolen fur, an adaptation that helps regulate their body temperature. During hot days, this fast-wicking fiber soaks up moisture and allows for a layer of dry air to rest atop the creature's skin. During the colder nights, this wool offers insulation from the desert's dramatic downshift in temperature. Mudhorn eggs are covered in the same wool as adults of the species, helping to keep them at a steady temperature when the mother leaves the nest to seek food. These absences are brief in duration: Mudhorn eggs are coveted by Jawas, who consider their contents a culinary delicacy and have been known to bribe more aggressive species to hunt the eggs on their behalf.

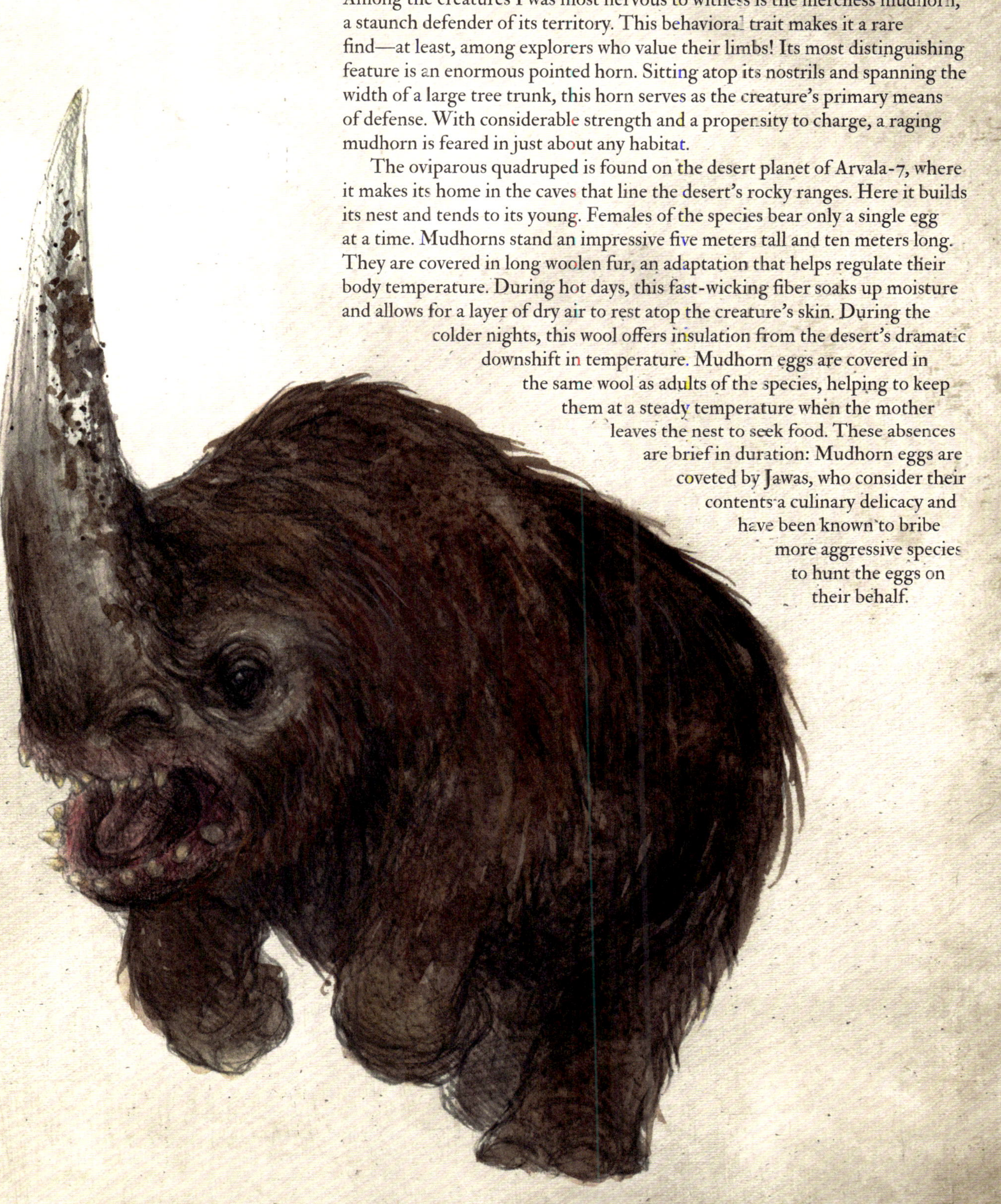

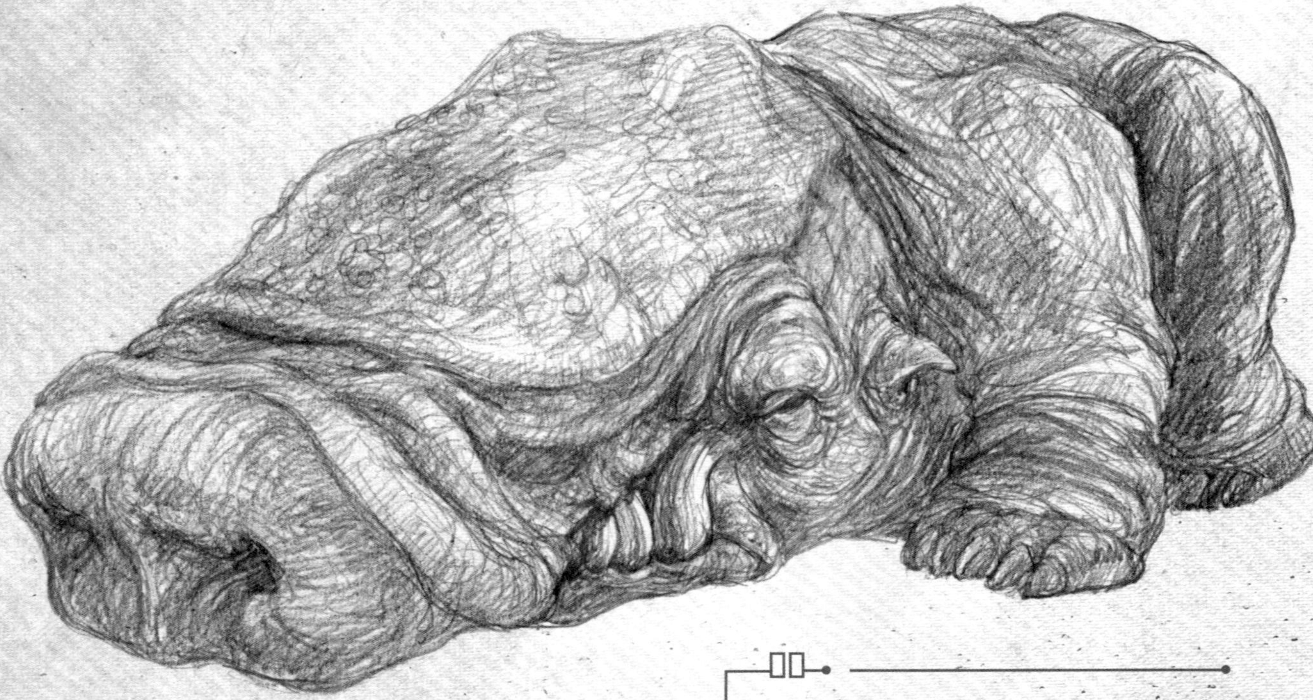

When excited, happabores snort like puffer pigs. They also can drink up to three hundred liters of water in a single day. (By the way, a full day on Jakku is about 26.8 hours.) These otherwise friendly creatures grow **exceptionally** aggressive when seeking out a water source.

— B8-T5

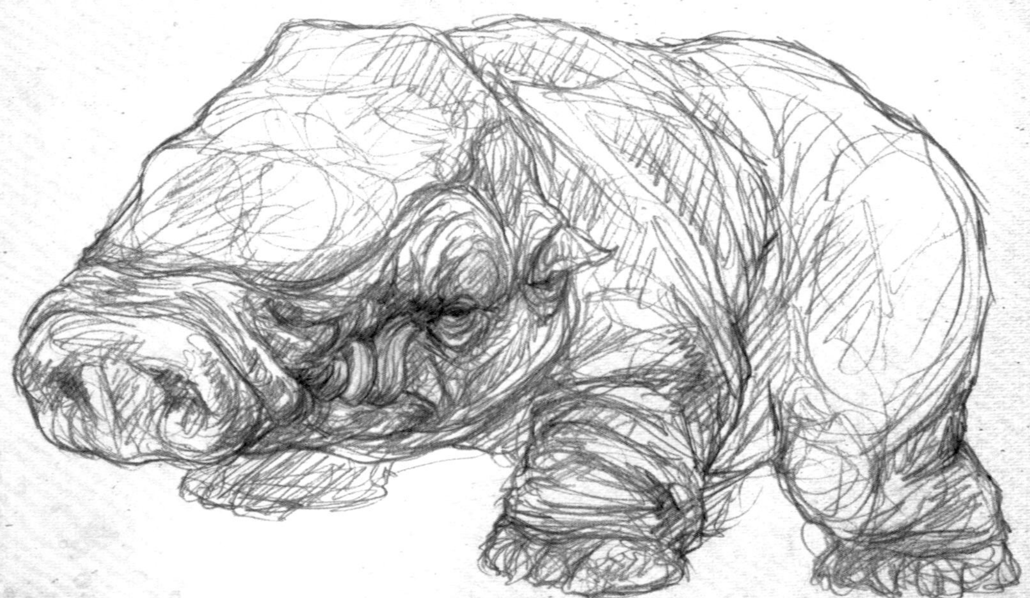

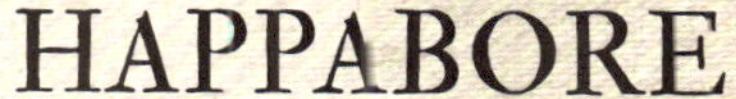

HAPPABORE

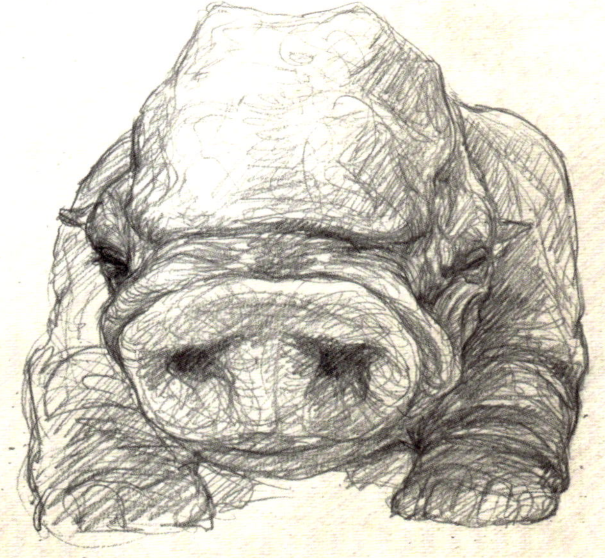

The massive mammalian happabore thrives in its harsh desert climate on the planet Jakku. Its thick gray skin leaves the creature nearly impervious to the heat. Additionally, the uppermost regions of its hide are coated in dense armor that both shields against the sun and offers perceptible protection against would-be predators. Deep-set wrinkles shelter the creature's four eyes from harsh solar rays and savage sandstorms, and flat teeth and powerful jaws deter any attacker that dares to come too close. Weighing in at 2,500 kilograms, the happabore averages 5.9 meters in length and 2.3 meters in height, with its unusually squat legs giving way to comparatively wide feet. Despite its numerous defenses, the creature is known across Jakku as an easygoing species whose innate desire to please its handler makes it well suited to domestication. Happabores are utilized across the Western Reaches by a multitude of handlers, who use the robust quadrupeds to haul junk, pull plows, and even ferry passengers.

Wide snouts with sizable nostrils support a heightened olfactory system, making the happabore uniquely adept at sniffing out subterranean tubers. The omnivore also consumes any available digestible plant life—although vegetation is a rare treat in its oft-arid ecosystem. A long tongue enables the species to consume significant amounts of liquid in a relatively short span, a key evolutionary element in a climate where water is perhaps the scarcest resource of all. This precious commodity is then stored within the happabore's bloodstream, sustaining the mammal as it navigates its barren landscape.

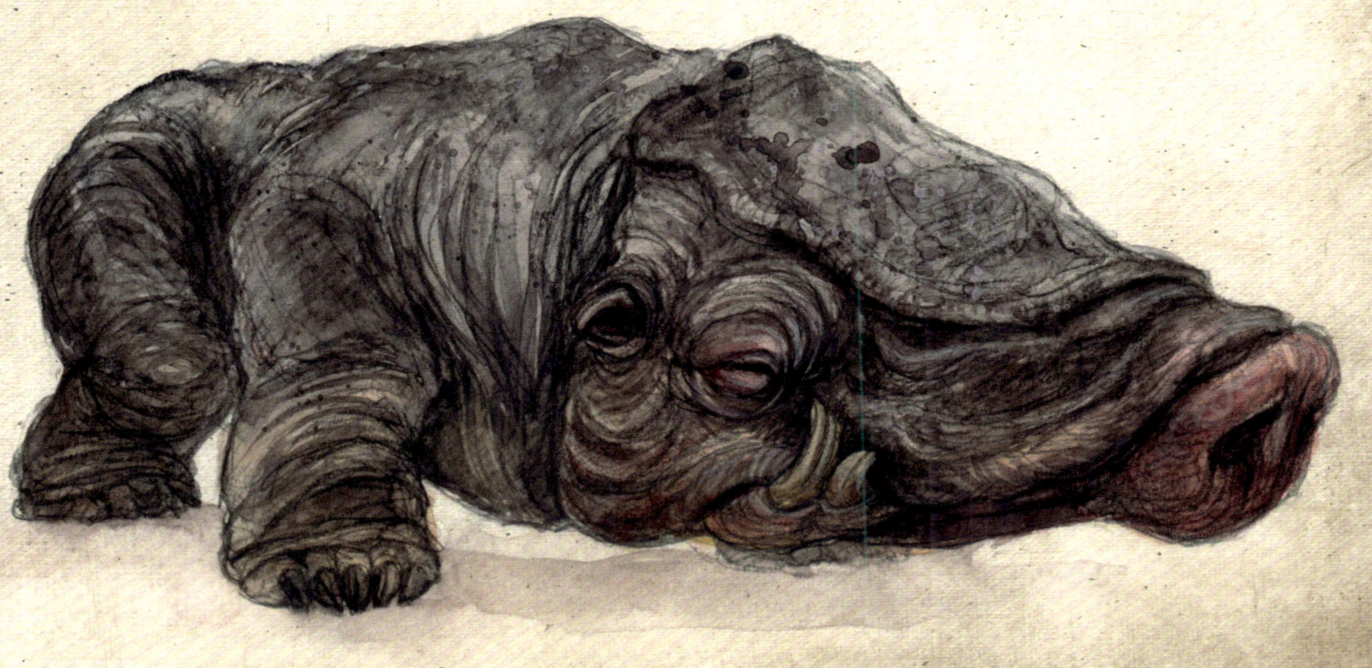

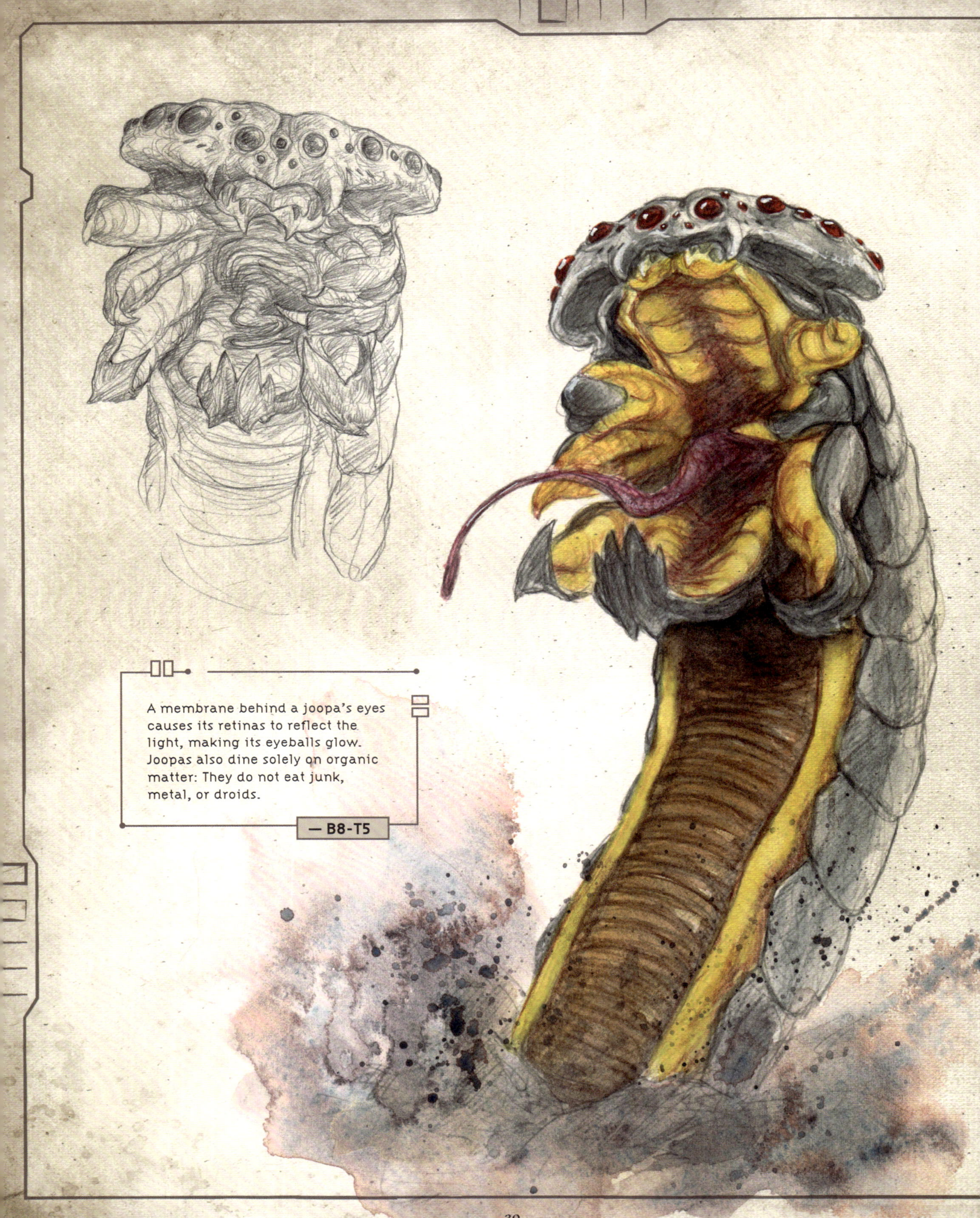
A membrane behind a joopa's eyes causes its retinas to reflect the light, making its eyeballs glow. Joopas also dine solely on organic matter: They do not eat junk, metal, or droids.
— B8-T5

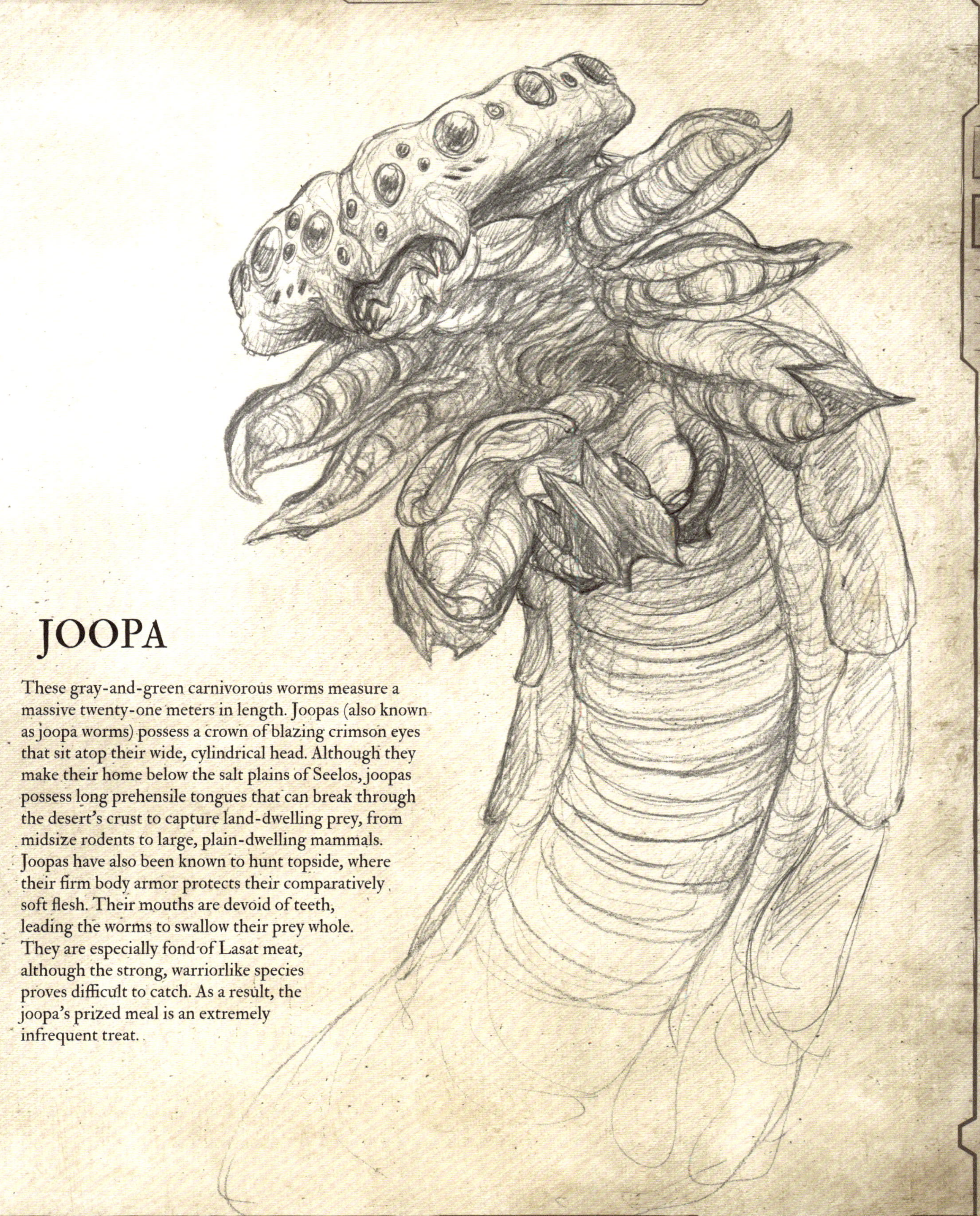

JOOPA

These gray-and-green carnivorous worms measure a massive twenty-one meters in length. Joopas (also known as joopa worms) possess a crown of blazing crimson eyes that sit atop their wide, cylindrical head. Although they make their home below the salt plains of Seelos, joopas possess long prehensile tongues that can break through the desert's crust to capture land-dwelling prey, from midsize rodents to large, plain-dwelling mammals. Joopas have also been known to hunt topside, where their firm body armor protects their comparatively soft flesh. Their mouths are devoid of teeth, leading the worms to swallow their prey whole. They are especially fond of Lasat meat, although the strong, warriorlike species proves difficult to catch. As a result, the joopa's prized meal is an extremely infrequent treat.

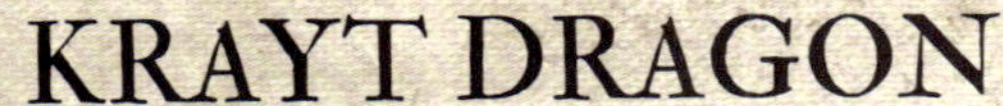

KRAYT DRAGON

Tatooine's apex predators are positively gargantuan—and exactly how large they can grow remains to be determined! Their elusive nature and strong survival tactics mean that few have been captured . . . and even fewer studied. (One does not, after all, *approach* the lethal krayt dragon to inquire of its measurements!) These carnivorous reptiles produce a poison known as krayt venom that they spit across great distances to ward off assailants. Contact with this venom is lethal—the highly acidic substance swiftly dissolves organic tissue. When retained internally, the dragon's venom serves as a digestive aid in breaking down its food.

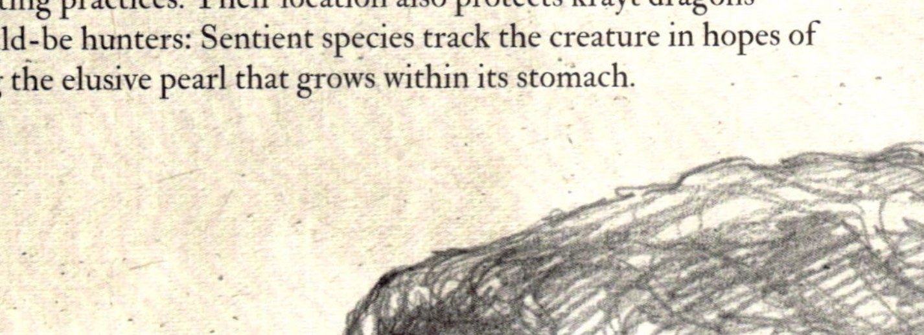

Of note, krayt dragons live among the canyons of Tatooine's Dune Sea. There they burrow beneath the sand, coming out to attack unsuspecting prey such as Jawas, Tuskens, and banthas. Krayt dragons have even been known to kill sarlaccs, consuming the massive creatures and then crawling into their pits and claiming the caverns as their homes. Because sarlacc pits are positioned near enough to the sand's surface for their occupant to sense the movements of prospective prey, krayt dragons find these subterranean spaces most advantageous for their hunting practices. Their location also protects krayt dragons from would-be hunters: Sentient species track the creature in hopes of capturing the elusive pearl that grows within its stomach.

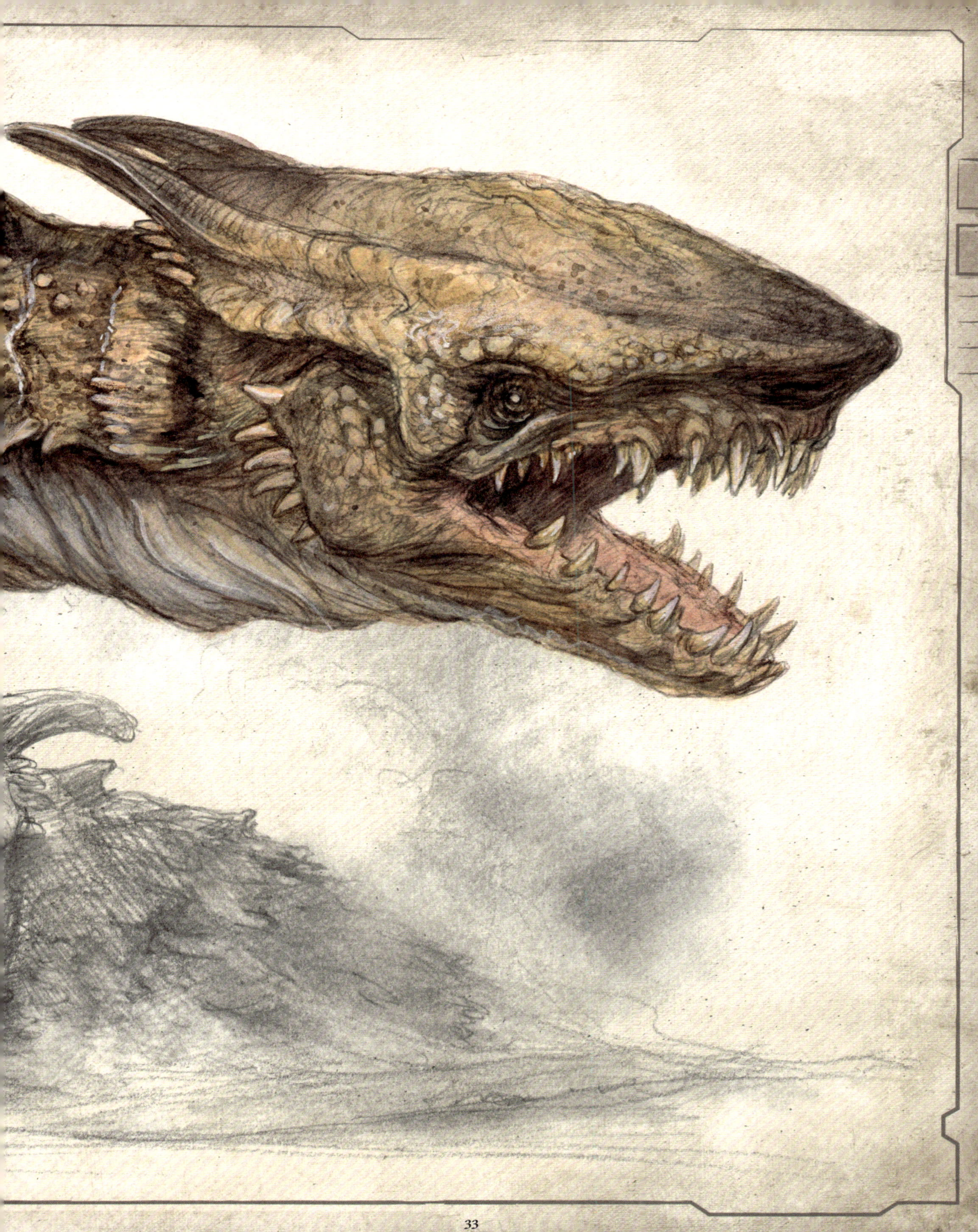

Several species of krayt dragons exist, including the sixteen-limbed, venom-spitting leviathan krayt dragon; the large greater krayt; and the smaller canyon krayt. Tatooine natives allege that a now-extinct species of the krayt had wings, although neither holographic evidence nor residual remains have substantiated this claim. The creatures are both feared and revered by Tuskens, who have been known to feed their beloved banthas to the predators in order to extend its sleep cycle and protect nearby Tusken settlements. The nomads also believed that krayt bones possessed magic. Accordingly, tribe members would collect the creatures' remains when they encountered them along their travels.

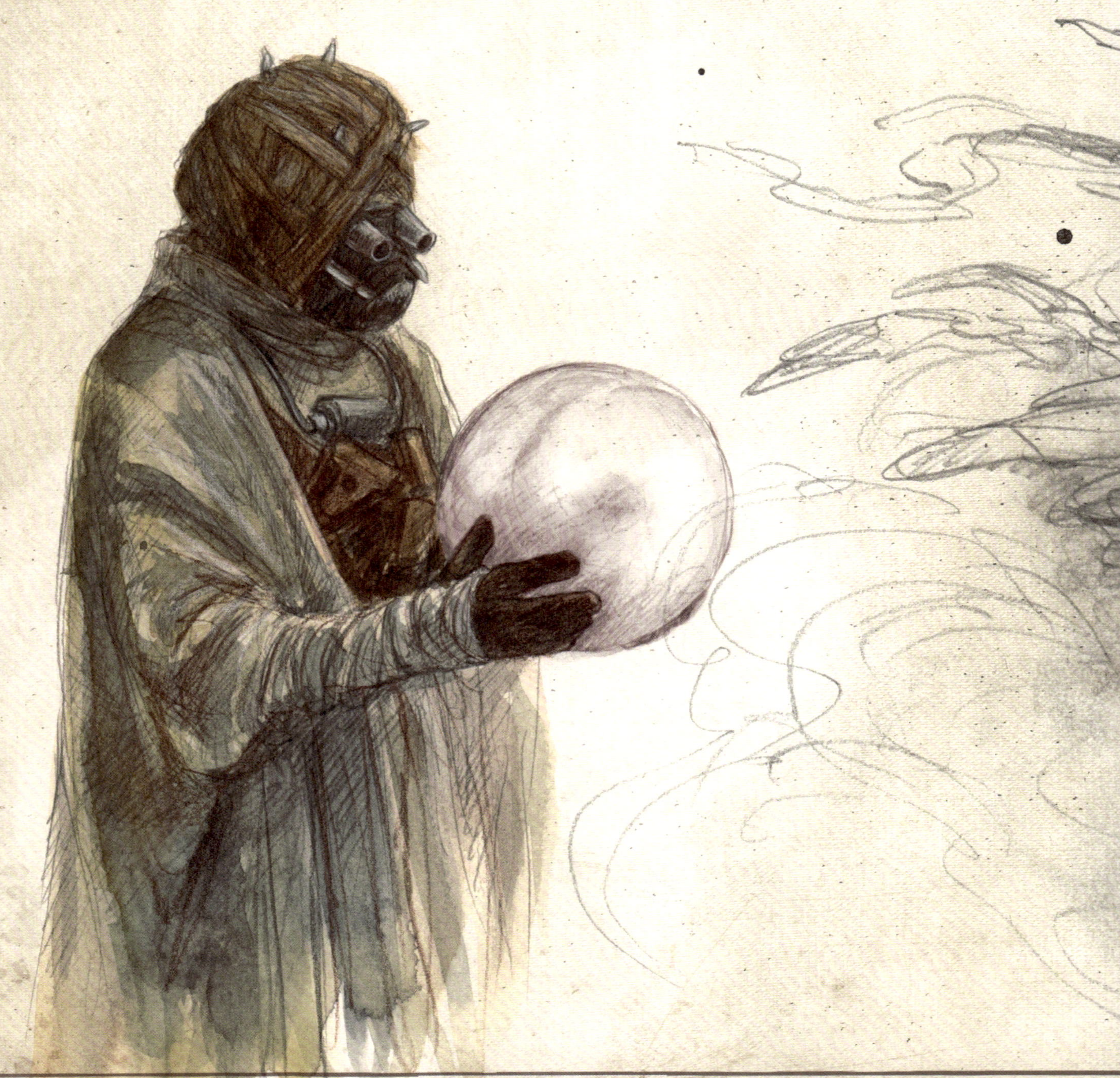

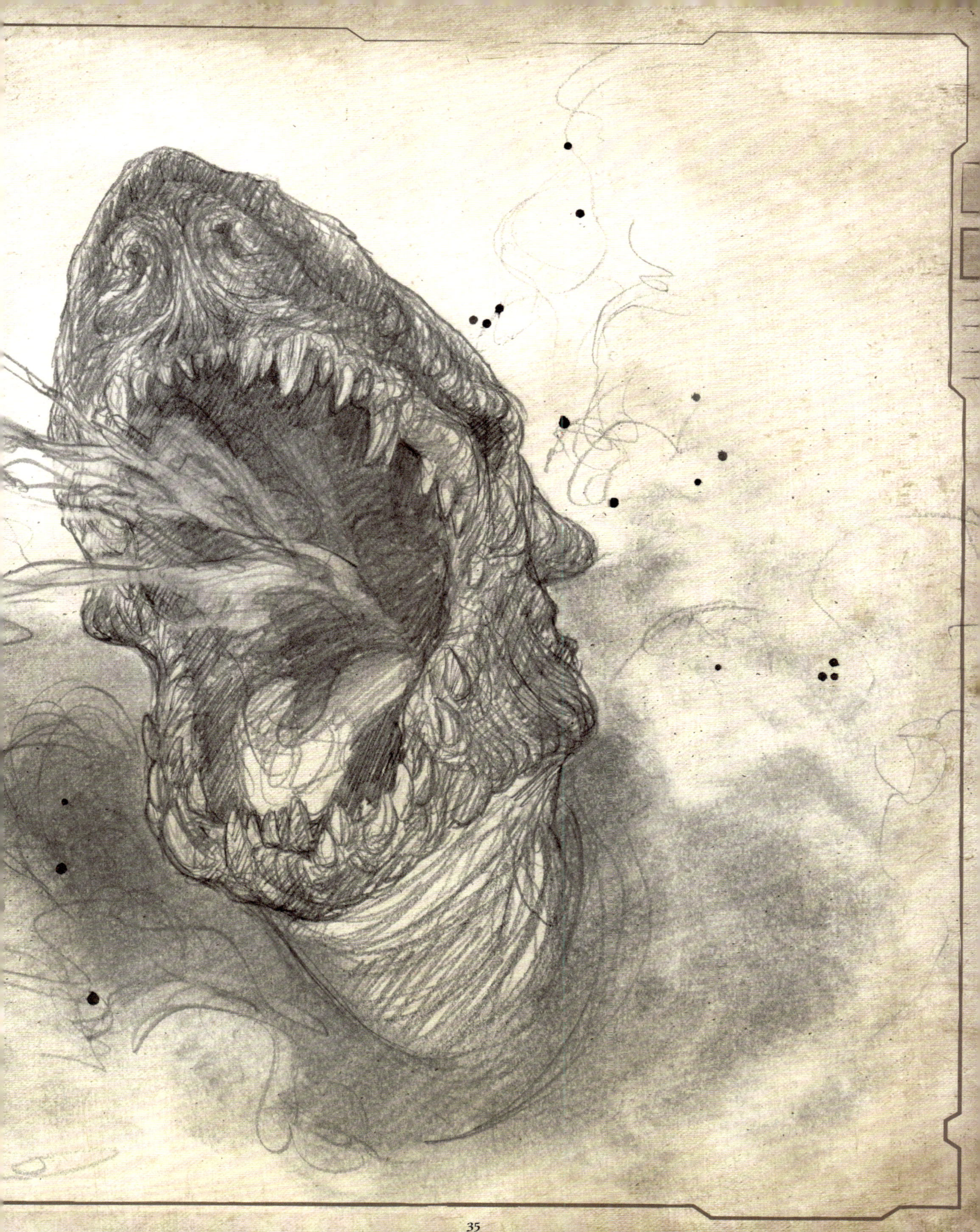

ICE SPIDER

Given this scientist's rather strong feelings about arachnids, I was very much dreading a run-in with Maldo Kreis's terrifying predators. Because the ice spider is known to swarm upon living prey and feast with their razor-sharp proboscises, I was only too happy to let my safari droid, B8-T5, take the lead on this particular study. Bait's findings confirmed what we have long believed to be true: These creatures make their homes in ice caves, stand up to sixteen meters in height, and are very protective of their eggs. Depending on their size, they have 6 to 10 legs, which connect to bulbous backsides built of toughened skin, a feature that makes larger specimens more resistant to blaster bolts. Beaked mouths are framed by fanged pedipalps, which serve two purposes—they function as sensory organs and can be used as a means of attack. There is disagreement amongst the scientific community as to whether the ice spider is connected to the krykna species of Atollon. Some seasoned spacefarers have even compared the ice spider to the knobby white spider of galactic legend.

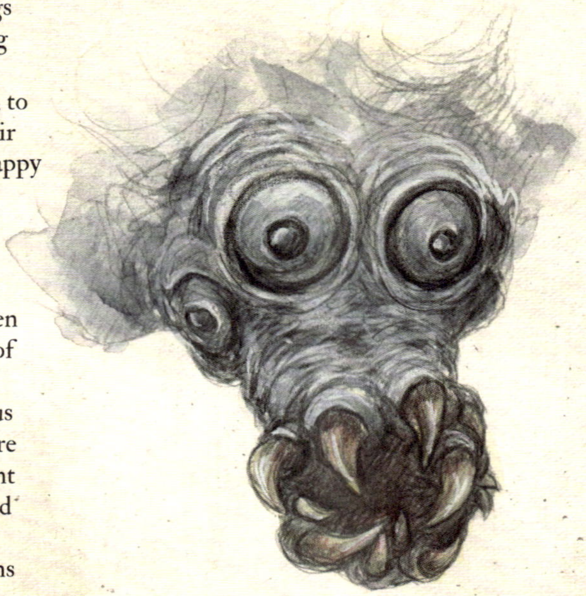

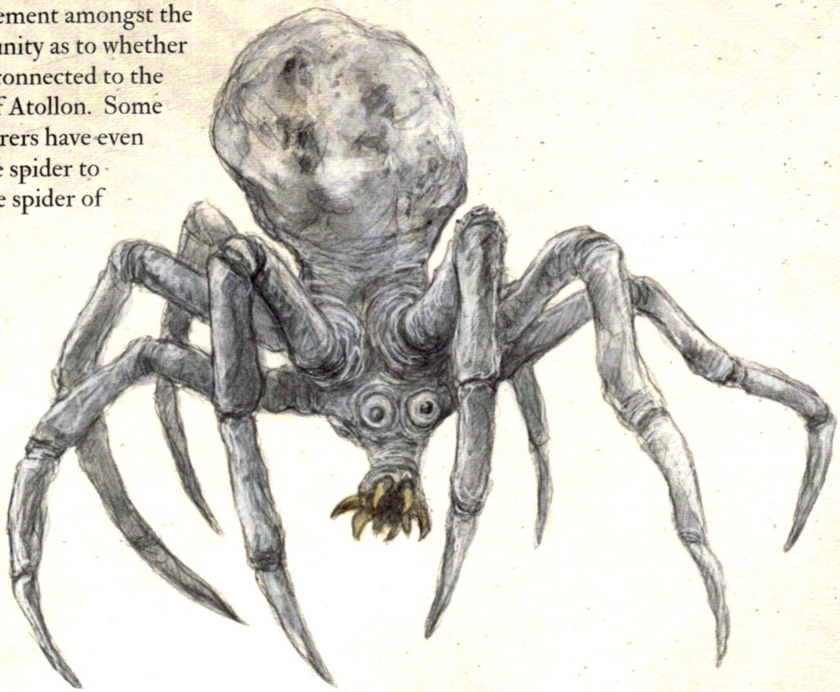

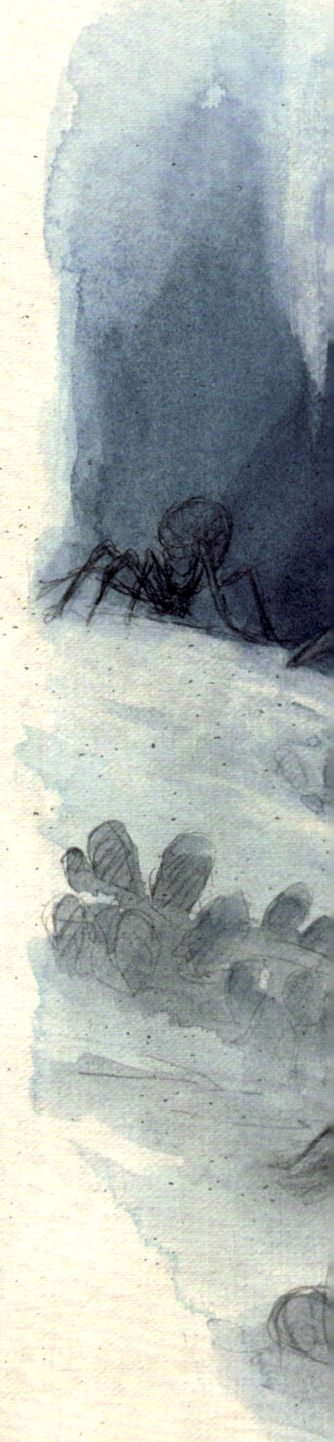

Ice spider caves can be typically found filled with hundreds of eggs. These creatures spin webs of ice strands everywhere, and all kinds of things get stuck in them—making anything potential prey. Given that, as well as the ice spider's shockingly rapid rate of movement, I was not enthusiastic about taking the lead on this particular study.

— B8-T5

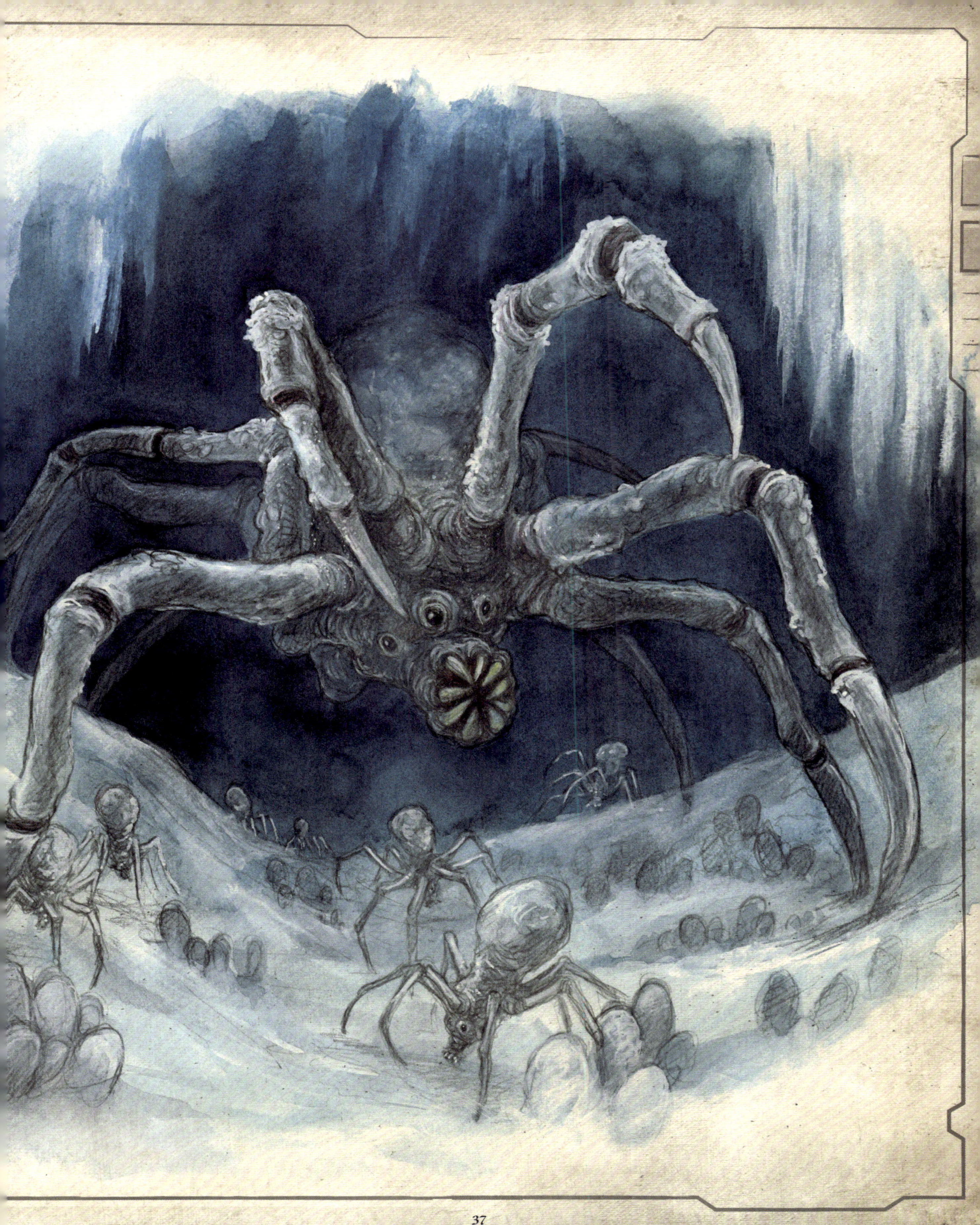

LUGGABEAST

The lumbering luggabeast is a cybernetically enhanced quadruped that owes its robotic movement to a multitude of modifications. Domesticated by the scavenging Teedos of Jakku, these beasts measure about 2.31 meters in height and are trained to carry heavy loads over great distances. At any given moment, their cargo nets may be filled with anything from scrap metal to wayward droids.

Mechanical systems increase the luggabeast's durability, enabling the creature to travel long distances without tiring. Sentient handlers have provided other cybernetic enhancements in an effort to resolve many of the issues that plague desert-dwelling species, such as exposure to the elements and a scarcity of food and water sources. Luggabeasts have been modified to receive nutrients via a series of wires, enabling the species to survive without needing to eat or drink. A permanent metallic mask is been fused to the luggabeast's head, protecting it from inclement weather, particularly Jakku's violent sandstorms. Additionally, luggabeasts are fitted with optical devices, to better serve their handlers in locating salvageable material. The creatures are also supplied with heavy coats of armor, to ward off predators and rival Teedos.

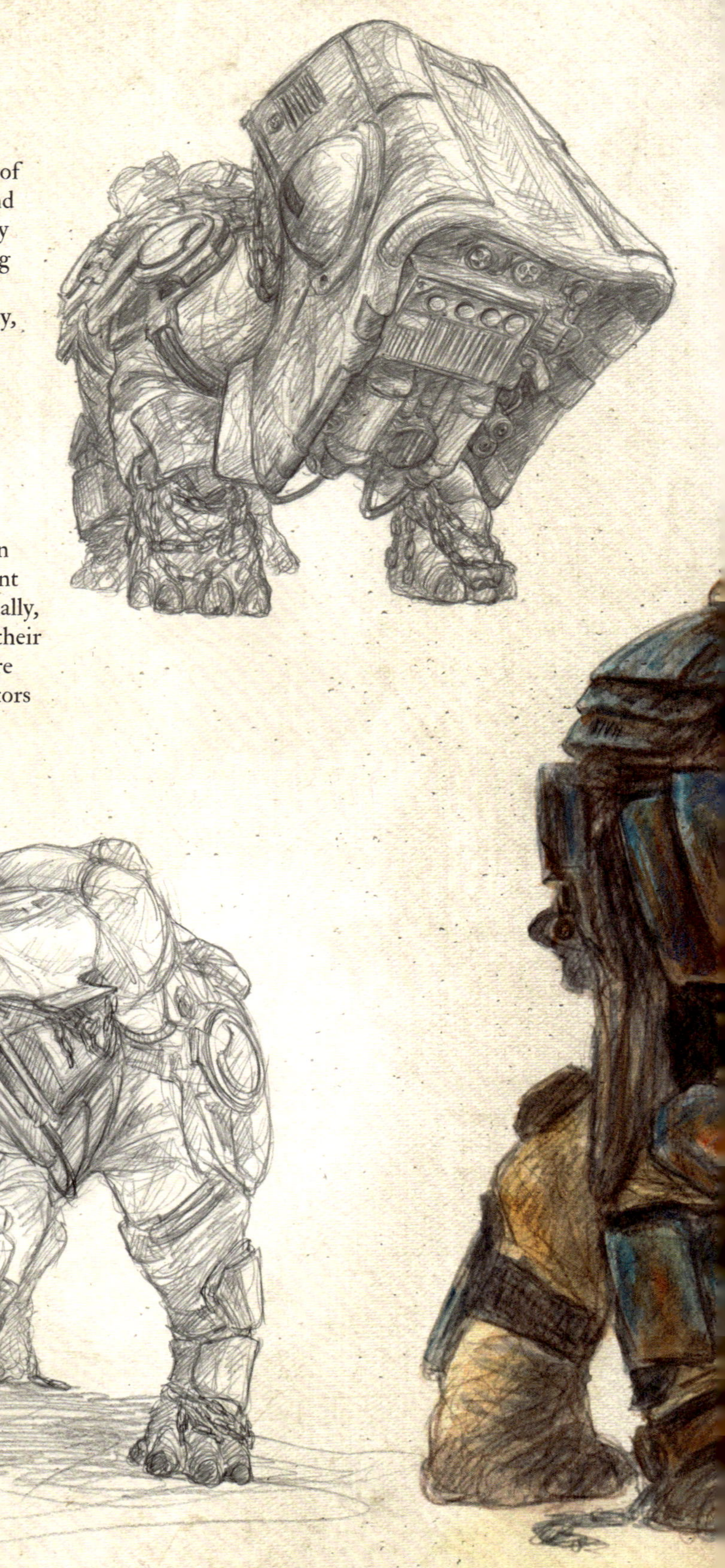

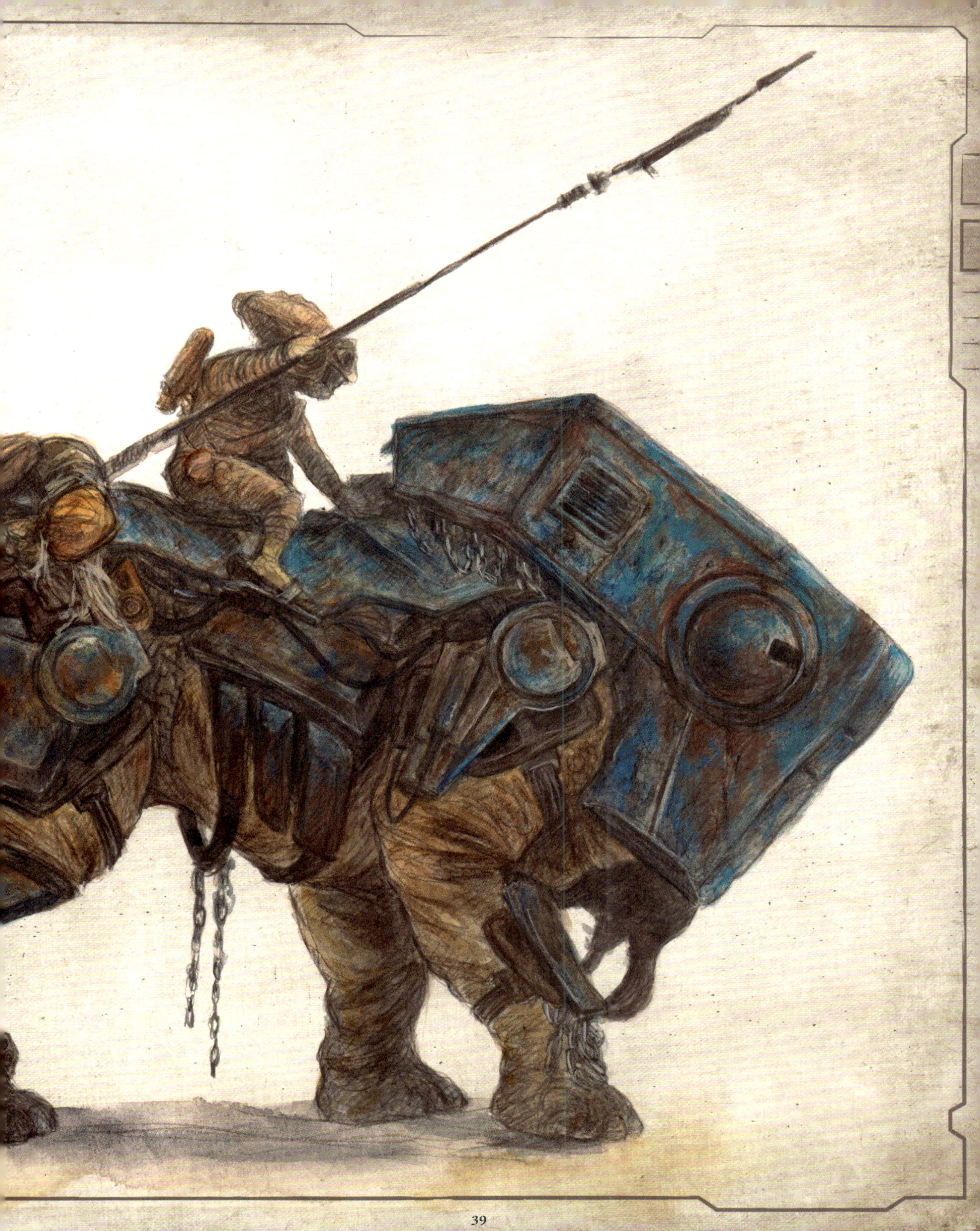

NIGHTWATCHER WORM

Measuring a mind-boggling twenty meters long (with particularly robust specimens coming in at six times that length), Jakku's nocturnal nightwatcher worm is among the planet's most elusive creatures. Despite infrequent sightings, these sharp-toothed behemoths inspire fear in Jakku's natives—not only because of their size, but also because of their propensity to consume anything that lies in their path. Their diet consists mostly of junk—a fitting choice for a region whose primary industry is scavenging—and the worms have pointed teeth and powerful jaws that allow them to grind anything from metal to bones. Potent stomach acids easily disintegrate any nondigestible material that the creatures consume. When the nightwatcher worm is unable to capture its prey, it bows its eyestalk and produces a low, pained wail.

Nightwatchers dwell in burrows beneath the sand, occasionally popping their head above ground to survey their surroundings. Glowing red eyes register movement, depth, and proximity of their prey. The creature's T-shaped head is frequently mistaken for an Arcona (hence the worm's nickname, the Arconan night terror). Although they are primarily found in the Sinking Fields, nightwatcher worms migrate with the sandstorms and have even been known to appear in the Goazon Badlands. They travel underground at the rate of a sprinting human—a fact that has earned them their other nickname, sandborers.

A nightwatcher's maw houses several blue tongues and produces substantial amounts of spittle. While searching for food, the subterranean creature relies on motion sensors within its skin to detect vibrations along Jakku's surface. When a vibration is registered, the worm bursts from the sand to attack. Captured prey is often held within the jaw, with consumption delayed until the nightwatcher vacates its hunting site. Communication occurs via a series of roars and sentient-like speech, creating the creature's highly unique language, Hideo.

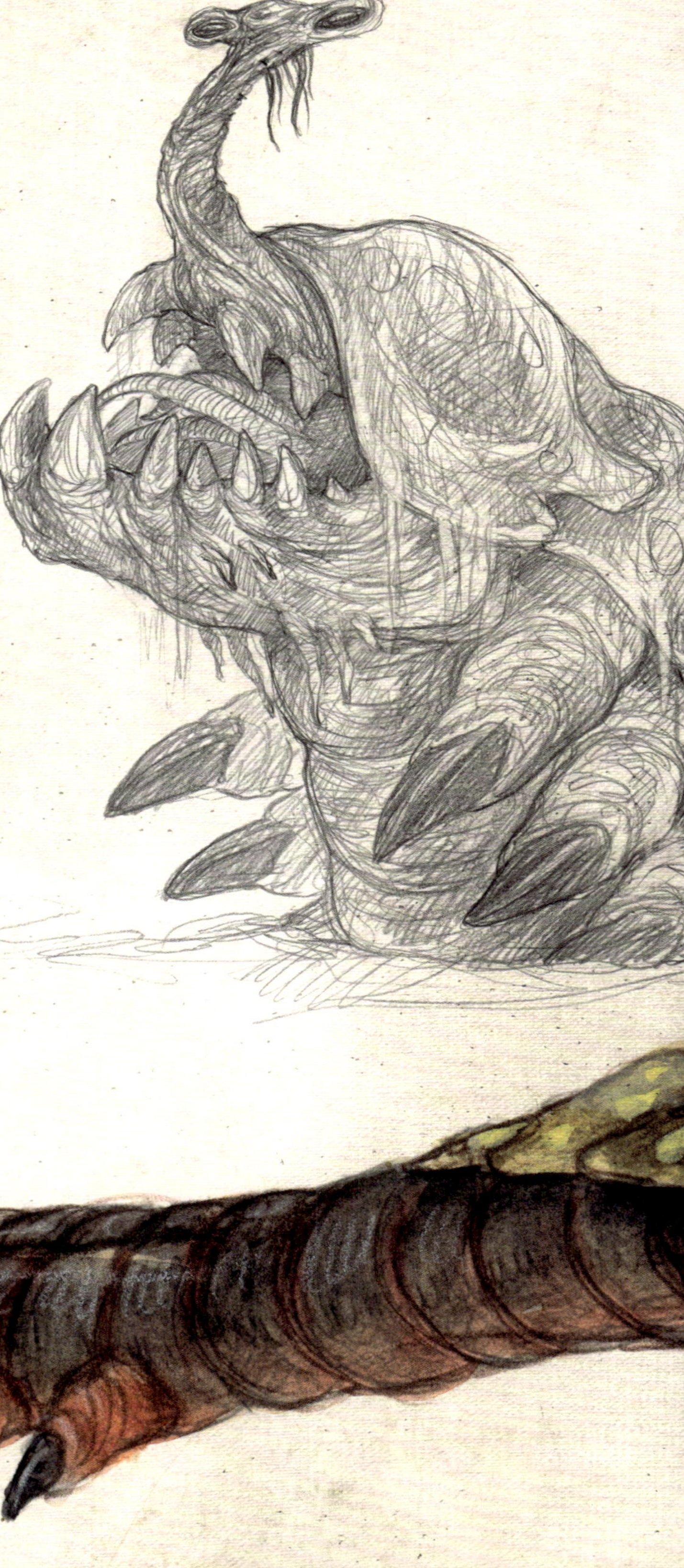

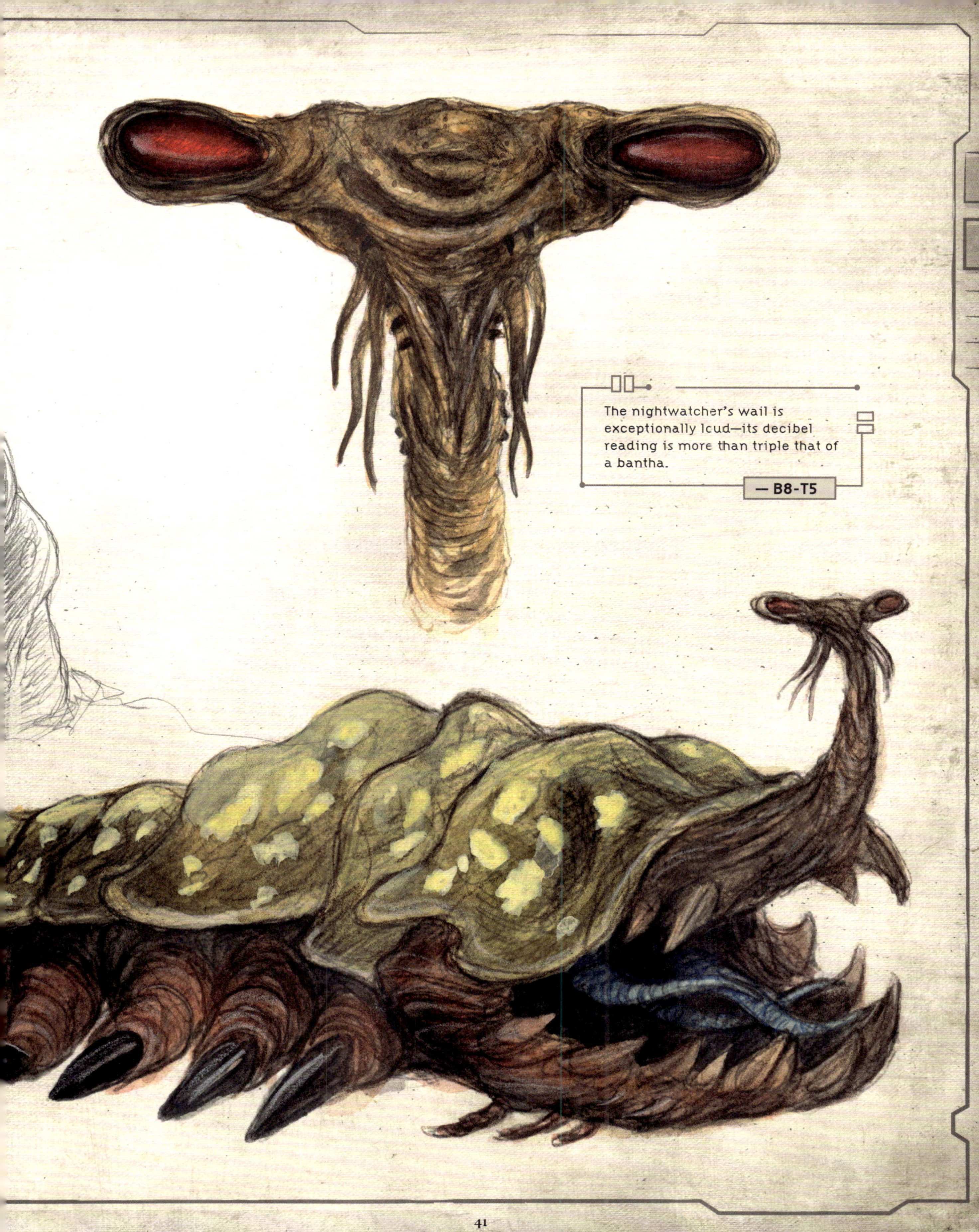
The nightwatcher's wail is exceptionally loud—its decibel reading is more than triple that of a bantha.
— B8-T5

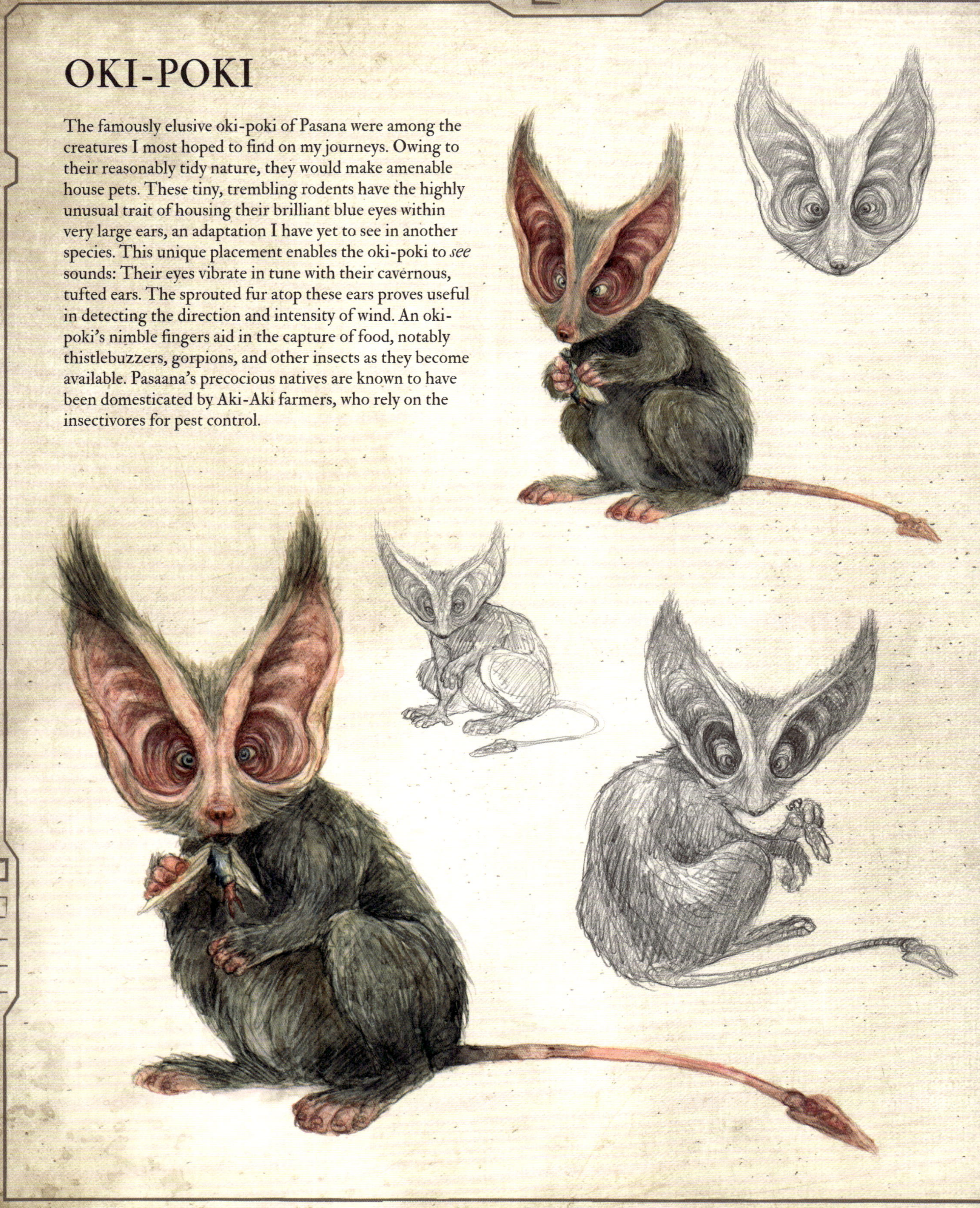

OKI-POKI

The famously elusive oki-poki of Pasana were among the creatures I most hoped to find on my journeys. Owing to their reasonably tidy nature, they would make amenable house pets. These tiny, trembling rodents have the highly unusual trait of housing their brilliant blue eyes within very large ears, an adaptation I have yet to see in another species. This unique placement enables the oki-poki to *see* sounds: Their eyes vibrate in tune with their cavernous, tufted ears. The sprouted fur atop these ears proves useful in detecting the direction and intensity of wind. An oki-poki's nimble fingers aid in the capture of food, notably thistlebuzzers, gorpions, and other insects as they become available. Pasaana's precocious natives are known to have been domesticated by Aki-Aki farmers, who rely on the insectivores for pest control.

ORRAY

Native to Geonosis, the wide-bodied, long-snouted orray was a domesticated species frequently tasked with ferrying heavy objects. The creatures were also called upon to transport passengers—from picadors to prisoners—within the Petranaki arena. An orray selected for such a role was first subjected to the removal of its tail; a metal cap was then placed atop the stump of its former appendage.

These four-legged reptiles stood two meters tall and three meters long. They were prized for their strength, resilience, and ability to haul heavy loads. Pronounced snouts were well adapted to digging in nests, and hearty teeth enabled the orray to crush eggs, a favorite food source. Despite their once-strong numbers, orray dropped into extinction following the fall of the Republic. Locating a rare orray skeleton within the arid dirt-pack of Geonosis remains one of my proudest moments.

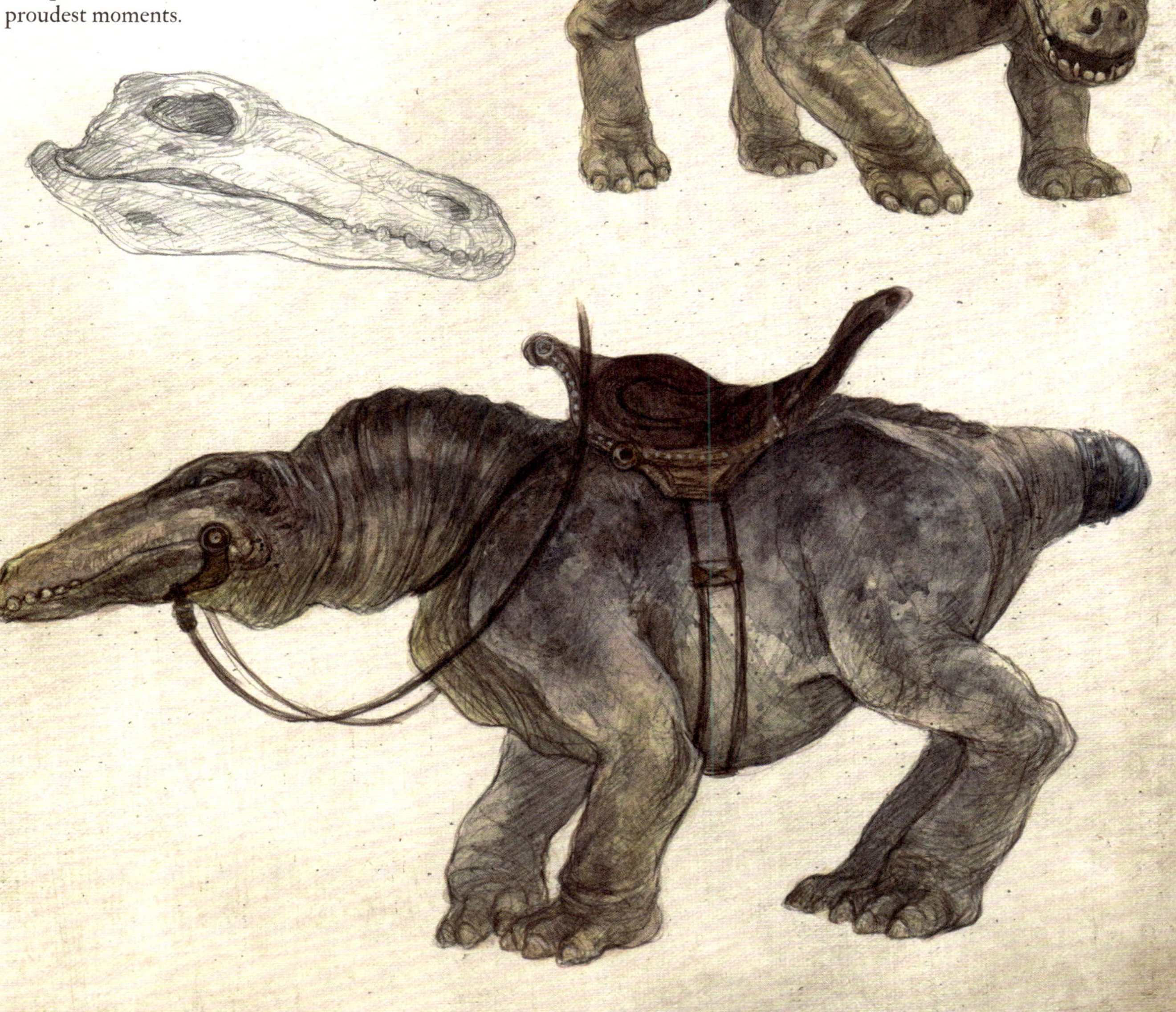

RANCOR

These terrifying reptilians stand at five meters tall and weigh approximately 1,650 kilograms. Believed to be native to the grottos and plains of Dathomir, they have been known to eat just about anything—from sentients to nonsentients—although their preferred diet is large herbivores. Despite their brutish appearance—and ability to cause excessive amounts of destruction—rancors are an innately benign species that give in to violence only when provoked. In the wild, the species has developed a symbiotic relationship with birds—the tiny avians clean the rancor's garishly yellowed teeth in exchange for food. The infamous Dathomir Nightsisters domesticated these naturally gentle giants, forging their bond with the creatures to expunge invaders from their homeworld, but the mutually beneficial relationship continued in the years that followed. Because of their significant strength (and propensity to pummel perceived threats), rancors have been shipped across the galaxy and employed as executioners, sentries, and combatants. Rancors have been spotted on Tatooine, Felucia, Koboh, and Vodran, where they roam freely, live peaceably alongside natives, and even serve in the courts of infamous crime lords. Domesticated rancors share a strong bond with their handlers. They imprint on the first person they see and remain devoted to that individual throughout their lives. Once such a bond is formed, a rancor will even permit its handler to ride atop its back, a feat I have yet to experience.

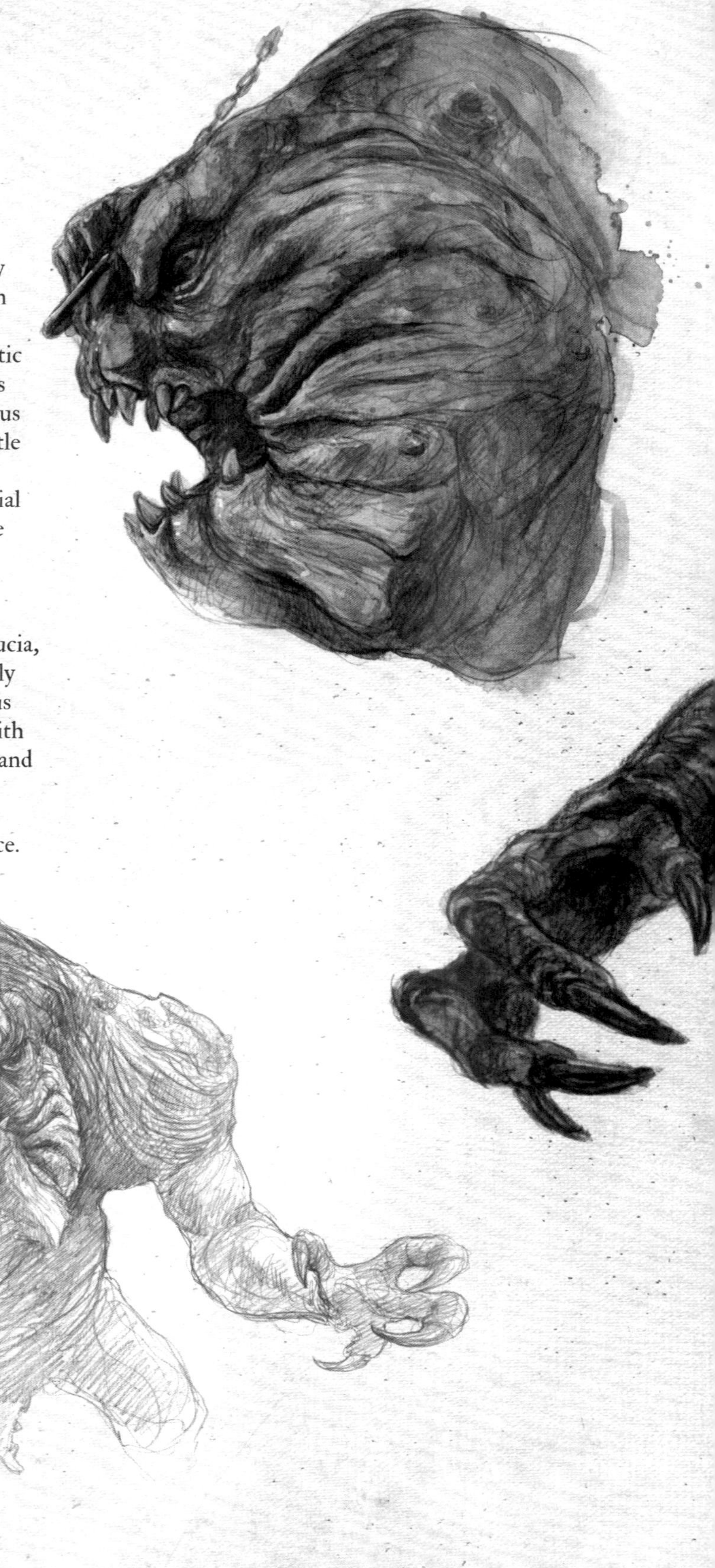

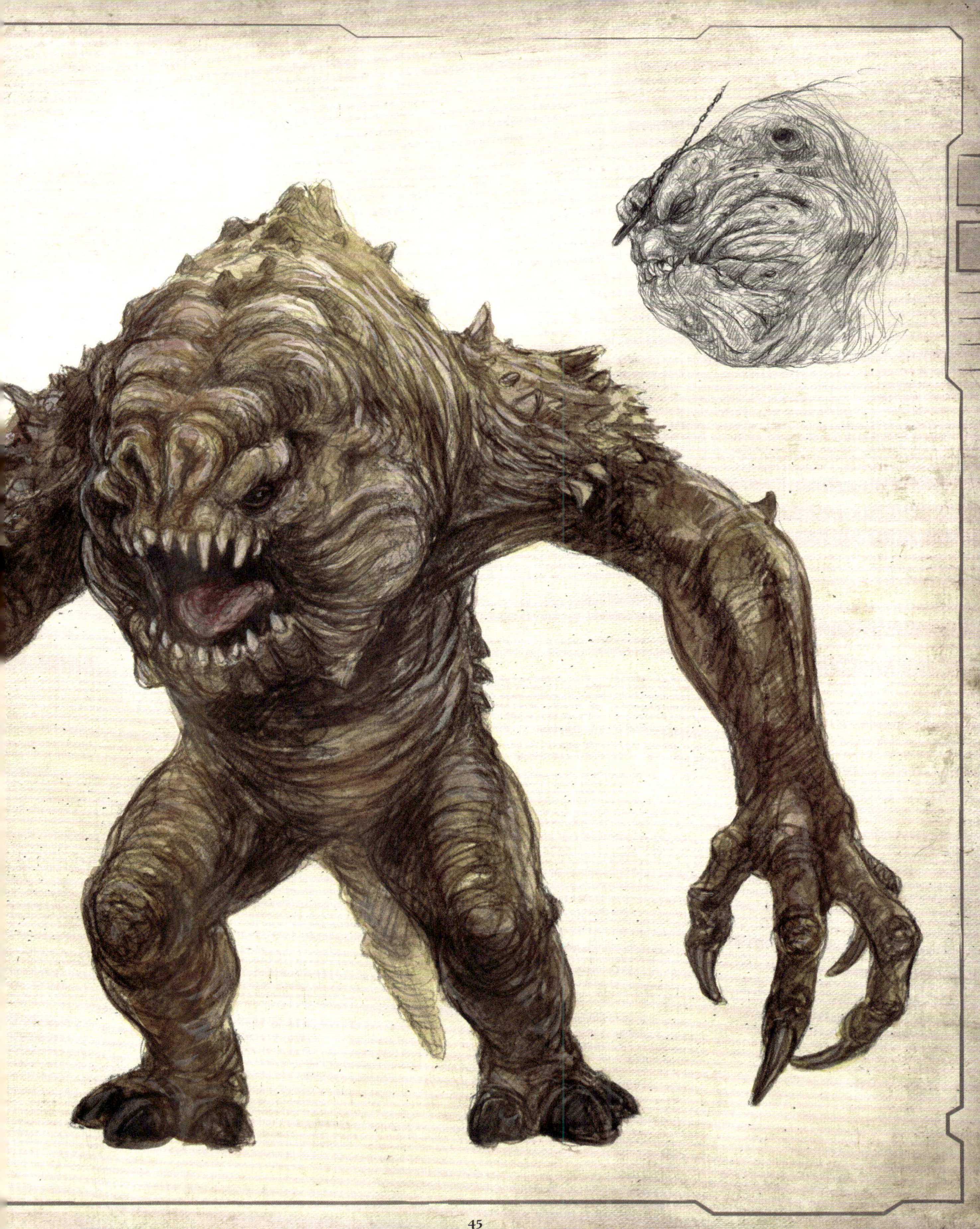

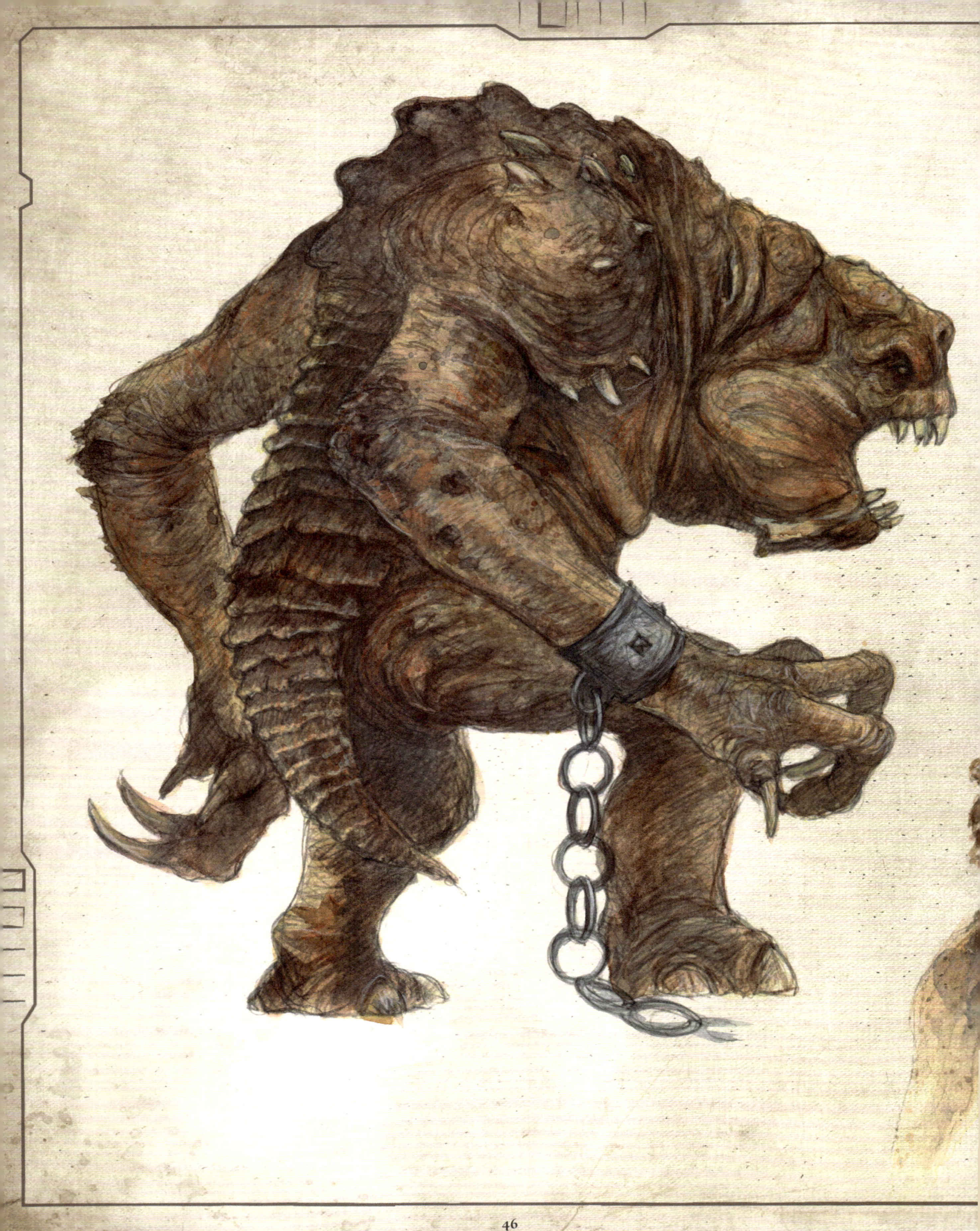

In addition to the primary species, there are several subspecies of rancors. Jungle rancors are native to Felucia, where they coexist peaceably with local farmers. Shadow rancors have a darker skin tone and a more destructive nature than the primary species. Rage rancors stand taller than their counterparts and possess a heightened level of anger. Wild rancors exist in groups called a crash, with a singular alpha exerting dominance over the rest of the group until he is challenged and defeated. Female rancors commonly give birth to twins, who remain with their mother until the age of three. During that time, the female teaches her offspring to survive in the wild. Upon reaching maturity, these young leave the nest and do not return.

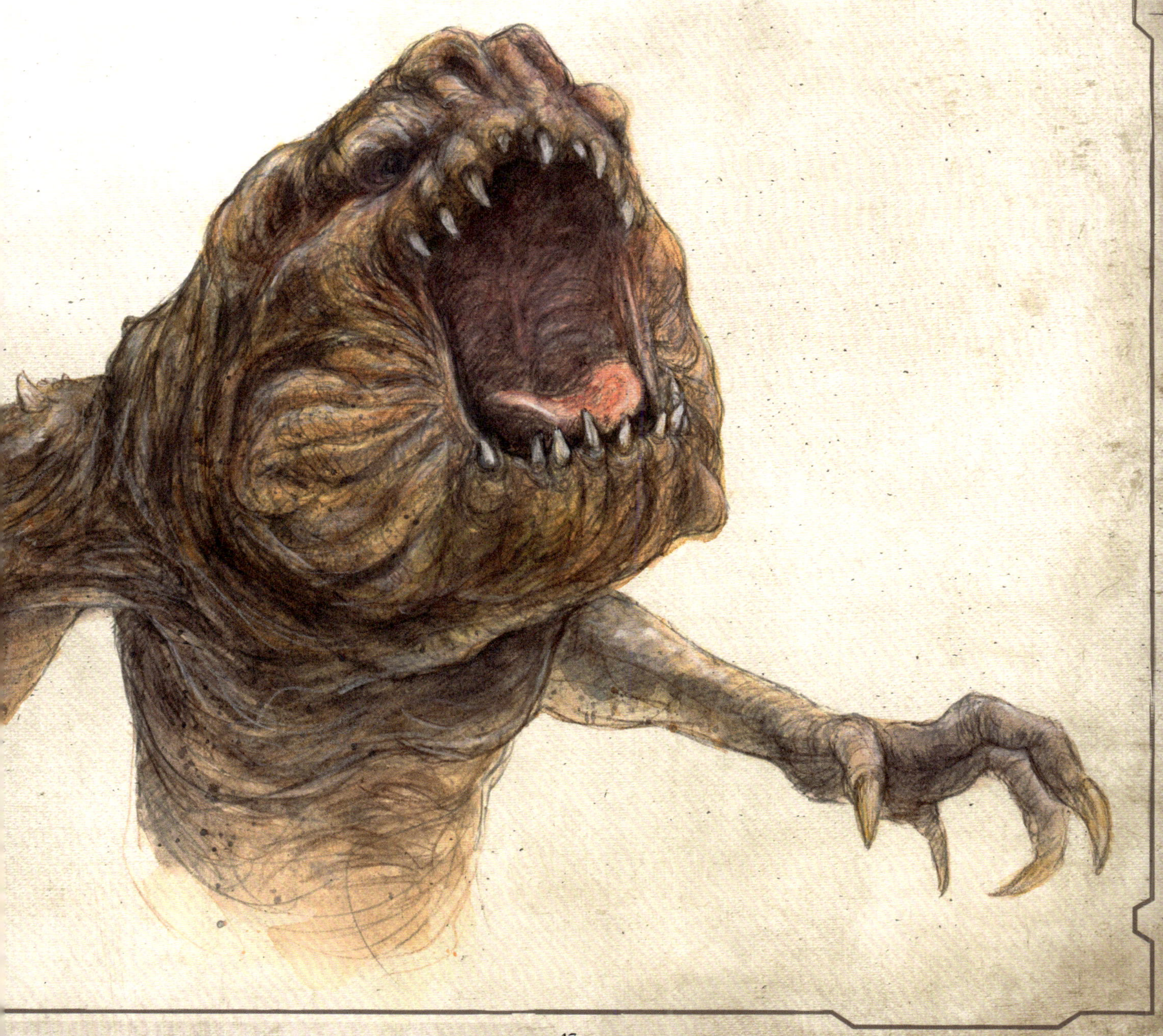

RONTO

These creatures are majestic saurians that stand up to 4.25 meters in height and possess a gentle nature that makes them the preferred mount of the highly skittish Jawas. Rontos can be seen across Tatooine, from Mos Espa to Mos Eisley, where they serve as the space port's ground transport. They've also been spotted ferrying Jawas and their goods between trading posts, and they are considered prized specimens among the menageries of well-to-do citizens. With small eyes and relatively poor eyesight, rontos are easily startled—and are likely to throw a rider if they're caught off guard. Regardless, their loyal nature and ability to haul heavy objects make rontos an ideal beast of burden for Tatooine's hardworking natives.

To compensate for their compromised eyesight, rontos have developed exceptional hearing—in no small part thanks to their long pointed ears. They also possesses a strong sense of smell, allowing the creatures to detect predators long before they see them. Other adaptations include facial skin flaps that can be shifted to cover a ronto's eyes during a sandstorm and the ability to expel heat through their skin. Perhaps best know in it's culinary form, ronto meat is often served up in wraps at popular destinations such as Batuu.

Despite their significant size, rontos can rear up on their hind legs, a behavior they exhibit when they're angry, startled, or ready to present a challenge to a nearby creature. The ronto's rearing behavior enables witnesses to observe the saurian's underside, which is slightly paler and significantly less calloused than the skin that coats the rest of its body. It is imperative to observe this behavior from a safe distance, lest one be inadvertently trampled.

— B8-T5

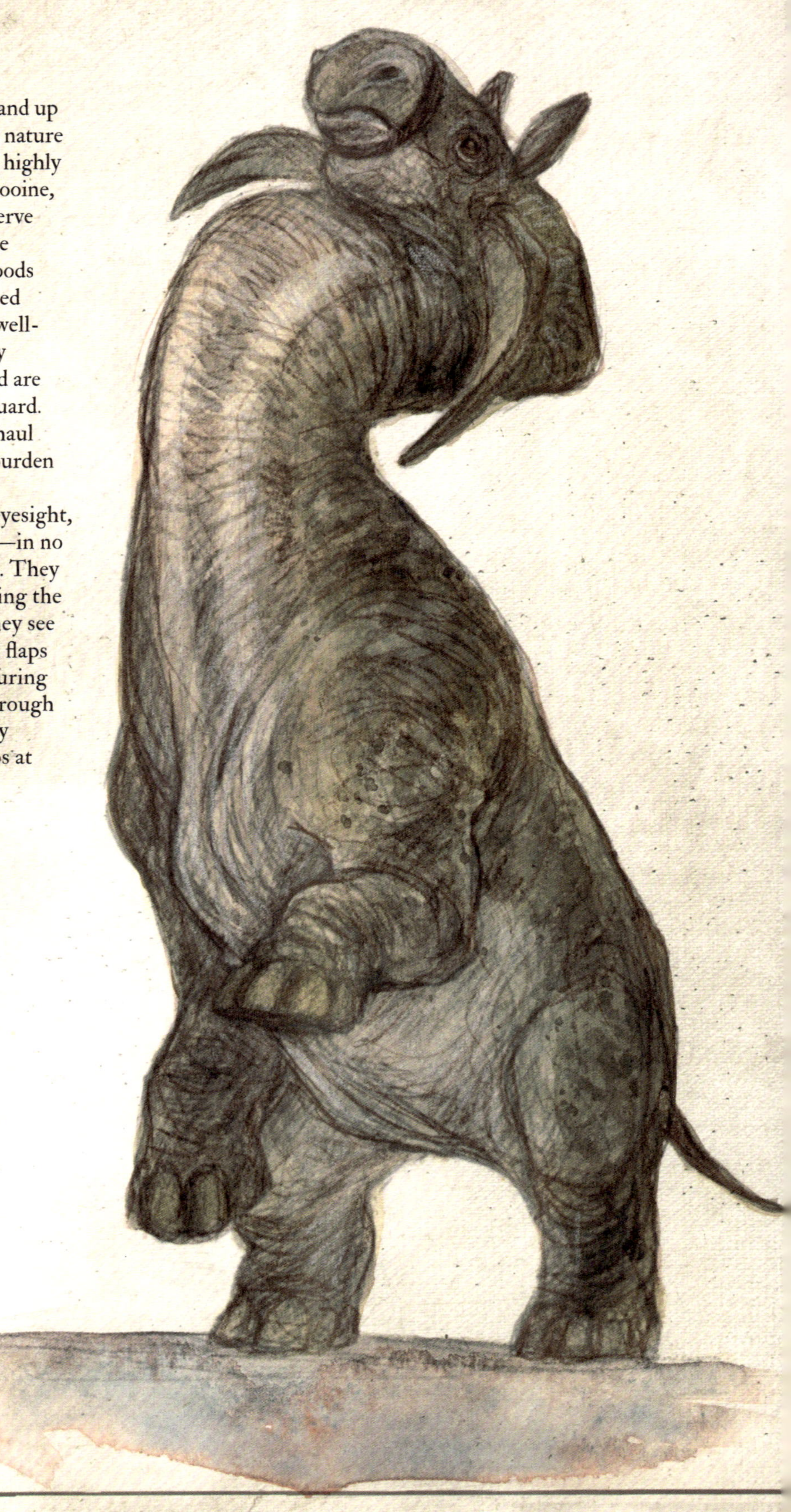

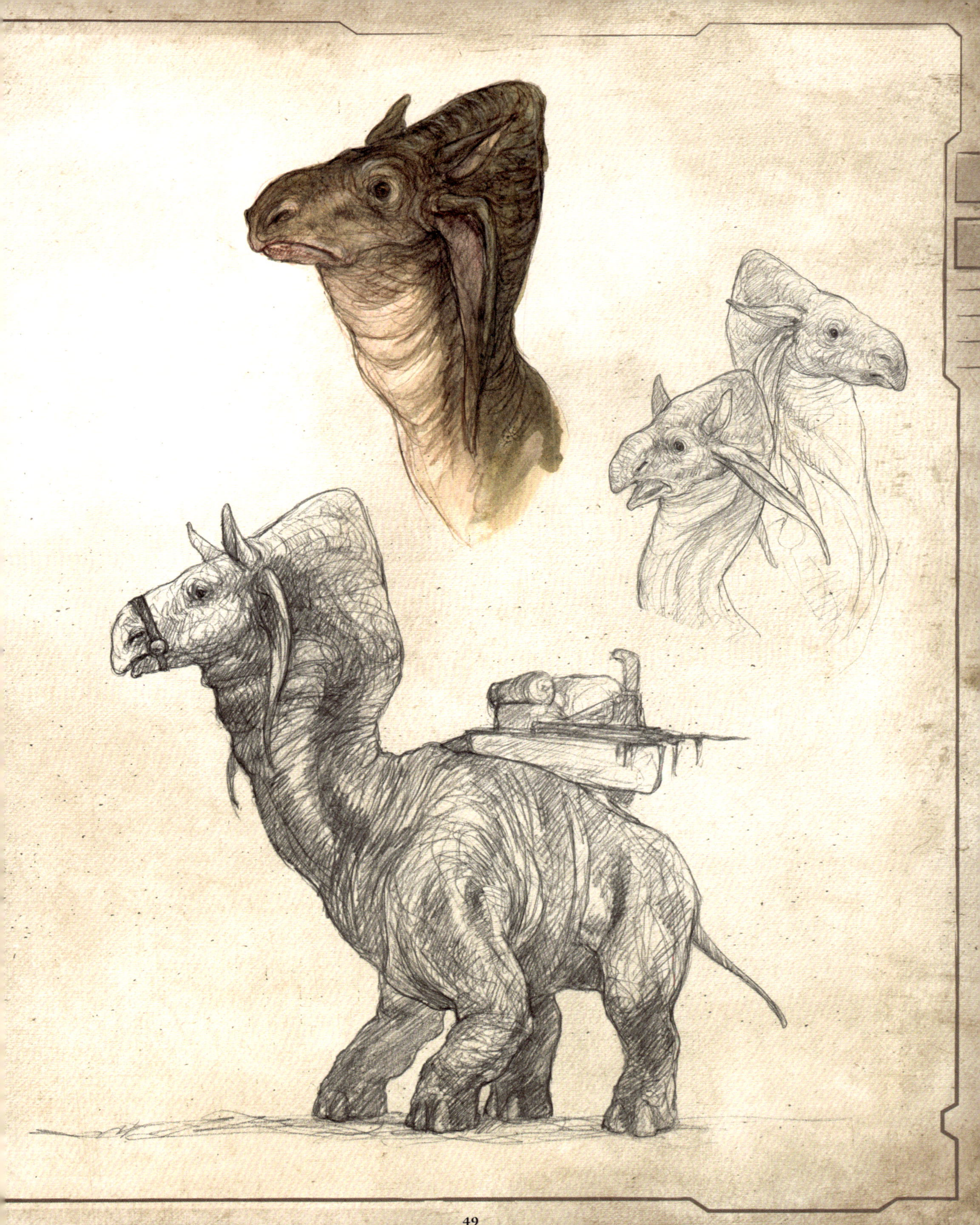

SARLACC

The all-powerful ancient sarlacc is feared by those who know of its massive maw, tenacious tentacles, and infinite rows of razor-sharp teeth. The ultimate desert predator, the sarlacc possesses a sharp beak within its maw, rendering it capable of crunching anything from armor to skulls. Because the creature usually swallows its prey whole, this beak is most likely an evolutionary holdover from a previous masticatory method. The sarlacc's scent glands release an odor known to attract nearby herbivores. Deft tentacles are quick to grab hold of any prospective prey. Once it consumes its food, a sarlacc's relatively weak stomach acid makes for slow digestion—some reports claim that a sarlacc can take up to one thousand years to digest its prey! Regardless of the duration, evidence suggests that the acid is strong enough to burn a hole through Imperial armor and would most likely kill an organic being long before digestion was completed. Whatever the truth may be, this scientist does *not* wish to investigate further!

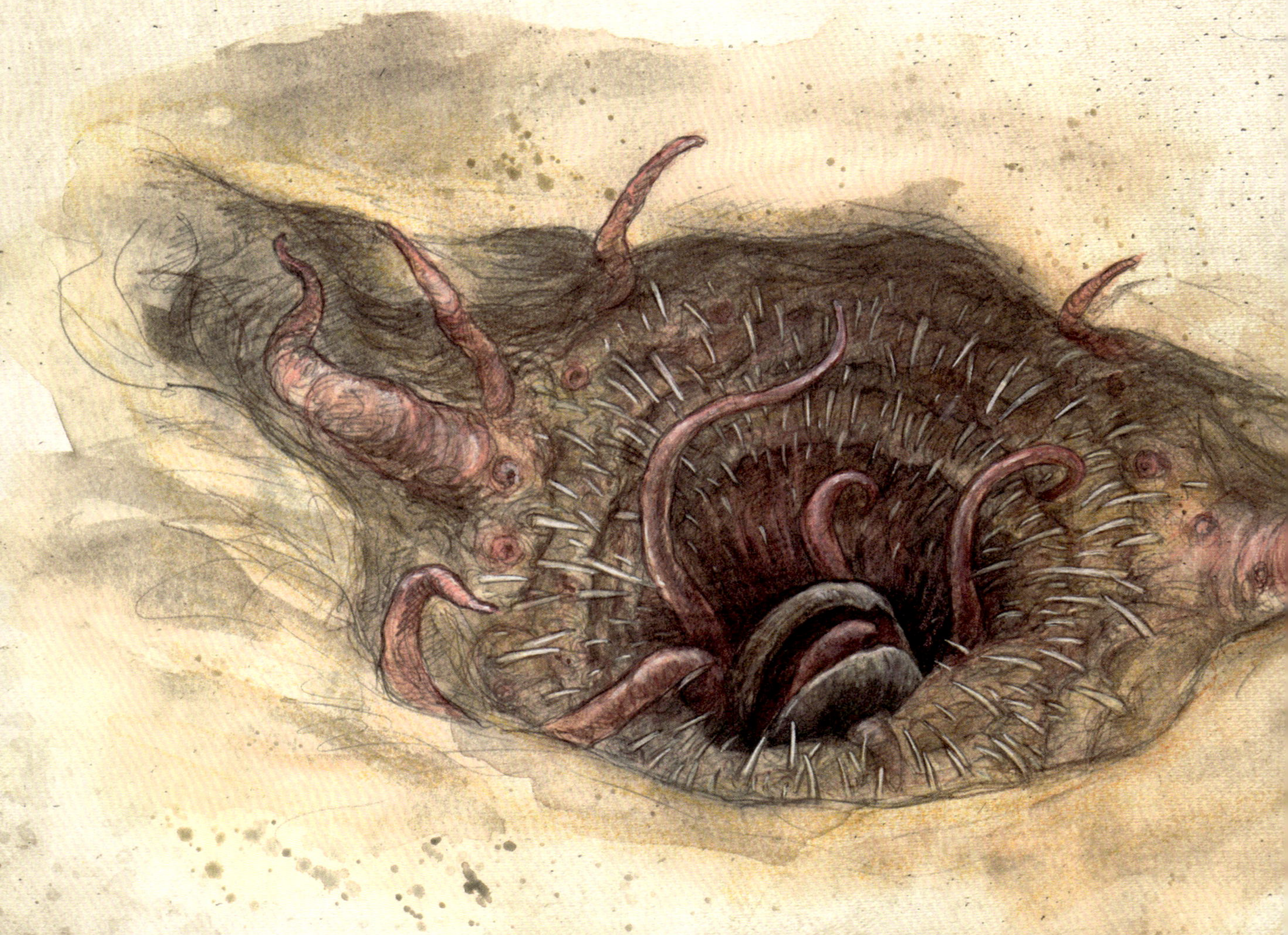

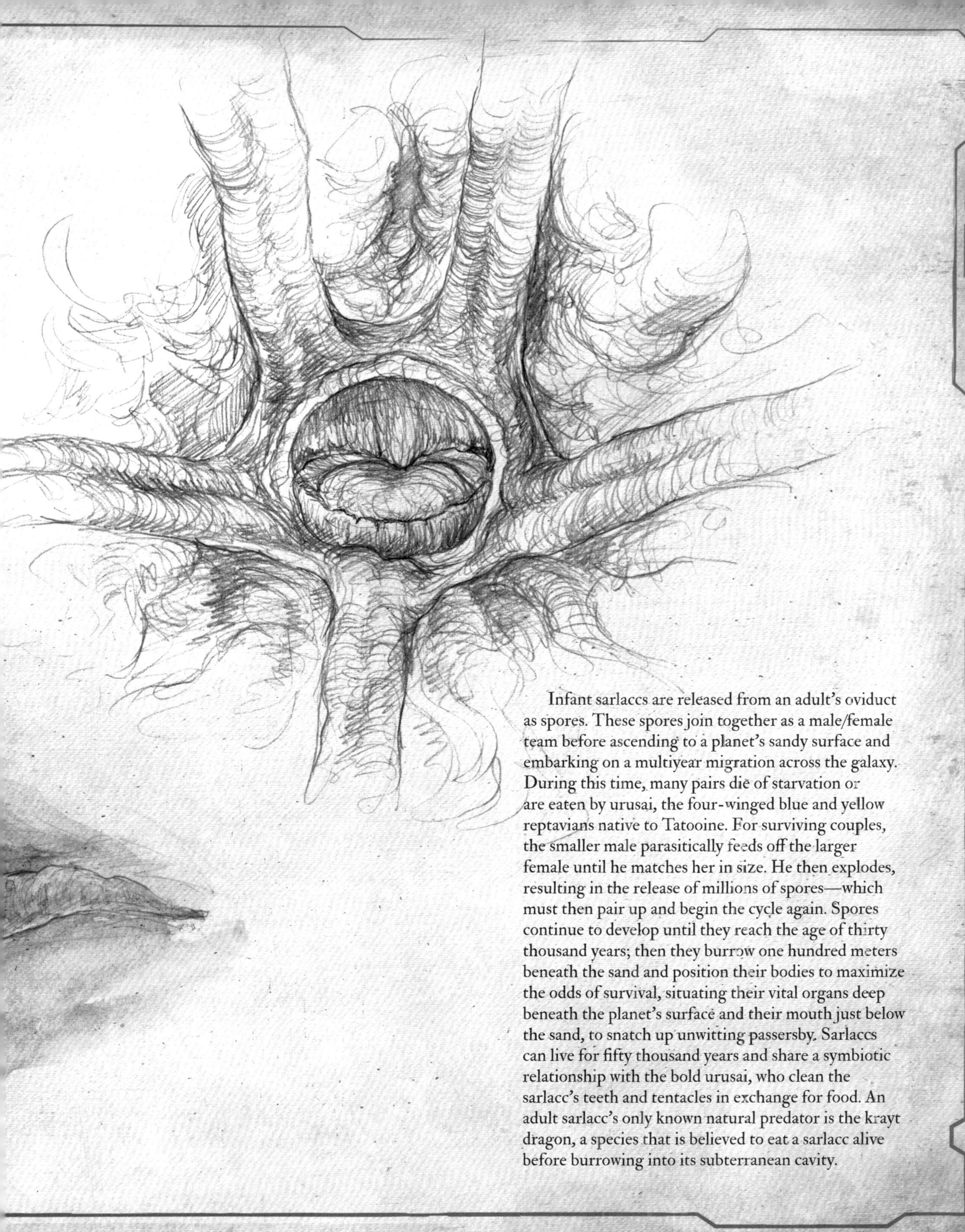

Infant sarlaccs are released from an adult's oviduct as spores. These spores join together as a male/female team before ascending to a planet's sandy surface and embarking on a multiyear migration across the galaxy. During this time, many pairs die of starvation or are eaten by urusai, the four-winged blue and yellow reptavians native to Tatooine. For surviving couples, the smaller male parasitically feeds off the larger female until he matches her in size. He then explodes, resulting in the release of millions of spores—which must then pair up and begin the cycle again. Spores continue to develop until they reach the age of thirty thousand years; then they burrow one hundred meters beneath the sand and position their bodies to maximize the odds of survival, situating their vital organs deep beneath the planet's surface and their mouth just below the sand, to snatch up unwitting passersby. Sarlaccs can live for fifty thousand years and share a symbiotic relationship with the bold urusai, who clean the sarlacc's teeth and tentacles in exchange for food. An adult sarlacc's only known natural predator is the krayt dragon, a species that is believed to eat a sarlacc alive before burrowing into its subterranean cavity.

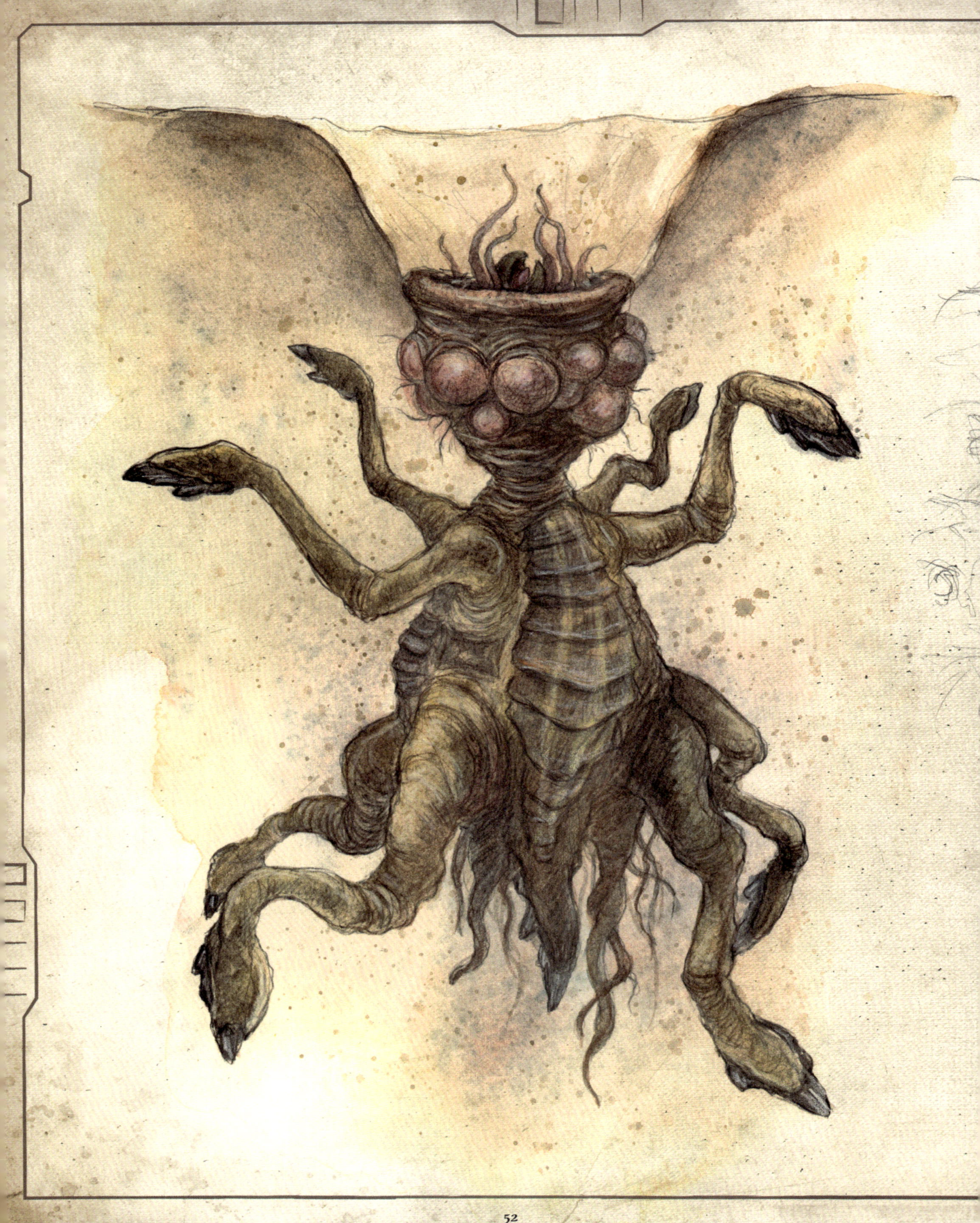

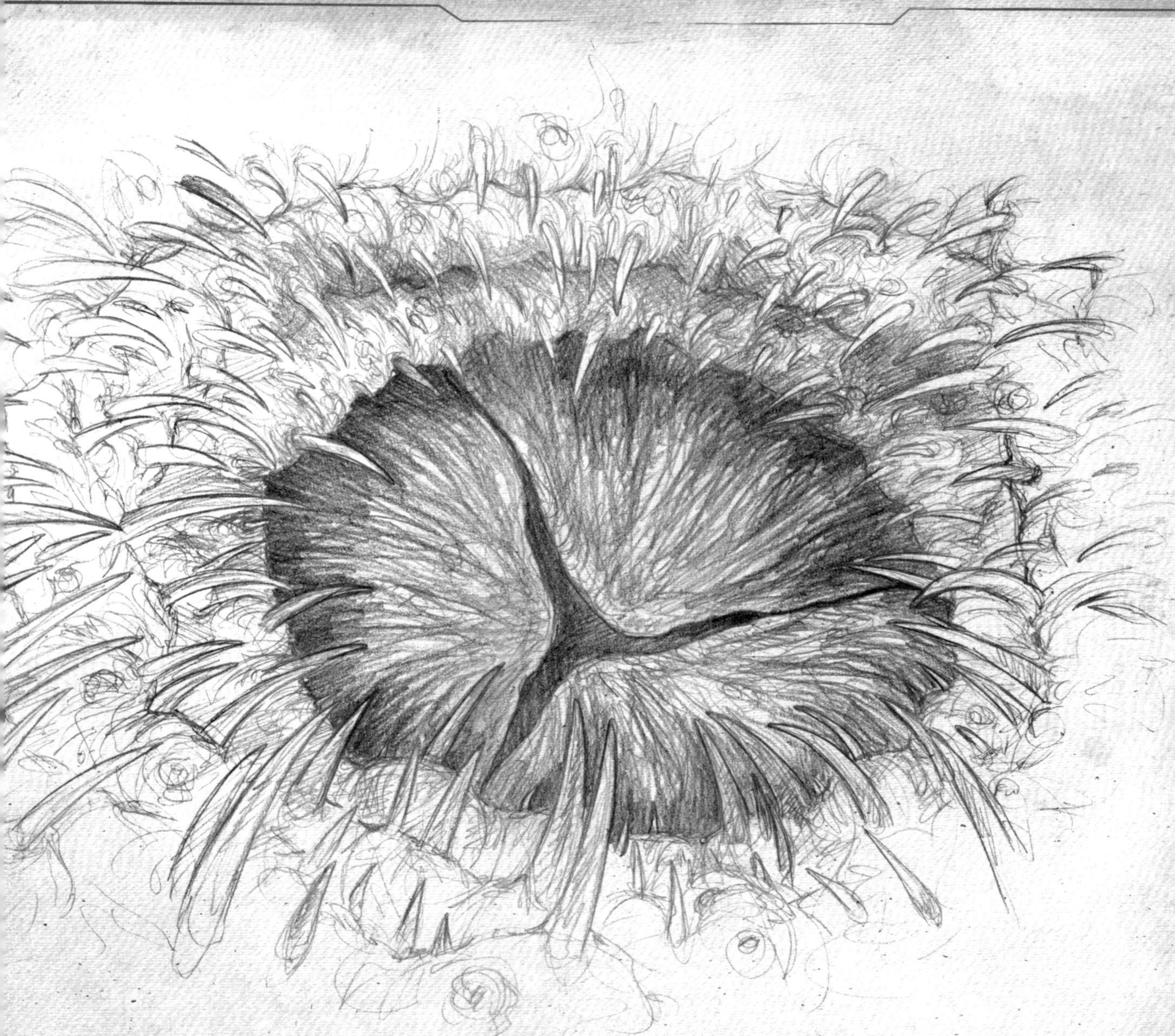

Sarlaccs live just beneath the surface of their various homeworlds, including Tatooine, I'vorcia Prime, Vodran, Felucia, and Pasaana. Their mobility is limited due to their substantial size—the average adult sarlacc measures three meters wide and one hundred meters long! Although young members of the species travel to capture food, fully grown adults—including the infamous Sarlacc that lived in Tatooine's Dune Sea—must wait for prey to come to them. When a food source approaches, the sarlacc uses its dexterous tentacles to sweep prey into its maw. Deadly rows of razor-sharp teeth prevent the victim from climbing to safety. Prey is swallowed whole before being digested across several stomachs, and death finally comes by means of toxic fumes, acid, or suffocation.

Because of the highly dangerous nature of the species—and the extremely low survival rate of those unwise (or unlucky!) enough to approach its maw—little research has been performed on the sarlacc. Consequently, there are still some within the scientific community who believe the creature to be nothing more than a highly evolved carnivorous plant. However, with the sarlacc's similarities to the rathtar and vixus—each of which relies on a similarly situated multitude of appendages to catch prey—it is the opinion of this scientist that the sarlacc is a carnivorous animal with distant biological ties to the aforementioned cephalopods. Thanks to the discovery of a recently deceased specimen, we now know that the sarlacc possesses an exoskeleton, which further debunks the carnivorous plant theory and leads to the conclusion that the creatures are, in fact, arthropods.

SCURRIER

Among the desert's more charming creatures, scurriers skitter across the sands of Tatooine in packs, which quickly disband in the face of a threat. Small, slight, and easily intimidated, scurriers were named for their agitated style of movement. With their tall ears, long tail, and wide snouts, they are easily identifiable as rodents. However, unlike others of their order, some scurriers have been known to grow antlers—the evolutionary purpose of these appendages is not known, given that scurriers do not commonly battle for dominance or exhibit aggressive tendencies toward their predators.

Despite having a quadrupedal bone structure, these diminutive creatures prefer to stand on two legs in order to optimize their view of their surroundings—and hopefully spot any predators before they're identified themselves! This position also enables the scurriers to free up their forelegs to dig for food. Although the positioning of their eyes along the side of their head easily identifies them as prey animals, their four nostrils allow them to pick up the scent of predators—often the scurrier evades capture before its opponent can attack.

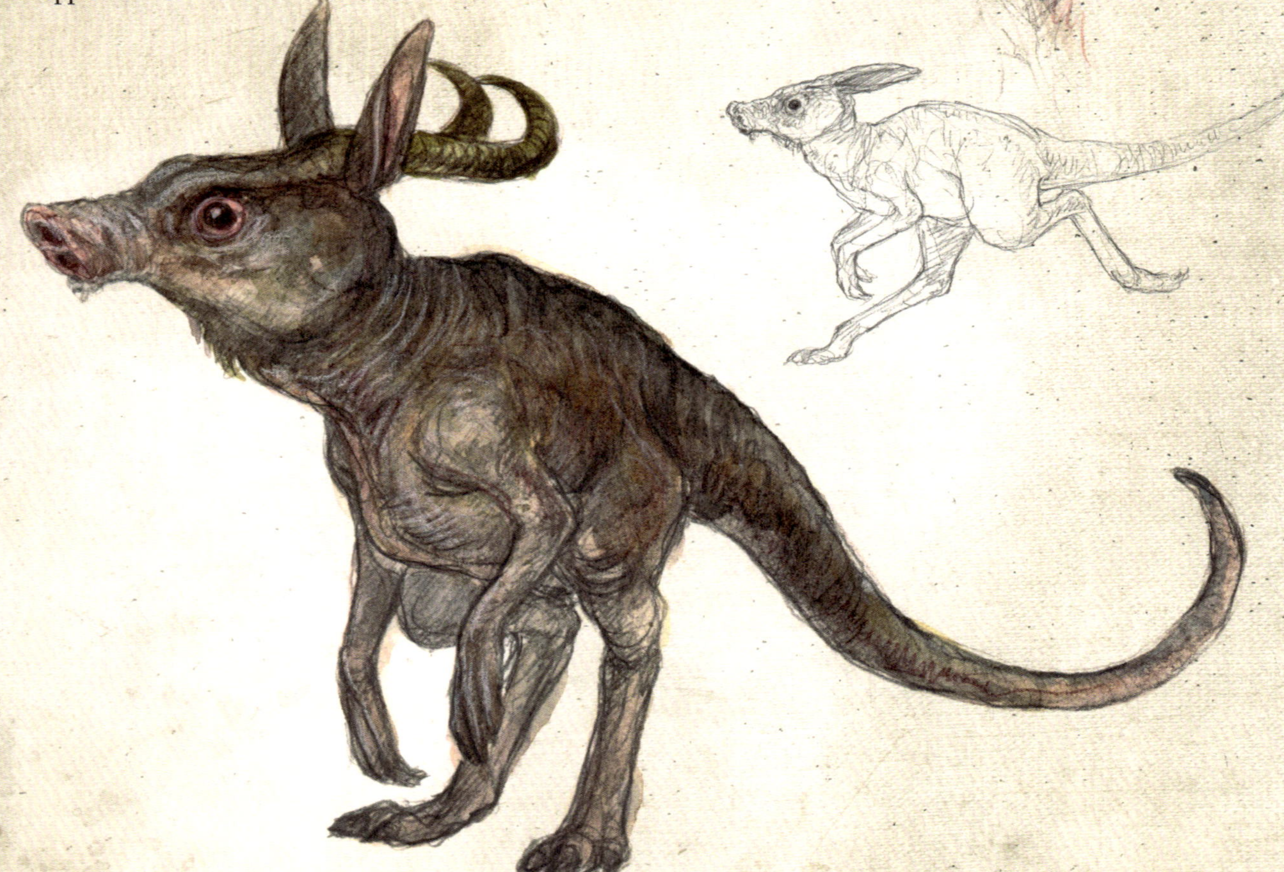

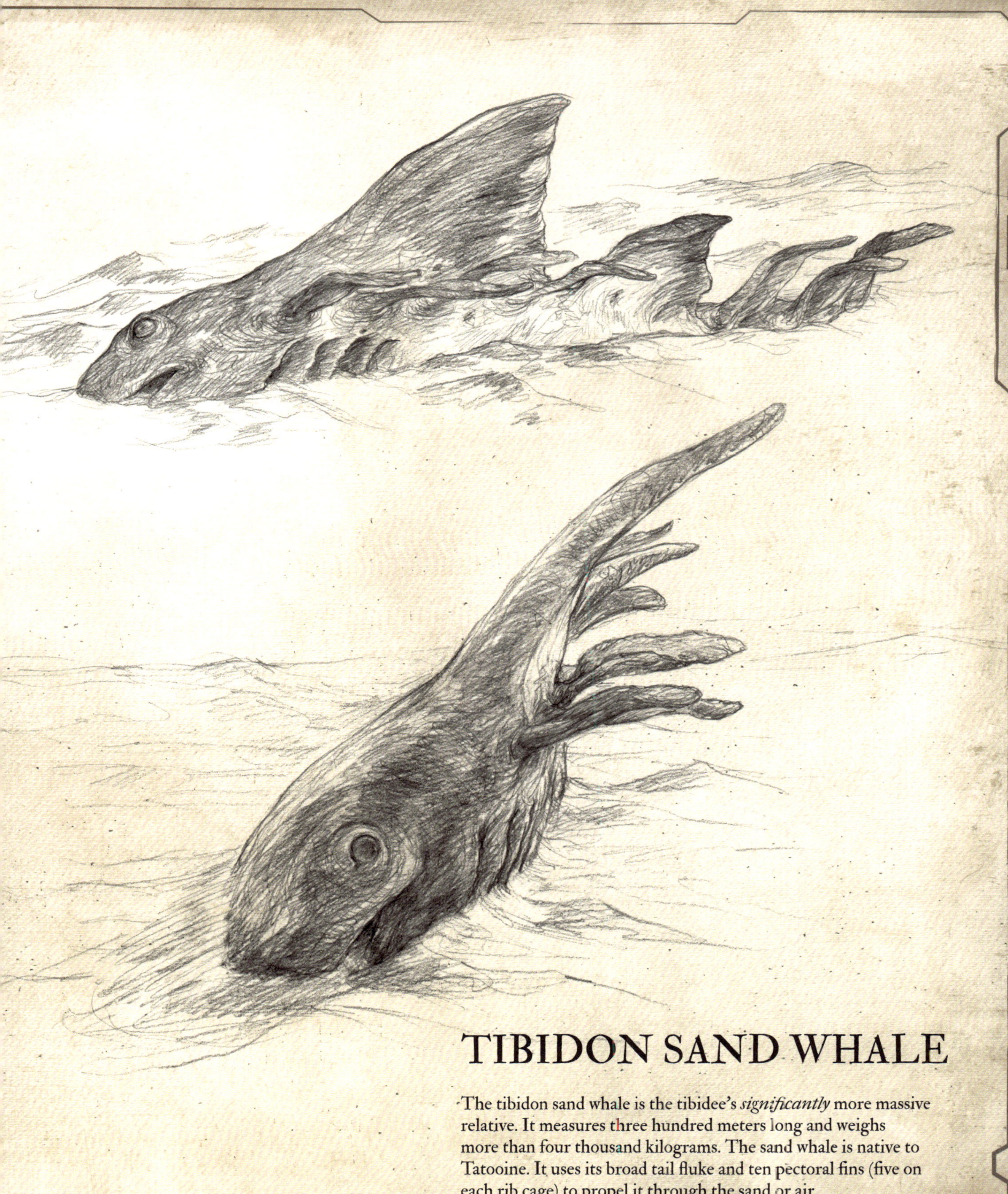

TIBIDON SAND WHALE

The tibidon sand whale is the tibidee's *significantly* more massive relative. It measures three hundred meters long and weighs more than four thousand kilograms. The sand whale is native to Tatooine. It uses its broad tail fluke and ten pectoral fins (five on each rib cage) to propel it through the sand or air.

TATOOINE SAND BEAST

Among the legion of dangers lurking beneath Tatooine is the dreaded sand beast, a six-limbed, thirty-meter behemoth with a long torso known for leaping from its subterranean lair to startle and slaughter unwitting prey. The beast's muscular appendages are capable of functioning as either arms or legs, allowing it to adapt to an opponent's fighting style by adopting a bipedal or quadrupedal stance. This carnivore is well adapted to hunting, with three fingers that end in broad, pointed claws and a mouth crowded with wide, sharpened teeth. Accordingly, its victims rarely escape capture—instead, they are most often shredded or ripped limb from limb. These adaptations, along with the creatures' thick armored skin and strong, muscular arms, all but guarantee that the sand beast remains at the top of Tatooine's food chain.

Much of what we know of this species comes from the accounts of Tuskens, who have had the misfortune of battling sand beasts on more than one occasion while traversing the Dune Sea. Those who survive an encounter earn the respect of Tusken chieftains, who are painfully aware of the risks these carnivores pose to the safety of their tribes.

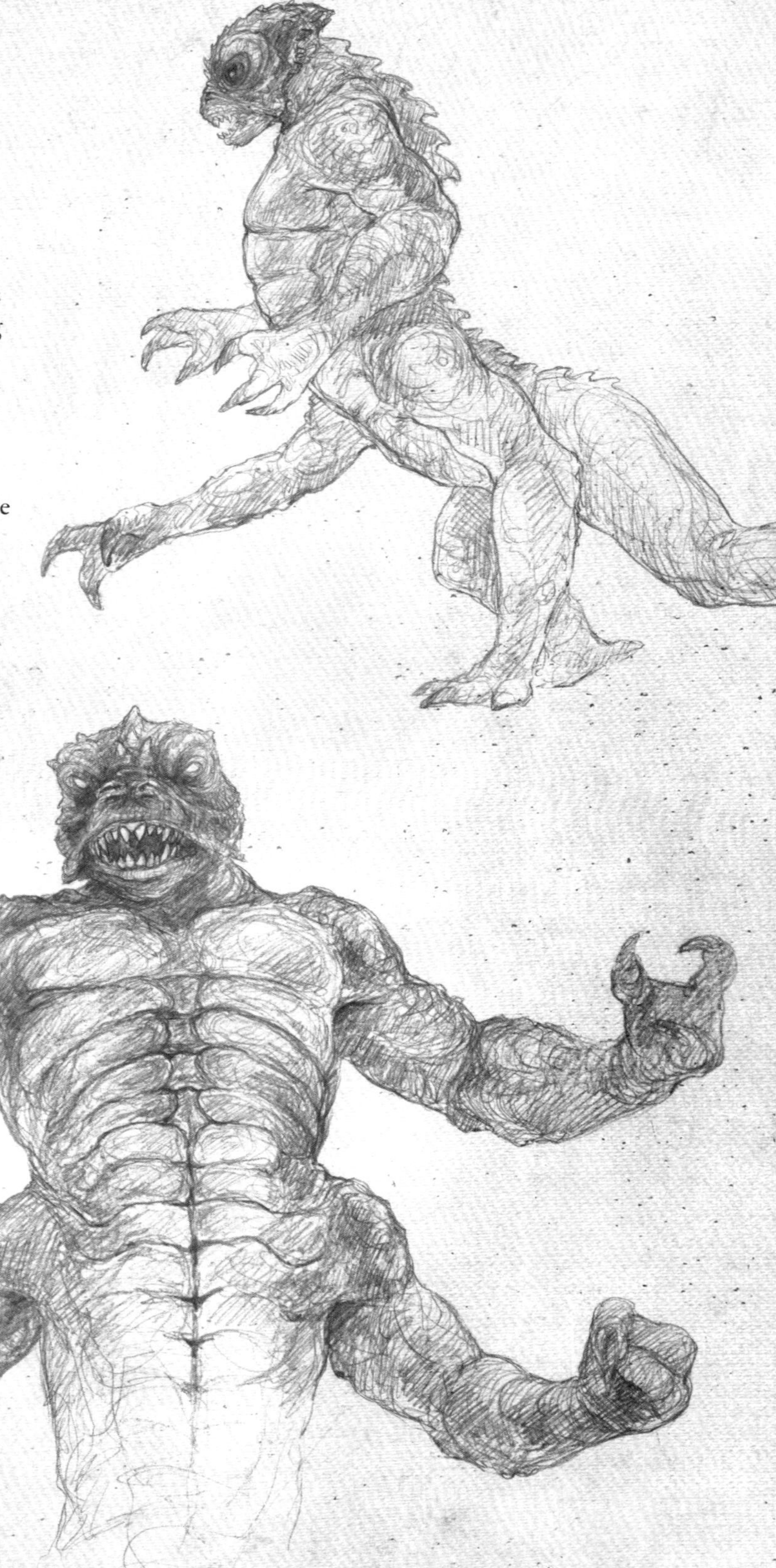

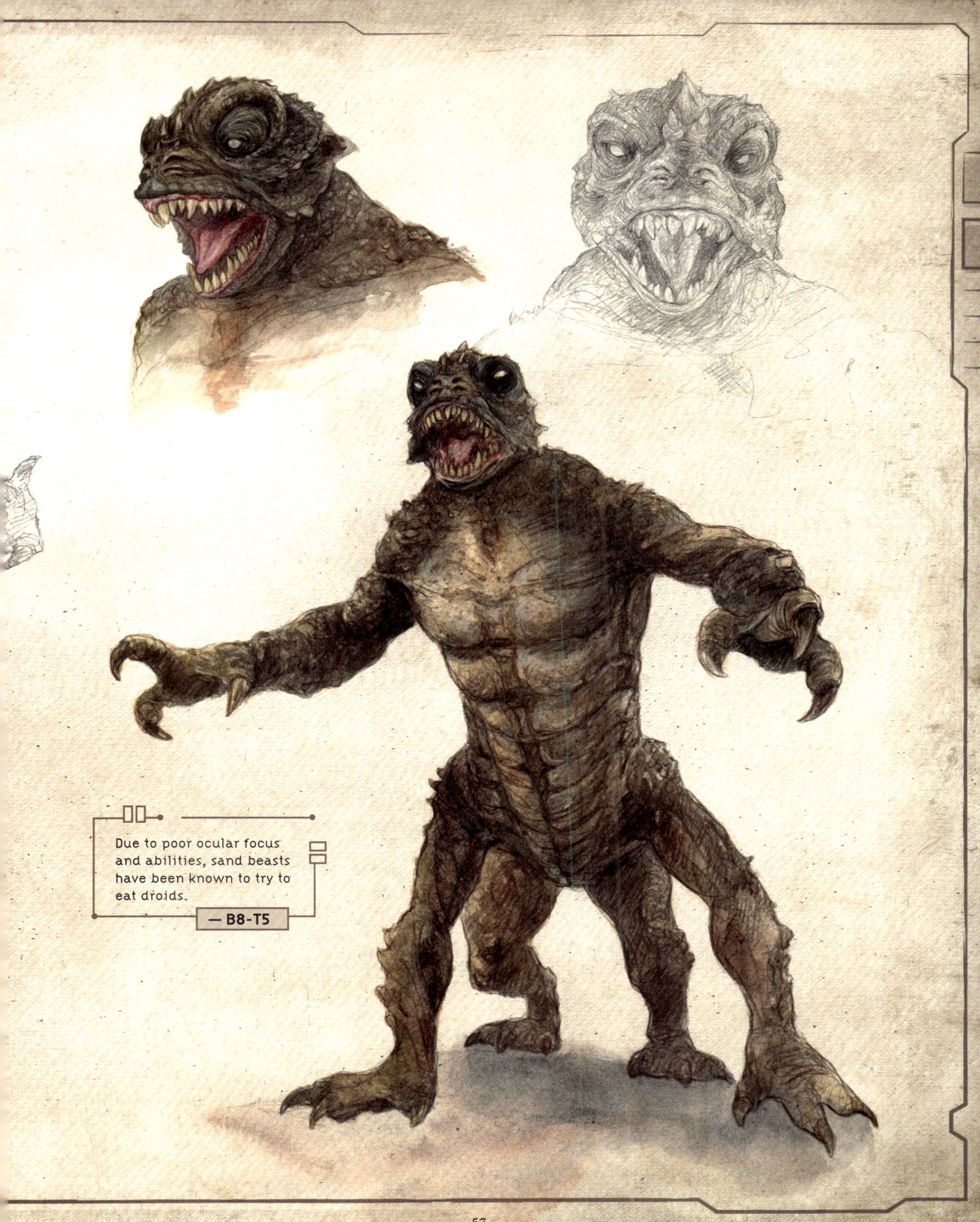

Due to poor ocular focus and abilities, sand beasts have been known to try to eat droids.
— B8-T5

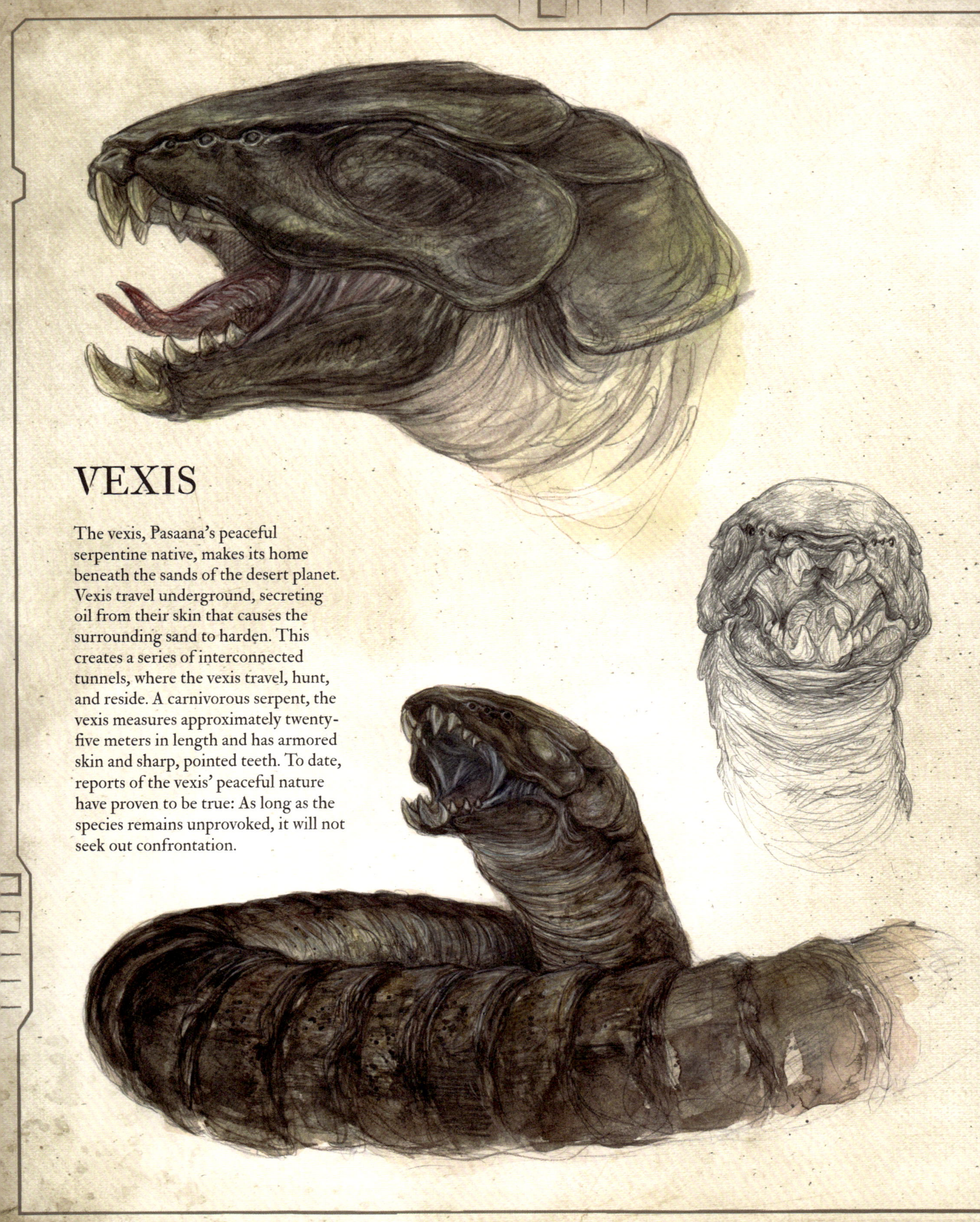

VEXIS

The vexis, Pasaana's peaceful serpentine native, makes its home beneath the sands of the desert planet. Vexis travel underground, secreting oil from their skin that causes the surrounding sand to harden. This creates a series of interconnected tunnels, where the vexis travel, hunt, and reside. A carnivorous serpent, the vexis measures approximately twenty-five meters in length and has armored skin and sharp, pointed teeth. To date, reports of the vexis' peaceful nature have proven to be true: As long as the species remains unprovoked, it will not seek out confrontation.

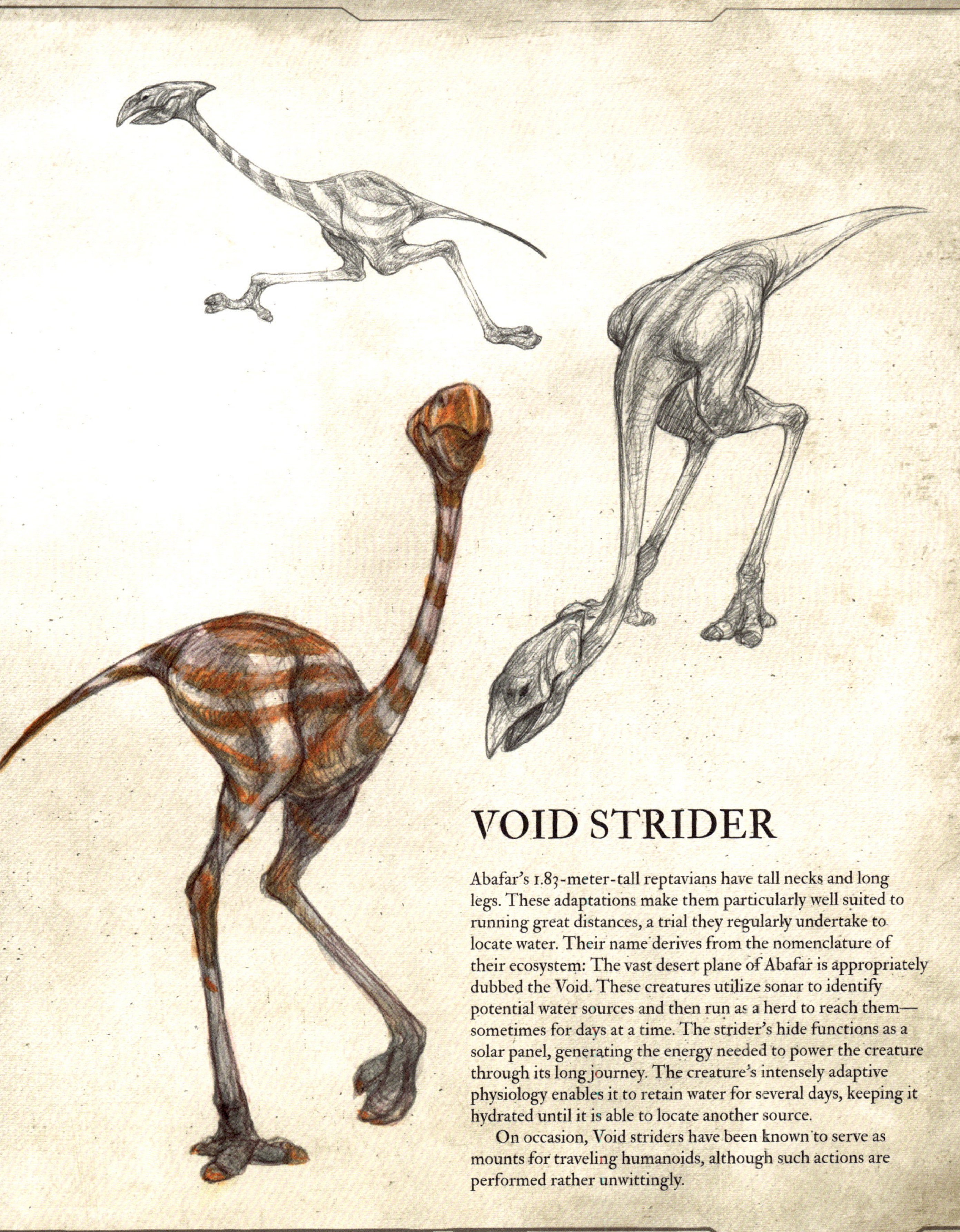

VOID STRIDER

Abafar's 1.83-meter-tall reptavians have tall necks and long legs. These adaptations make them particularly well suited to running great distances, a trial they regularly undertake to locate water. Their name derives from the nomenclature of their ecosystem: The vast desert plane of Abafar is appropriately dubbed the Void. These creatures utilize sonar to identify potential water sources and then run as a herd to reach them—sometimes for days at a time. The strider's hide functions as a solar panel, generating the energy needed to power the creature through its long journey. The creature's intensely adaptive physiology enables it to retain water for several days, keeping it hydrated until it is able to locate another source.

On occasion, Void striders have been known to serve as mounts for traveling humanoids, although such actions are performed rather unwittingly.

WOMP RAT

Tatooine's red-eyed rodents are the bane of any moisture farmer's existence. Measuring two meters in length and sporting a sea of sharply pointed canines within their narrow jaws, the womp rat is known for chewing cables . . . as well as anything else it can sink its teeth into. This unfortunate habit has led farmers to hunt their nefarious nemeses for sport, and local pilots—particularly those who fly in Beggar's Canyon—use the fleeing rodents for target practice.

A womp rat's bumpy skin is covered in tufts of gray or brown hair along the length of its back, and a prehensile tail helps the rodent right itself if it is caught off balance. In addition to chewing cables, womp rats feed on smaller creatures, using their three-clawed paws or ferocious fangs to capture their prey. Womp rats prefer to hunt in packs, although a solitary member of the species might also resort to eating the garbage left outside one of Tatooine's many moisture farms. Groups of womp rats have been known to swarm the residents of the desert planet, leading locals to fear these oft-aggressive rodents.

But despite their predatory tendencies, womp rats often find themselves cast as prey to larger, carnivorous creatures. Krayt dragons and dewbacks readily feast on womp rat flesh, and Tuskens remove the rodents' tusks and repurpose them as decorative clothing adornments.

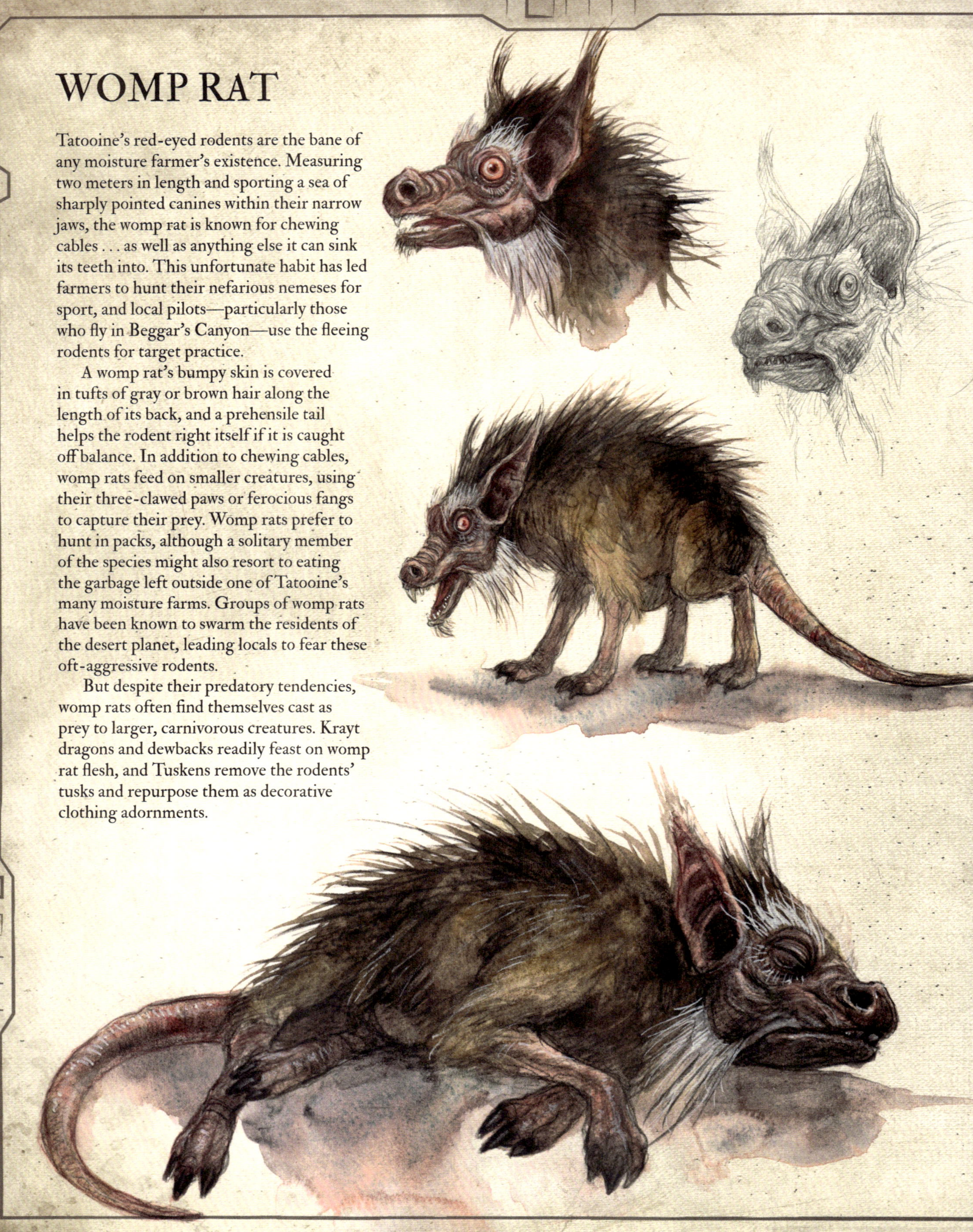

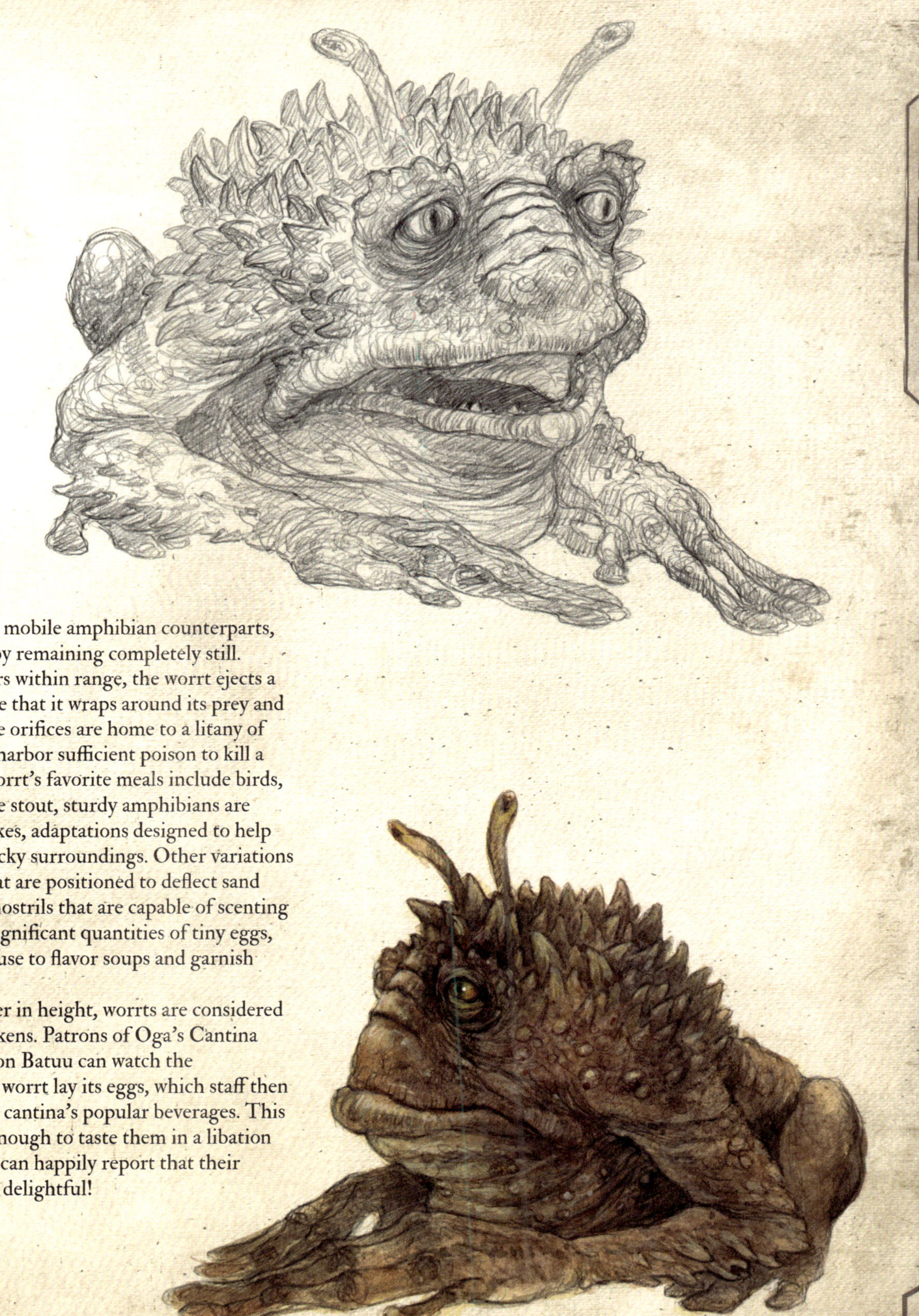

WORRT

Unlike its smaller, more mobile amphibian counterparts, the worrt lures its prey by remaining completely still. When a creature wanders within range, the worrt ejects a purple prehensile tongue that it wraps around its prey and drags into its jaws. These orifices are home to a litany of venom-laced teeth that harbor sufficient poison to kill a fully grown bantha. A worrt's favorite meals include birds, rodents, and insects. The stout, sturdy amphibians are covered in warts and spikes, adaptations designed to help the animal blend into rocky surroundings. Other variations include broad eyelids that are positioned to deflect sand from the eyes and twin nostrils that are capable of scenting predators. Females lay significant quantities of tiny eggs, which locals gather and use to flavor soups and garnish beverages.

At almost half a meter in height, worrts are considered a hearty delicacy by Tuskens. Patrons of Oga's Cantina at Black Spire Outpost on Batuu can watch the establishment's resident worrt lay its eggs, which staff then harvest and mix into the cantina's popular beverages. This scientist was fortunate enough to taste them in a libation called Jabba Juice—and can happily report that their popping texture is quite delightful!

FOREST AND JUNGLE CREATURES

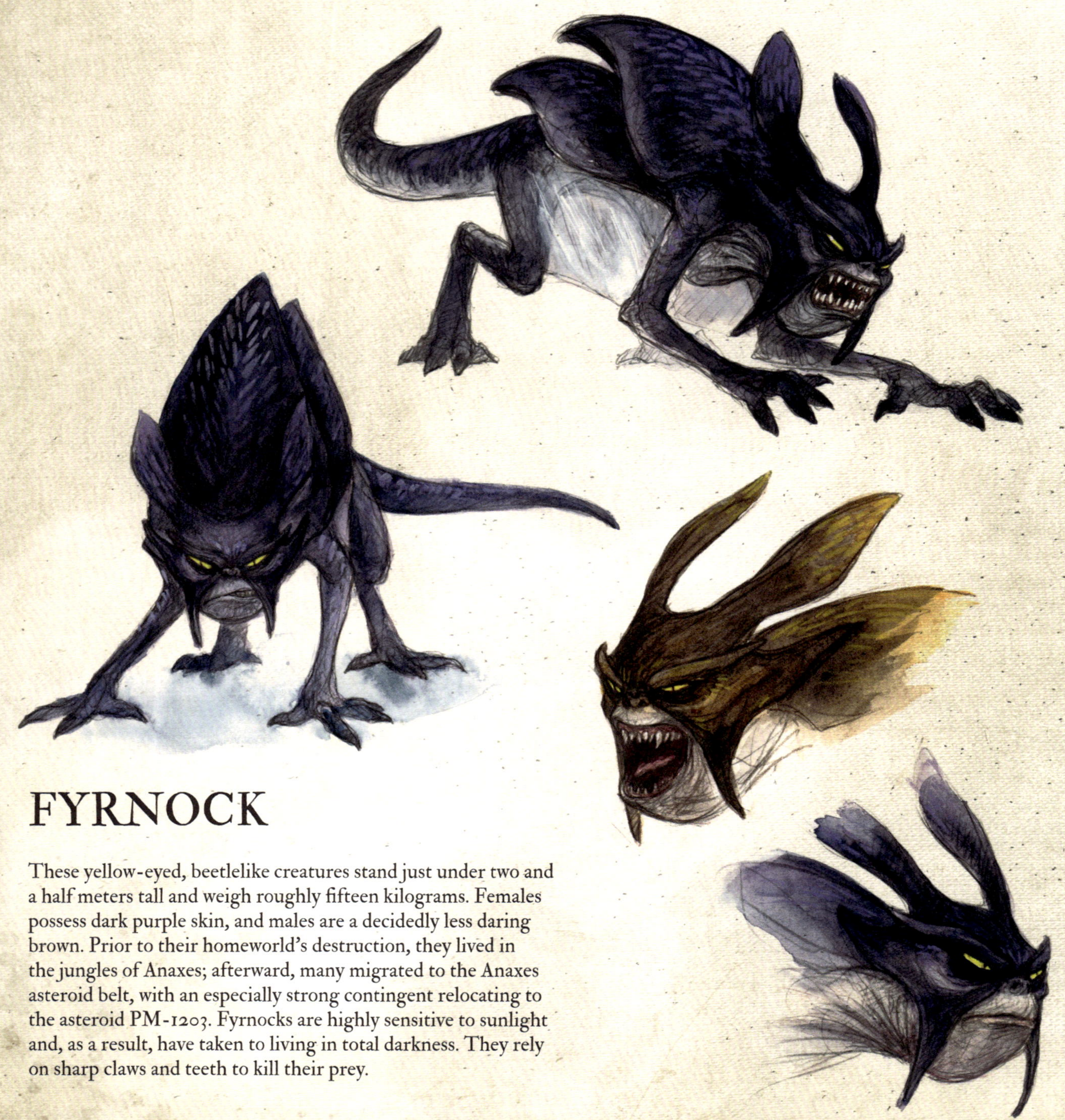

FYRNOCK

These yellow-eyed, beetlelike creatures stand just under two and a half meters tall and weigh roughly fifteen kilograms. Females possess dark purple skin, and males are a decidedly less daring brown. Prior to their homeworld's destruction, they lived in the jungles of Anaxes; afterward, many migrated to the Anaxes asteroid belt, with an especially strong contingent relocating to the asteroid PM-1203. Fyrnocks are highly sensitive to sunlight and, as a result, have taken to living in total darkness. They rely on sharp claws and teeth to kill their prey.

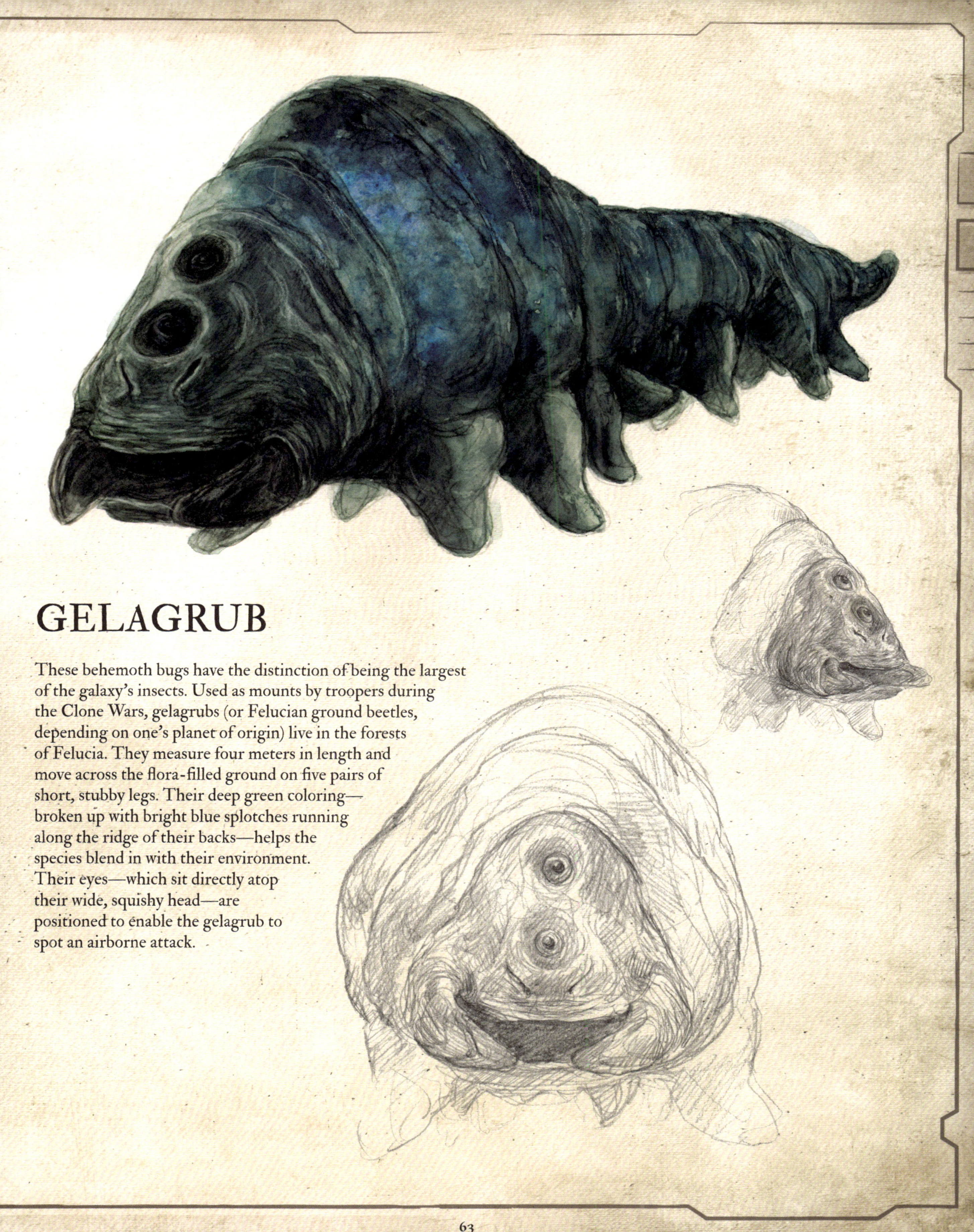

GELAGRUB

These behemoth bugs have the distinction of being the largest of the galaxy's insects. Used as mounts by troopers during the Clone Wars, gelagrubs (or Felucian ground beetles, depending on one's planet of origin) live in the forests of Felucia. They measure four meters in length and move across the flora-filled ground on five pairs of short, stubby legs. Their deep green coloring—broken up with bright blue splotches running along the ridge of their backs—helps the species blend in with their environment. Their eyes—which sit directly atop their wide, squishy head—are positioned to enable the gelagrub to spot an airborne attack.

GHHHK

Bith's native insectoids are easily recognized throughout the galaxy as one of the creatures depicted in the popular hologame dejarik. But fierce as they are on the board, they are even more so in their native environment: They hold the title of Bith's apex predator. They have four limbs and two antennae, and their strong musculature makes them a mighty opponent—in person or otherwise!

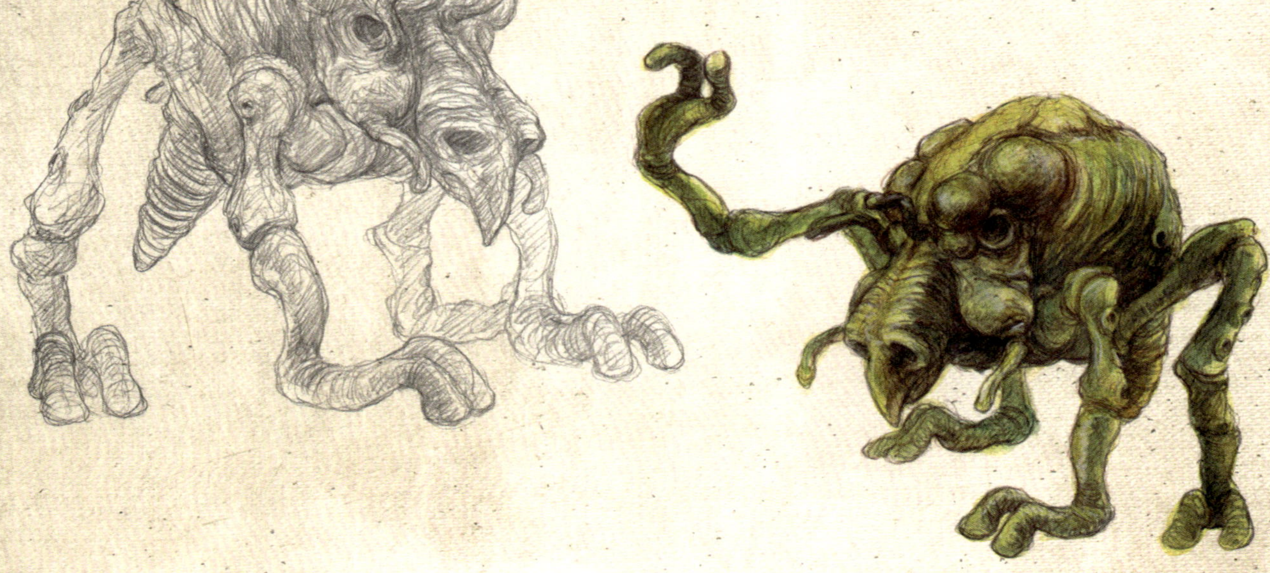

KOUHUN

These fifty-six-legged arthropods are highly poisonous—one injection is capable of killing its victim within minutes. They are thirty centimeters long and boast a venomous stingers that they use to deliver deadly doses of poison. They live on Indoumodo, where they make their homes in swamps and work in packs to hunt creatures as large as canines. Their abilities to move silently and track prey by reading body heat make them valuable assets to bounty hunters, who use them as assassins.

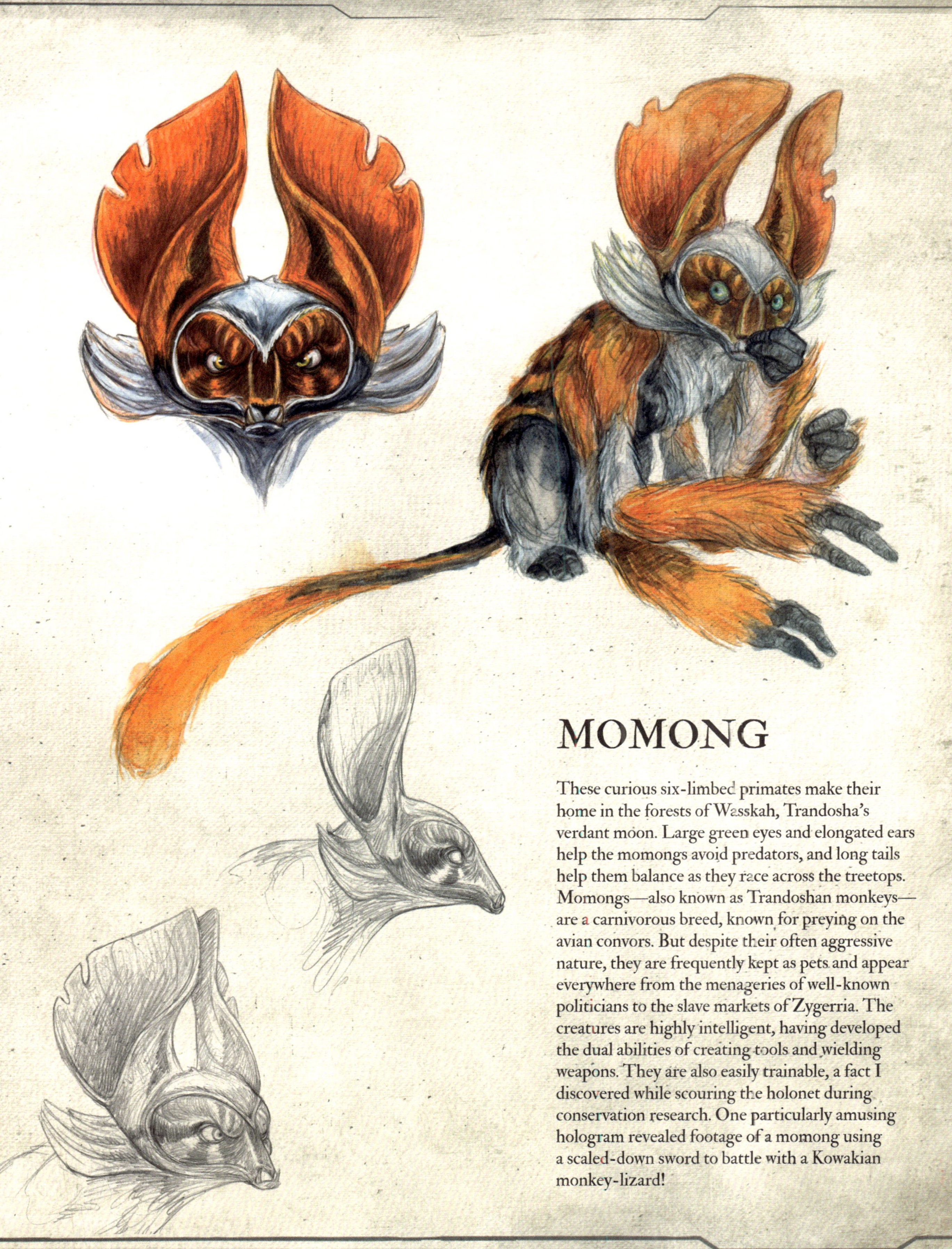

MOMONG

These curious six-limbed primates make their home in the forests of Wasskah, Trandosha's verdant moon. Large green eyes and elongated ears help the momongs avoid predators, and long tails help them balance as they race across the treetops. Momongs—also known as Trandoshan monkeys—are a carnivorous breed, known for preying on the avian convors. But despite their often aggressive nature, they are frequently kept as pets and appear everywhere from the menageries of well-known politicians to the slave markets of Zygerria. The creatures are highly intelligent, having developed the dual abilities of creating tools and wielding weapons. They are also easily trainable, a fact I discovered while scouring the holonet during conservation research. One particularly amusing hologram revealed footage of a momong using a scaled-down sword to battle with a Kowakian monkey-lizard!

NEXU

Nexu are native to Cholganna but have been spotted on Zhanox, Vodran, Saleucami, and even Geonosis, where they are used as gladiators in the infamous Petranaki arena. As my travels took me into the forest regions, I looked forward to seeing any number of the "big game" creatures whose pelts are prized by hunters throughout the galaxy. Specifically, I hoped to run into the predatory nexu—at a safe distance, of course! The feline's predatory practices are legendary, relying on its sharp claws, sharper teeth, spinal spikes, and no fewer than four blazing-red eyeballs to source its prey. The nexu utilizes multiple methods of sight, using two of its eyes for visual tracking and the others as infrared sensors to detect body heat. This combination makes the nexu more lethal than a gundark because it can follow movement regardless of atmospheric phenomena.

Nexu measure roughly four and a half meters in length and just less than one meter in height (with a body mass of two hundred twenty-five kilograms), making them sizable opponents. However, a nexu's comparatively slight frame and surprisingly weak skeletal structure renders the beast susceptible to attack. A well-placed blow can stun the feline, putting it into a near-catatonic state. They have forked double tails that they whip violently in acts of aggression. They are lithe of foot and capable of covering great distances in very little time, making the predatory nexu a beast that is *not* to be trifled with.

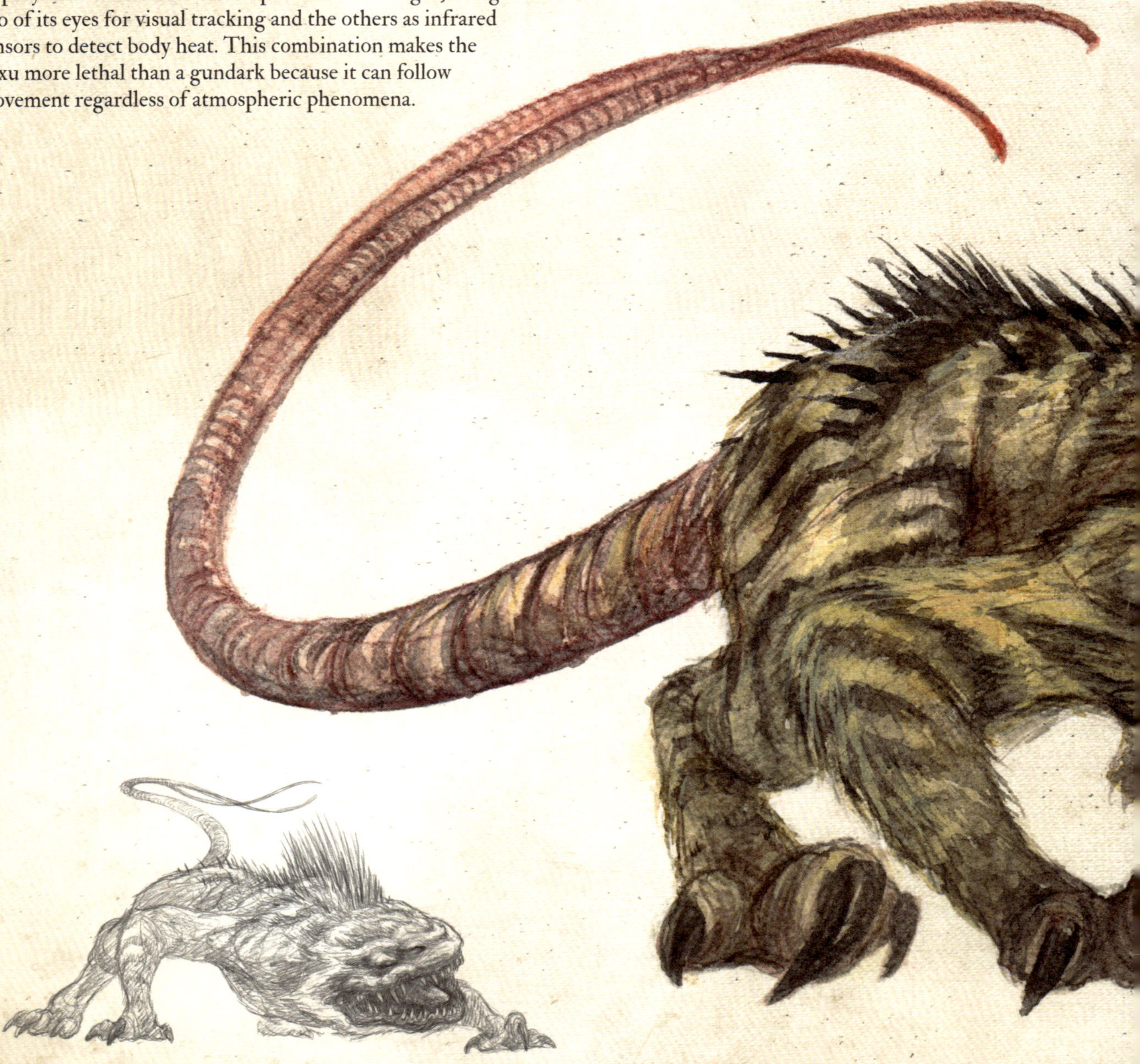

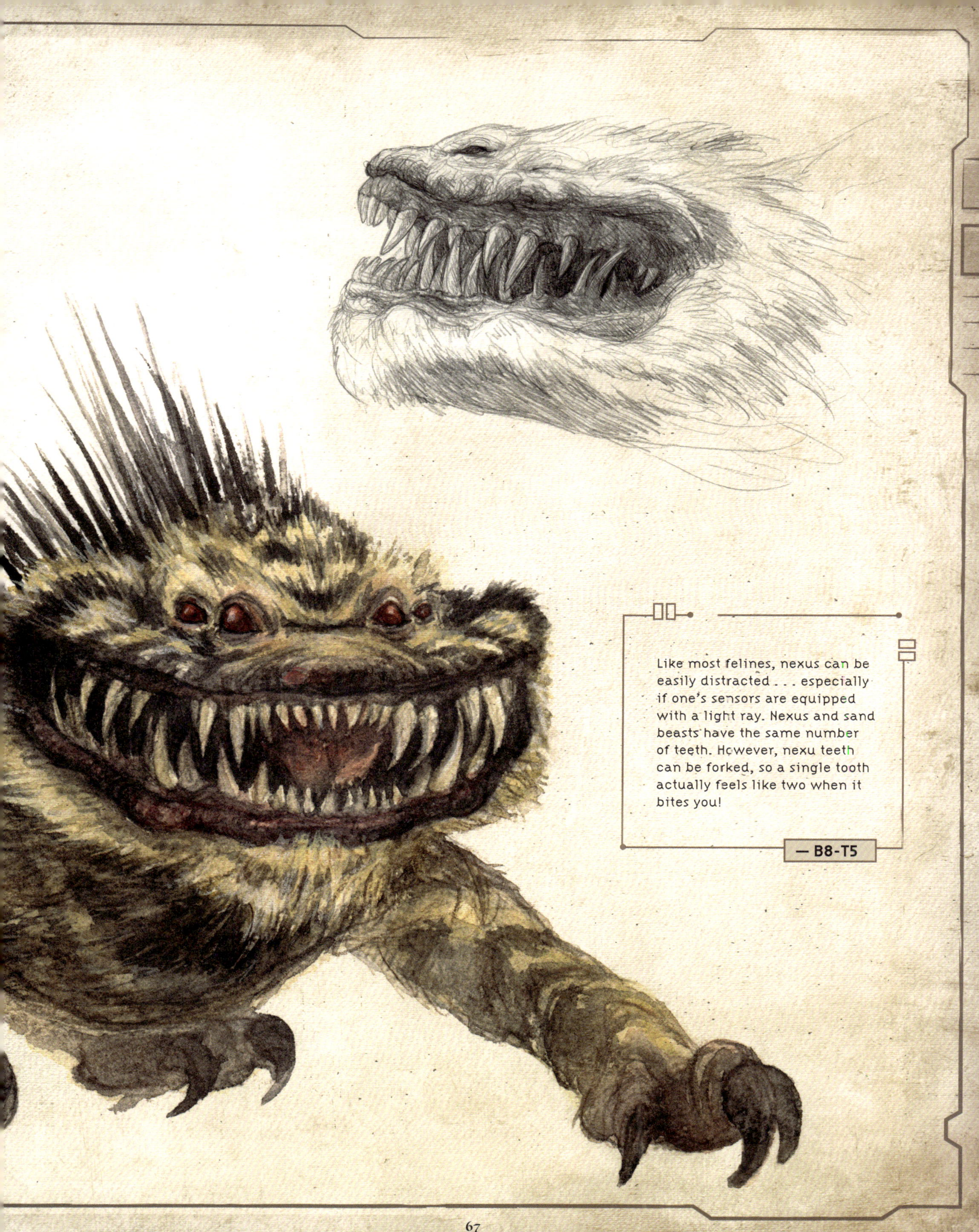

Like most felines, nexus can be easily distracted . . . especially if one's sensors are equipped with a light ray. Nexus and sand beasts have the same number of teeth. However, nexu teeth can be forked, so a single tooth actually feels like two when it bites you!

— B8-T5

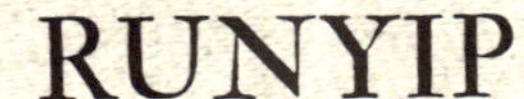

RUNYIP

Yavin 4's forest-dwelling quadrupeds are especially curious creatures. With stout legs, a rotund midsection, tall antlers, and a wide, malleable snout, they appear to be an amalgam of several different animals. Further examination reveals that each of their varied components serves as an adaptation to the creature's unique role within its ecosystem. Flexible snouts make the runyip well suited to a life of foraging, enabling it to move over, around, and even through foliage in search of food. A striped hide serves as camouflage in the sun-dappled forests, and long antlers and front-toe claws deter predators. These gentle herbivores subsist on a diet of roots and plants, and they spend much of their time attempting to evade the forest's aggressive piranha beetles. Their hides are frequently used to craft goods—even famed Resistance pilot Poe Dameron is said to have worn a jacket made from runyip leather!

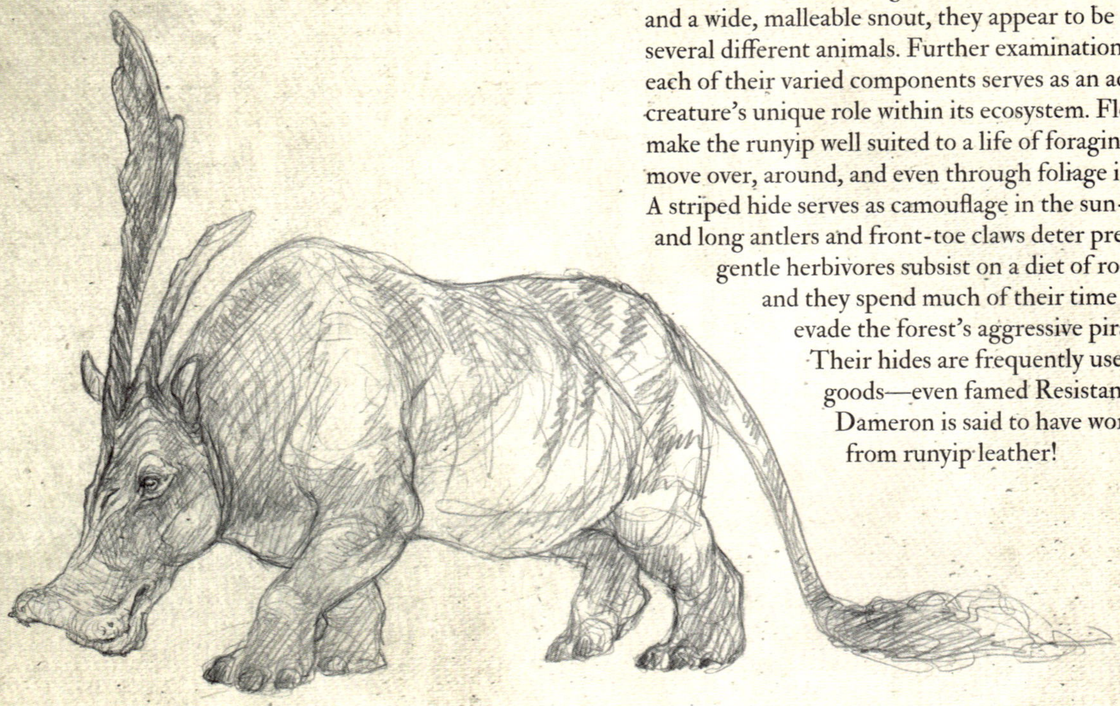

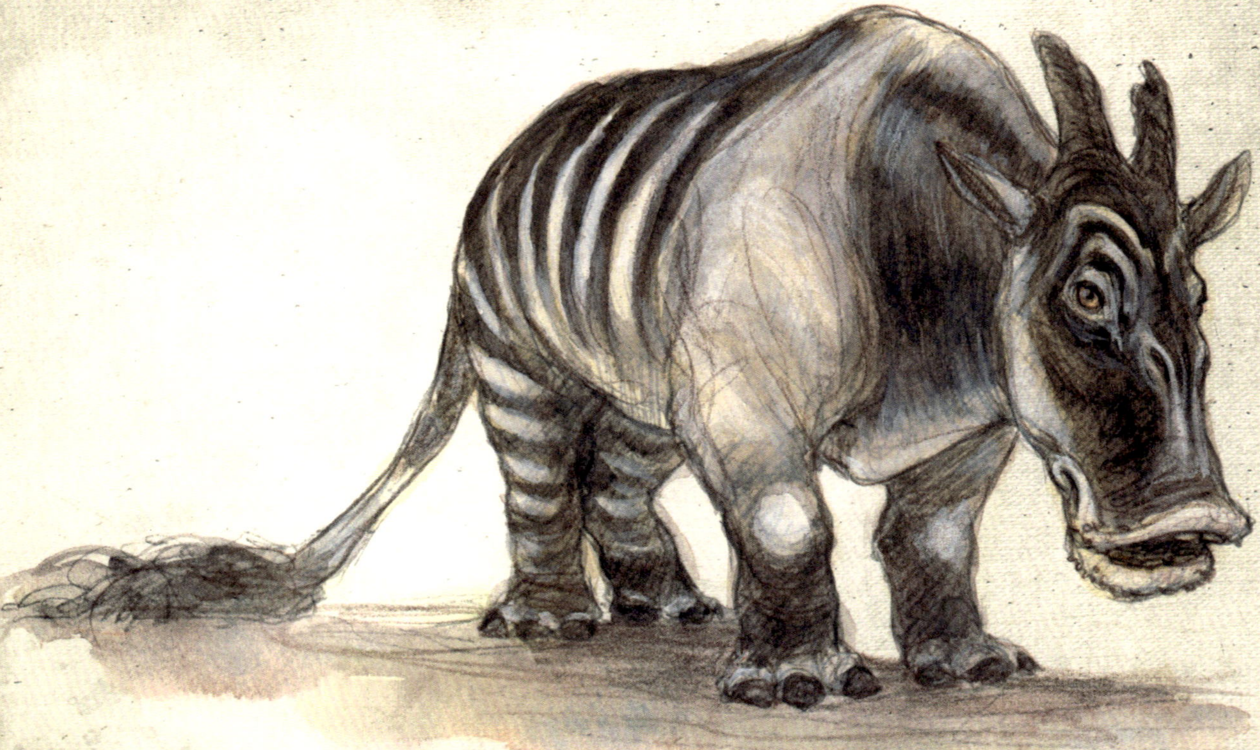

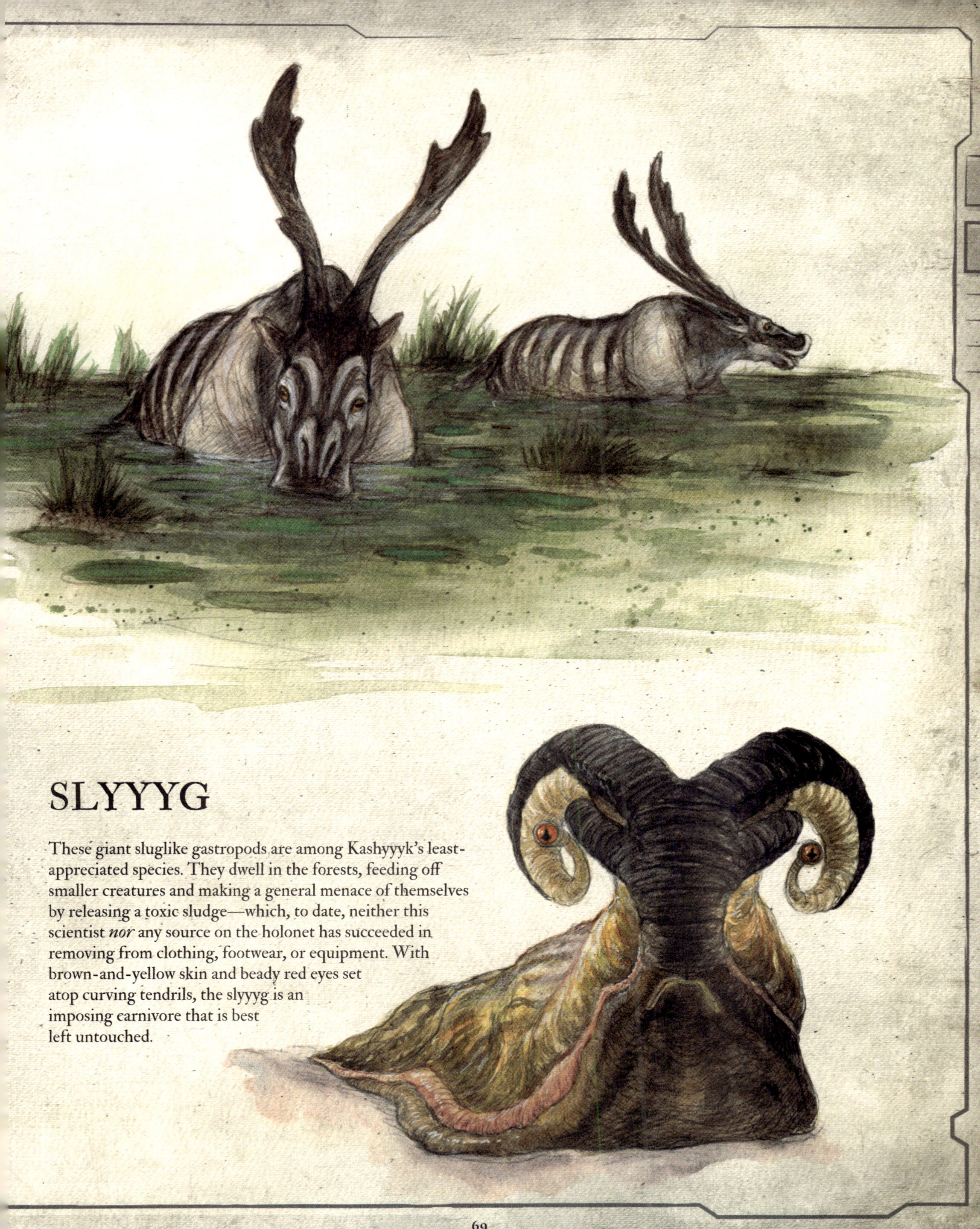

SLYYYG

These giant sluglike gastropods are among Kashyyyk's least-appreciated species. They dwell in the forests, feeding off smaller creatures and making a general menace of themselves by releasing a toxic sludge—which, to date, neither this scientist *nor* any source on the holonet has succeeded in removing from clothing, footwear, or equipment. With brown-and-yellow skin and beady red eyes set atop curving tendrils, the slyyyg is an imposing carnivore that is best left untouched.

WYYYSCHOKK

Not being particularly partial to arachnids, I was none too excited to come upon a member of Kashyyyk's enormous spider species. The wyyyschokk stands a shade taller than two meters and has eight eyes, eight legs, and a wide, bulbous body topped with rows of wiry black hair. The creature's dark coloring—and the smattering of dark yellow along its back—helps it blend into its forest environment. Its ability to excrete a weblike substance from its mandibles ensures that it ensnares plenty of prey that can range from rodents to avians and even to Wookiees! Wyyyschokk have been known to drop from the treetops to attack unwitting passersby, and their webs are said to cover up to 15 percent of Kashyyyk's forests. Adult wyyyschokks lay up to one thousand eggs per year, which they protect in strong egg sacs comprised of saliva, webbing, and lymphatic secretions. At birth, their young spend five days eating this sac before they emerge to attack and devour anything and everything they see.

The wyyyschokk's white-and-cream subspecies, the albino wyyyschokk, lives within the subterranean areas of Kashyyyk's forests. The albino is more aggressive than its counterpart, possessing a lifespan that can last for centuries. It spits venom, paralyzing its prey and rendering it helpless before it feeds off its victim's brain.

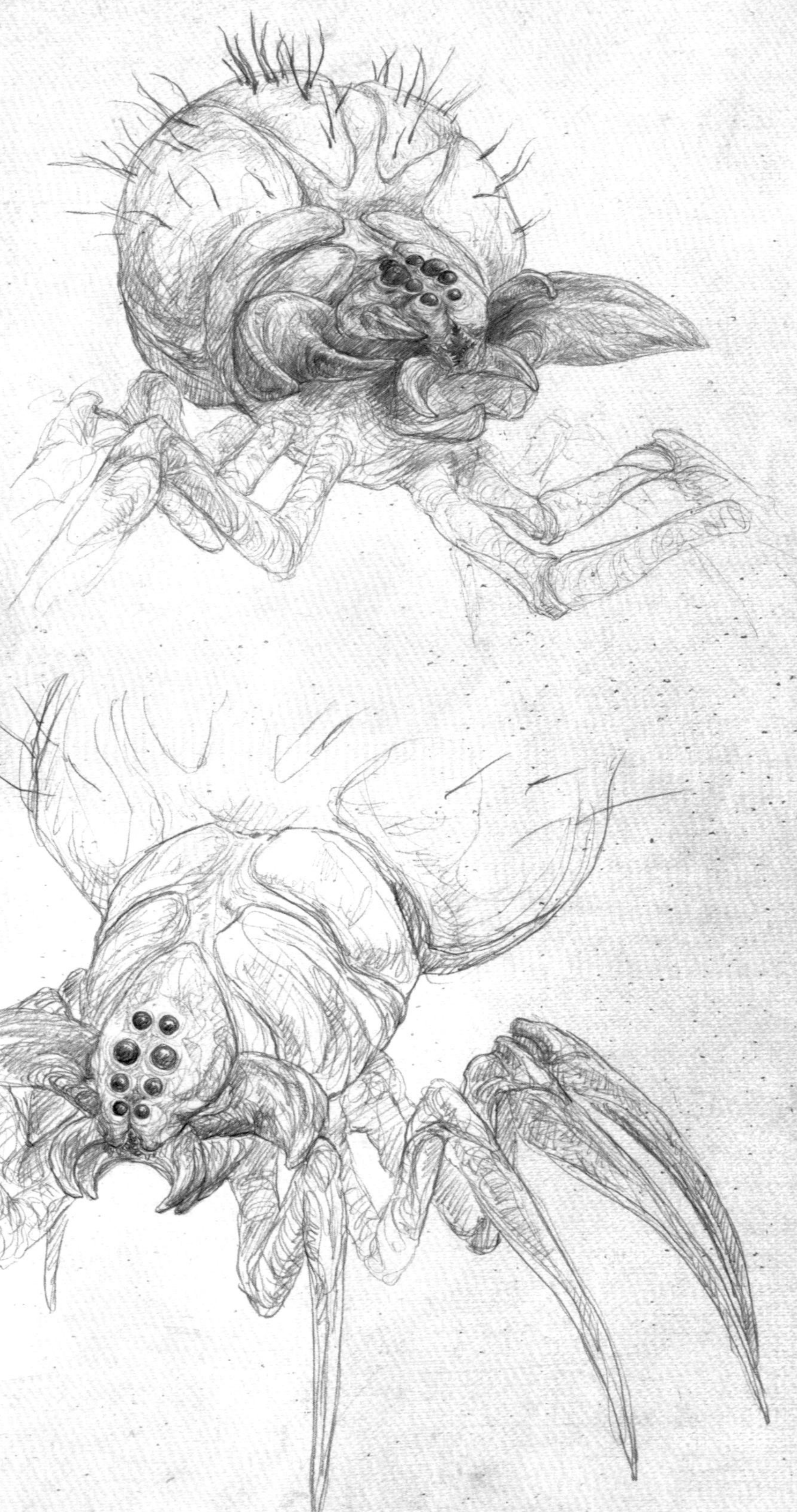

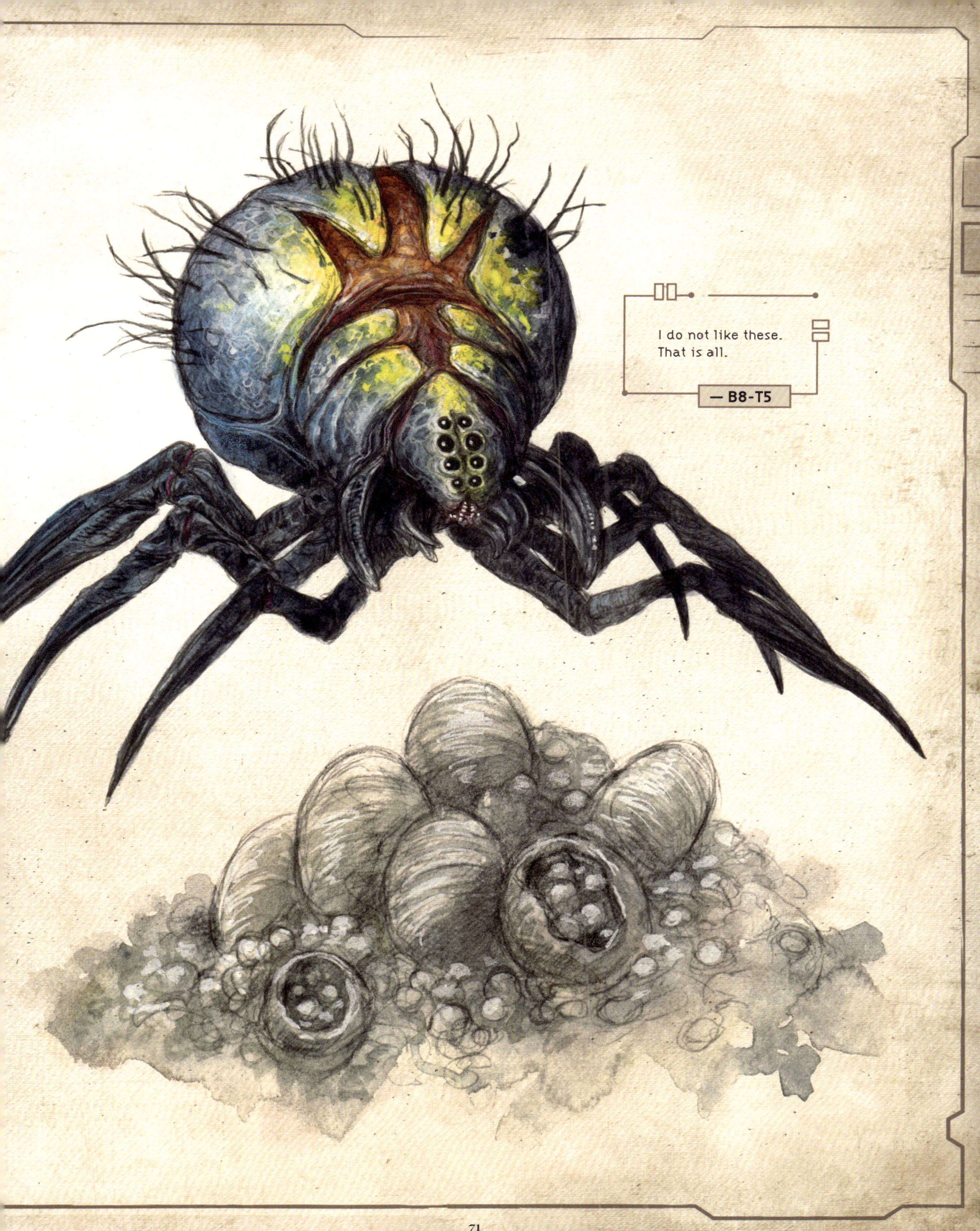
I do not like these.
That is all.
— B8-T5

ZILLO BEAST

In days of yore, the infamous zillo beasts roamed their homeworld of Malastare, slaughtering the native Dugs and attacking any other beings that dared to cross their path. Long considered to be untamable, the zillo beast lived alone, interacting among its species only long enough to breed before returning to its solitary existence. The creatures sustained themselves on electric energy; they attached themselves to a power source and drew strength from its current. Once connected to a source, the beasts would power up, regenerating lost or damaged limbs and expanding until they'd reached their full size and strength. An adult zillo beast could measure up to ninety-seven meters in height and weigh up to sixty-thousand metric tons.

These beasts boasted a nearly indestructible hide, with armored plates that proved impenetrable by blaster fire, explosions, and, as rumor had it, lightsabers. Gaps in the armor, however, could be pierced, leaving the creatures vulnerable to attack at close proximity. The creatures were highly mobile, scurrying across their environment on four legs while maneuvering their eight-spiked tail, for both balance and defense. Adult zillos grew an additional arm atop their backs that boasted the same grasping fingers and sharp claws as their other appendages. The creatures' glowing green eyes were capable of night vision, and their talons and teeth could easily slice through metal.

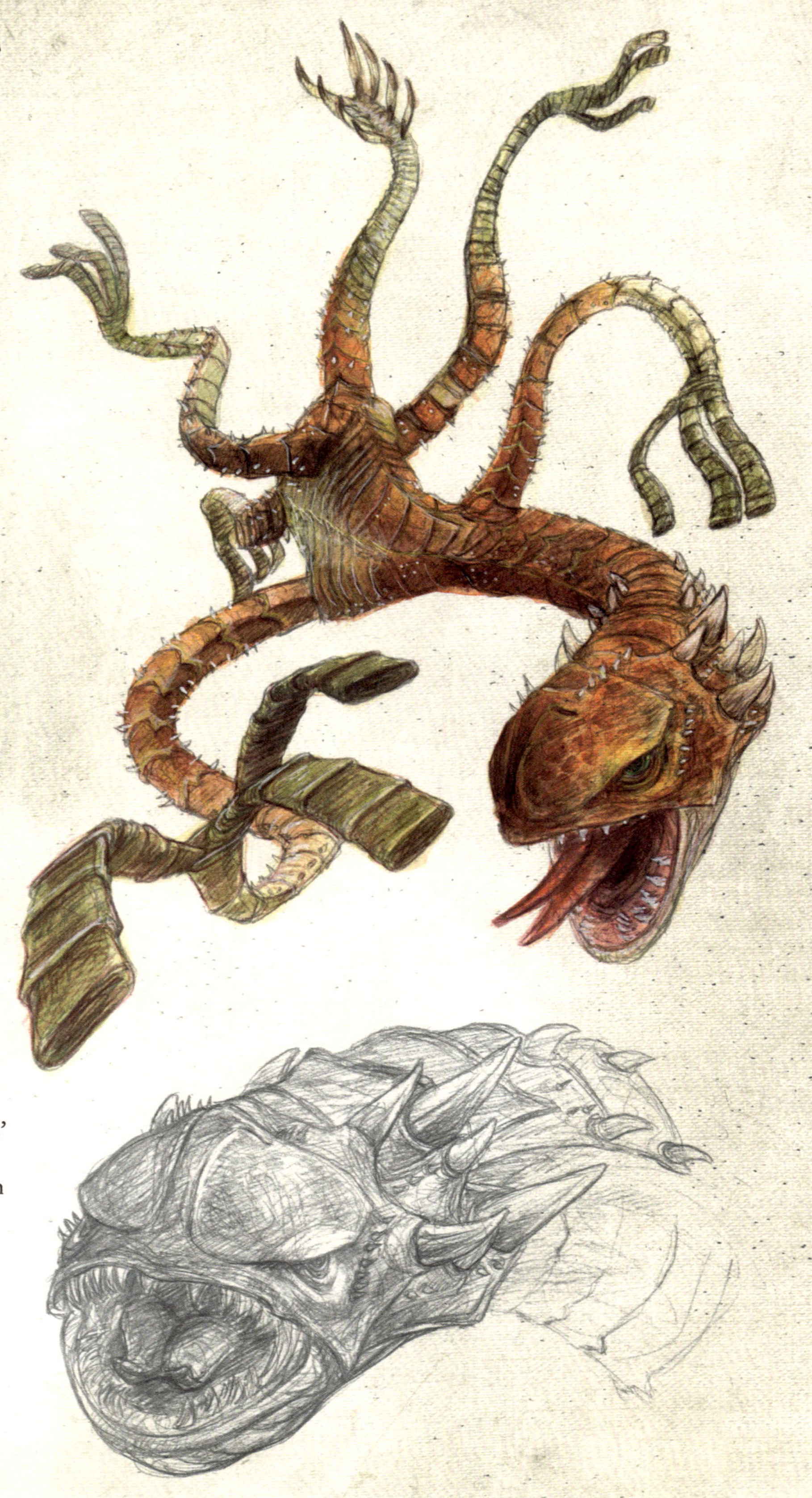

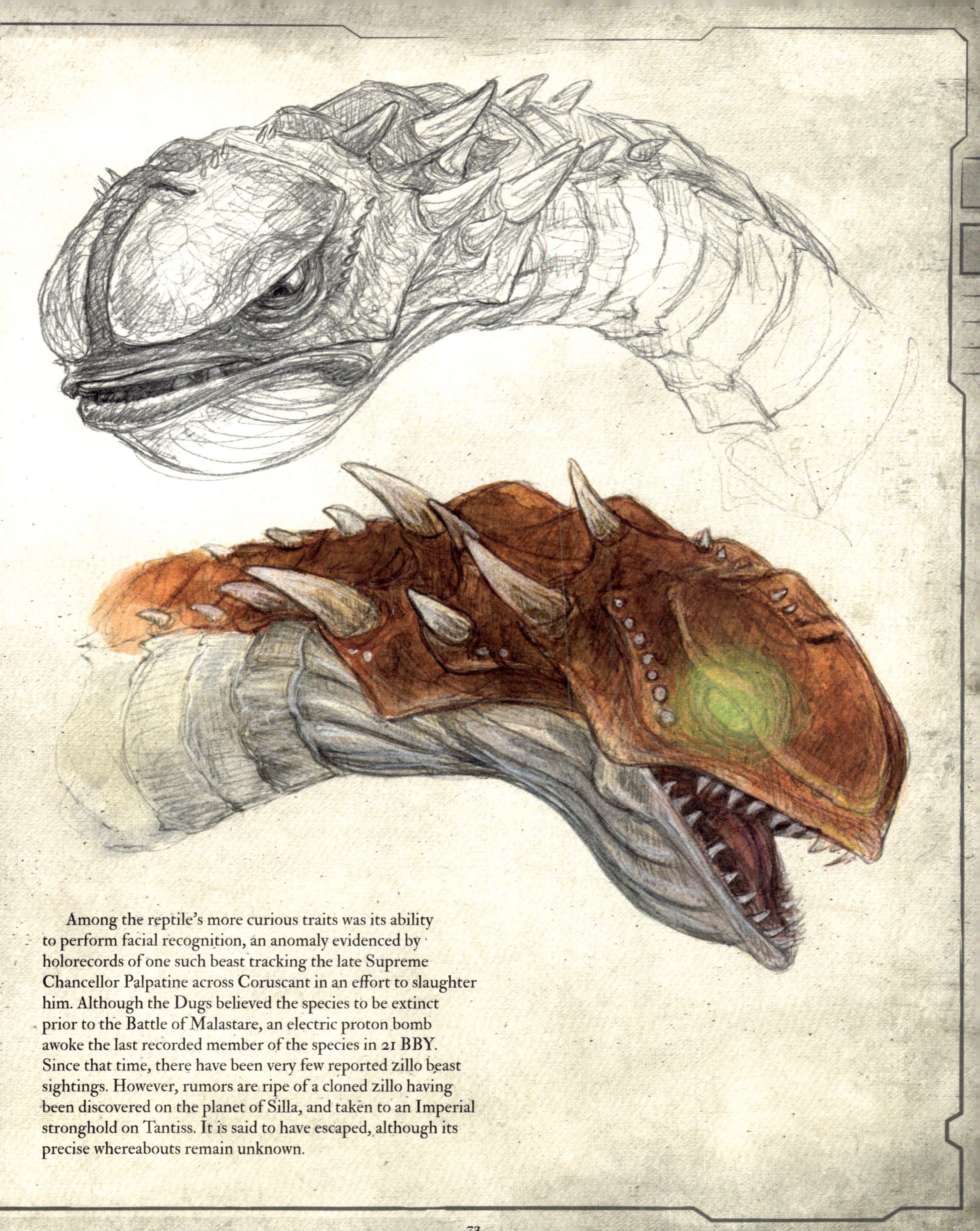

Among the reptile's more curious traits was its ability to perform facial recognition, an anomaly evidenced by holorecords of one such beast tracking the late Supreme Chancellor Palpatine across Coruscant in an effort to slaughter him. Although the Dugs believed the species to be extinct prior to the Battle of Malastare, an electric proton bomb awoke the last recorded member of the species in 21 BBY. Since that time, there have been very few reported zillo beast sightings. However, rumors are ripe of a cloned zillo having been discovered on the planet of Silla, and taken to an Imperial stronghold on Tantiss. It is said to have escaped, although its precise whereabouts remain unknown.

GRASSLAND CREATURES

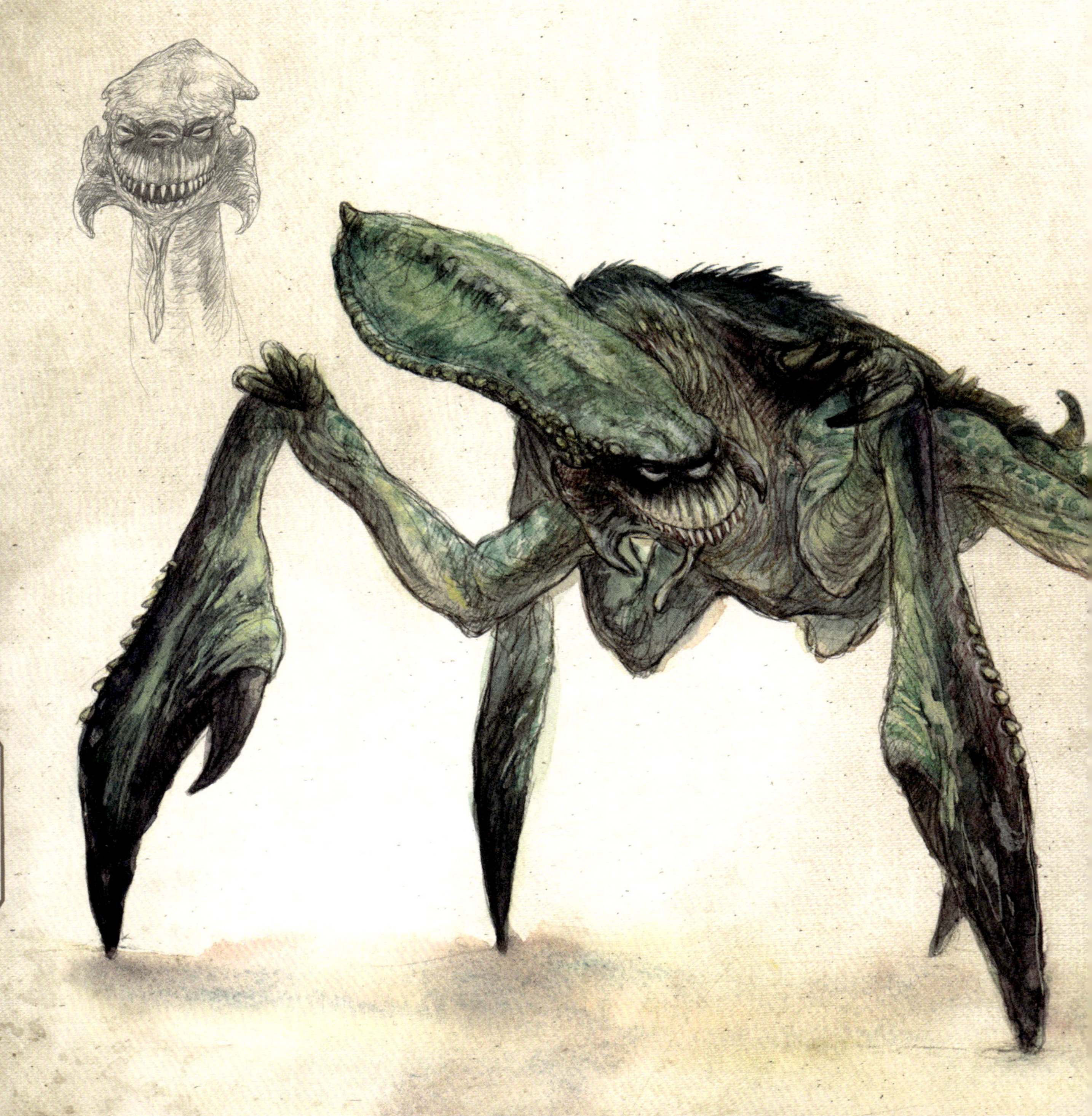

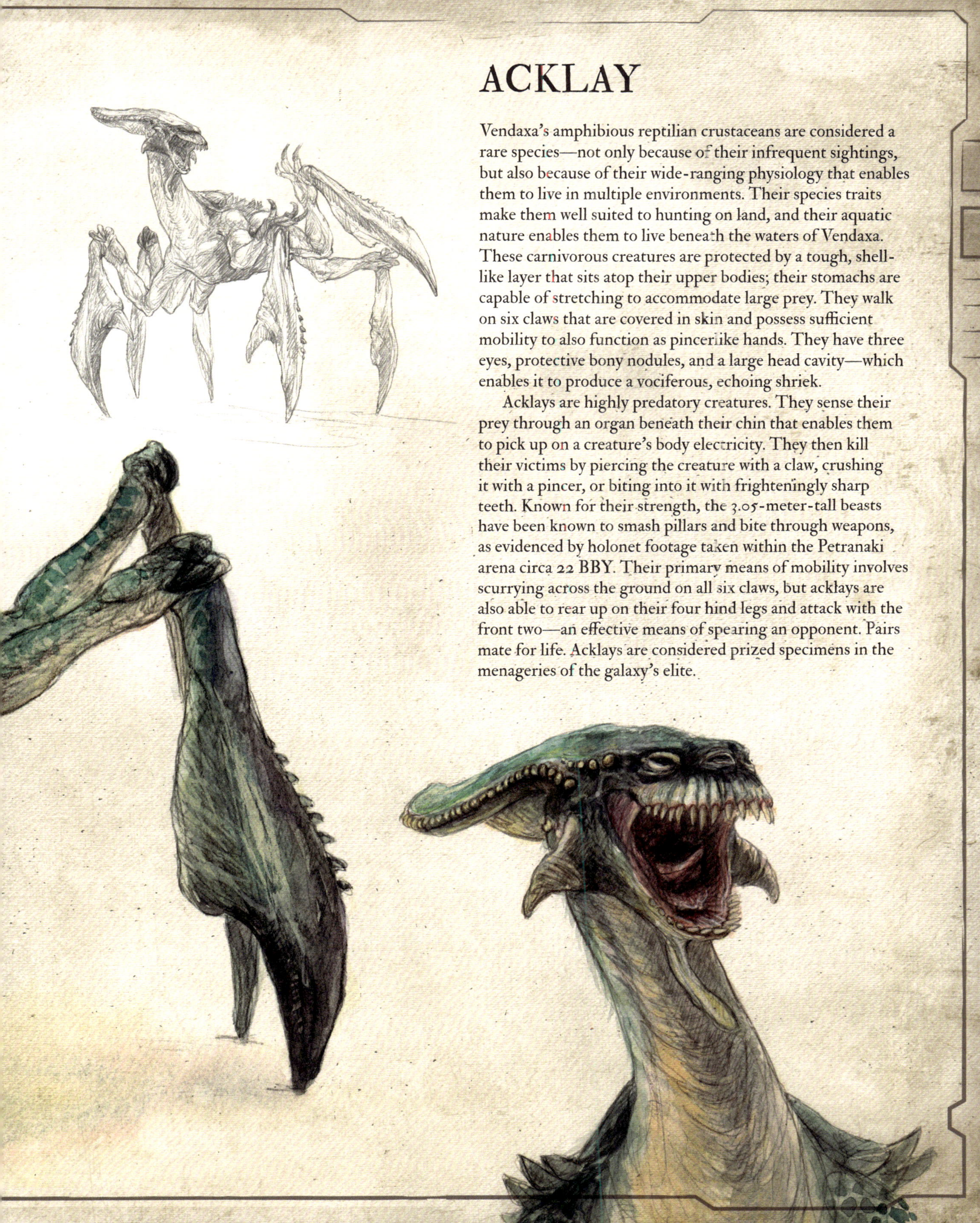

ACKLAY

Vendaxa's amphibious reptilian crustaceans are considered a rare species—not only because of their infrequent sightings, but also because of their wide-ranging physiology that enables them to live in multiple environments. Their species traits make them well suited to hunting on land, and their aquatic nature enables them to live beneath the waters of Vendaxa. These carnivorous creatures are protected by a tough, shell-like layer that sits atop their upper bodies; their stomachs are capable of stretching to accommodate large prey. They walk on six claws that are covered in skin and possess sufficient mobility to also function as pincerlike hands. They have three eyes, protective bony nodules, and a large head cavity—which enables it to produce a vociferous, echoing shriek.

Acklays are highly predatory creatures. They sense their prey through an organ beneath their chin that enables them to pick up on a creature's body electricity. They then kill their victims by piercing the creature with a claw, crushing it with a pincer, or biting into it with frighteningly sharp teeth. Known for their strength, the 3.05-meter-tall beasts have been known to smash pillars and bite through weapons, as evidenced by holonet footage taken within the Petranaki arena circa 22 BBY. Their primary means of mobility involves scurrying across the ground on all six claws, but acklays are also able to rear up on their four hind legs and attack with the front two—an effective means of spearing an opponent. Pairs mate for life. Acklays are considered prized specimens in the menageries of the galaxy's elite.

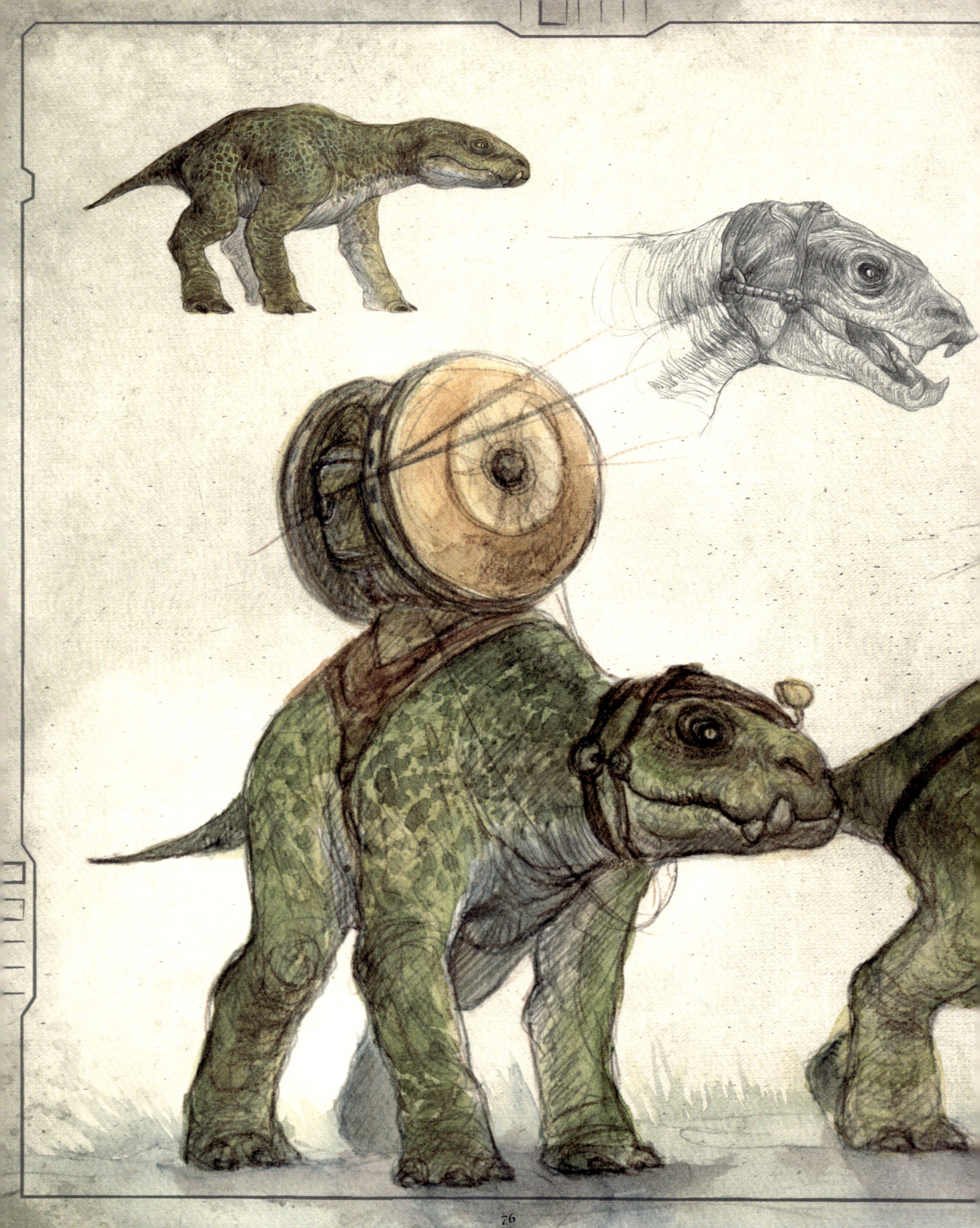

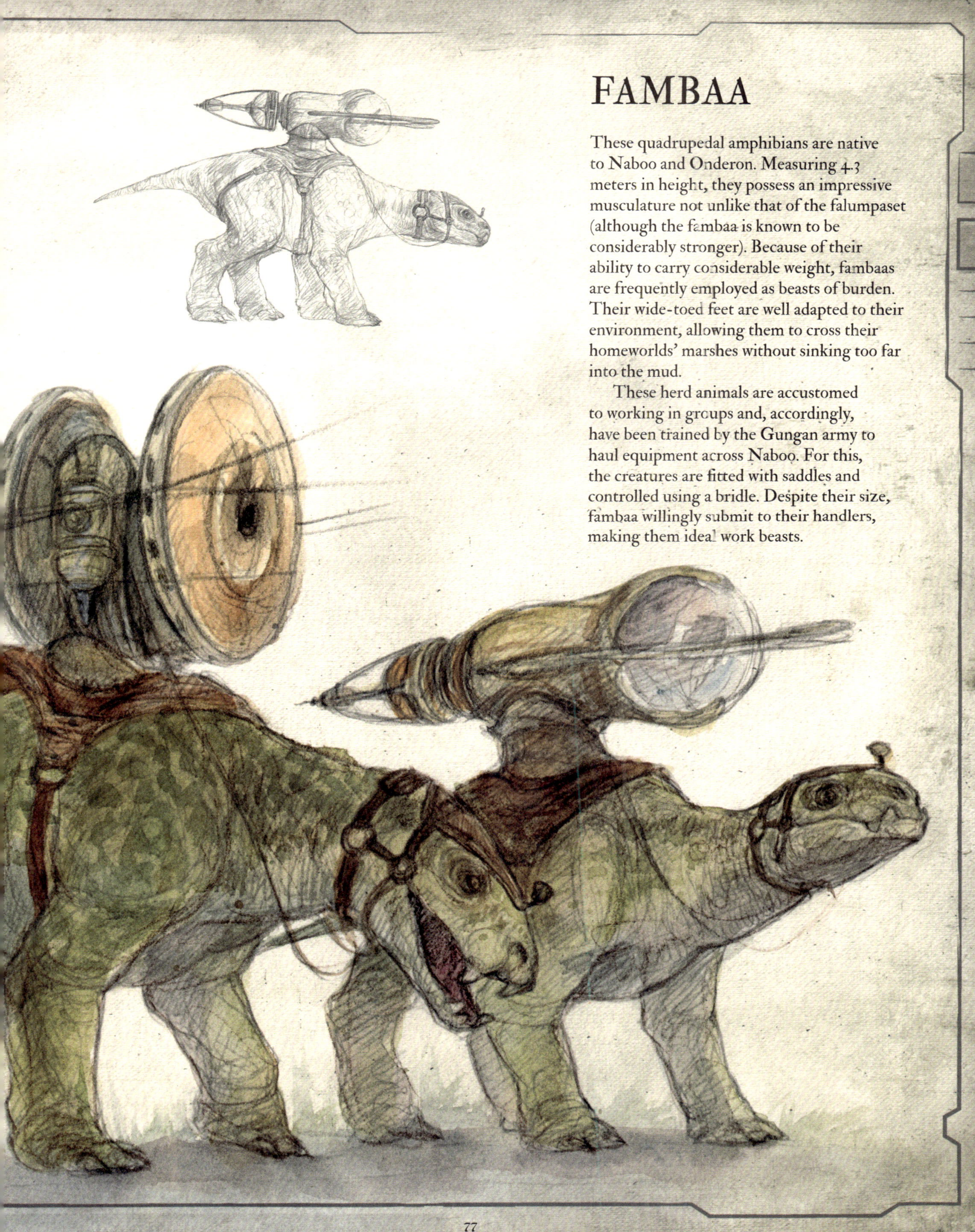

FAMBAA

These quadrupedal amphibians are native to Naboo and Onderon. Measuring 4.3 meters in height, they possess an impressive musculature not unlike that of the falumpaset (although the fambaa is known to be considerably stronger). Because of their ability to carry considerable weight, fambaas are frequently employed as beasts of burden. Their wide-toed feet are well adapted to their environment, allowing them to cross their homeworlds' marshes without sinking too far into the mud.

These herd animals are accustomed to working in groups and, accordingly, have been trained by the Gungan army to haul equipment across Naboo. For this, the creatures are fitted with saddles and controlled using a bridle. Despite their size, fambaa willingly submit to their handlers, making them ideal work beasts.

FALUMPASET

The fambaa's smaller, slighter counterparts have longer necks and narrower legs than their sizable amphibian colleagues. Falumpasets are herbivorous mammals who favor the forests, swamps, and plains of both Naboo and Onderon. They are strong swimmers, with long limbs that enable them to cut through swamps at a surprising speed. They live in herds among family groupings, and their willingness to work together to survive makes for easy domestication—the Gungans often employ the beasts as haulers in their army.

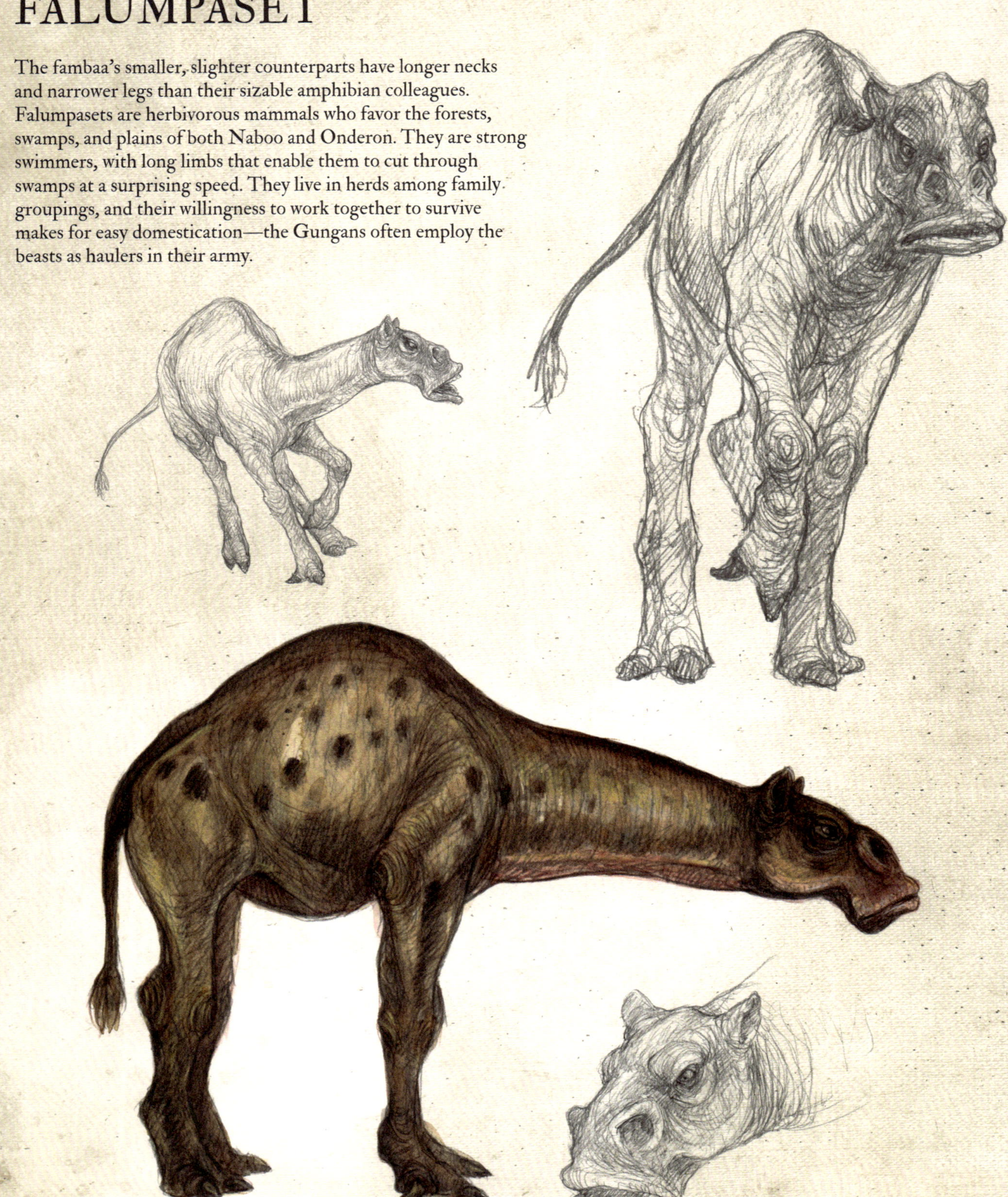

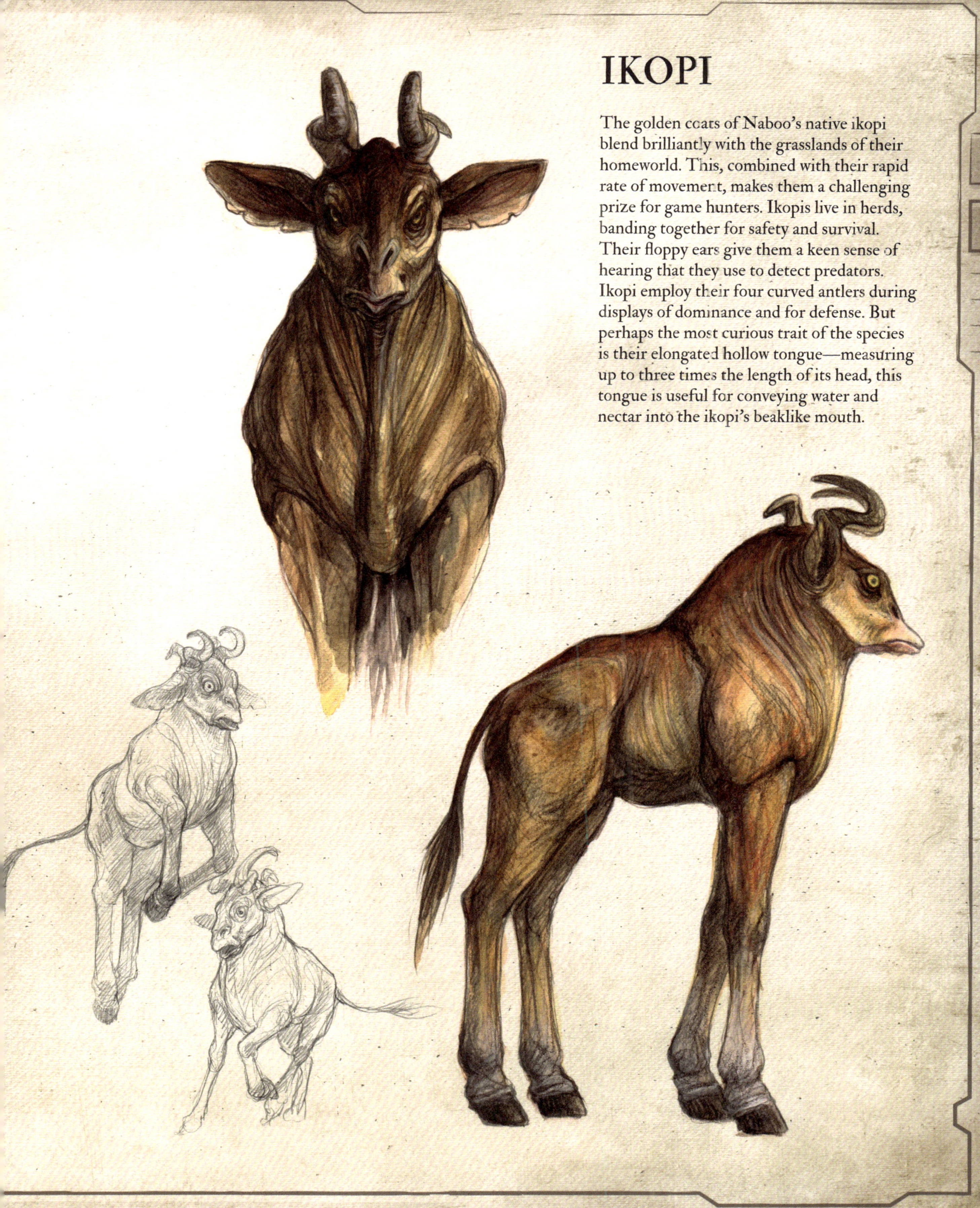

IKOPI

The golden coats of Naboo's native ikopi blend brilliantly with the grasslands of their homeworld. This, combined with their rapid rate of movement, makes them a challenging prize for game hunters. Ikopis live in herds, banding together for safety and survival. Their floppy ears give them a keen sense of hearing that they use to detect predators. Ikopi employ their four curved antlers during displays of dominance and for defense. But perhaps the most curious trait of the species is their elongated hollow tongue—measuring up to three times the length of its head, this tongue is useful for conveying water and nectar into the ikopi's beaklike mouth.

LOTH-CAT

Among the galaxy's most captivating creatures—and one of the species I very much hope to see in the wild—Loth-cats are a subspecies of the feline tooka. These furry mammals are native to Lothal. They use their sharp teeth and claws to hunt smaller creatures—including their preferred delicacy, the Loth-rat. Loth-cats have unpredictable personalities, sometimes greeting a stranger with a wave of their tail and a contented purr, and other times adopting a hunting position and emitting an enraged growl. It is this unpredictability that makes them so endearing: With Loth-cats, one *always* knows exactly where one stands.

Measuring just under one meter in length and weighing up to ten kilograms, the Loth-cat's most distinctive features are its triangular ears and wide, expressive tails. They are tireless hunters that have been known to stalk prey for days at a time. They prefer to live alone, joining with others of their species only long enough to breed and raise their young, which are known as kits. The Loth-cat is rarely capable of domestication, and it should be noted that, even in captivity, these felines are prone to destructive episodes. The famed Jedi Kanan Jarrus is said to have attempted to teach his Padawan, Ezra Bridger, by instructing him to train a temperamental Loth-cat. It is also said this lesson ended in the aforementioned Padawan being attacked, proving that Loth-cats might seem adorable but are often best left at a distance.

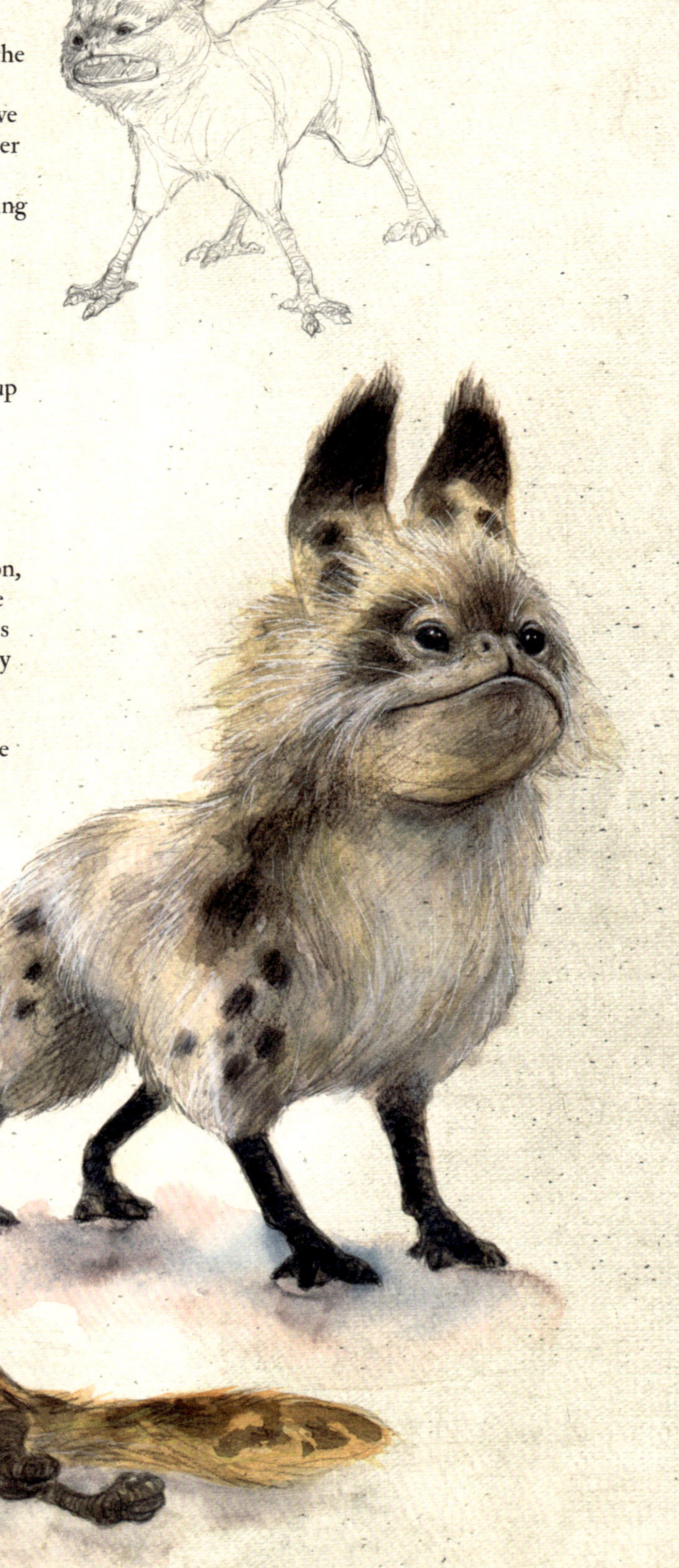

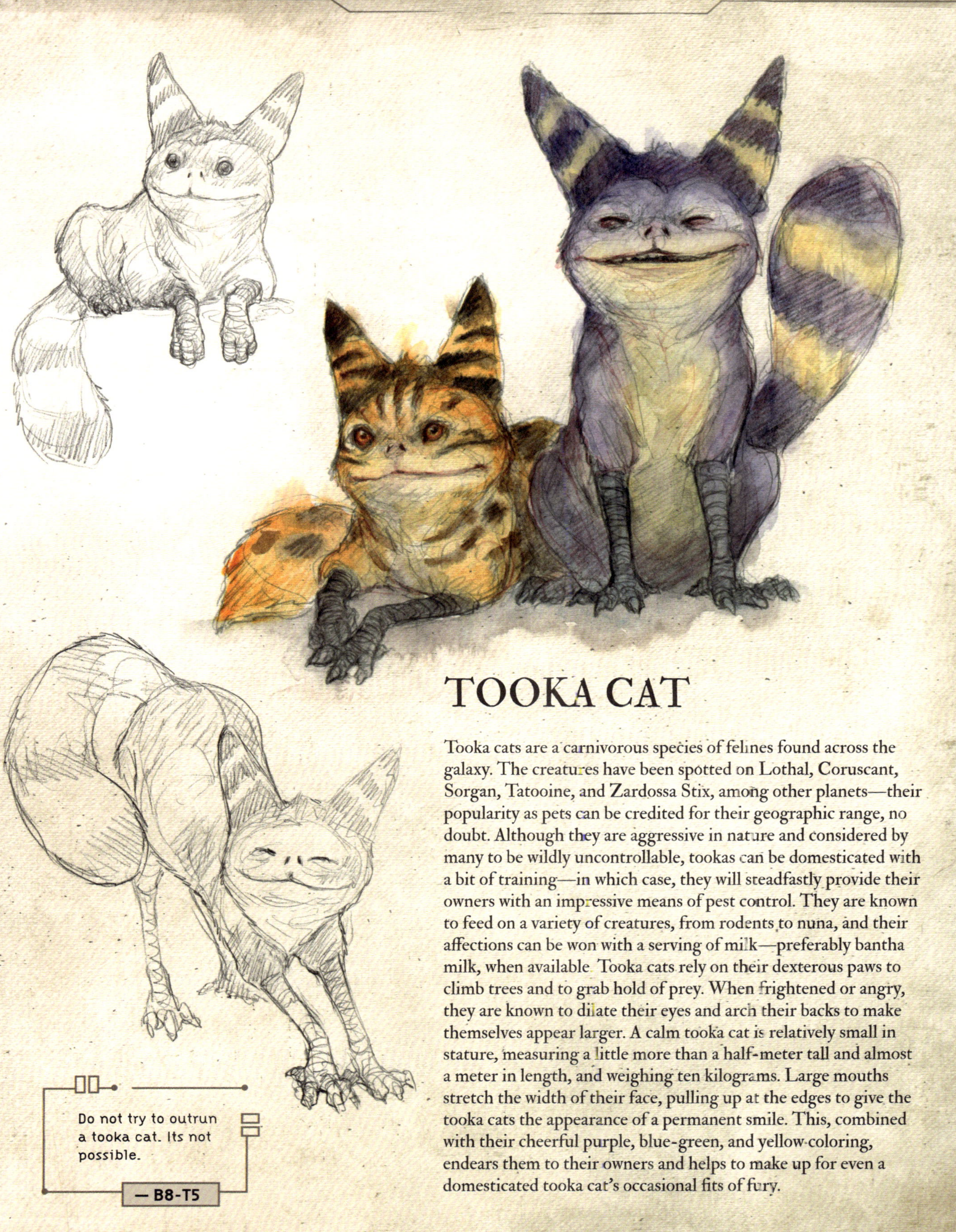

TOOKA CAT

Tooka cats are a carnivorous species of felines found across the galaxy. The creatures have been spotted on Lothal, Coruscant, Sorgan, Tatooine, and Zardossa Stix, among other planets—their popularity as pets can be credited for their geographic range, no doubt. Although they are aggressive in nature and considered by many to be wildly uncontrollable, tookas can be domesticated with a bit of training—in which case, they will steadfastly provide their owners with an impressive means of pest control. They are known to feed on a variety of creatures, from rodents to nuna, and their affections can be won with a serving of milk—preferably bantha milk, when available. Tooka cats rely on their dexterous paws to climb trees and to grab hold of prey. When frightened or angry, they are known to dilate their eyes and arch their backs to make themselves appear larger. A calm tooka cat is relatively small in stature, measuring a little more than a half-meter tall and almost a meter in length, and weighing ten kilograms. Large mouths stretch the width of their face, pulling up at the edges to give the tooka cats the appearance of a permanent smile. This, combined with their cheerful purple, blue-green, and yellow coloring, endears them to their owners and helps to make up for even a domesticated tooka cat's occasional fits of fury.

Do not try to outrun a tooka cat. Its not possible.

— B8-T5

LOTH-WOLF

The seldom-seen mystical Loth-wolves are said to be a natural embodiment of the Force, acting as guardians between the light side and the planet of Lothal. Standing 2.6 meters tall and 5.85 meters long, these larger-than-life wolves communicate with one another through a series of emotive howls. They are able to speak Galactic Basic, a language they use to communicate with sentient creatures as the need arises. Loth-wolves are believed to be nearly as old as Lothal, appearing in cave paintings made by the earliest residents of the planet. Although they were feared by these early Lothalites, over time, the residents grew to revere the wolves, speaking of them in oral histories and including the creatures in a popular children's rhyme.

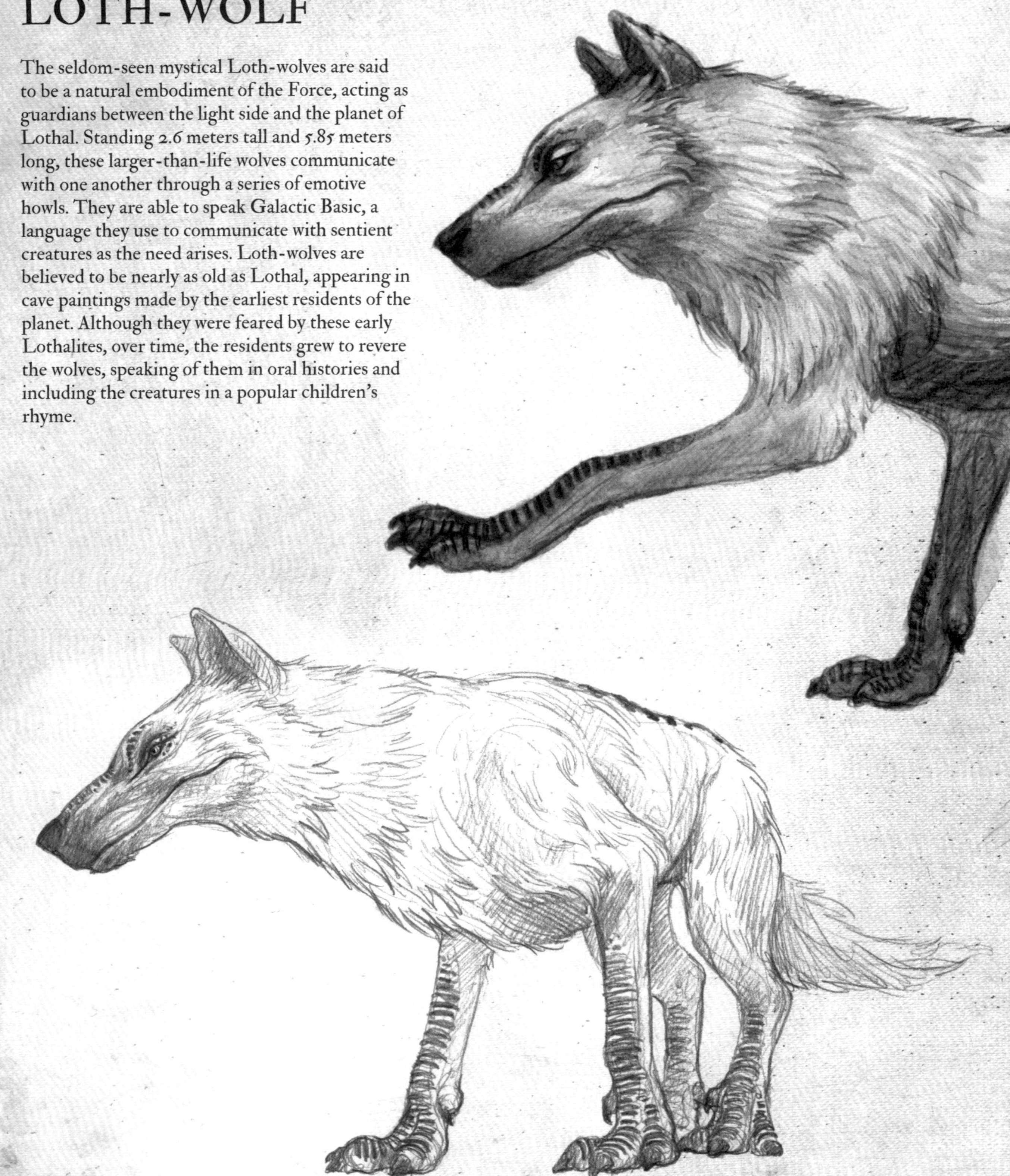

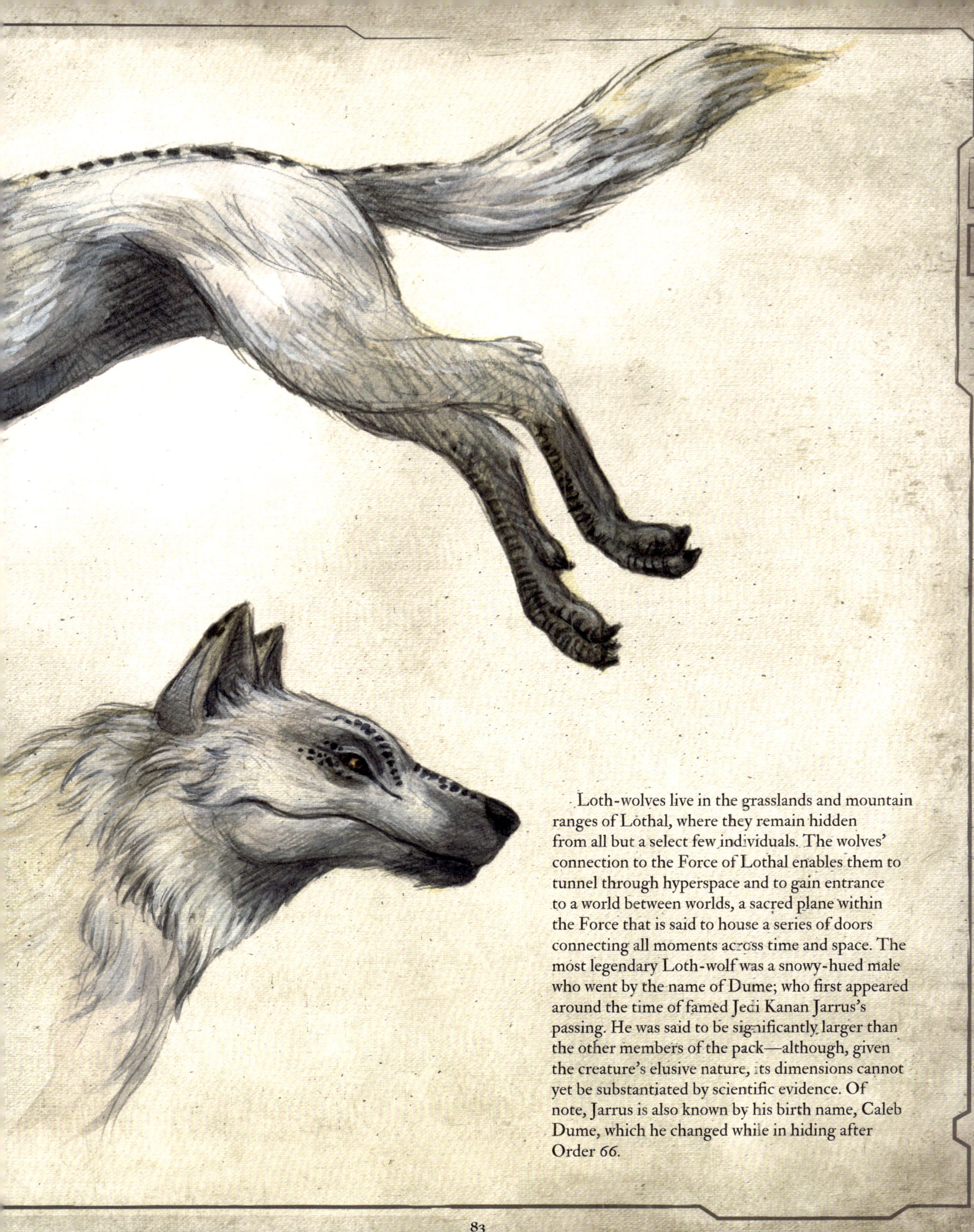

Loth-wolves live in the grasslands and mountain ranges of Lothal, where they remain hidden from all but a select few individuals. The wolves' connection to the Force of Lothal enables them to tunnel through hyperspace and to gain entrance to a world between worlds, a sacred plane within the Force that is said to house a series of doors connecting all moments across time and space. The most legendary Loth-wolf was a snowy-hued male who went by the name of Dume; who first appeared around the time of famed Jedi Kanan Jarrus's passing. He was said to be significantly larger than the other members of the pack—although, given the creature's elusive nature, its dimensions cannot yet be substantiated by scientific evidence. Of note, Jarrus is also known by his birth name, Caleb Dume, which he changed while in hiding after Order 66.

Nerfs have three times the number of scent glands that similarly sized livestock do. This evolutionary adaptation is designed to make it easier for them to identify one herd from another, ensuring that they don't get lost. These creatures smell every bit as wretched as rumors may have led you to believe. Beings that have the ability to shut off their olfactory sensors are advised to do so.

— B8-T5

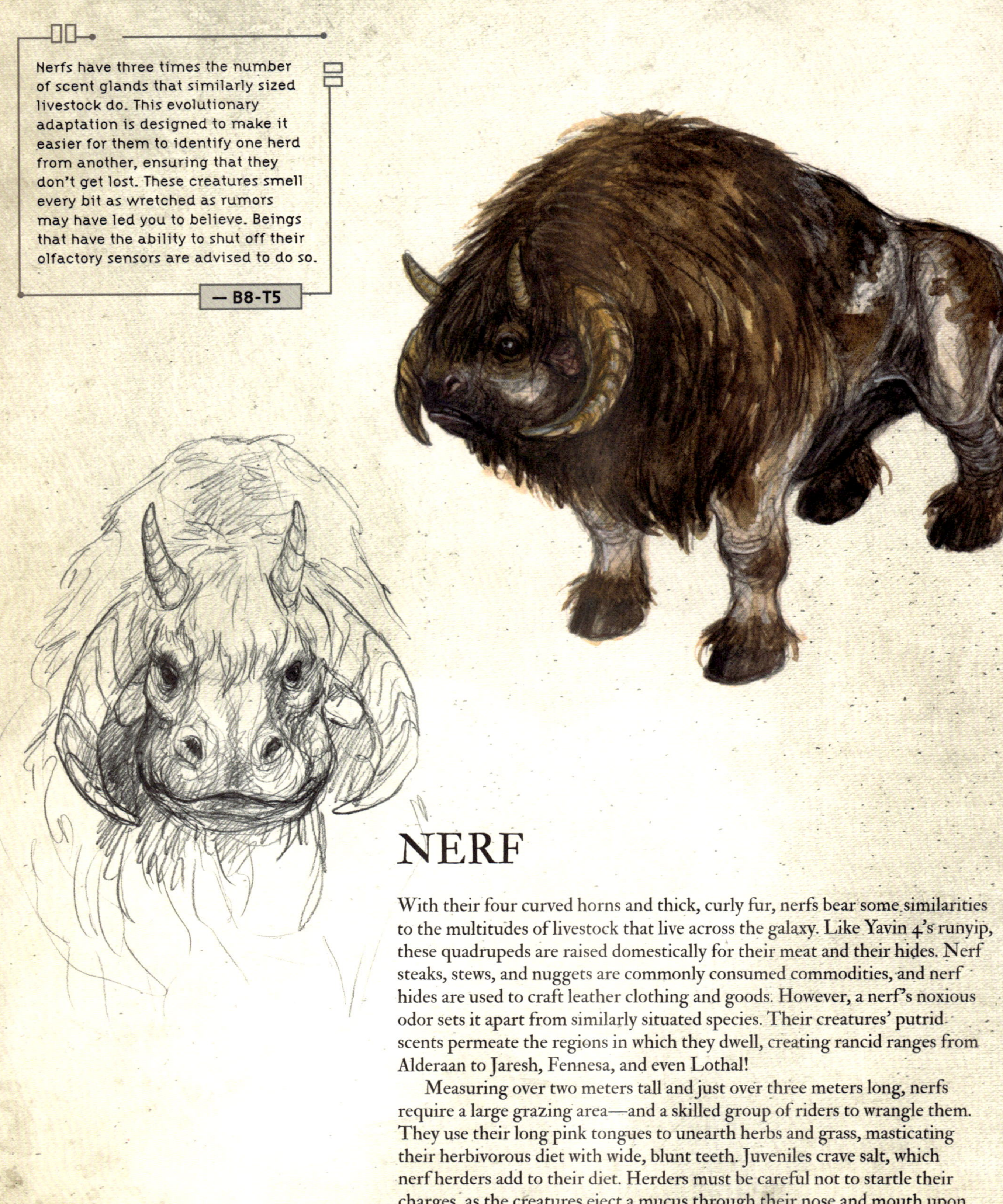

NERF

With their four curved horns and thick, curly fur, nerfs bear some similarities to the multitudes of livestock that live across the galaxy. Like Yavin 4's runyip, these quadrupeds are raised domestically for their meat and their hides. Nerf steaks, stews, and nuggets are commonly consumed commodities, and nerf hides are used to craft leather clothing and goods. However, a nerf's noxious odor sets it apart from similarly situated species. Their creatures' putrid scents permeate the regions in which they dwell, creating rancid ranges from Alderaan to Jaresh, Fennesa, and even Lothal!

Measuring over two meters tall and just over three meters long, nerfs require a large grazing area—and a skilled group of riders to wrangle them. They use their long pink tongues to unearth herbs and grass, masticating their herbivorous diet with wide, blunt teeth. Juveniles crave salt, which nerf herders add to their diet. Herders must be careful not to startle their charges, as the creatures eject a mucus through their nose and mouth upon experiencing a scare.

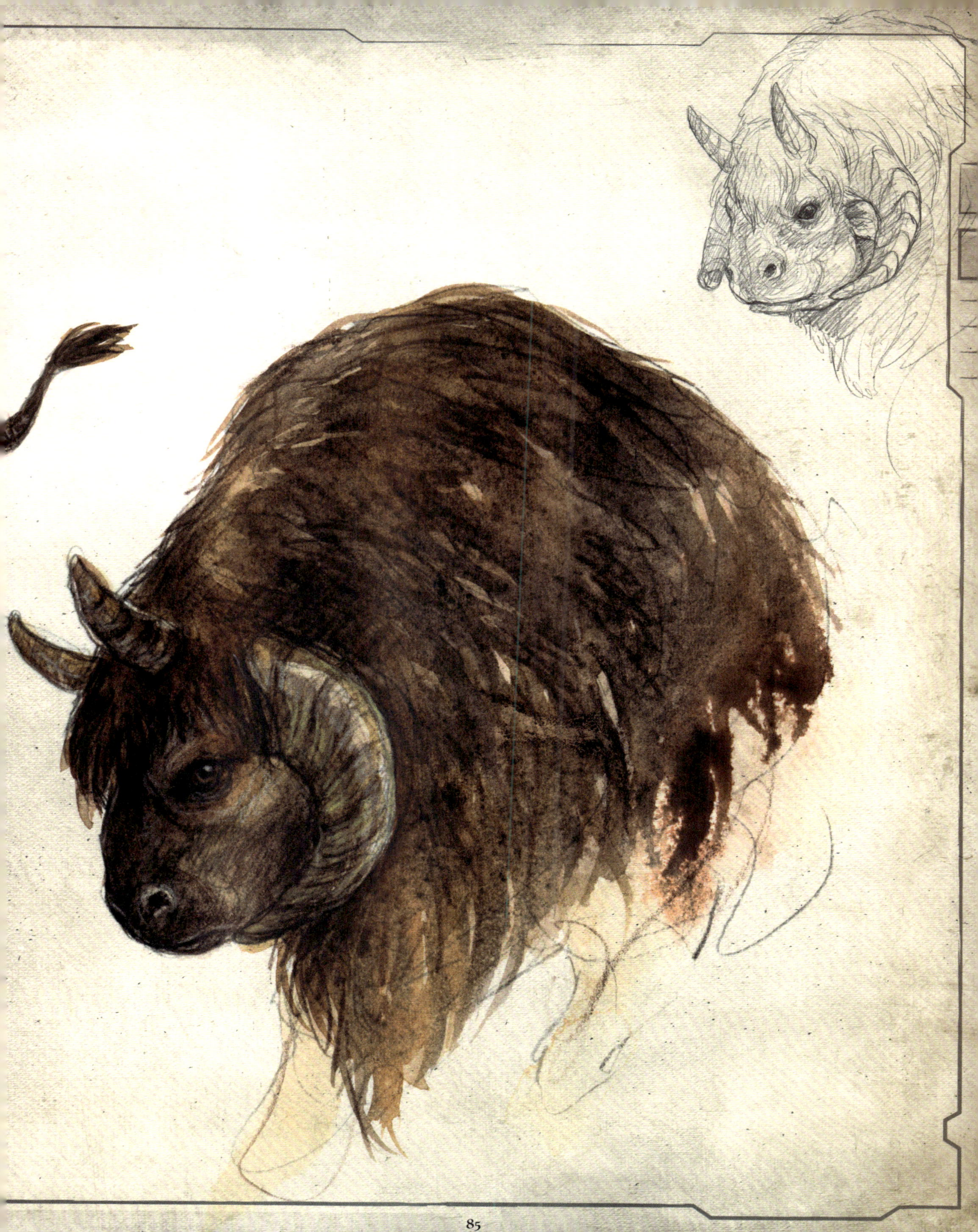

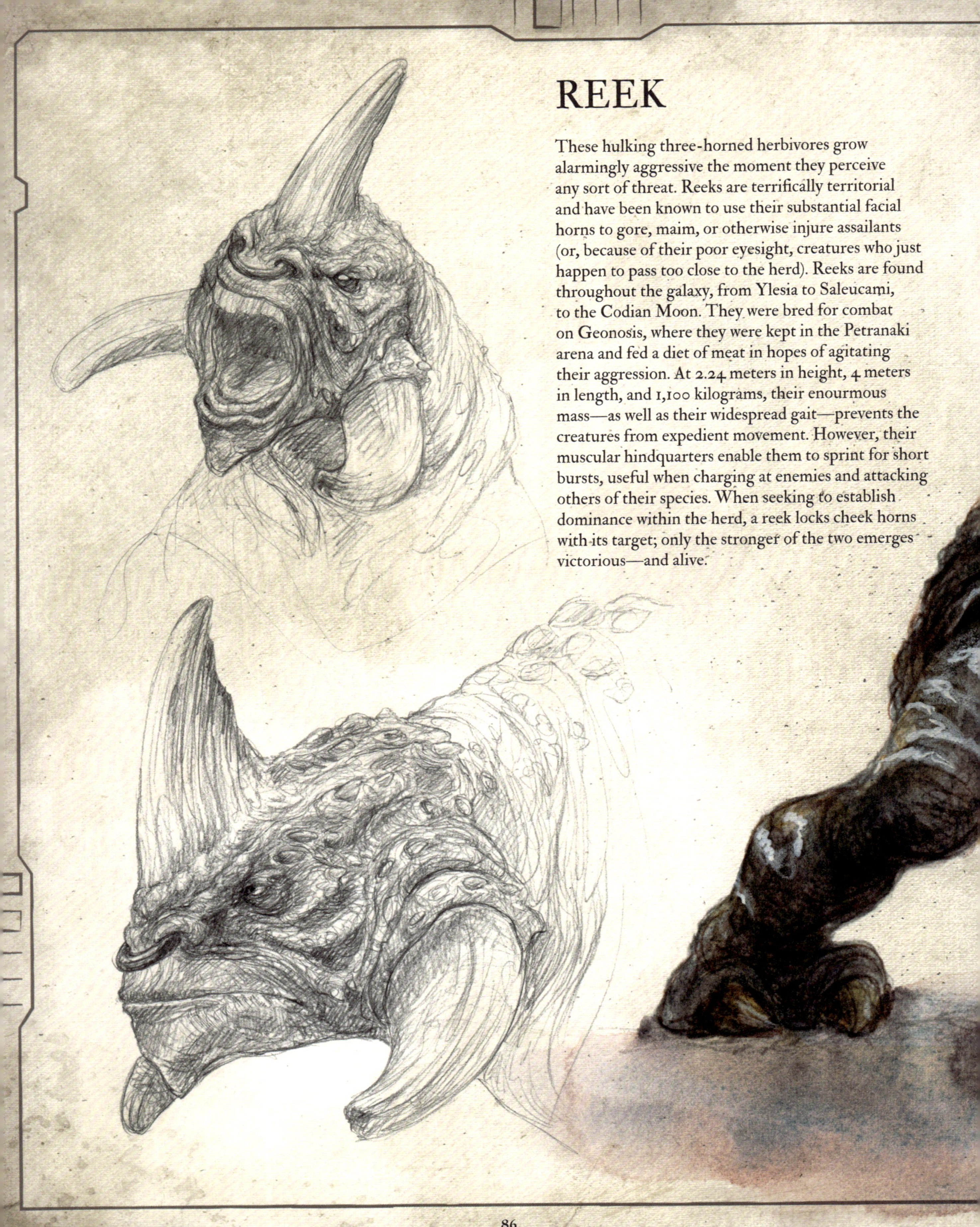

REEK

These hulking three-horned herbivores grow alarmingly aggressive the moment they perceive any sort of threat. Reeks are terrifically territorial and have been known to use their substantial facial horns to gore, maim, or otherwise injure assailants (or, because of their poor eyesight, creatures who just happen to pass too close to the herd). Reeks are found throughout the galaxy, from Ylesia to Saleucami, to the Codian Moon. They were bred for combat on Geonosis, where they were kept in the Petranaki arena and fed a diet of meat in hopes of agitating their aggression. At 2.24 meters in height, 4 meters in length, and 1,100 kilograms, their enourmous mass—as well as their widespread gait—prevents the creatures from expedient movement. However, their muscular hindquarters enable them to sprint for short bursts, useful when charging at enemies and attacking others of their species. When seeking to establish dominance within the herd, a reek locks cheek horns with its target; only the stronger of the two emerges victorious—and alive.

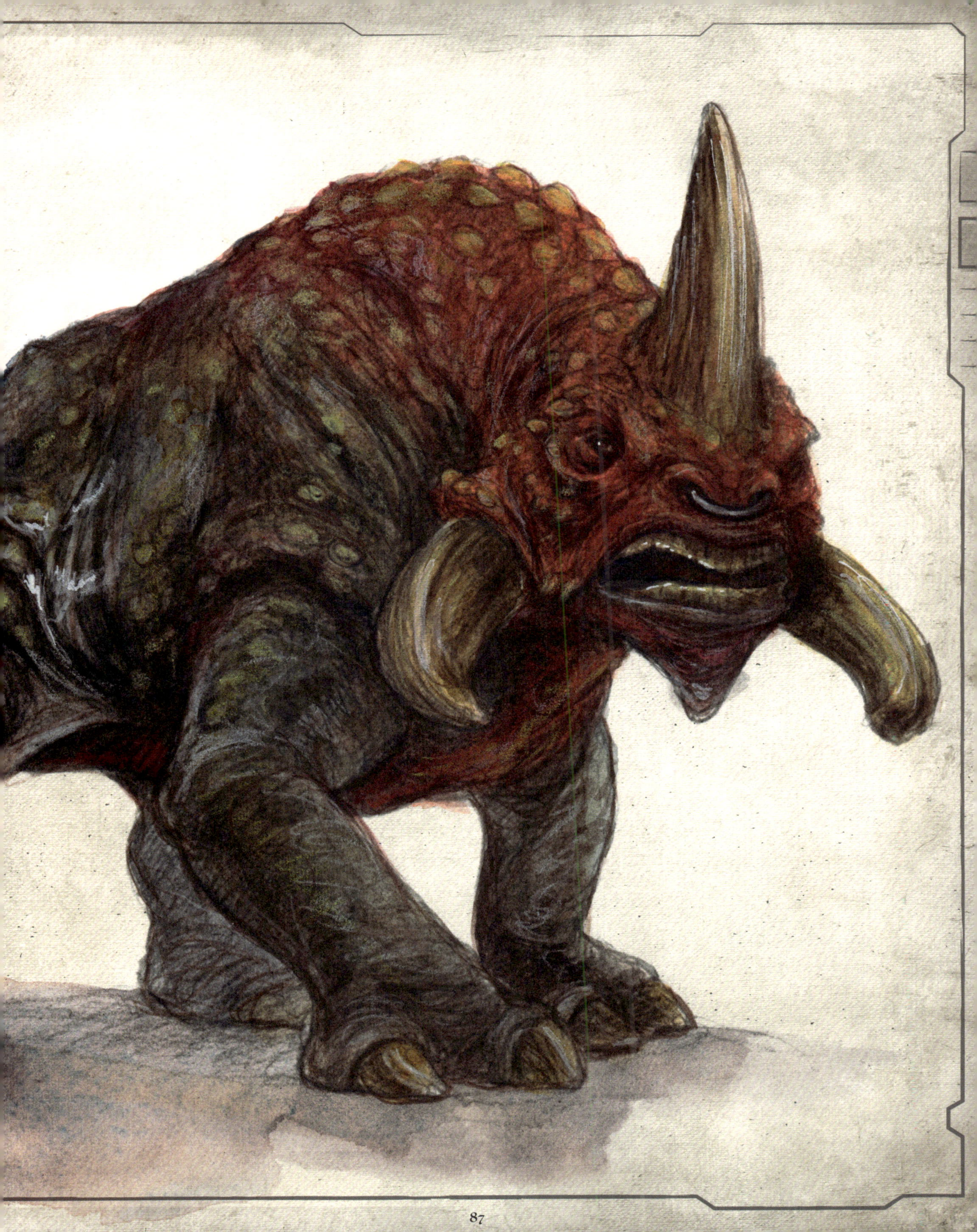

ORBAK

These herbivorous herd animals are related to fathiers, bordoks, tris, and pulgas. Their heavy coats of black or white hair sit atop their lightly bowed backs. They live on planets across the galaxy, with one especially strong herd making its home on the ocean moon of Kef Bir. Orbaks have long, flat snouts and two curved tusks that they use to uproot vegetation when feeding. Steady hooves help them navigate new terrain, and their loyal nature makes them ideal mounts for those with the patience to train them. Domesticated orbaks can be fitted with saddles and collars; specimens on frontier planets work in transport, agriculture, and even warfare.

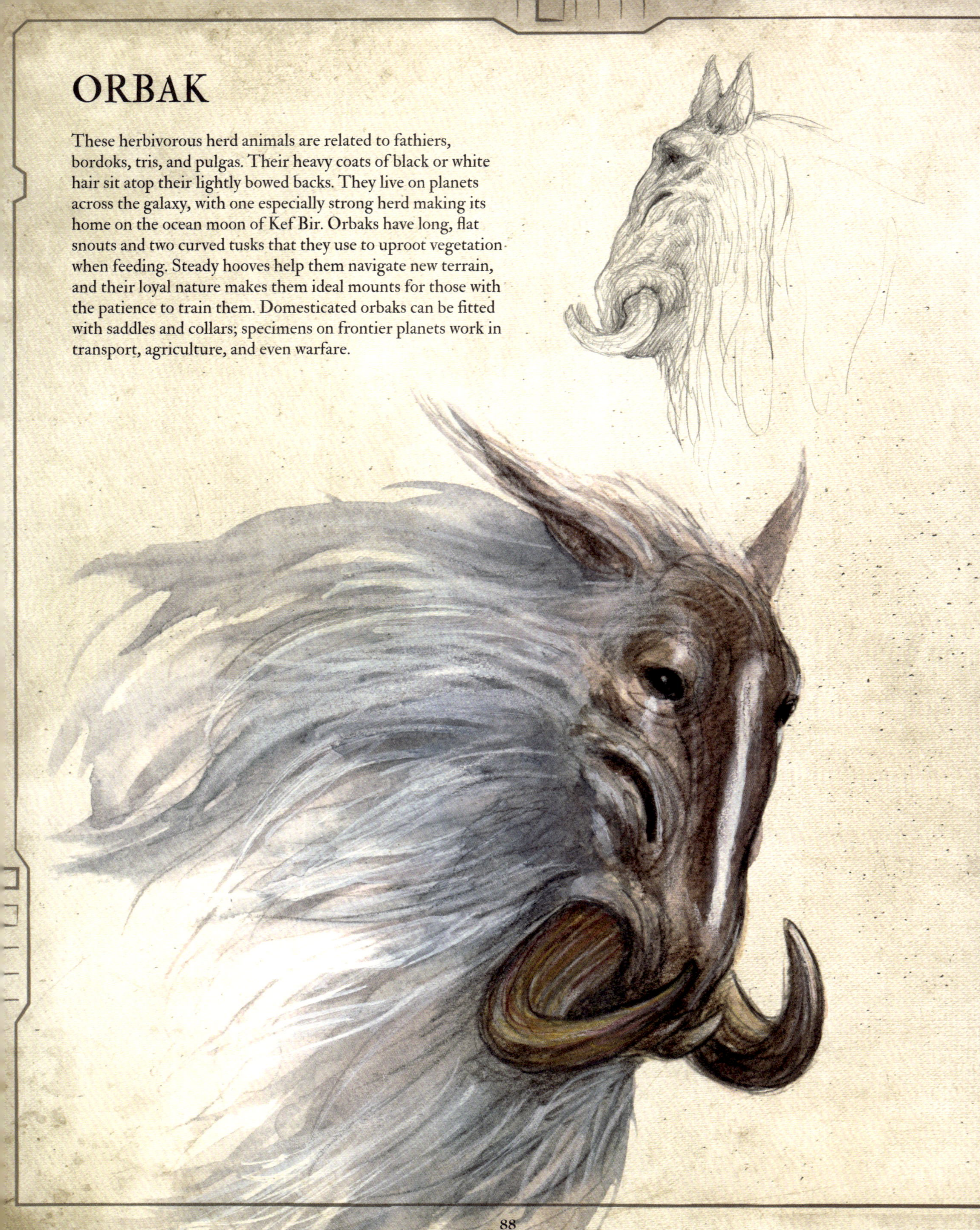

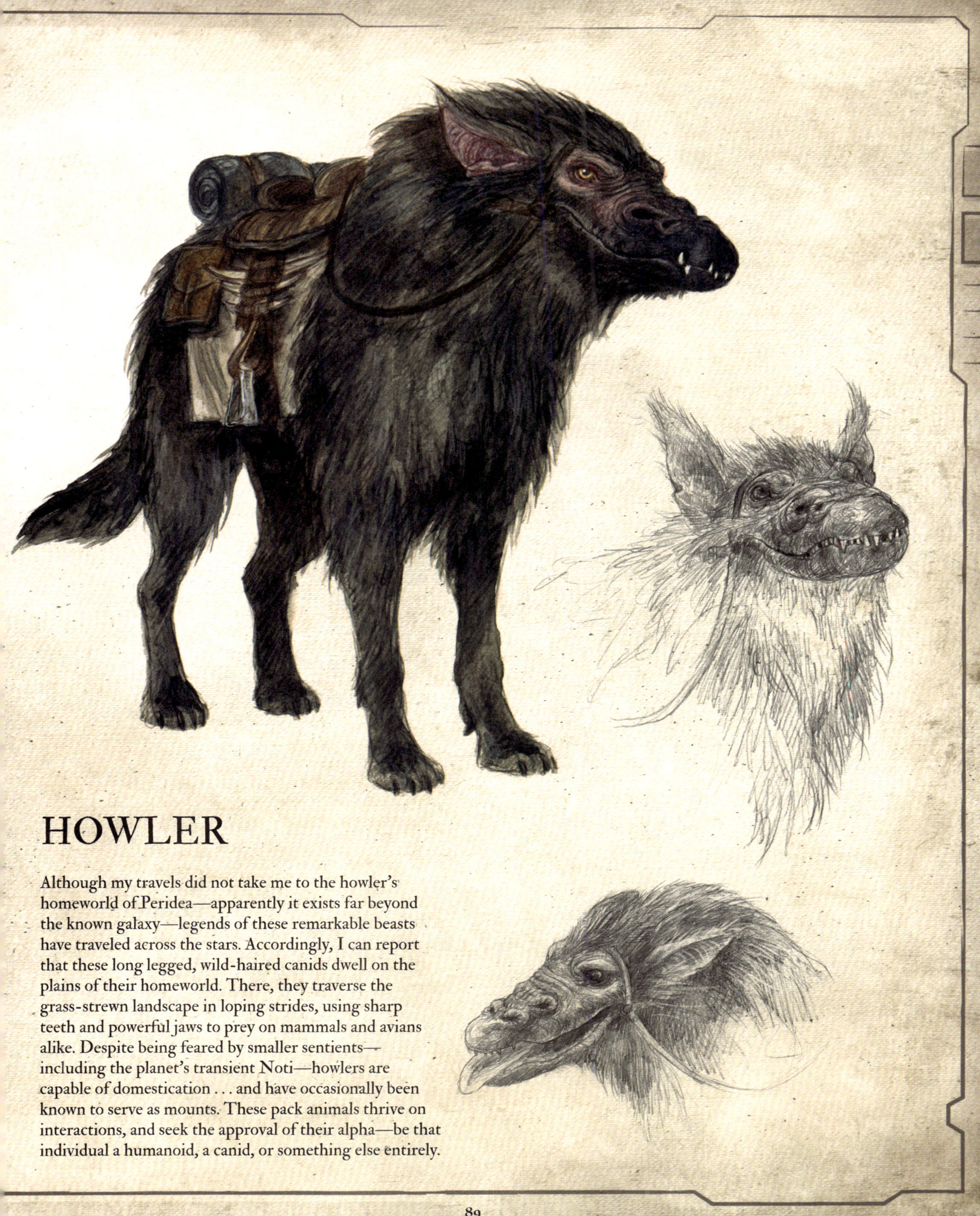

HOWLER

Although my travels did not take me to the howler's homeworld of Peridea—apparently it exists far beyond the known galaxy—legends of these remarkable beasts have traveled across the stars. Accordingly, I can report that these long legged, wild-haired canids dwell on the plains of their homeworld. There, they traverse the grass-strewn landscape in loping strides, using sharp teeth and powerful jaws to prey on mammals and avians alike. Despite being feared by smaller sentients—including the planet's transient Noti—howlers are capable of domestication . . . and have occasionally been known to serve as mounts. These pack animals thrive on interactions, and seek the approval of their alpha—be that individual a humanoid, a canid, or something else entirely.

SHAAK

Naboo's most uniquely proportioned mammals appear barely able to stand. With their short legs and enormous backsides, shaaks seem to be in a constant state of nearly tipping over! But these 1.8-meter-tall herbivores are well aware of their limitations. They move slowly and carefully across the grasslands of Naboo, systematically avoiding the swamps, where an excess of predators makes them particularly vulnerable. Shaak are popular livestock among Gungan farmers, who find the grazers to be of tremendous use. Shaak hides are sold for leather, their meat is made into steaks and chops, and their droppings are repurposed as fertilizer, thus enhancing the value of a farmer's land.

Shaaks are unusually susceptible to the Blue Shadow Virus, a disease that kills the creatures instantly, despite offering an excruciating forty-eight-hour survival rate in other species, sparing them continued suffering.

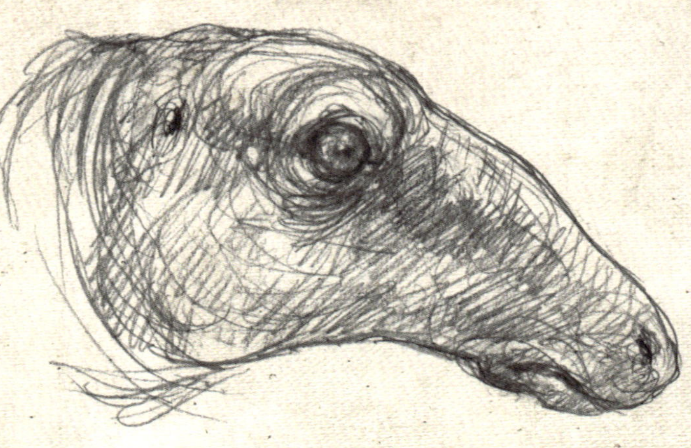

Because of their uneven proportions, shaaks are prone to tipping over. The fatty tissue in their bulbous backsides makes them bounce back upright when they fall over! This fatty tissue also enables shaaks to float, providing an additional survival mechanism in their swamp-rich environment.

— B8-T5

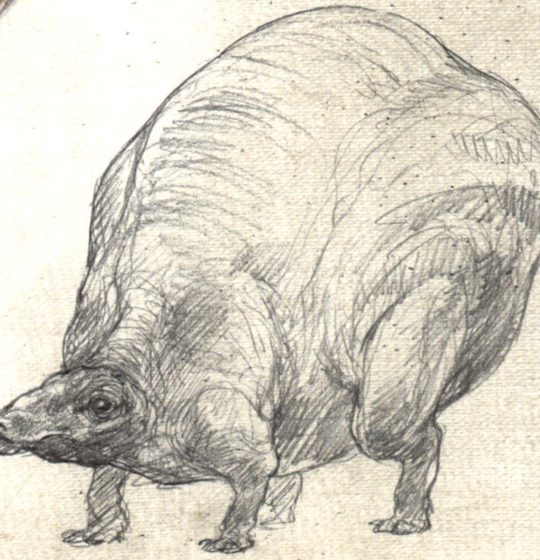

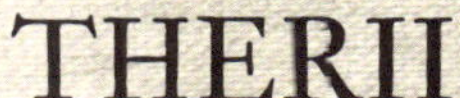

THERII

The floppy-eared, twin-tusked therii makes its home on the planets of Pacara and Batuu. It has soft, reddish-brown fur and short, two-toed hooves. Therii are an herbivorous species whose preferred diet includes the leaves and stems of oats, wheat, and corn—although they have been known to beg Batuu tourists for snacks of popped grains. Therii use their ears both for hearing and as a means of expression: They often show contentment by flapping them wildly!

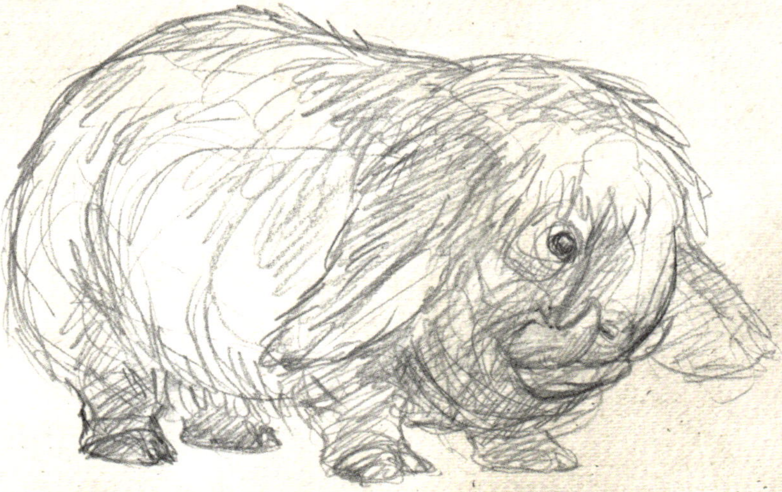

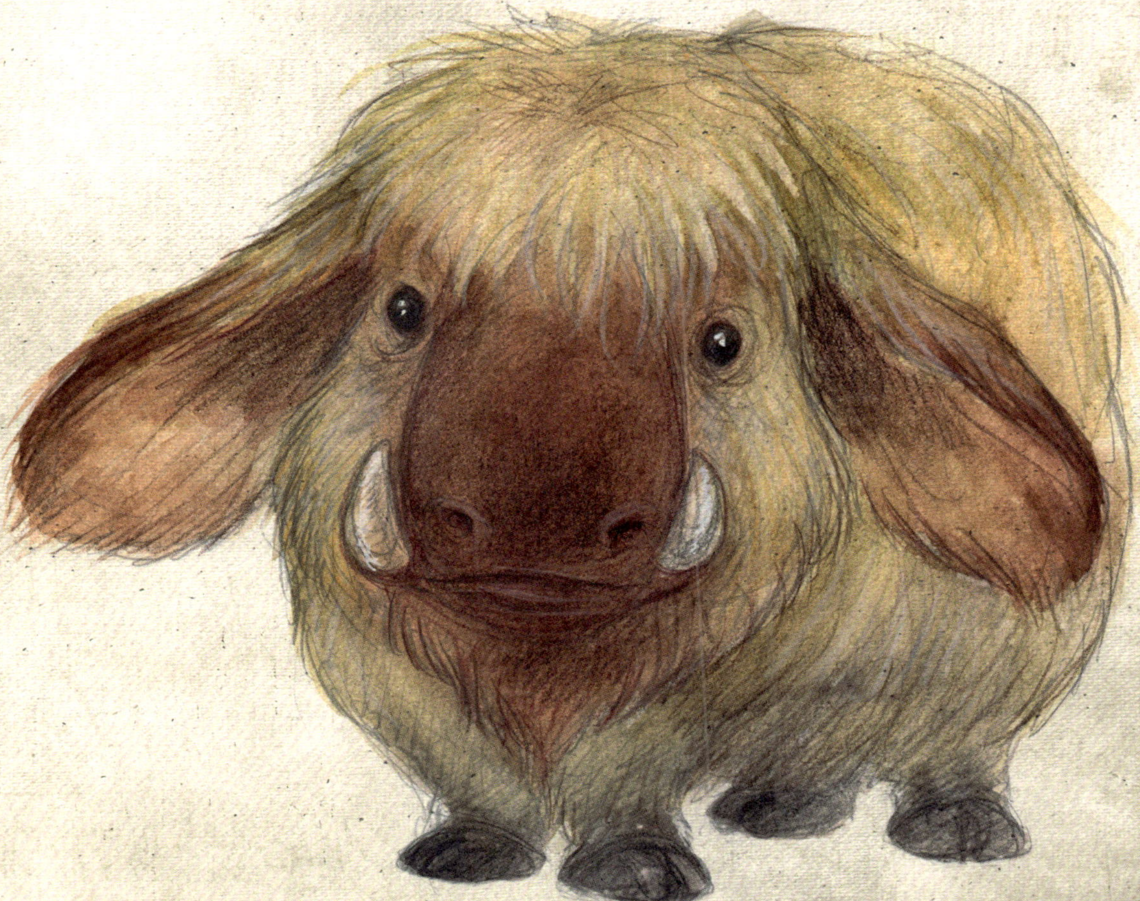

ICE AND SNOW CREATURES

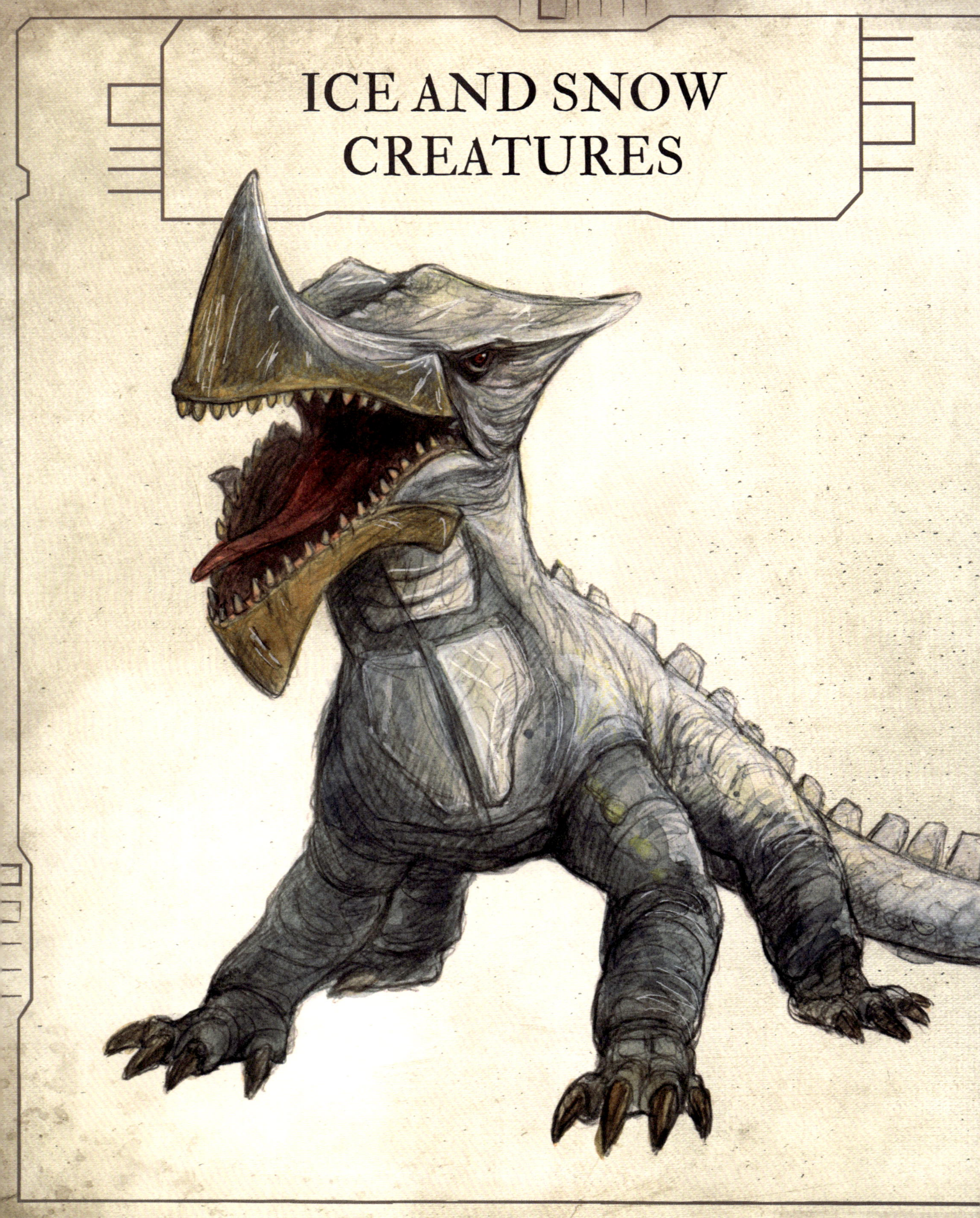

BONZAMI

These four-legged ice dwellers are native to the Geonosis moon of Bahryn. Standing at around 14.75 meters tall and 13 meters long, they boast intimidating rows of sharp, gray spikes on their backs. These reptilian creatures possess a pair of horns, one atop and one below their powerful jaws. Their skin is resistant to blaster bolts, ensuring that they retain the upper hand in most battles—including those against sentient beings. They can, however, be deterred with high amounts of heat and fierce surges of electricity; this makes the bo-rifle, used by the Honor Guard of Lasan, a particularly effective weapon to use against them.

Bonzami hunt both alone and in packs, using their razor-sharp teeth and piercing, hornlike head spikes to attack their prey. A heavy layer of white fur allows them to withstand Bahryn's frigid temperatures, and their thick hides further aid in temperature regulation.

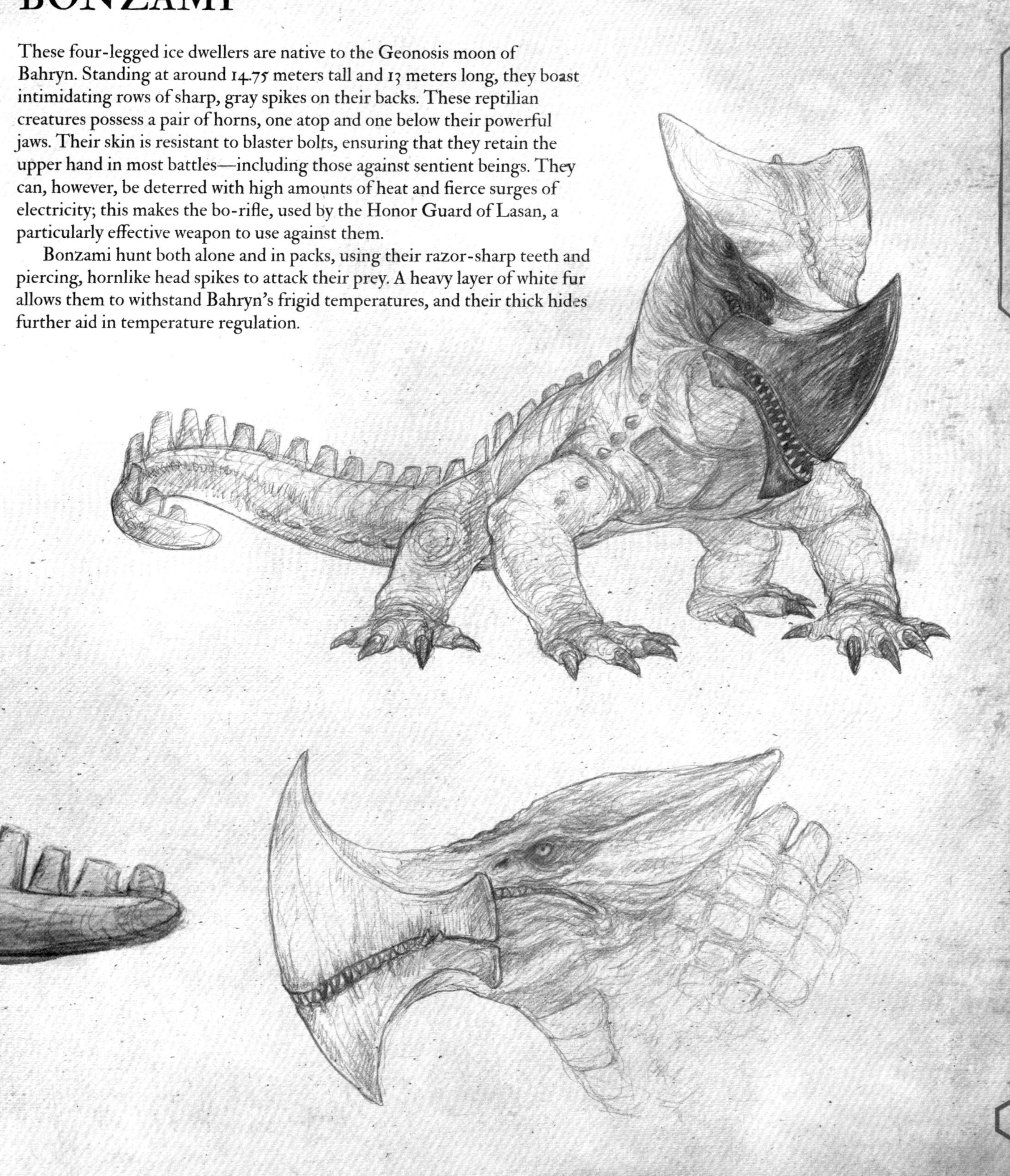

KOD'YOK

Vandor's peaceful, twin-horned natives roam the snowy plains of their homeworld in herds that can exceed fifty members. Standing roughly two meters tall and measuring a little more than one and a half meters long, kod'yoks make for a common method of transport. Throughout time, they have been hunted for their hides, which are made into a variety of leather goods. This practice has rapidly diminished the kod'yok population, with numbers that continue to sit just above the endangered level. Their long brown wool offers warmth in Vandor's frosty climate, and steady hooves enable the kod'yok to traverse icy surfaces with relative ease. The creatures produce a sweet milk favored by young ones. Their meat is easily cooked into steaks, stews, and chops, making kod'yok in all its forms a staple of the Vandorian diet.

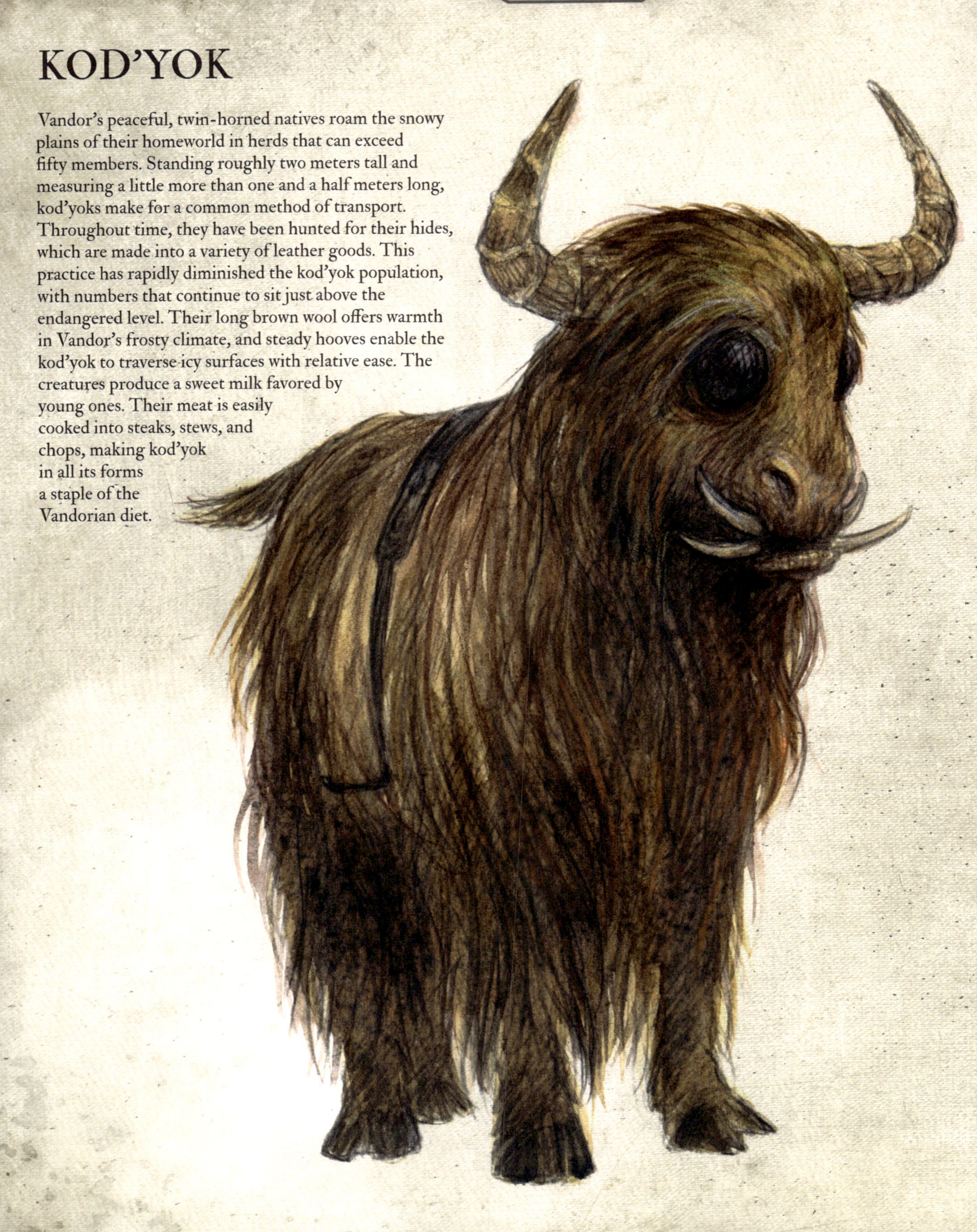

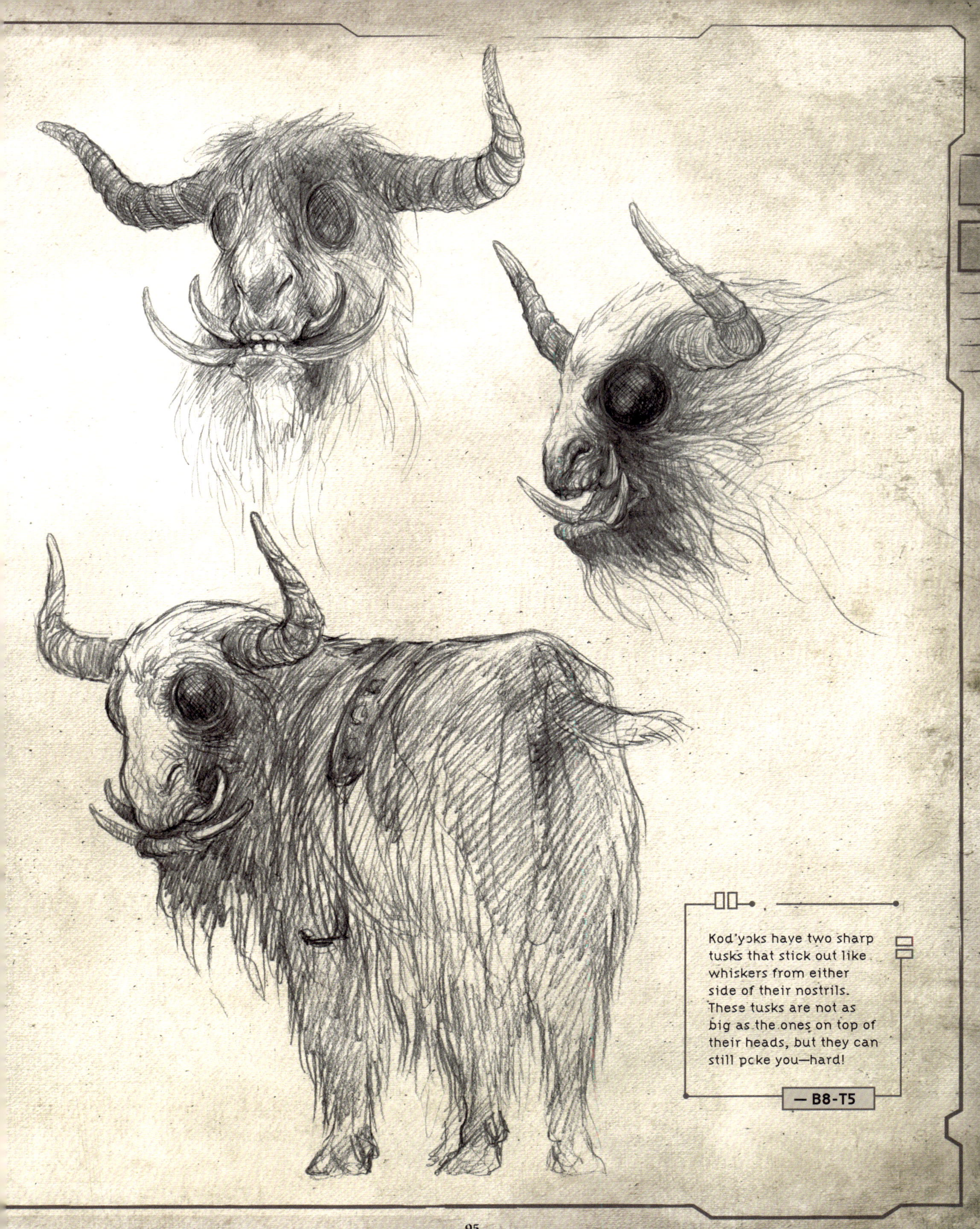
Kod'yoks have two sharp tusks that stick out like whiskers from either side of their nostrils. These tusks are not as big as the ones on top of their heads, but they can still poke you—hard!
— B8-T5

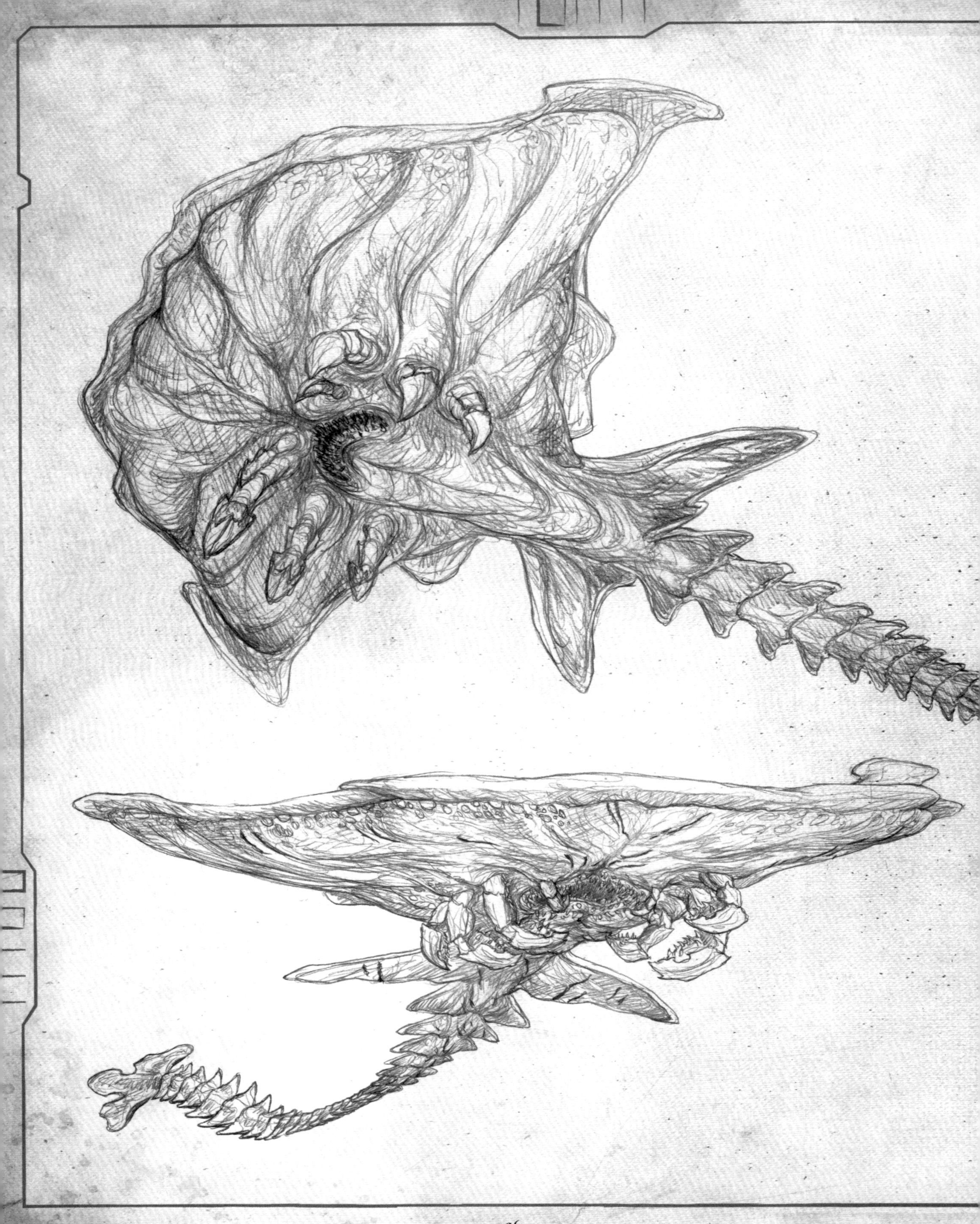

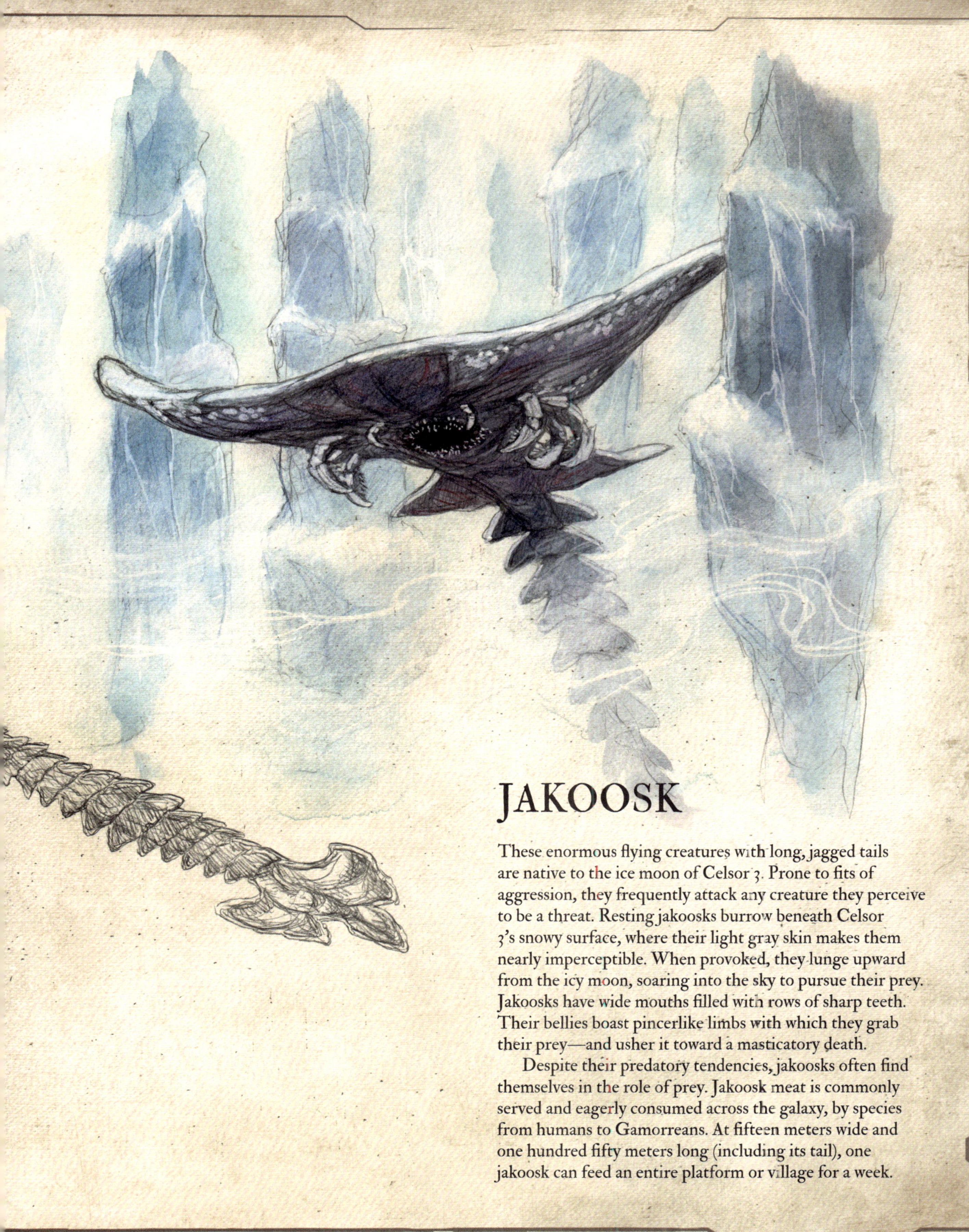

JAKOOSK

These enormous flying creatures with long, jagged tails are native to the ice moon of Celsor 3. Prone to fits of aggression, they frequently attack any creature they perceive to be a threat. Resting jakoosks burrow beneath Celsor 3's snowy surface, where their light gray skin makes them nearly imperceptible. When provoked, they lunge upward from the icy moon, soaring into the sky to pursue their prey. Jakoosks have wide mouths filled with rows of sharp teeth. Their bellies boast pincerlike limbs with which they grab their prey—and usher it toward a masticatory death.

Despite their predatory tendencies, jakoosks often find themselves in the role of prey. Jakoosk meat is commonly served and eagerly consumed across the galaxy, by species from humans to Gamorreans. At fifteen meters wide and one hundred fifty meters long (including its tail), one jakoosk can feed an entire platform or village for a week.

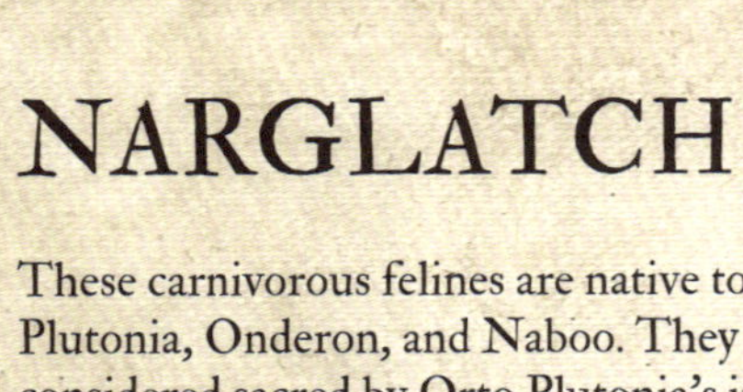

NARGLATCH

These carnivorous felines are native to Orto Plutonia, Onderon, and Naboo. They are considered sacred by Orto Plutonia's indigenous Talz, who ride atop the majestic cats (and also consume their meat). Narglatches measure at 6.2 meters in length, and have sharp claws, piercing fangs, and a brilliant, blue coat—the latter of which has led to them to be hunted by those who value narglatch pelts, including the Trandoshans.

Narglatch cubs are frequently sold as pets and to traveling carnivals. However, the animal's temperament diminishes greatly with age, leading many owners to release their captives as they near adolescence. For this reason, residents of planets such as Coruscant must often be on alert for escaped feline threats.

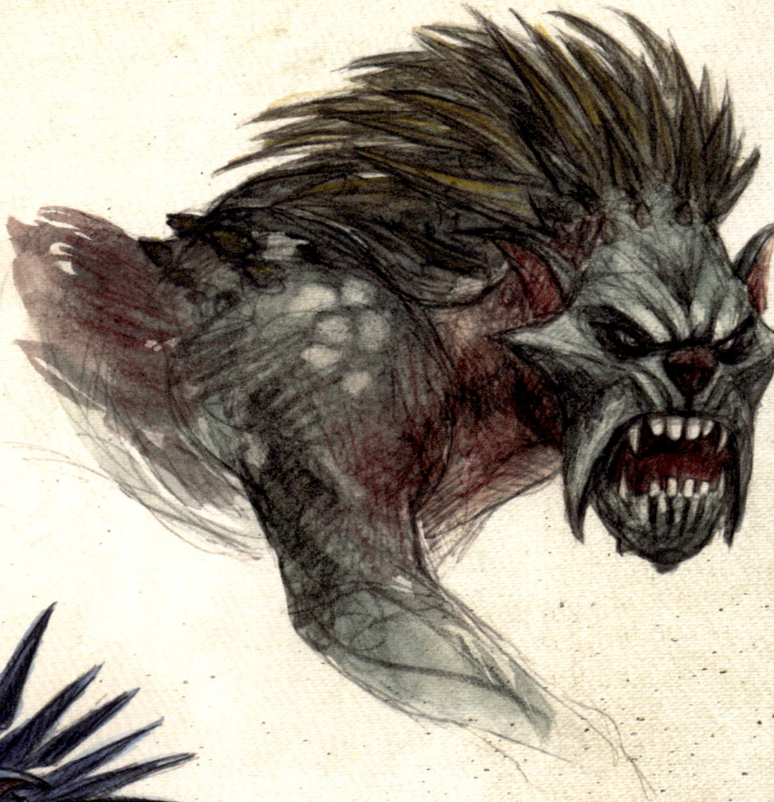

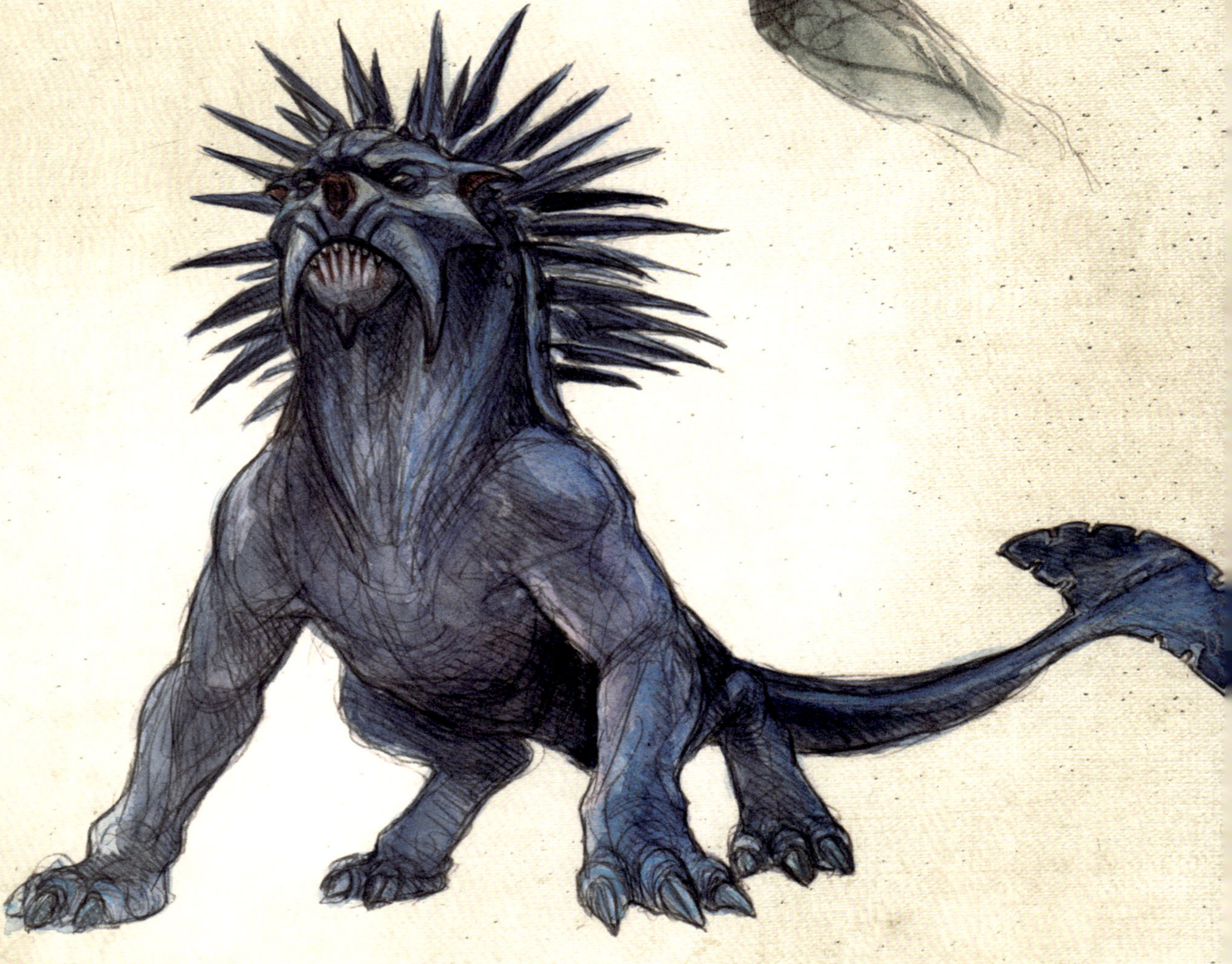

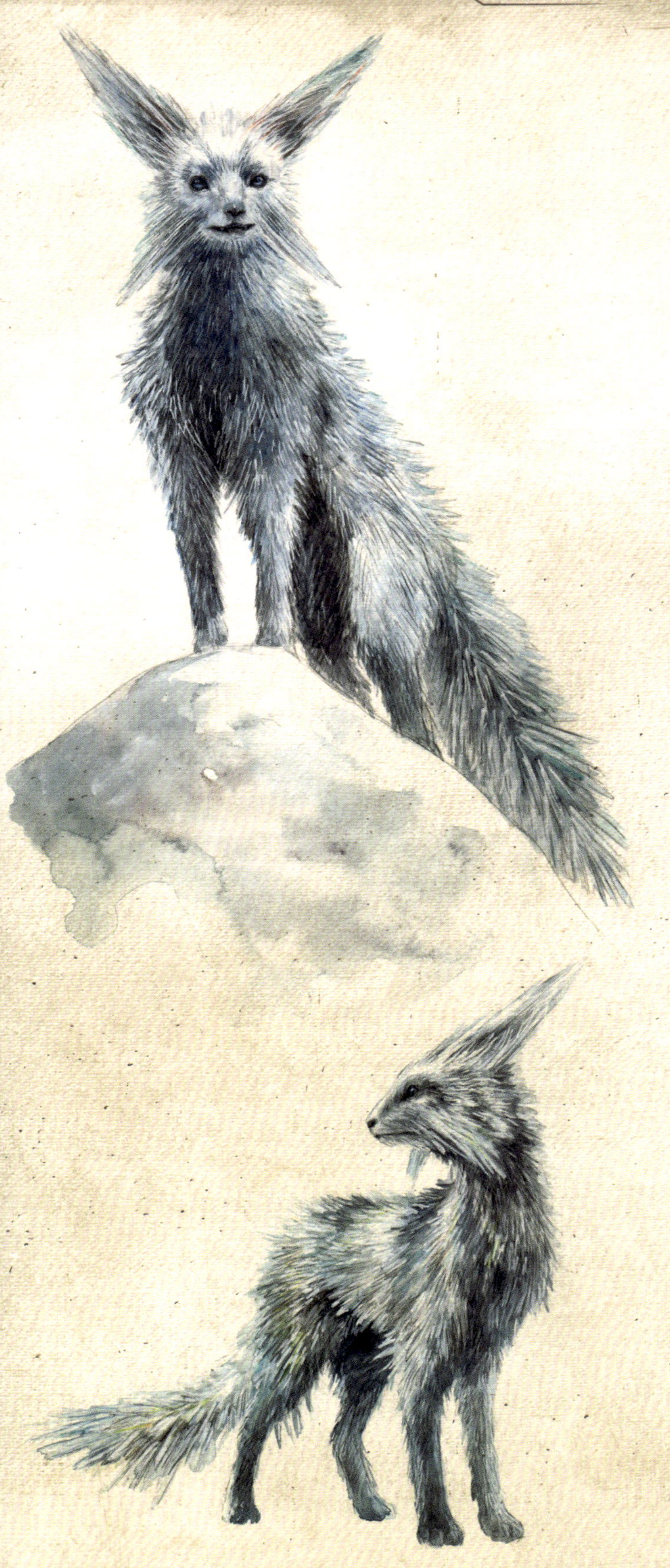

VULPTEX

Vulptices are a small canine species. They have a standing height of a mere c.51 meters, with their pointed, crystalline ears making up a good portion of that size. Their rapid rate of movement—along with their habit of weaving in and out of their pack—confuses predators, making these omnivores difficult to catch. The vulptices live among Crait's highland caves and canyons, migrating across the flats to reach their well-concealed dens. Because they frequent the planet's rocky caverns—and, accordingly, must navigate tight spaces on a regular basis—vulptices rely on facial bristles spanning the width of their bodies to ascertain whether they can fit into a passage. With their vibrant, crystalline bristles, these creatures also emit the sound of melodic chimes as they race across Crait's salt flats, a defensive mechanism used to warn of approaching danger.

The creatures are able to see in low light, enabling the cave dwellers to navigate their subterranean spaces. The respected xenobiologist Paqin Mesoli believed the creatures dwell in two locations, with some dens located beneath Crait's salty surface and others sitting higher atop Crait's caverns. They live in family packs called skulks, with up to four families residing in one den at a time. They work together to survive, hunting in groups and brushing their bristles against nearby surfaces to communicate among their species. They rely on sharp claws and long snouts to dig tubers and burrowing mammals from beneath the planet's salty crust, and they reserve the bulk of their activity for dawn and dusk—times when their prey actively forages for food. Vulptices develop strong bonds within their species and have even been known to help those outside it, as evidenced by a Resistance account circa 34 ABY of a particular vulptex guiding a human party to safety.

Vulptices will chase almost anything, and their strong jaws ensure that, once they have you in their grasp, you're unlikely to escape. Each vulptex pack has its own way of calling to one another using their crystal bristles, almost like a family song.

—B8-T5

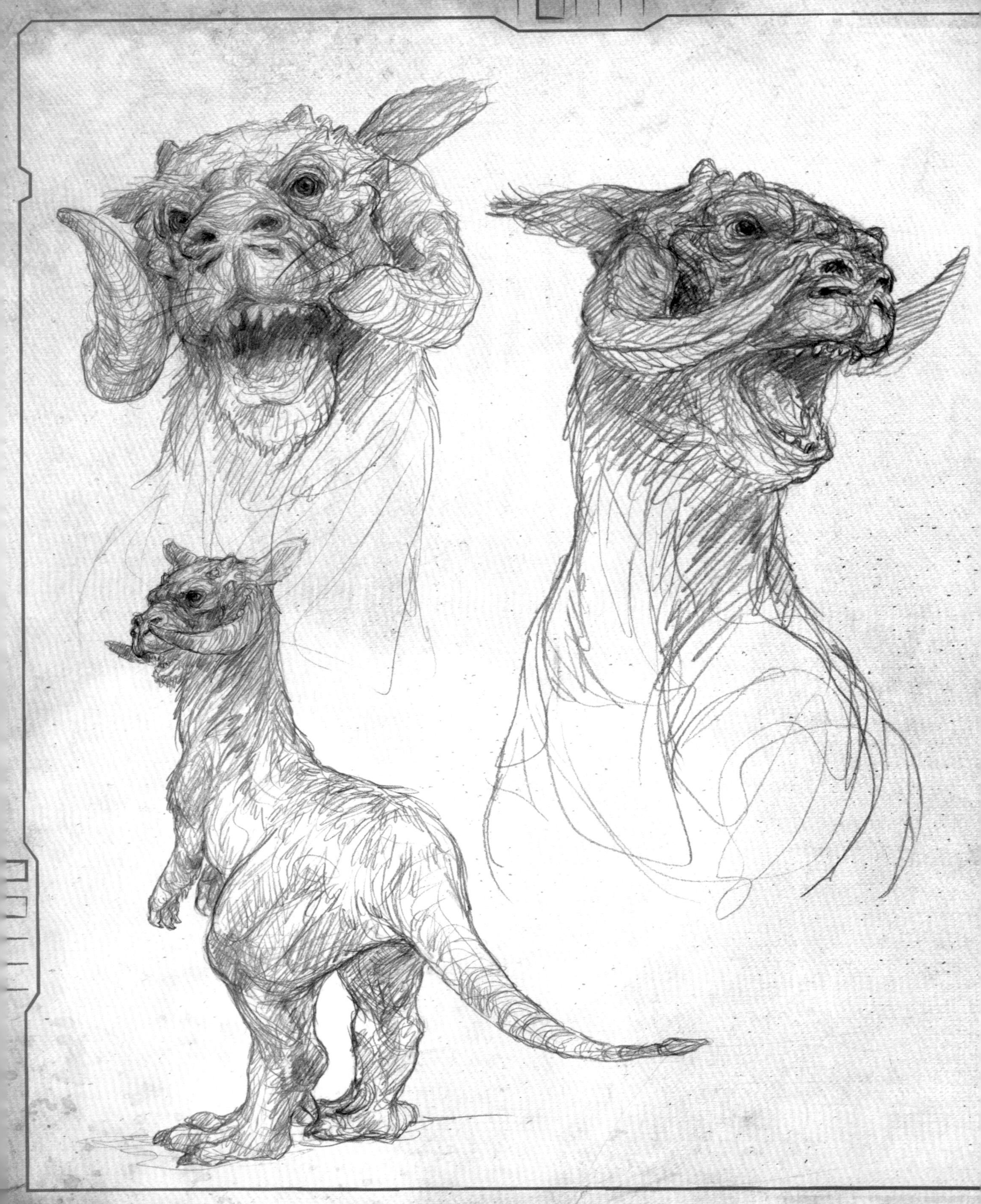

TAUNTAUN

After spending time studying wildlife on Hoth, this scientist can confirm that the tauntaun's reputation as Hoth's most rancid-smelling reptomammal is, in fact, *warranted*! This is due to the fact that the tauntaun expels a thick, pungent oil in order to attract a mate. (The oil is also used to communicate among others of its species.) Some suspect that the tauntaun's dense layers of coarse woolen fur also contribute to its odiferous scent. The species relies on this coat to remain warm within its icy habitat, with its fur wicking away moisture and also clinging valiantly to old scents, much like that of a mudhorn. Tauntauns feed on a variety of sources, including Hoth hogs, ice scrabblers, ice plants, and lichen.

Thick skin and layers of fatty blubber—along with their habit of burrowing beneath the snow for warmth—help tauntauns regulate their body heat in Hoth's frigid atmosphere, where the nighttime air can drop to below negative sixty degrees. The creatures have twin sets of nostrils—one large and one small—that they alternate in use to better control their body temperature. Tauntauns activate their larger nostrils during physical exertion to maximize oxygen flow; they use their smaller nostrils while grazing because the diminished proportions prove more effective than their larger counterparts in obstructing snow. Their long tails improve balance while running and also enable the bipedal beasts to literally cover their tracks, avoiding visual detection by predators such as the wampa. The creatures' four wide toes, which are independent of their fifth, elevated dew claw, are connected by a webbed layer of fur-coated skin that offers surety of step on the ice planet's unsteady surface.

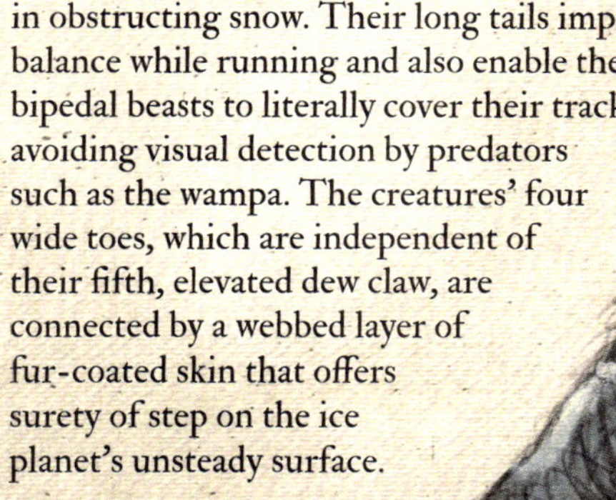

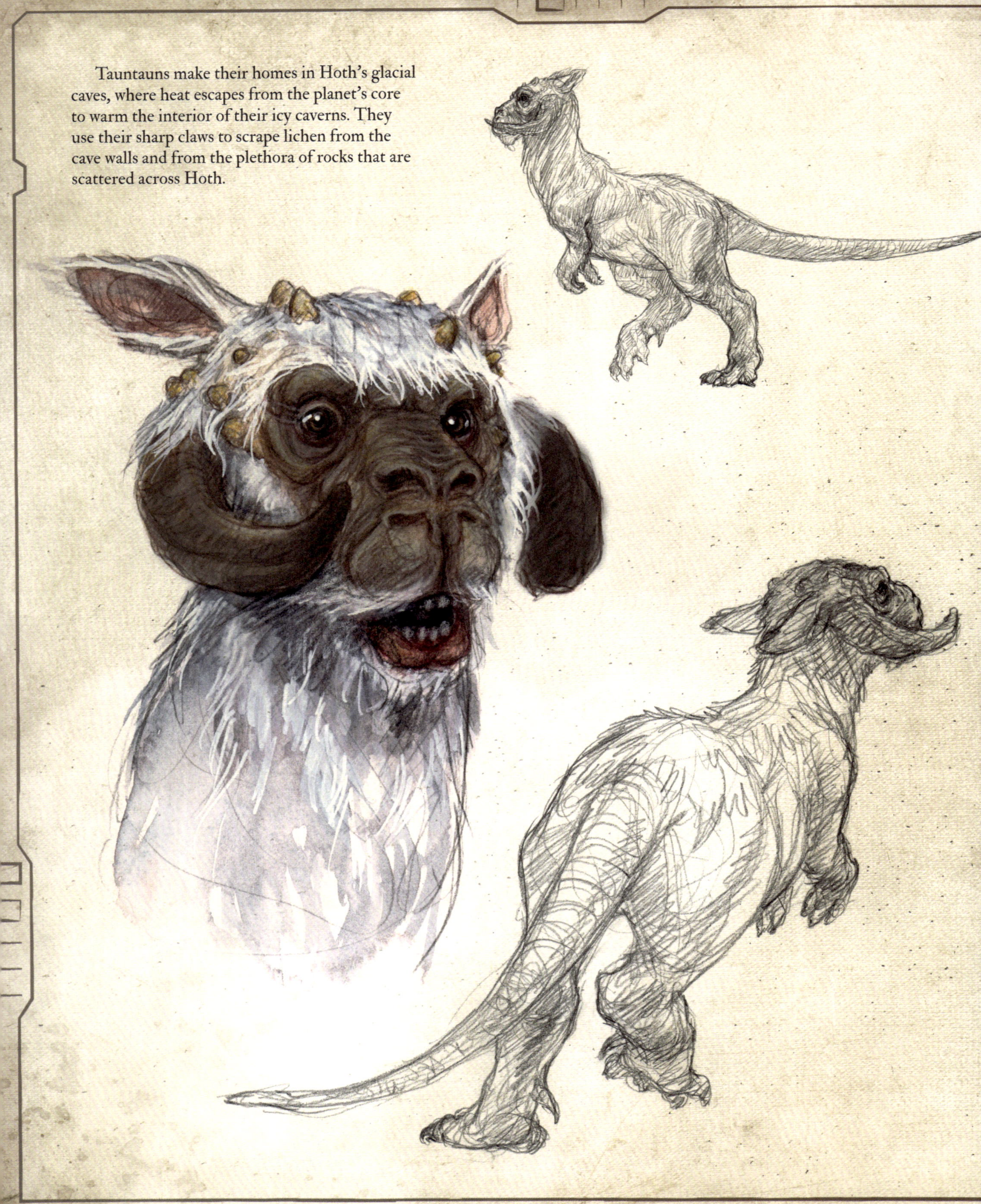

Tauntauns make their homes in Hoth's glacial caves, where heat escapes from the planet's core to warm the interior of their icy caverns. They use their sharp claws to scrape lichen from the cave walls and from the plethora of rocks that are scattered across Hoth.

Tauntauns are easily domesticated. They were used as mounts by members of the Rebel forces around the time of the Battle of Hoth. They stand 2.7 meters tall at the shoulder, and they run at speeds of ninety kilometers per hour. They live in matriarchal herds of up to twenty-five members, within which they give birth to live young, known as tauntlets. There are fifteen known subspecies of tauntauns, with additional numbers believed to exist in the more remote—and, as of yet, unstudied—regions of the glacial planet.

> Hoth natives say that tauntauns smell the least awful to most senitent creatures immediately after shedding their fur. The period following tauntaun shedding season is also the ideal time to visit Hoth because of the decrease in aggression among wampas. Maybe they don't like the smell, either.
>
> — B8-T5

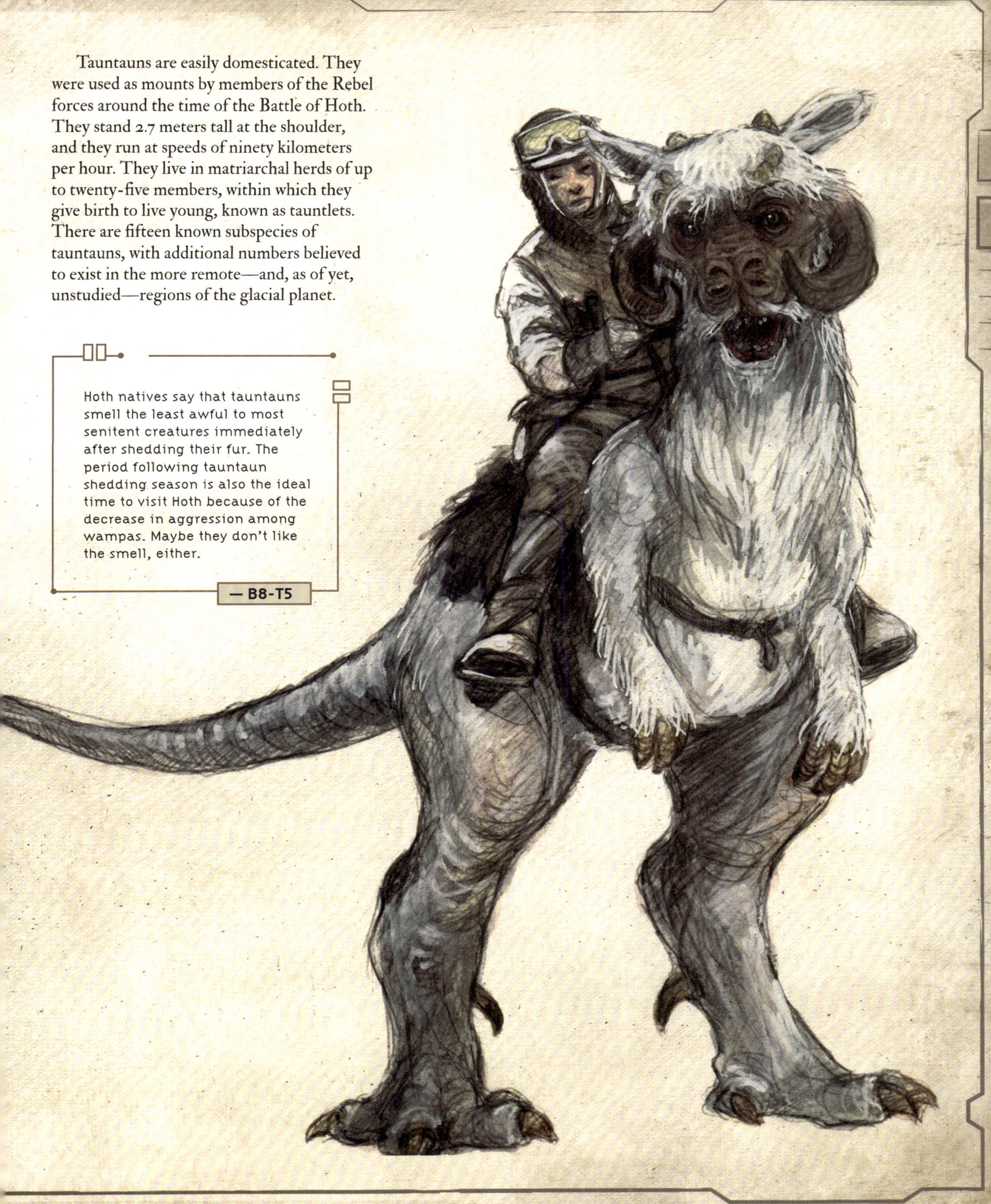

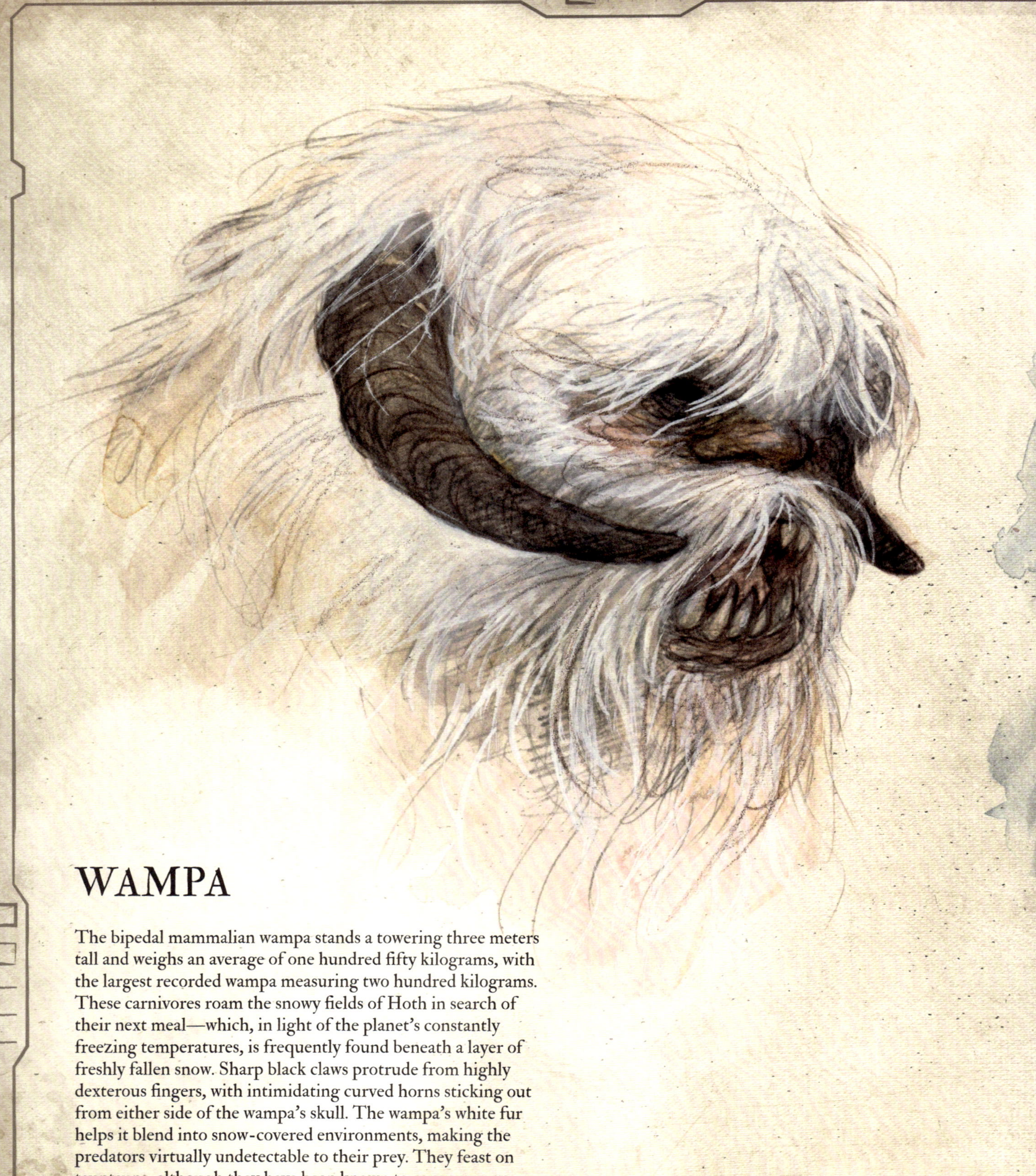

WAMPA

The bipedal mammalian wampa stands a towering three meters tall and weighs an average of one hundred fifty kilograms, with the largest recorded wampa measuring two hundred kilograms. These carnivores roam the snowy fields of Hoth in search of their next meal—which, in light of the planet's constantly freezing temperatures, is frequently found beneath a layer of freshly fallen snow. Sharp black claws protrude from highly dexterous fingers, with intimidating curved horns sticking out from either side of the wampa's skull. The wampa's white fur helps it blend into snow-covered environments, making the predators virtually undetectable to their prey. They feast on tauntauns, although they have been known to consume any available food source—including humans!

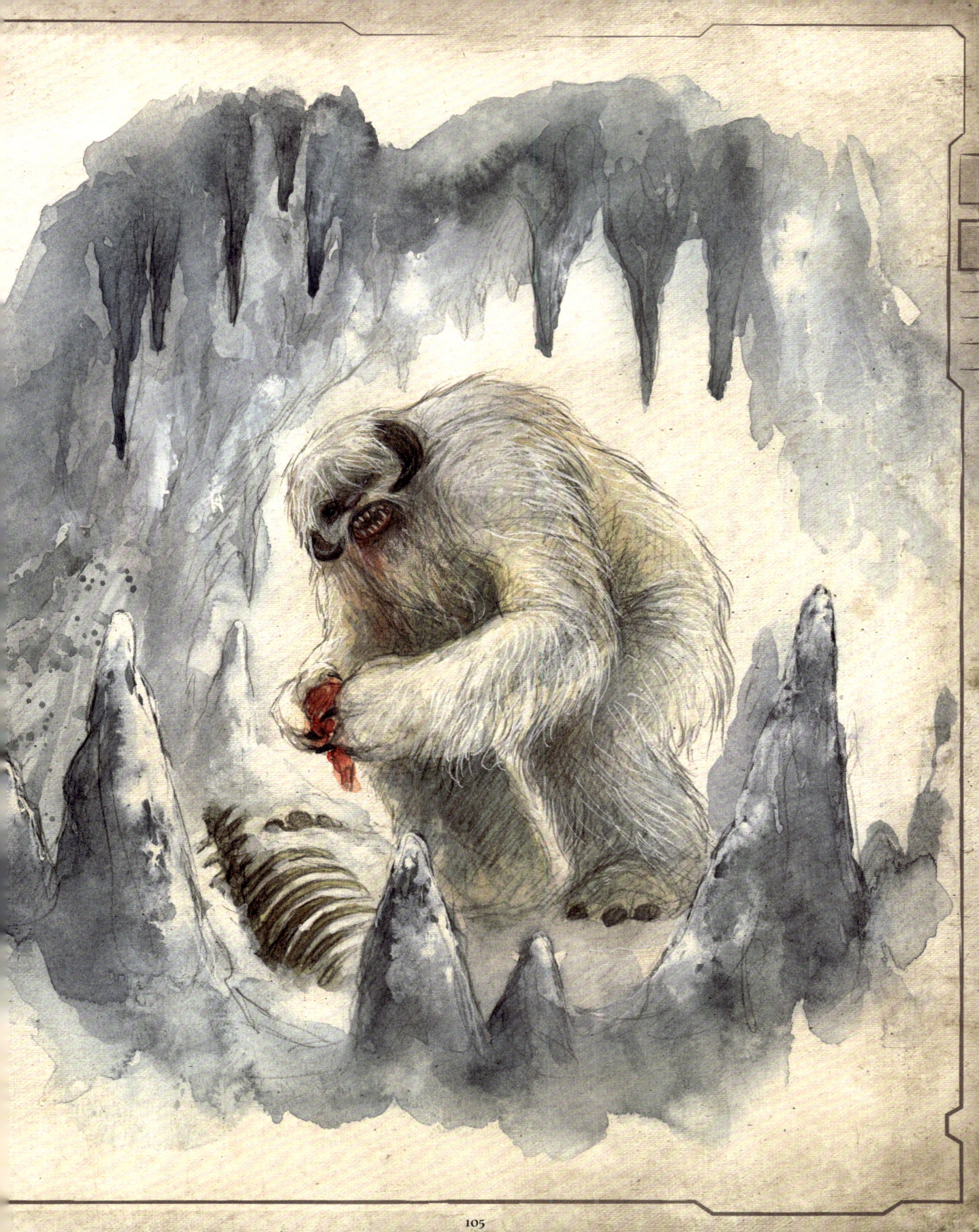

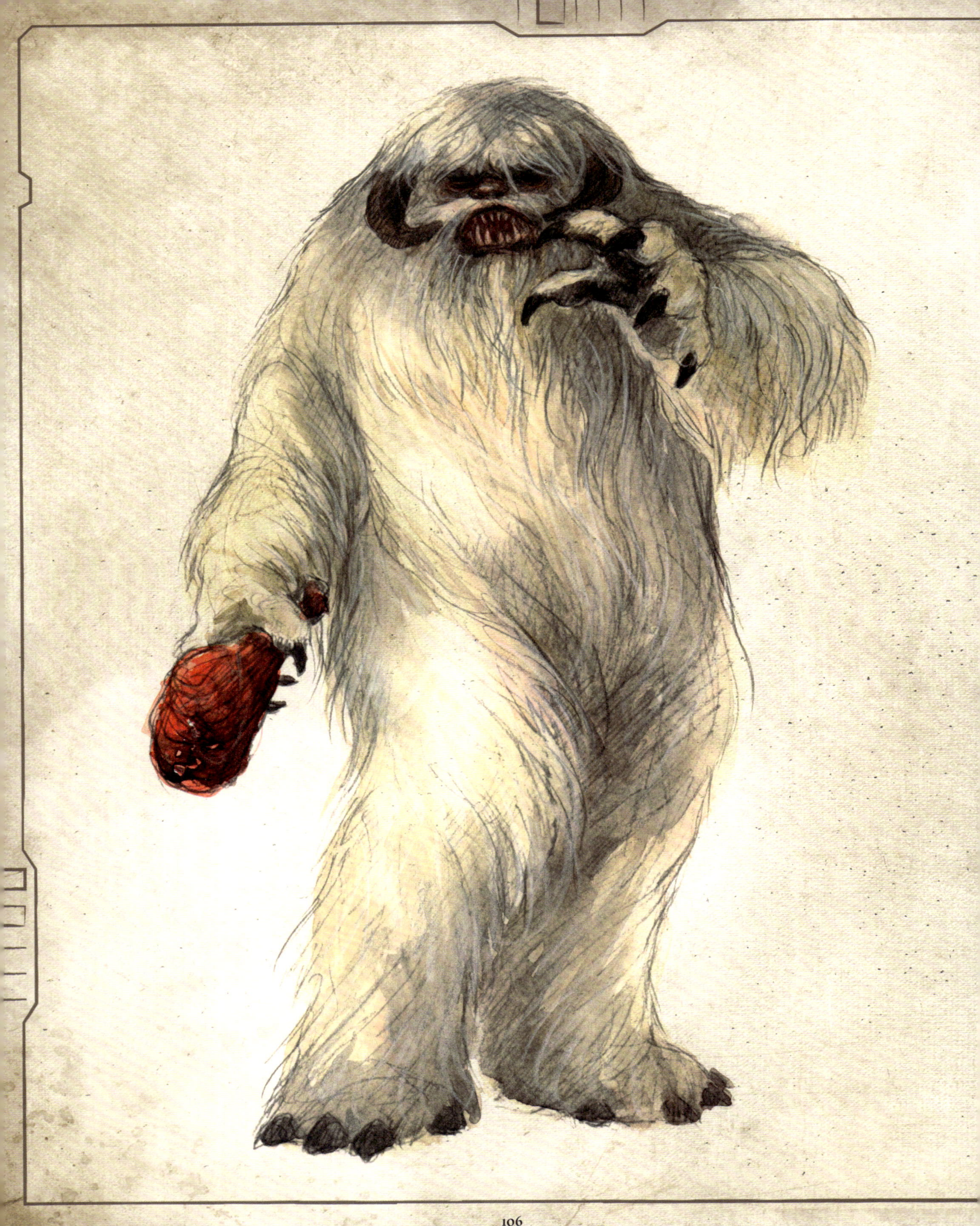

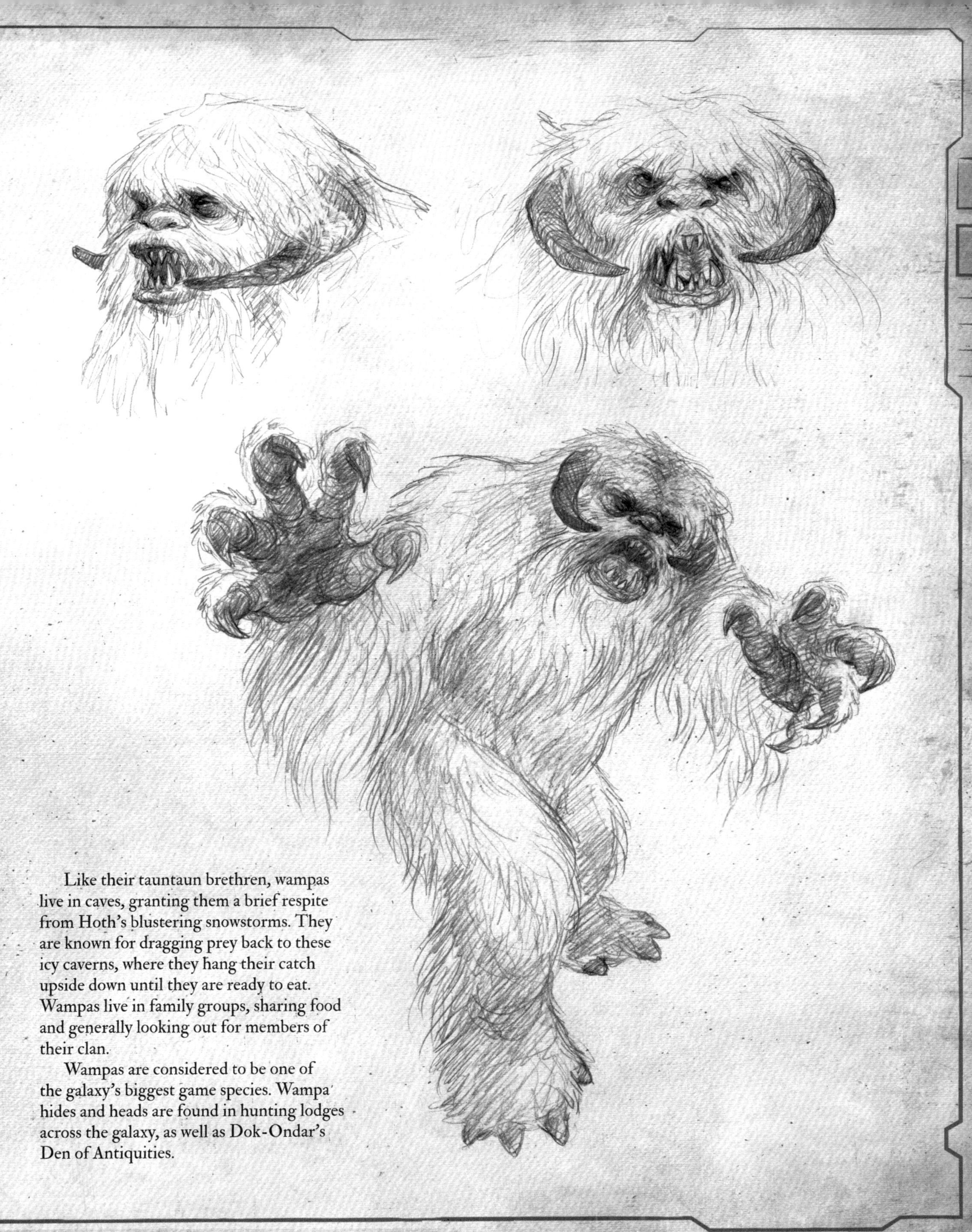

Like their tauntaun brethren, wampas live in caves, granting them a brief respite from Hoth's blustering snowstorms. They are known for dragging prey back to these icy caverns, where they hang their catch upside down until they are ready to eat. Wampas live in family groups, sharing food and generally looking out for members of their clan.

Wampas are considered to be one of the galaxy's biggest game species. Wampa hides and heads are found in hunting lodges across the galaxy, as well as Dok-Ondar's Den of Antiquities.

MOUNTAINS, ROCKY PLAINS, AND VOLCANIC CREATURES

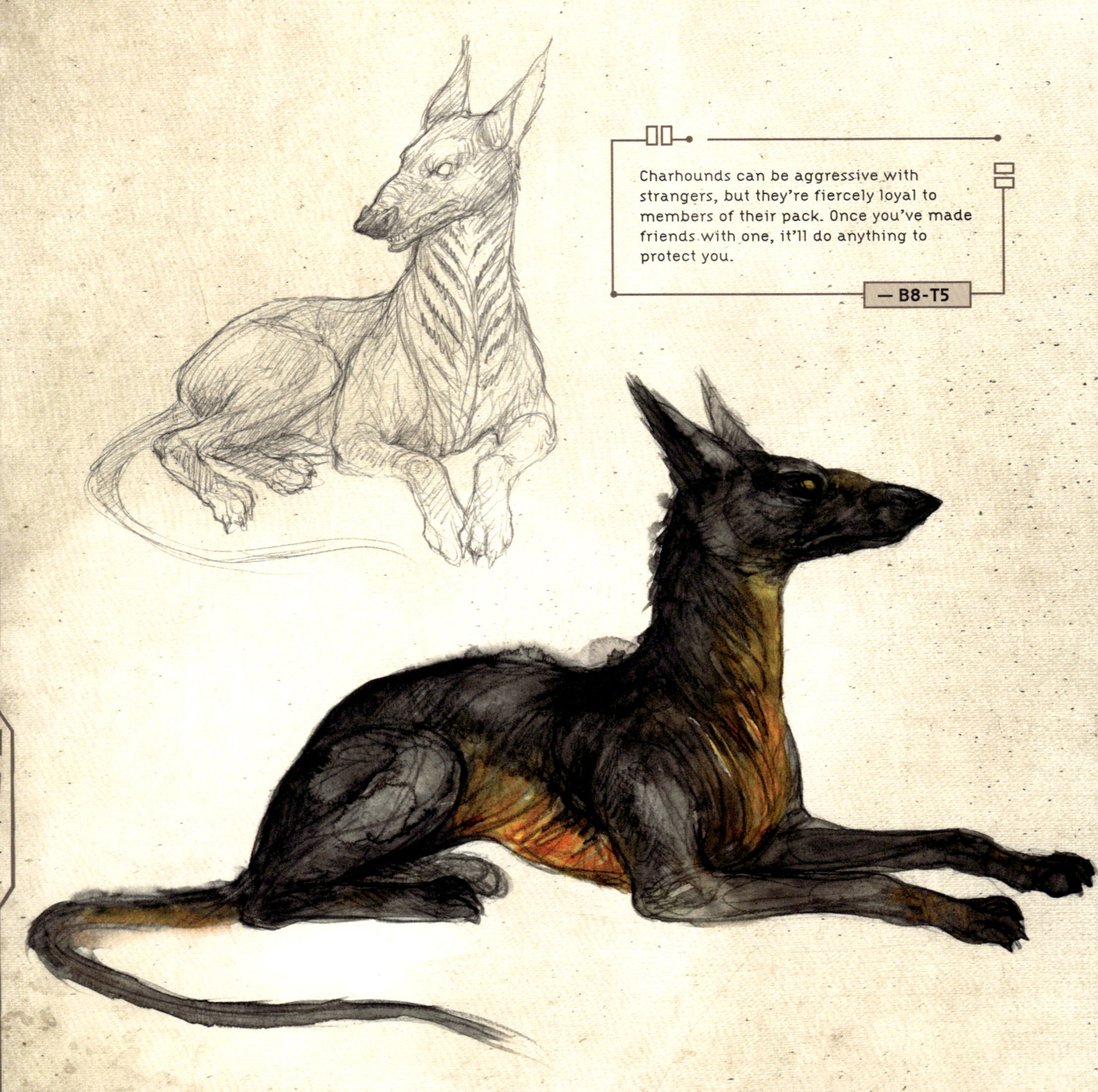

Charhounds can be aggressive with strangers, but they're fiercely loyal to members of their pack. Once you've made friends with one, it'll do anything to protect you.

— B8-T5

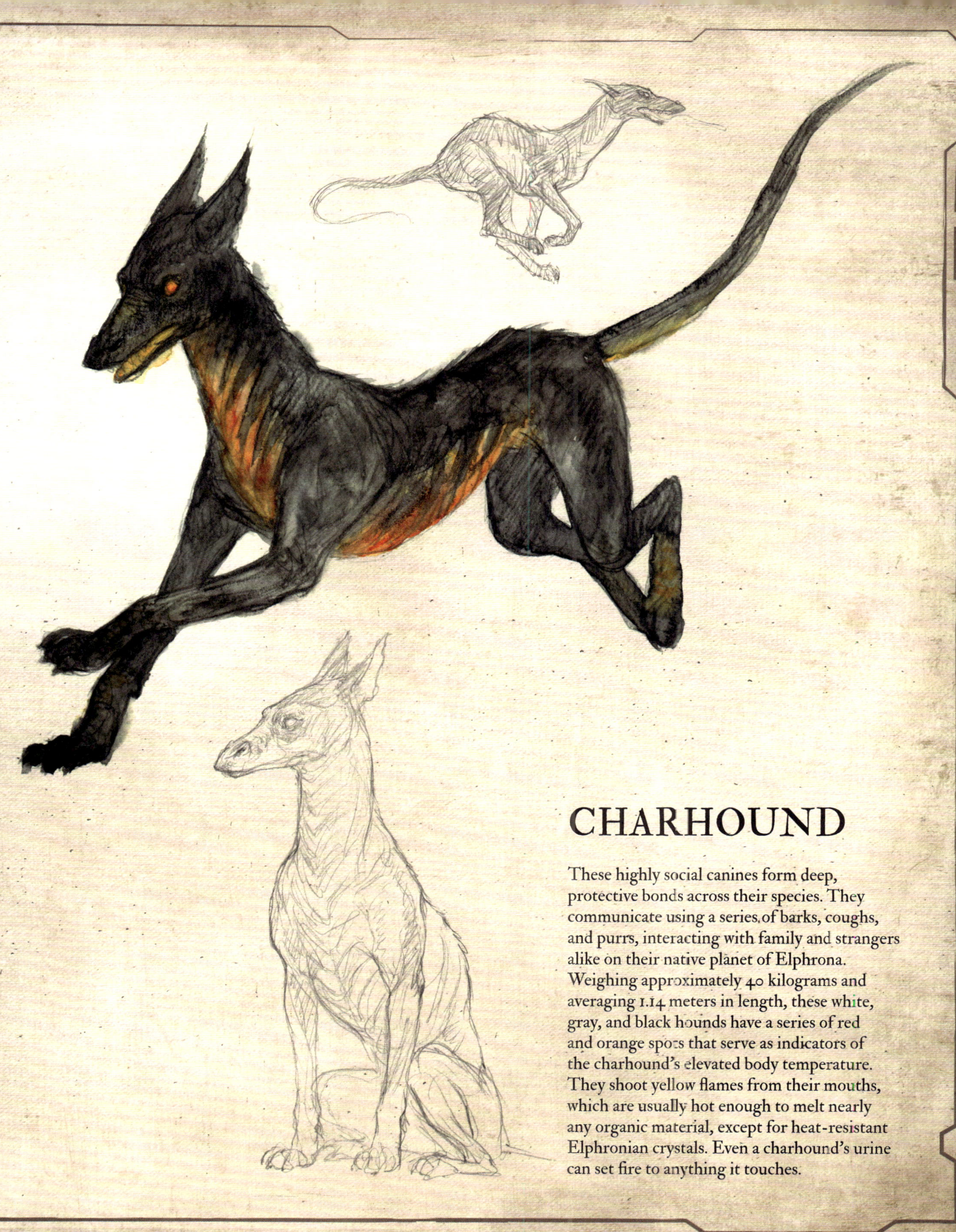

CHARHOUND

These highly social canines form deep, protective bonds across their species. They communicate using a series of barks, coughs, and purrs, interacting with family and strangers alike on their native planet of Elphrona. Weighing approximately 40 kilograms and averaging 1.14 meters in length, these white, gray, and black hounds have a series of red and orange spots that serve as indicators of the charhound's elevated body temperature. They shoot yellow flames from their mouths, which are usually hot enough to melt nearly any organic material, except for heat-resistant Elphronian crystals. Even a charhound's urine can set fire to anything it touches.

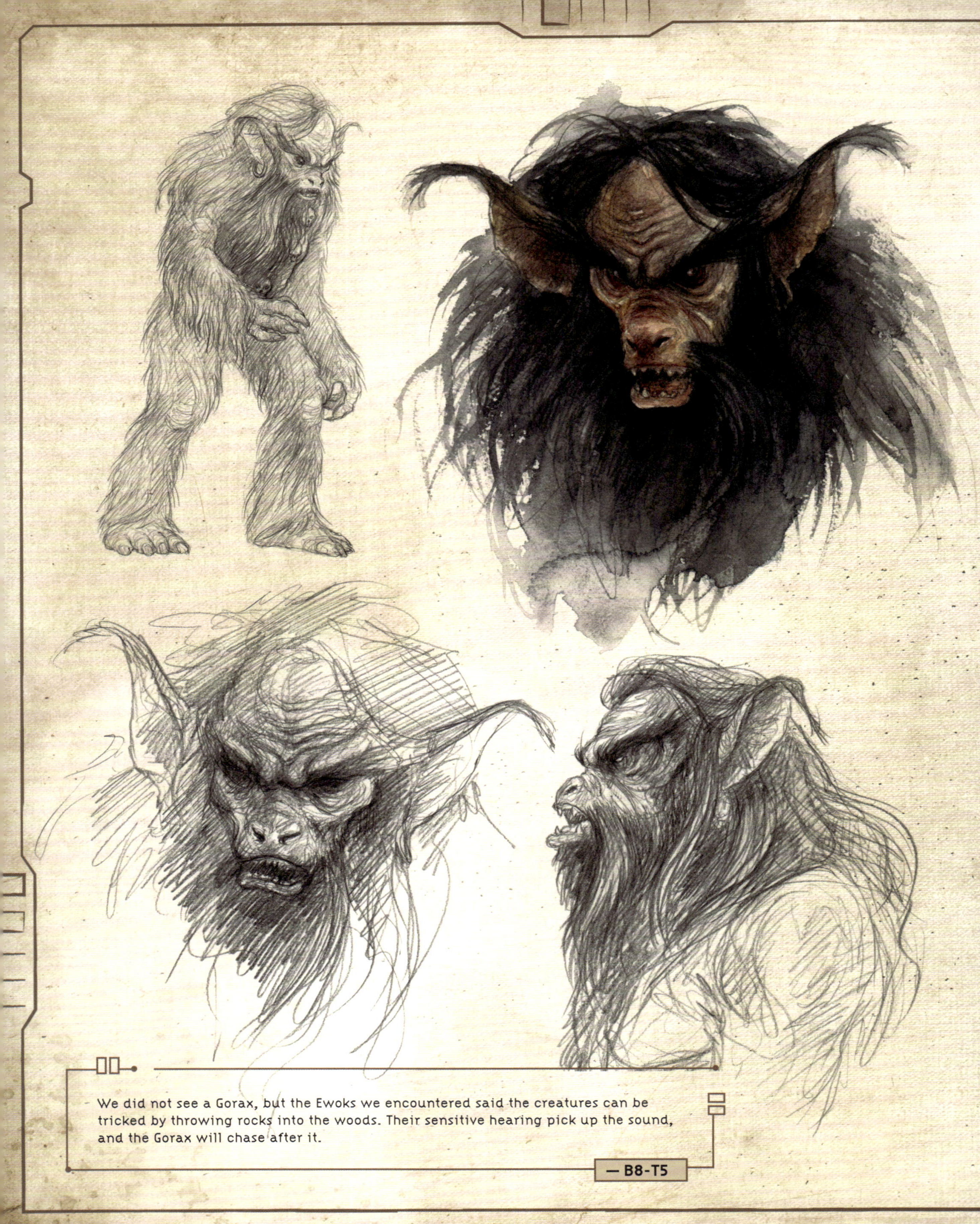

We did not see a Gorax, but the Ewoks we encountered said the creatures can be tricked by throwing rocks into the woods. Their sensitive hearing pick up the sound, and the Gorax will chase after it.

— B8-T5

GORAX

These enormous Endorian humanoids are known to attack Ewok villages and generally wreak havoc on the peaceful Forest Moon. Standing up to 8.6 meters in height, the gorax towers over its diminutive Endorian counterparts. Pointed ears give the creature a heightened sense of hearing, which it uses to track prey across the mountain ranges. Gorax have thick dark fur that recedes at their hands, feet, and face; they have long arms that end in four fingers, which they use to capture their prey. These carnivorous creatures eat Ewoks, Endorian chickens, and other small animals. Although they're believed to be rather unintelligent, they do exhibit some traits of higher life forms, including uprooting trees to use as weapons and donning articles of protective clothing.

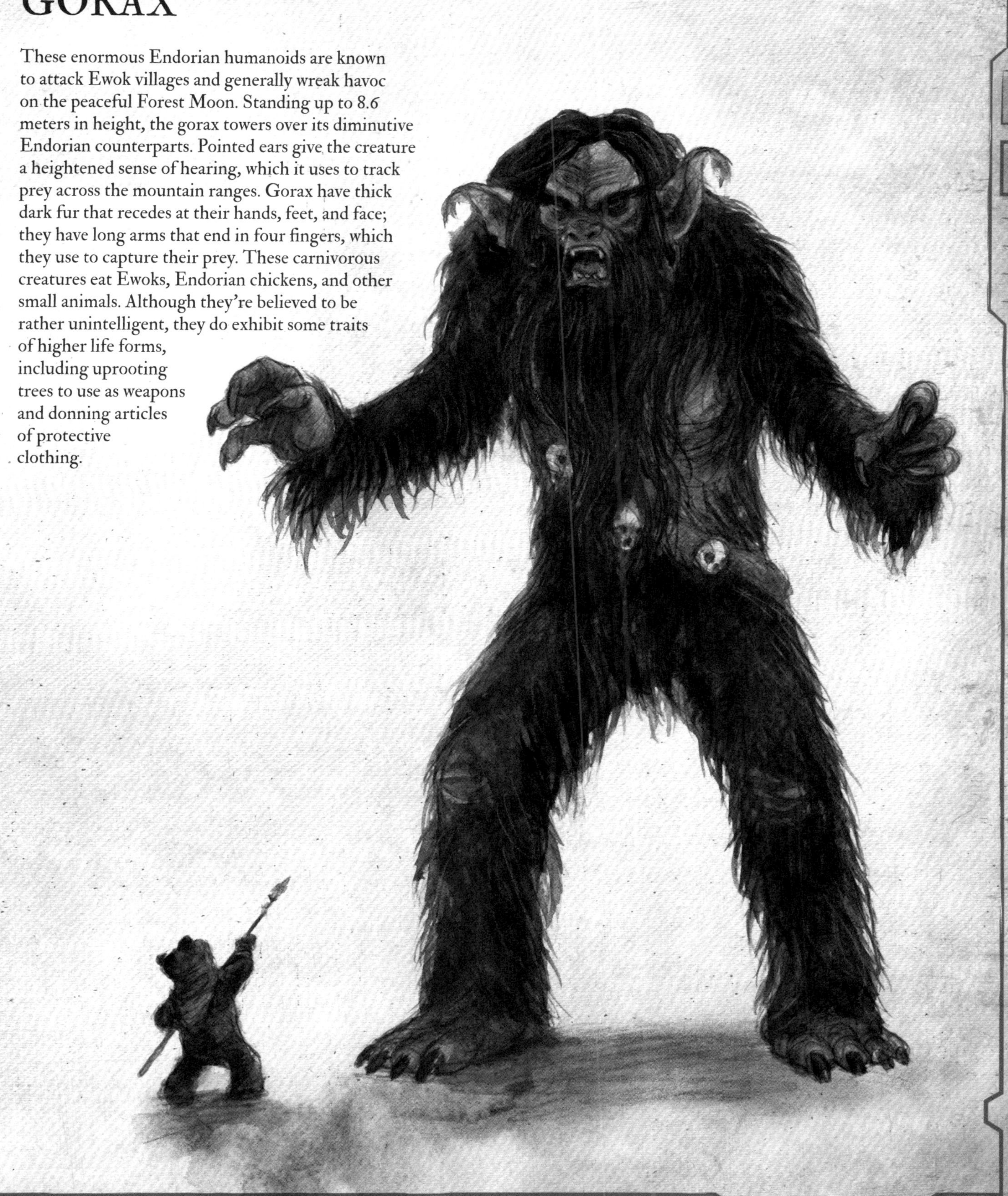

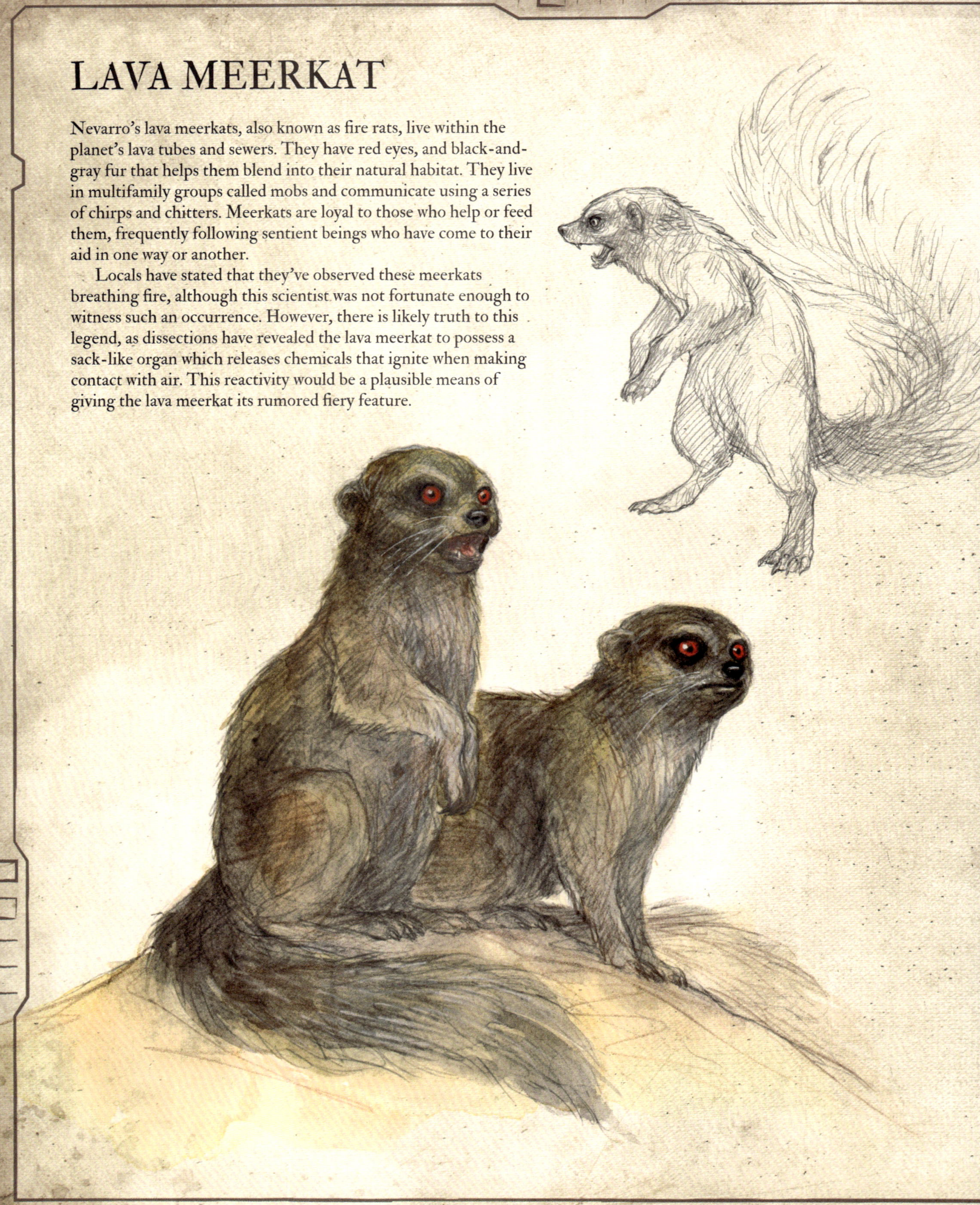

LAVA MEERKAT

Nevarro's lava meerkats, also known as fire rats, live within the planet's lava tubes and sewers. They have red eyes, and black-and-gray fur that helps them blend into their natural habitat. They live in multifamily groups called mobs and communicate using a series of chirps and chitters. Meerkats are loyal to those who help or feed them, frequently following sentient beings who have come to their aid in one way or another.

Locals have stated that they've observed these meerkats breathing fire, although this scientist was not fortunate enough to witness such an occurrence. However, there is likely truth to this legend, as dissections have revealed the lava meerkat to possess a sack-like organ which releases chemicals that ignite when making contact with air. This reactivity would be a plausible means of giving the lava meerkat its rumored fiery feature.

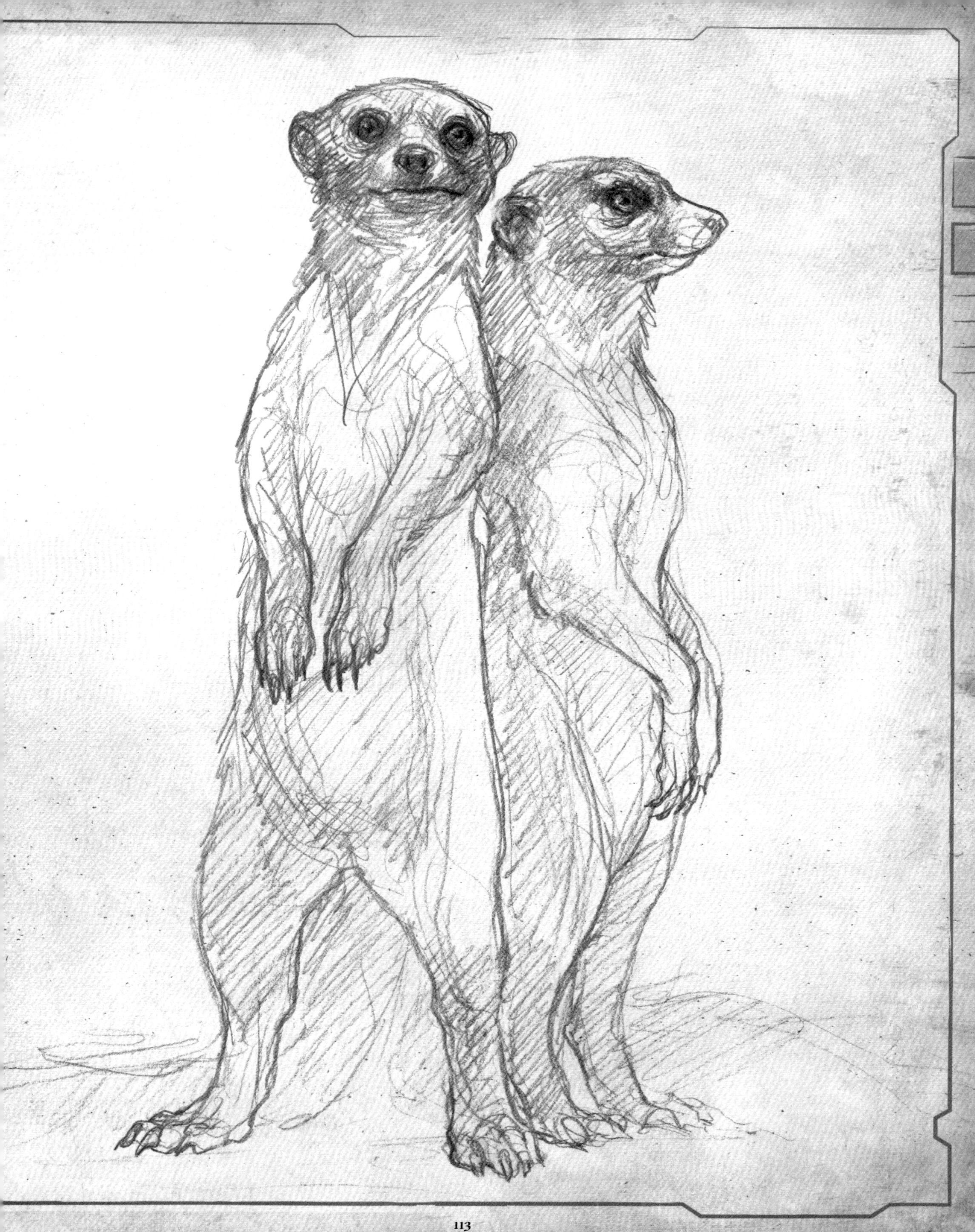

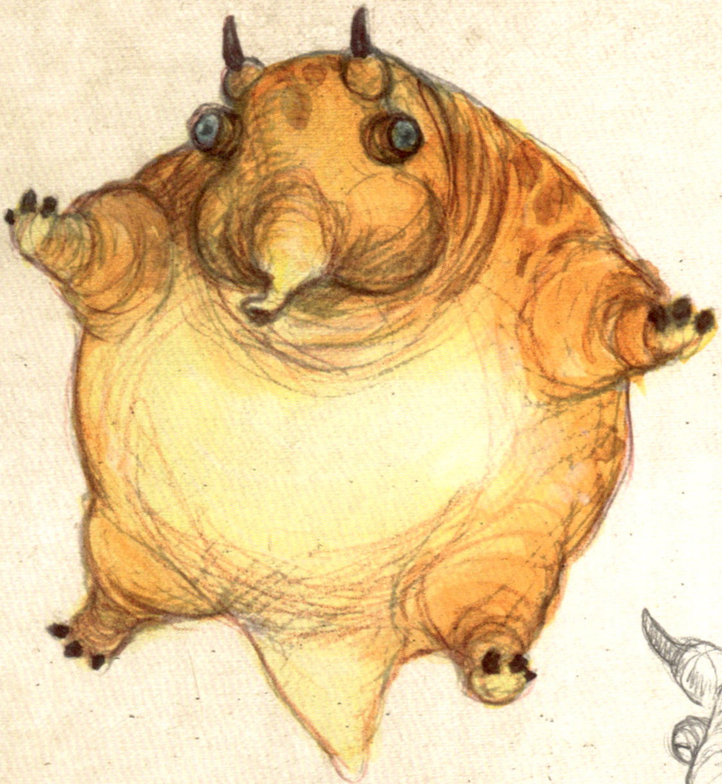

Puffer pigs make the most peculiar noises. Their low grunt sounds like a cross between a squeal and a groan. And despite their lack of fingers, these creatures can climb up a ladder, which they do by wedging their toes on either side of the rungs and leaping upward.

— B8-T5

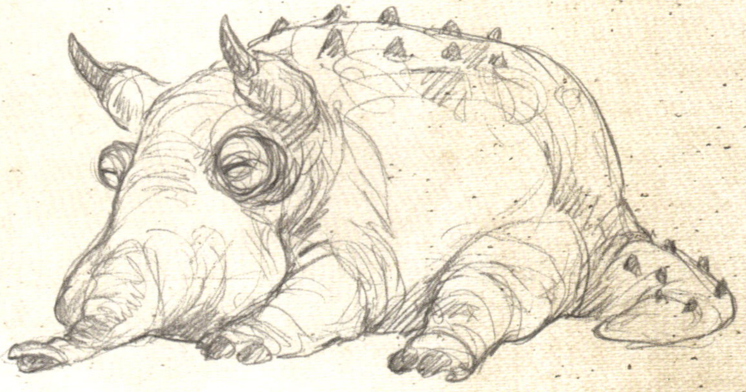

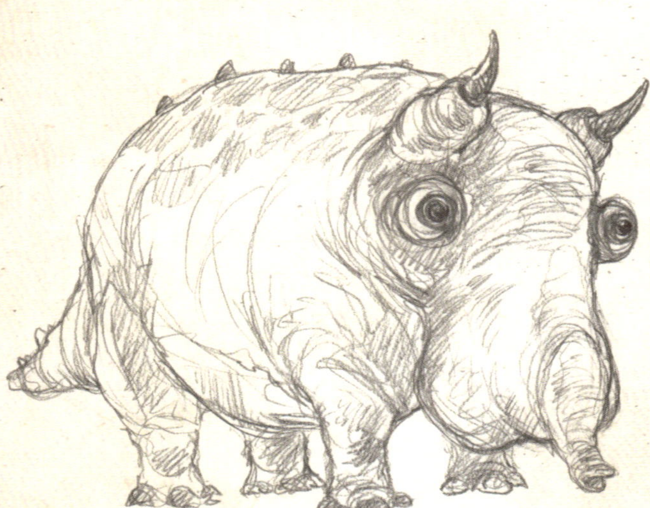

PUFFER PIG

These herbivorous mammals live among the mines of the red-rocked realm of Kyryll's World. When threatened, they expand their bodies, puffing up to increase their size and hopefully deter any predators. An uninflated puffer pig measures just less than one meter long and slightly more than half a meter tall—when frightened, it can grow up to nine meters in length and sixty centimeters in height. Puffer pigs communicate using low squeals. They are raised as livestock on Batuu, where residents and visitors alike dine on puffer pig bacon and stuffed puffer pig.

Puffer pigs are perhaps the most popular species to inhabit Kyryll's World. They are able to sniff out precious minerals, with a single pig rumored to be as effective at locating valuable items as twelve mining scanners. Accordingly, the Mining Guild is willing to pay large sums for the creatures, which smugglers track for a hefty fee.

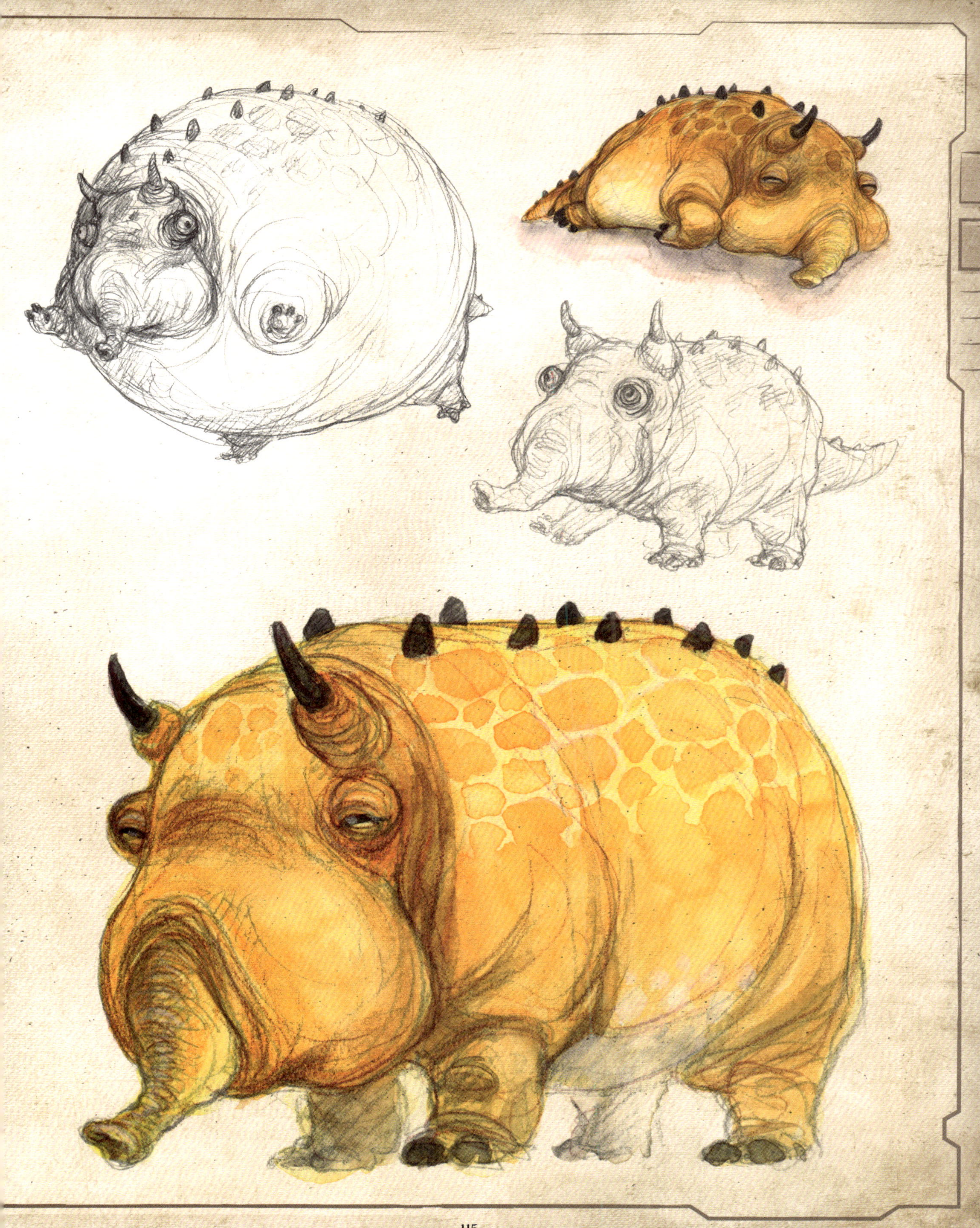

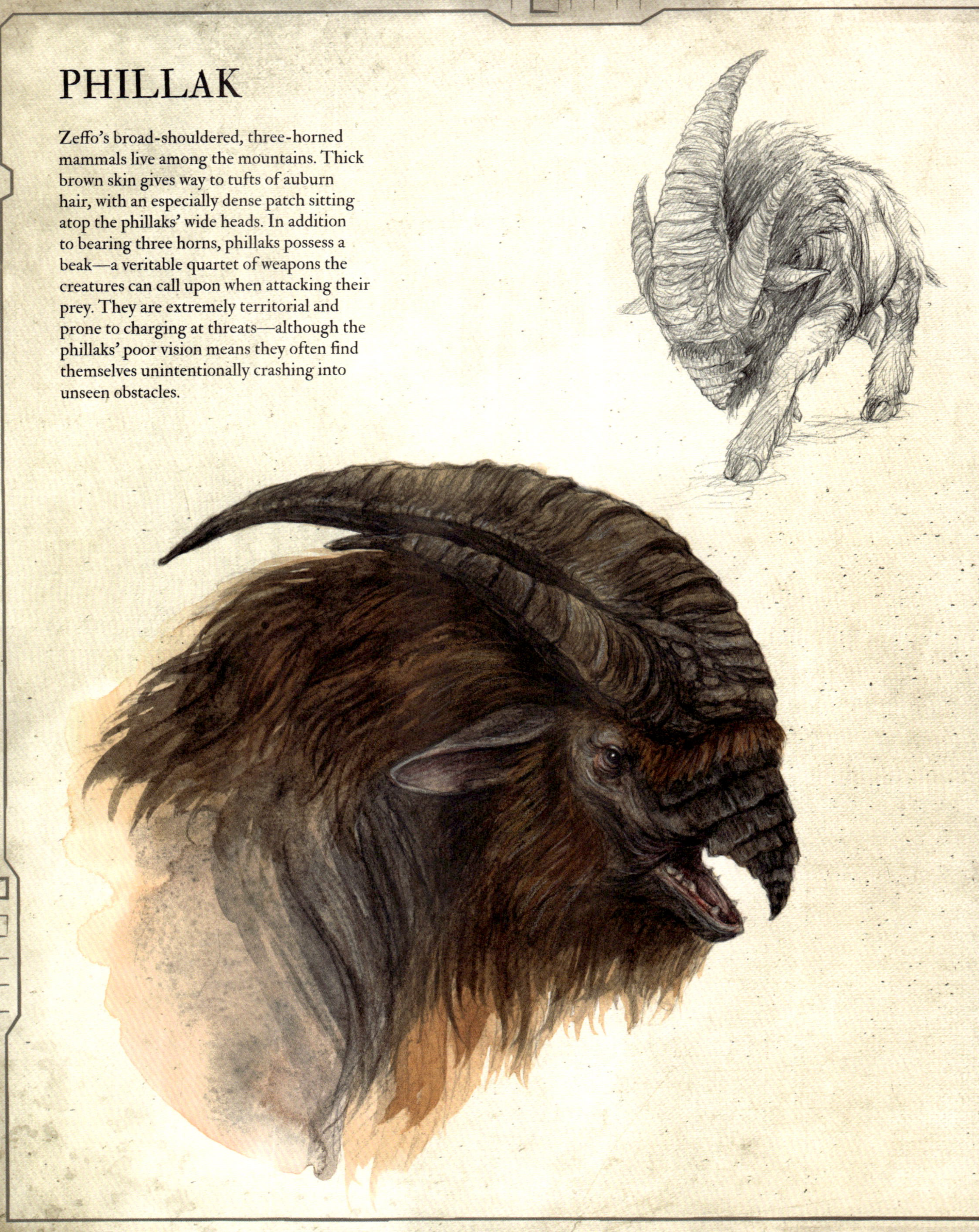

PHILLAK

Zeffo's broad-shouldered, three-horned mammals live among the mountains. Thick brown skin gives way to tufts of auburn hair, with an especially dense patch sitting atop the phillaks' wide heads. In addition to bearing three horns, phillaks possess a beak—a veritable quartet of weapons the creatures can call upon when attacking their prey. They are extremely territorial and prone to charging at threats—although the phillaks' poor vision means they often find themselves unintentionally crashing into unseen obstacles.

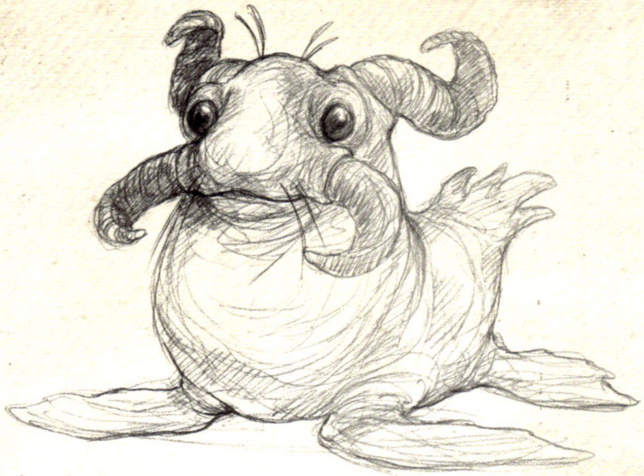

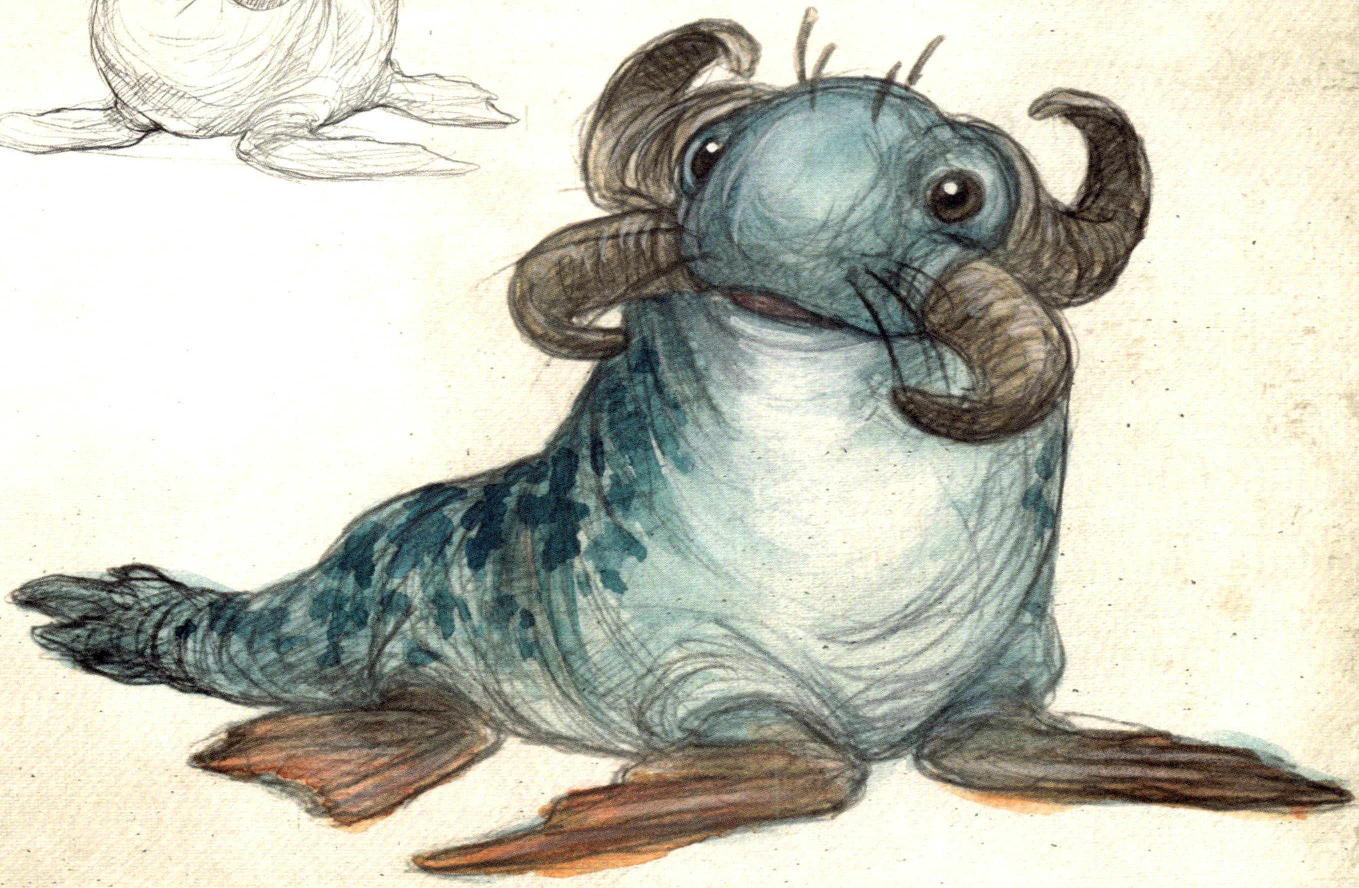

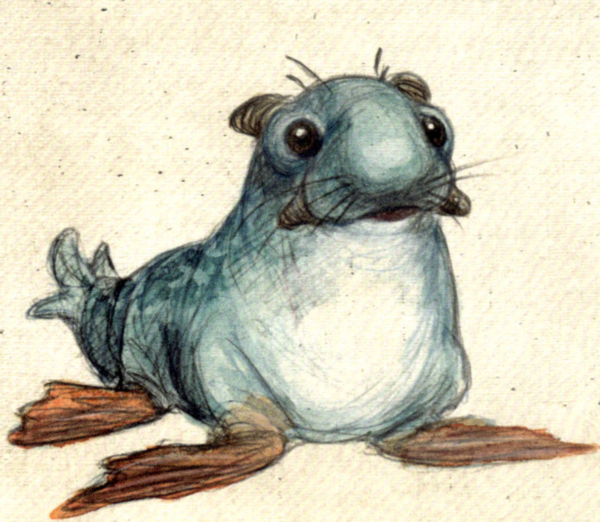

WELLAGRIN

These blubbery blue-and-orange mountain dwellers have four curved horns and a highly curious nature. Wide pectoral fins and raised tail flippers help them waddle over, swim under, and travel through their snowy environment; coarse whiskers and wide eyes help them perceive changes in wind and proximity of predators. These domesticated mammals make an annual migration across their homeworld of Andraven, moving from their stables to the orchards. They live in family groups called herds and respond to the calls of their shepherd's flute.

URBAN CREATURES

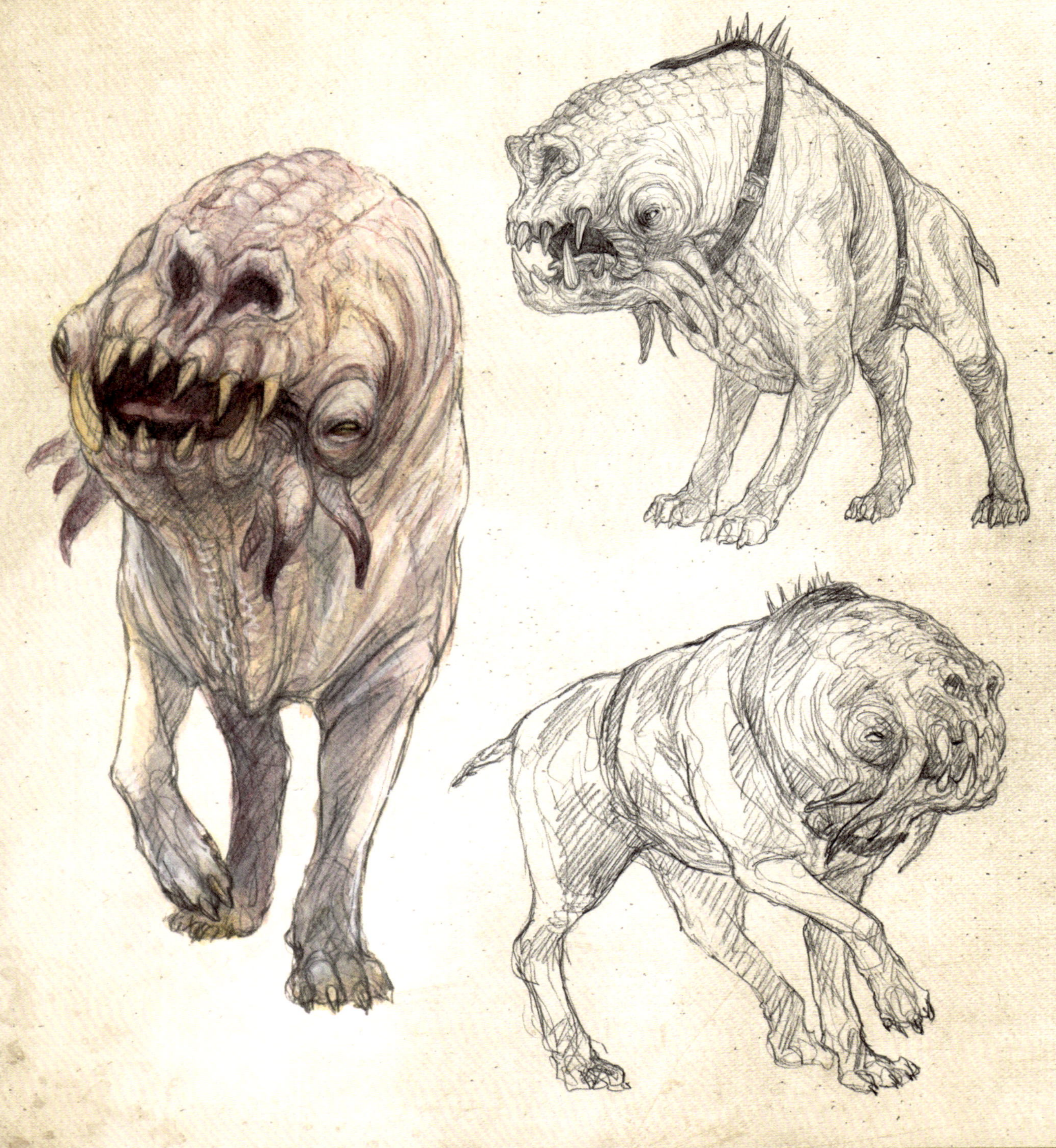

CORELLIAN HOUND

Corellia's imposing canids are known for their brutal bark, piercing teeth, and rabid demeanor. With their impressive sense of smell and often relentless nature, they are frequently employed as trackers or sent on hunting missions. Their teeth are capable of regeneration, ensuring their reputation as formidable foes. With some hounds weighing up to one hundred kilograms and standing seventy centimeters, their size has made them a popular attack dog with the criminal gangs that operate in the underworlds of Corellia.

These hounds harbor a bony ridge between their head and shoulders, along with three spiked tendrils that rest below each cheek. On Corellia, they are known as Sibian hounds; natives of Ushruu refer to them as snarlers.

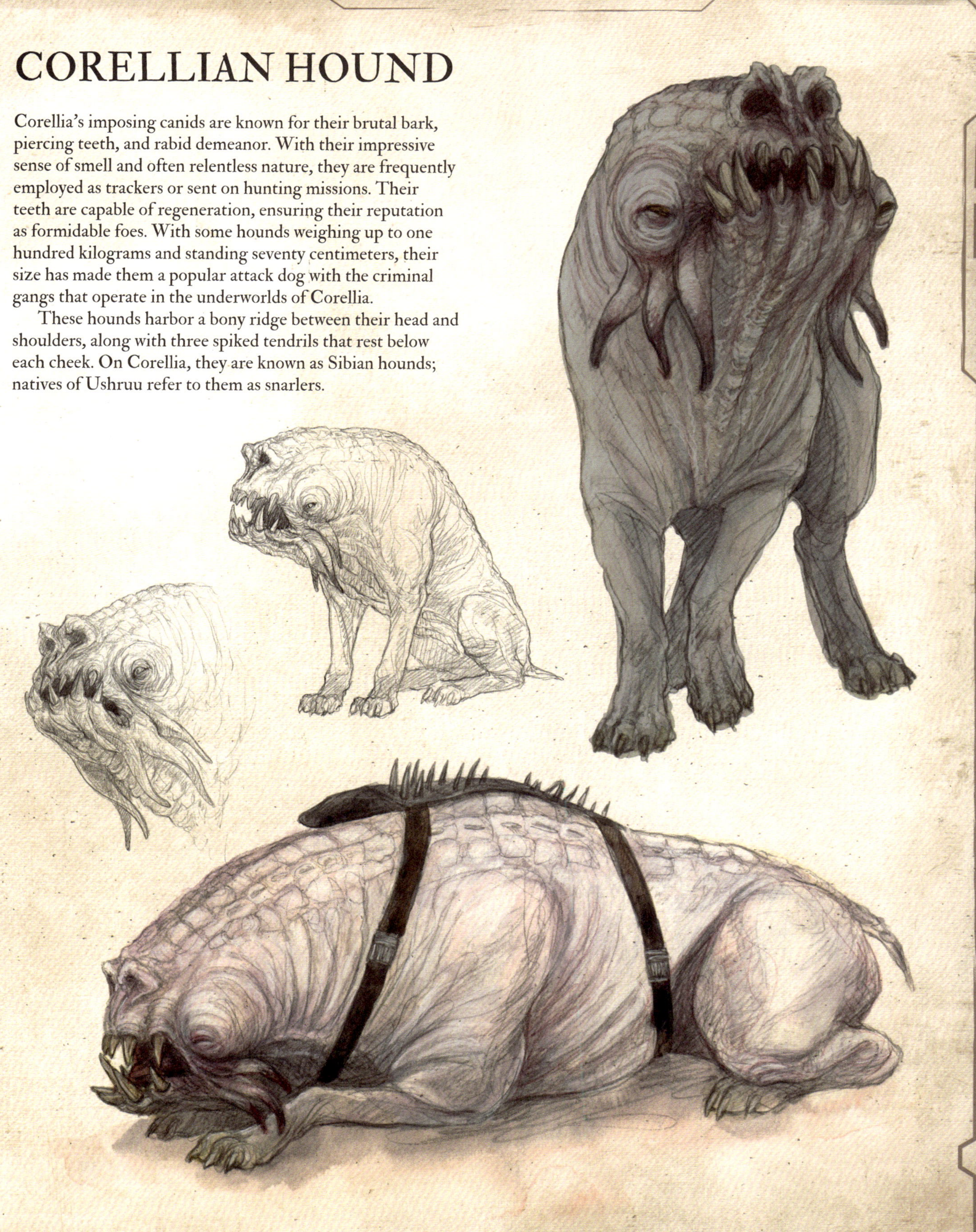

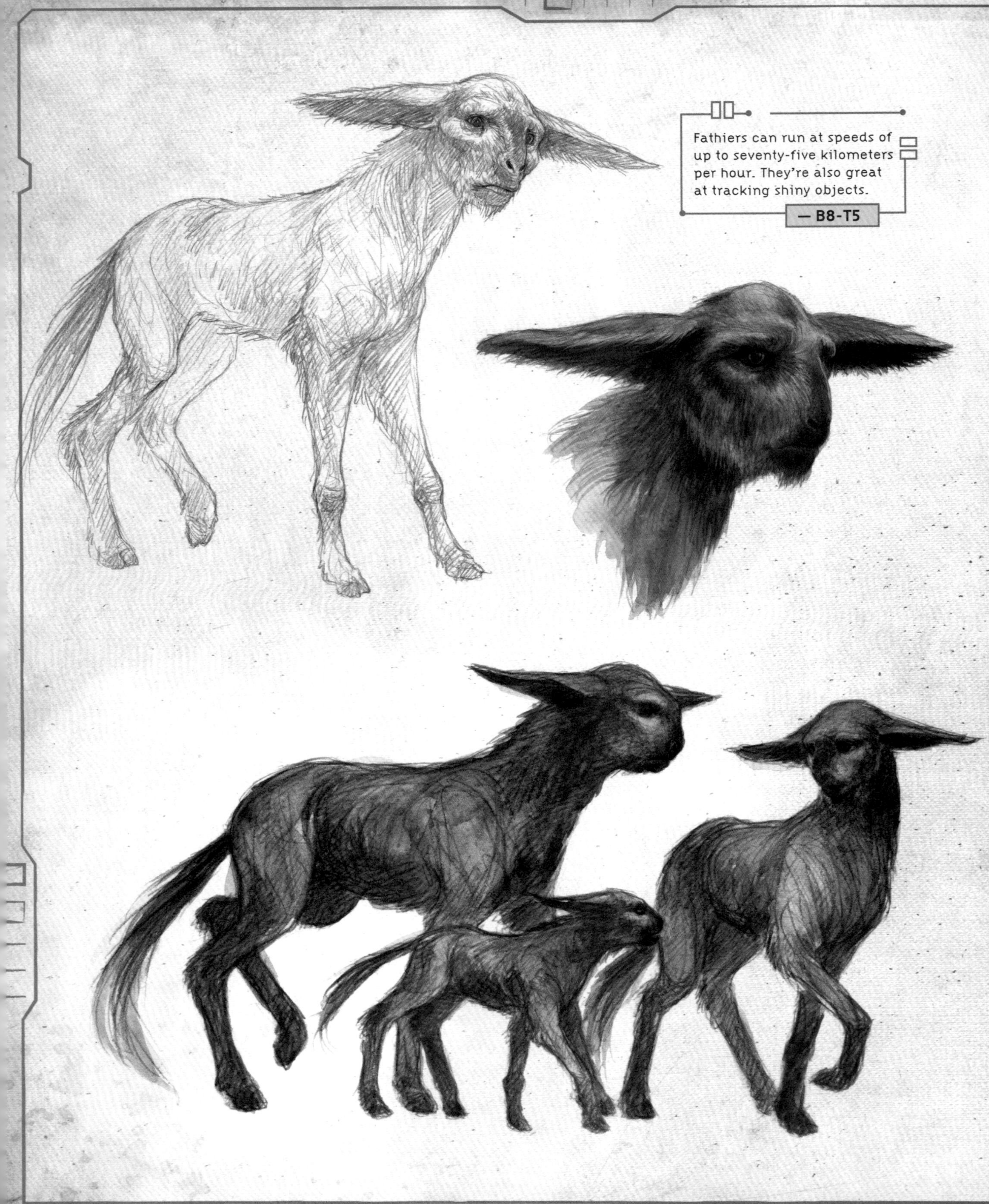
Fathiers can run at speeds of up to seventy-five kilometers per hour. They're also great at tracking shiny objects.
— B8-T5

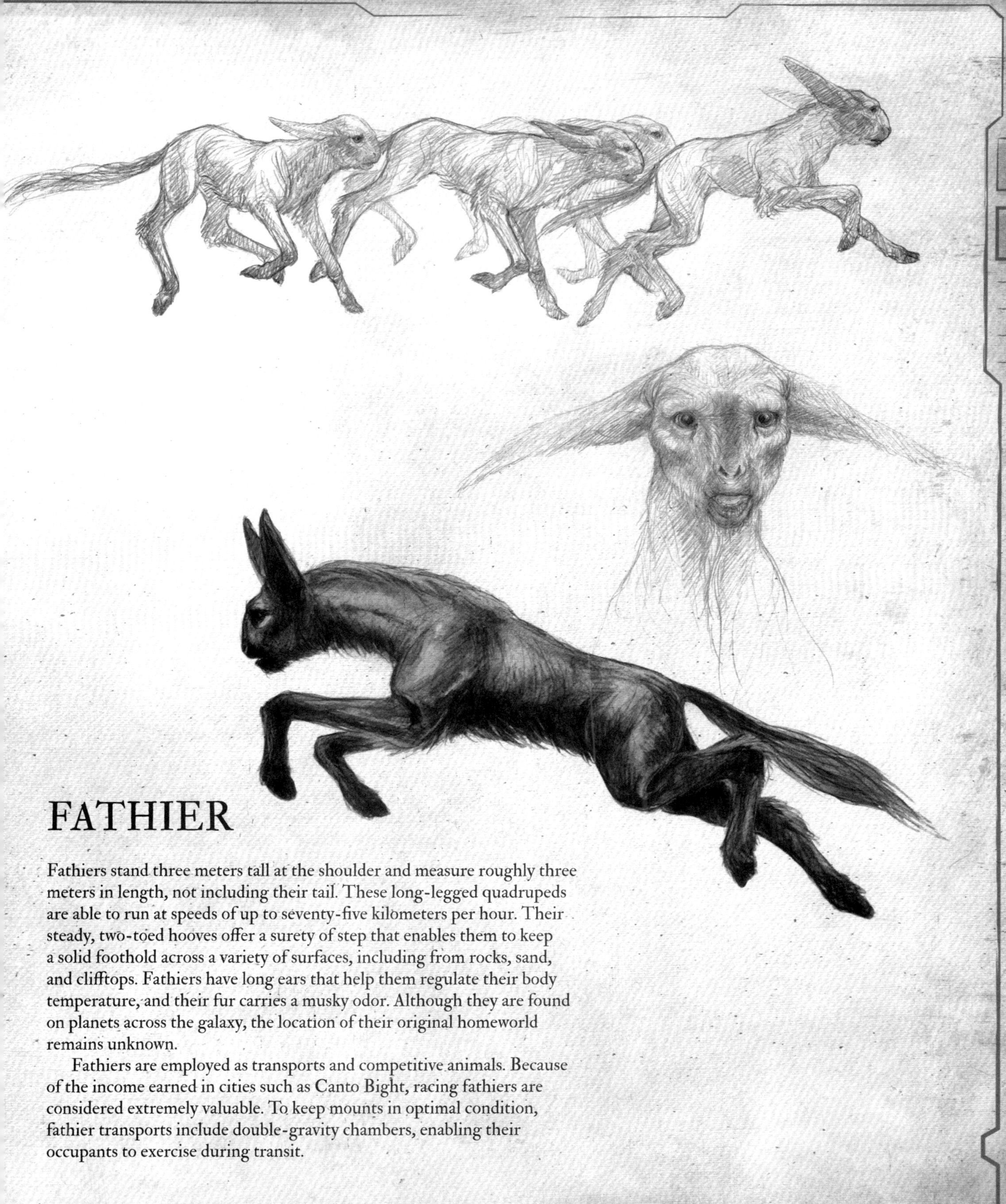

FATHIER

Fathiers stand three meters tall at the shoulder and measure roughly three meters in length, not including their tail. These long-legged quadrupeds are able to run at speeds of up to seventy-five kilometers per hour. Their steady, two-toed hooves offer a surety of step that enables them to keep a solid foothold across a variety of surfaces, including from rocks, sand, and clifftops. Fathiers have long ears that help them regulate their body temperature, and their fur carries a musky odor. Although they are found on planets across the galaxy, the location of their original homeworld remains unknown.

Fathiers are employed as transports and competitive animals. Because of the income earned in cities such as Canto Bight, racing fathiers are considered extremely valuable. To keep mounts in optimal condition, fathier transports include double-gravity chambers, enabling their occupants to exercise during transit.

KOWAKIAN MONKEY-LIZARD

These multihued, cantankerous creatures stand between fifty-eight and seventy centimeters in height and weigh an average of twelve kilograms. They are native to the planet Kowak, where they eat insects, worms, and small rodents. They are highly intelligent and have developed the ability to mimic most languages, from Huttese to Galactic Basic. However, their most common form of communication is their wild, jubilant laughter. Their playful nature and eagerness to live among a family group make them popular pets across the galaxy. However, they must be monitored closely—their natural curiosity can get them into trouble. According to the holonet, one Kowakian monkey-lizard once wielded a blaster, and another even commandeered a pirate tank!

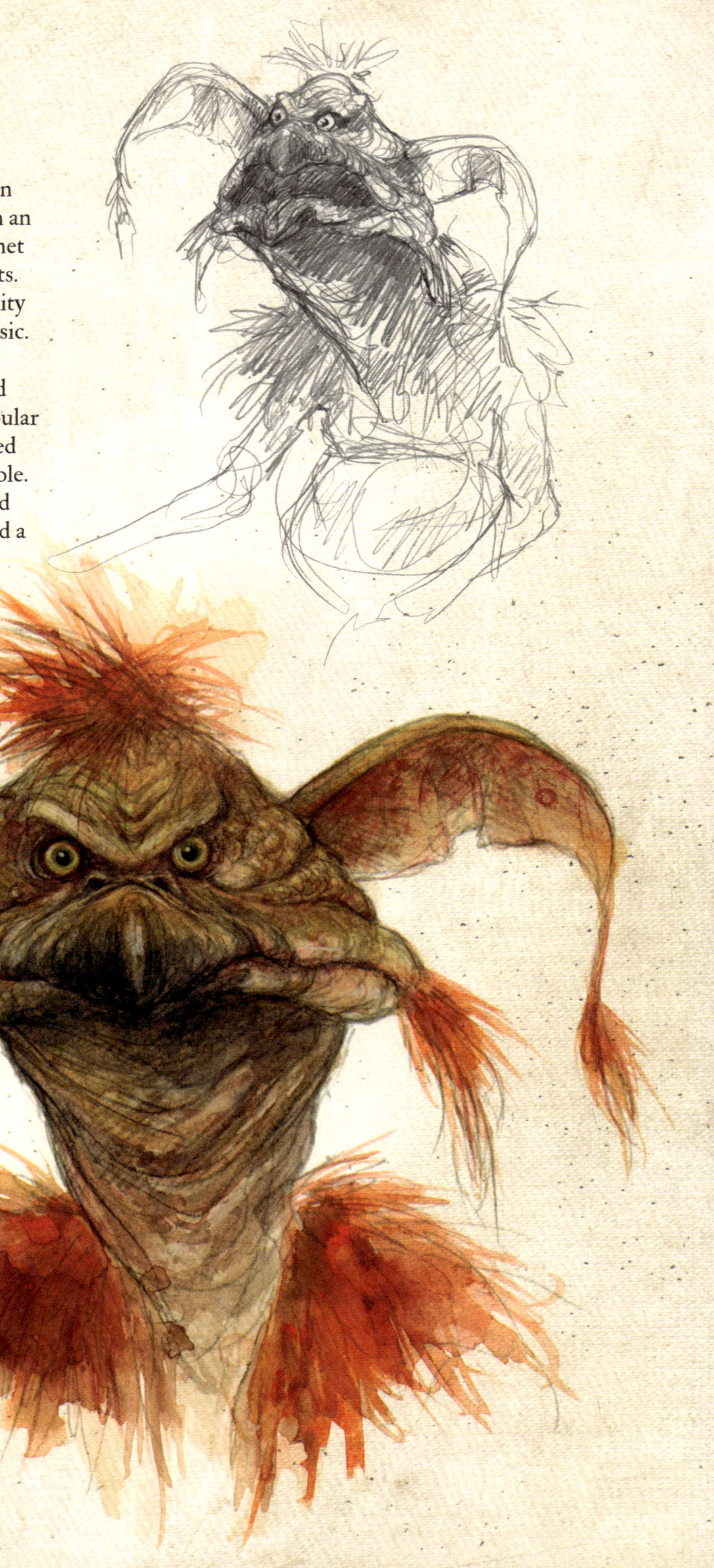

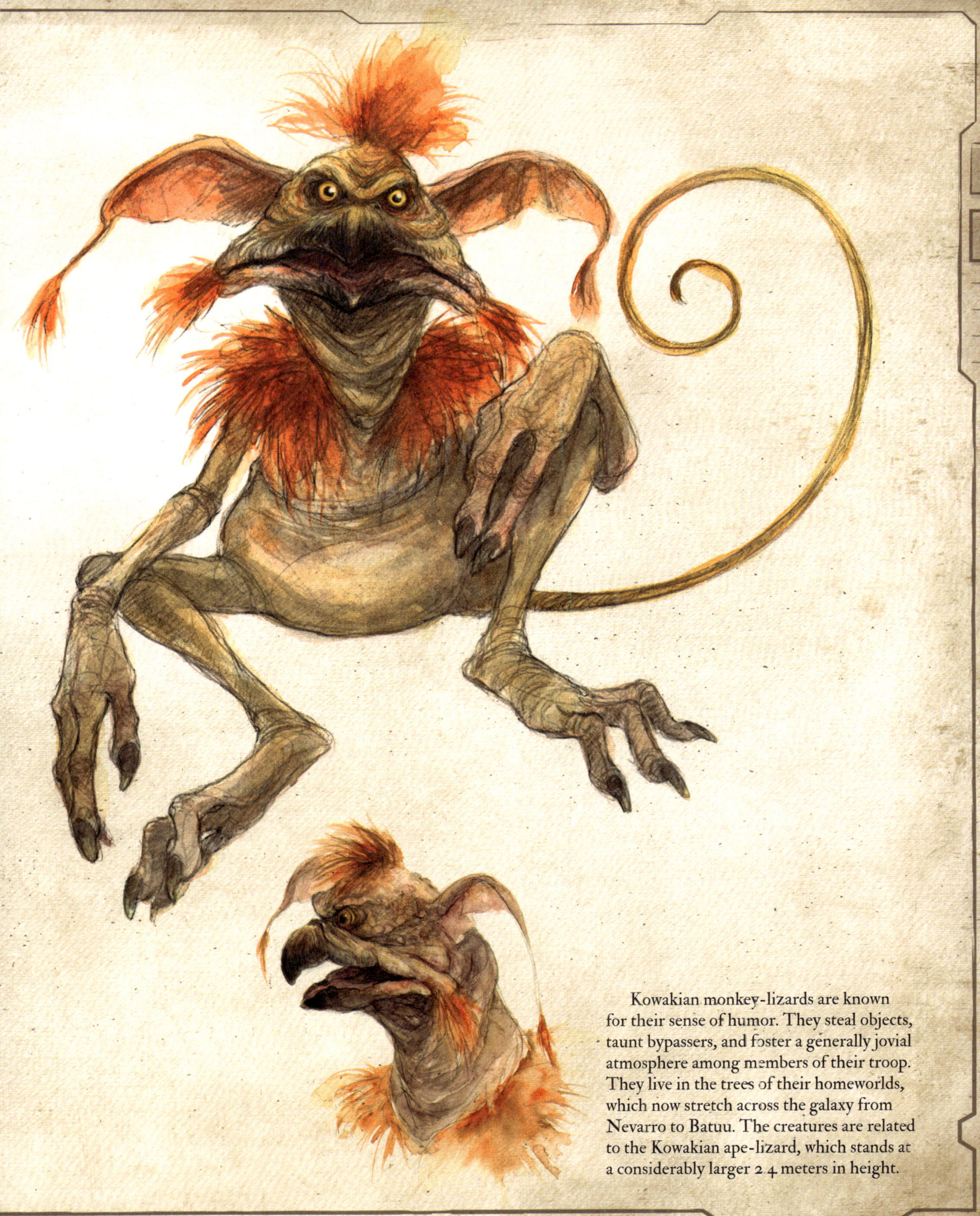

Kowakian monkey-lizards are known for their sense of humor. They steal objects, taunt bypassers, and foster a generally jovial atmosphere among members of their troop. They live in the trees of their homeworlds, which now stretch across the galaxy from Nevarro to Batuu. The creatures are related to the Kowakian ape-lizard, which stands at a considerably larger 2.4 meters in height.

VOORPAK

Considered the preferred pet on Naboo, these fluffy, six-legged mammals are among the planet's most endearing creatures. They stand at sixty centimeters tall and have two tufted balls that sit atop their seemingly smiling faces. With bright blue eyes and a fondness for being held, voorpaks easily endear themselves to their owners. Wild voorpaks live among the rocky outcroppings of Naboo, raising litters of up to five voorlings in well-concealed dens. These carnivores feed on smaller mammals and seek to evade capture from trappers, who sell their fur for use in clothing.

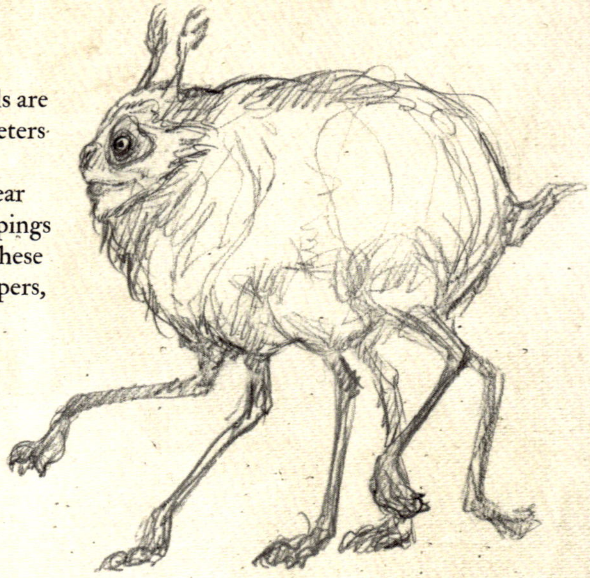

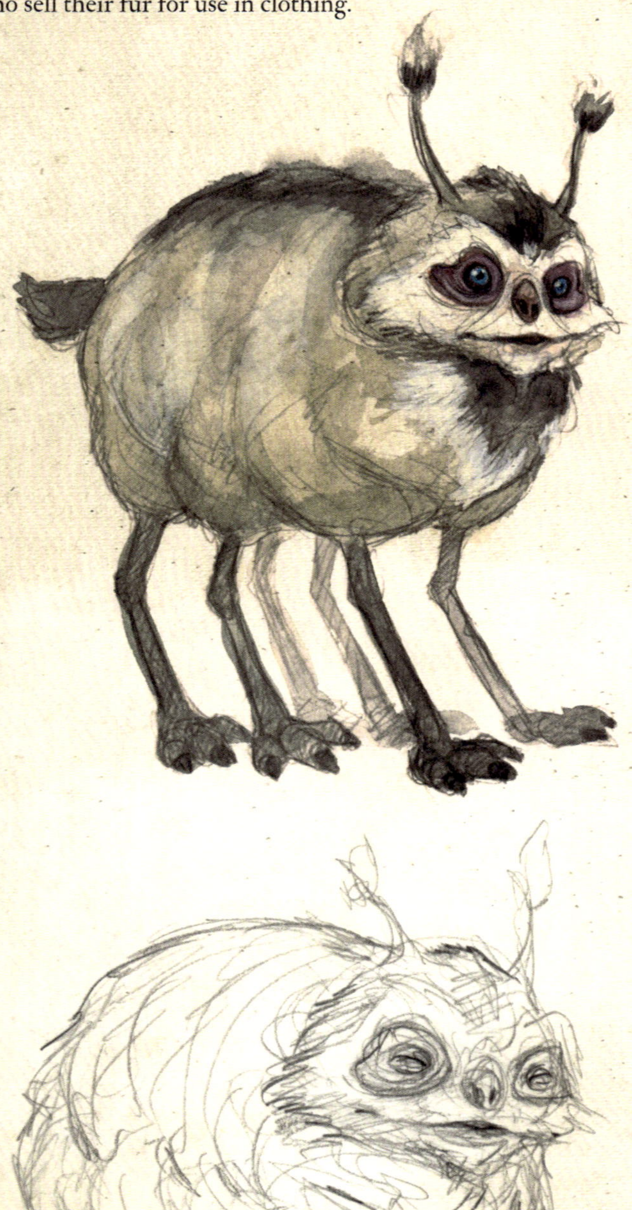

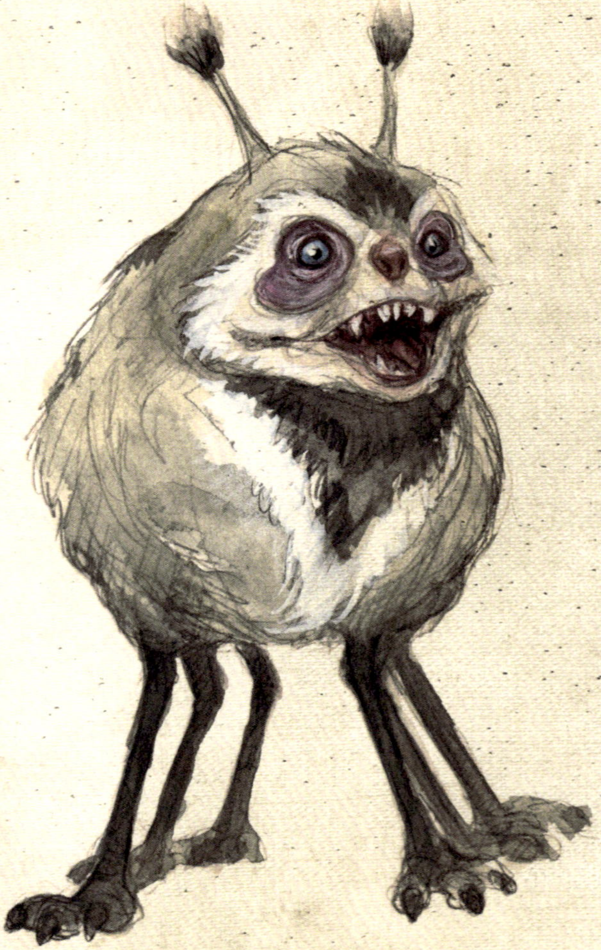

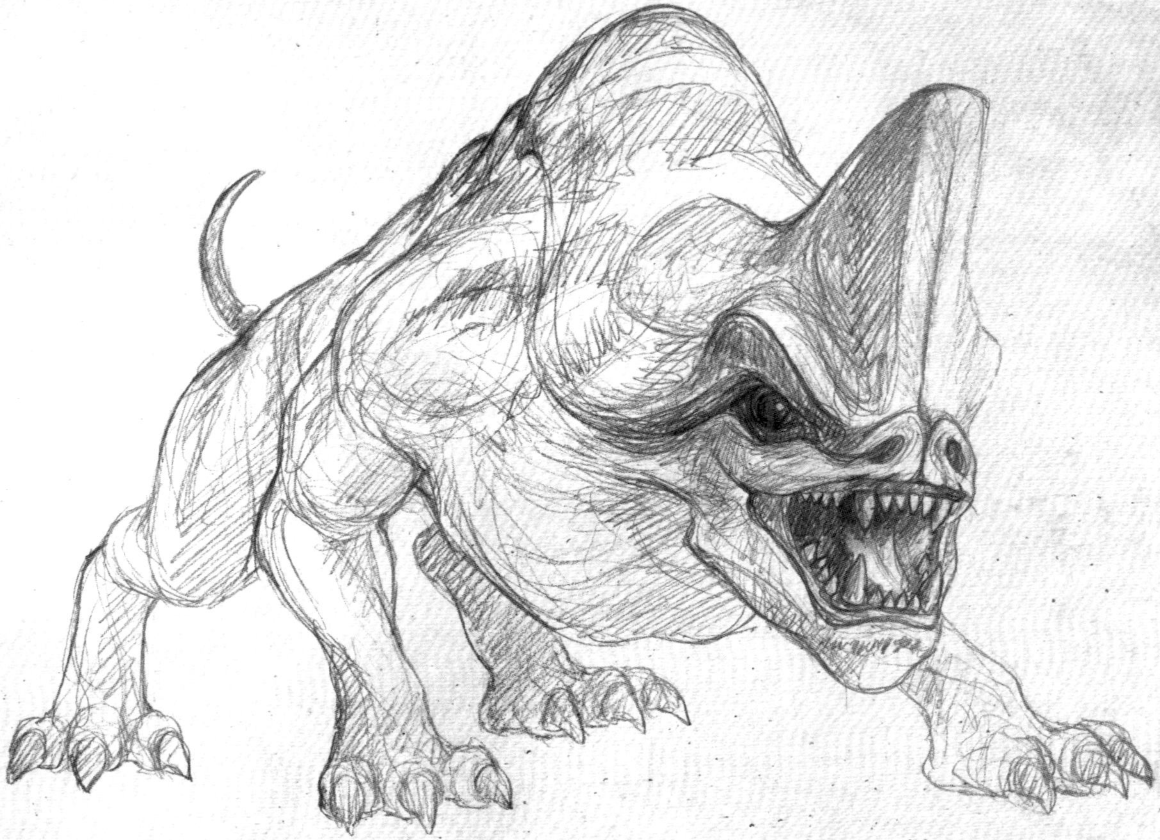

LURCA

Fiercely aggressive and widely feared, Wayland's intimidating and muscular lurca are not to be trifled with. The canid's physical features serve as a warning to would-be challengers. Its wide haunches, muscular legs, and sharp teeth silently communicate a predatory nature, while the bony ruff protruding from a snubbed nose enhances resonance of the lurca's fearsome bark. While they are typically used to secure the perimeter of Mount Tantiss, the often feral lurcas are difficult to domesticate—though select members of the species are said to be outfitted with special collars that are controlled by Imperial droids, which can affect their behavior. This scientist has not yet been brave enough to approach a lurca.

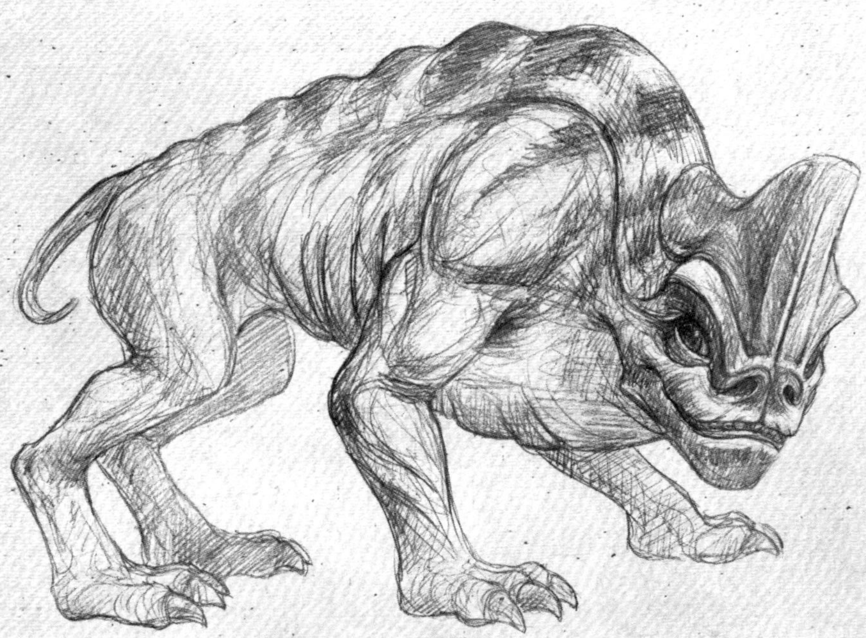

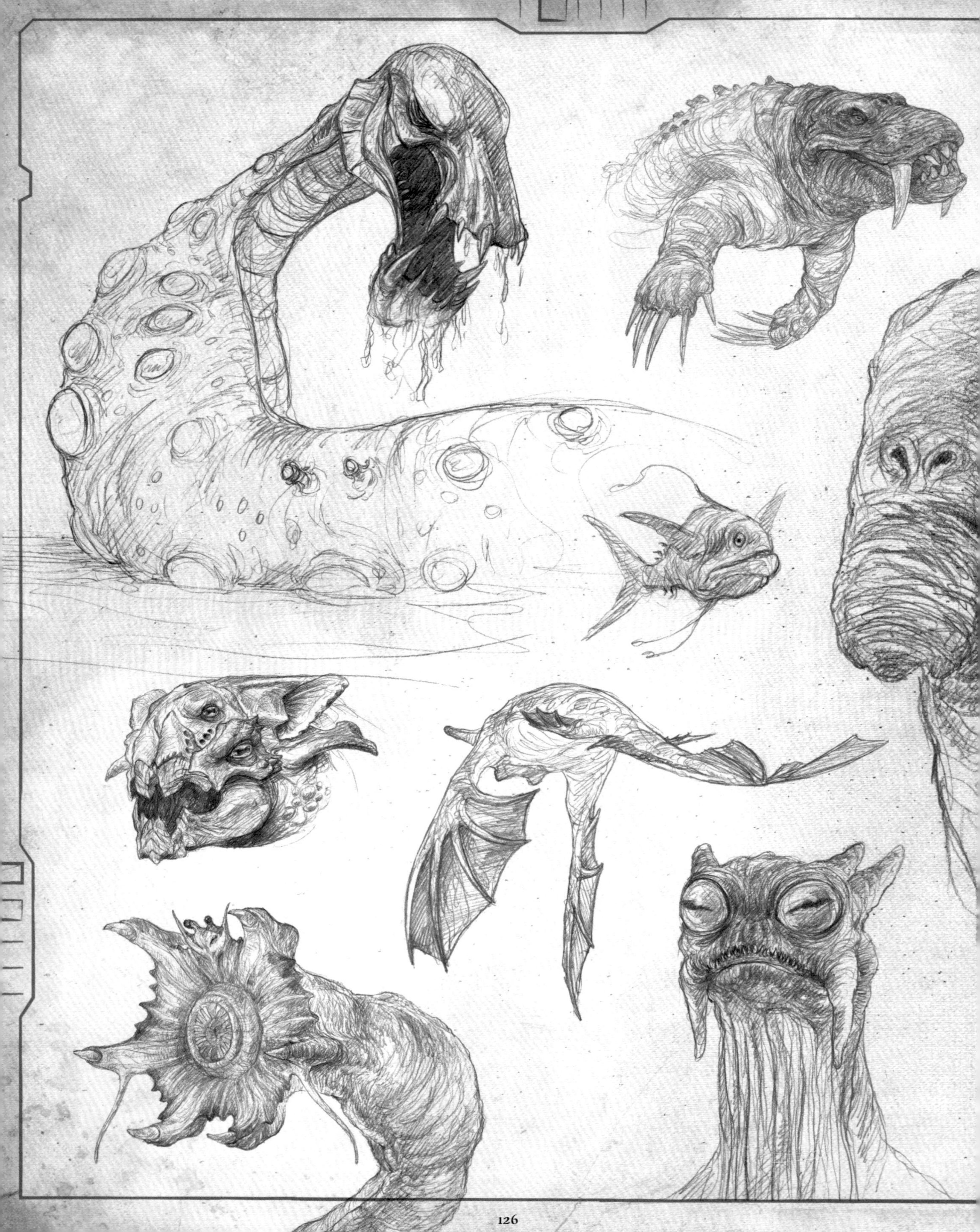

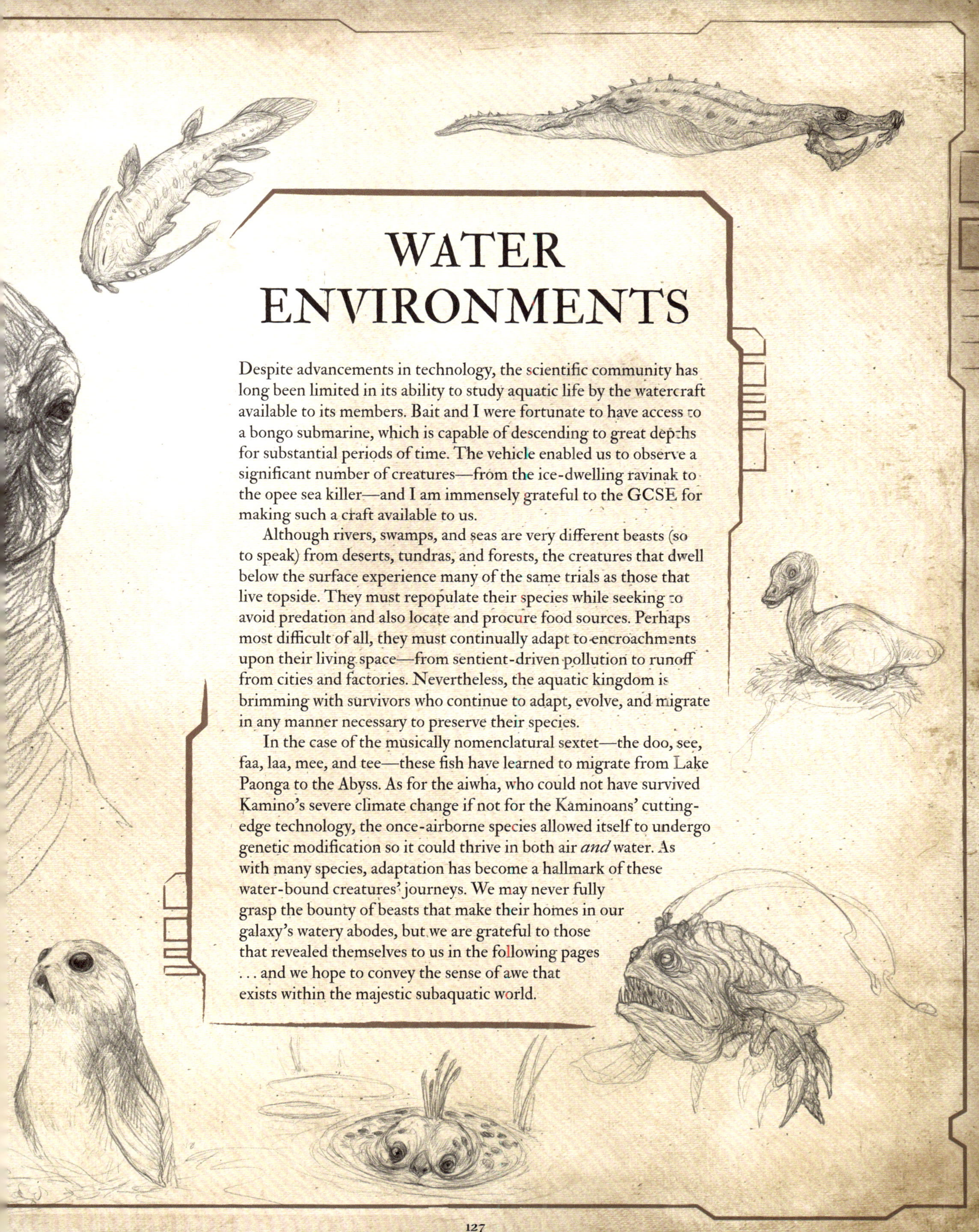

WATER ENVIRONMENTS

Despite advancements in technology, the scientific community has long been limited in its ability to study aquatic life by the watercraft available to its members. Bait and I were fortunate to have access to a bongo submarine, which is capable of descending to great depths for substantial periods of time. The vehicle enabled us to observe a significant number of creatures—from the ice-dwelling ravinak to the opee sea killer—and I am immensely grateful to the GCSE for making such a craft available to us.

Although rivers, swamps, and seas are very different beasts (so to speak) from deserts, tundras, and forests, the creatures that dwell below the surface experience many of the same trials as those that live topside. They must repopulate their species while seeking to avoid predation and also locate and procure food sources. Perhaps most difficult of all, they must continually adapt to encroachments upon their living space—from sentient-driven pollution to runoff from cities and factories. Nevertheless, the aquatic kingdom is brimming with survivors who continue to adapt, evolve, and migrate in any manner necessary to preserve their species.

In the case of the musically nomenclatural sextet—the doo, see, faa, laa, mee, and tee—these fish have learned to migrate from Lake Paonga to the Abyss. As for the aiwha, who could not have survived Kamino's severe climate change if not for the Kaminoans' cutting-edge technology, the once-airborne species allowed itself to undergo genetic modification so it could thrive in both air *and* water. As with many species, adaptation has become a hallmark of these water-bound creatures' journeys. We may never fully grasp the bounty of beasts that make their homes in our galaxy's watery abodes, but we are grateful to those that revealed themselves to us in the following pages . . . and we hope to convey the sense of awe that exists within the majestic subaquatic world.

COASTAL CREATURES

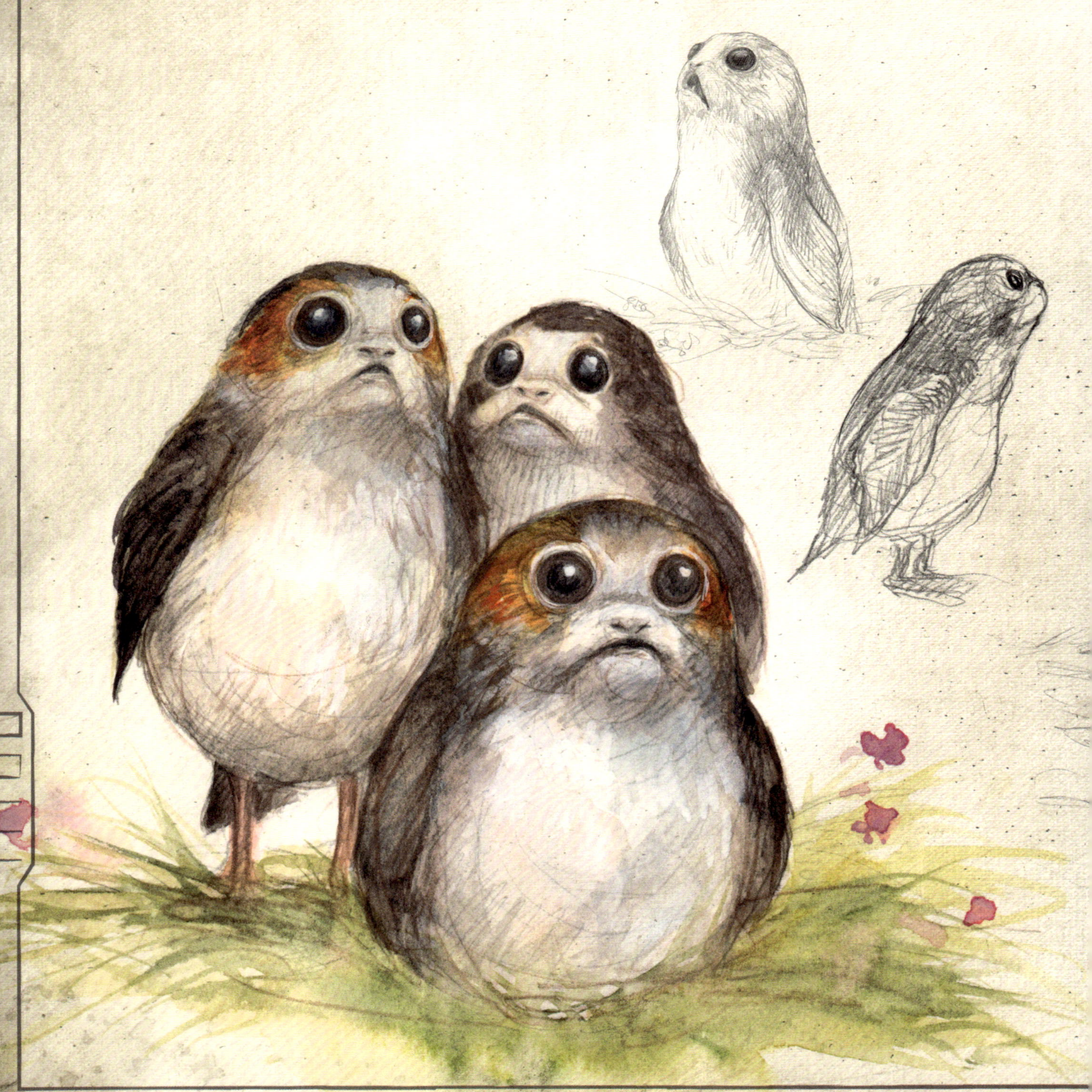

PORG

Ahch-To's adorable seabirds, with their short yellow legs, stout white bellies, and big black eyes, now live far beyond the borders of the ancient world, having expanded their territory after a number of them stowed away aboard the *Millennium Falcon* around 34 ABY, where they promptly built a nest among the cables. In fact, they are even sold as pets in the creature stall of Black Spire Outpost on Batuu.

Porgs feed primarily on fish, which they must procure by hunting with their claws because, curiously, they lack a beak. Webbed feet help propel porgs through water, while also offering stability when rapidly running across Ahch-To's rocky terrain. These avians stand between eighteen and twenty-six centimeters in height, with males measuring slightly larger than their female counterparts. Males are also distinguishable by the smattering of orange plumage located near their eyes. Both sexes have a dense coat of feathers, including a waterproof outer layer and a fluffier underlayer. This combination helps porgs stay warm in Ahch-To's often bracing temperatures. Their white, brown, and tan coloring provides camouflage, protecting them from predators—including the local Lanai, island visitors, and larger, taloned avians.

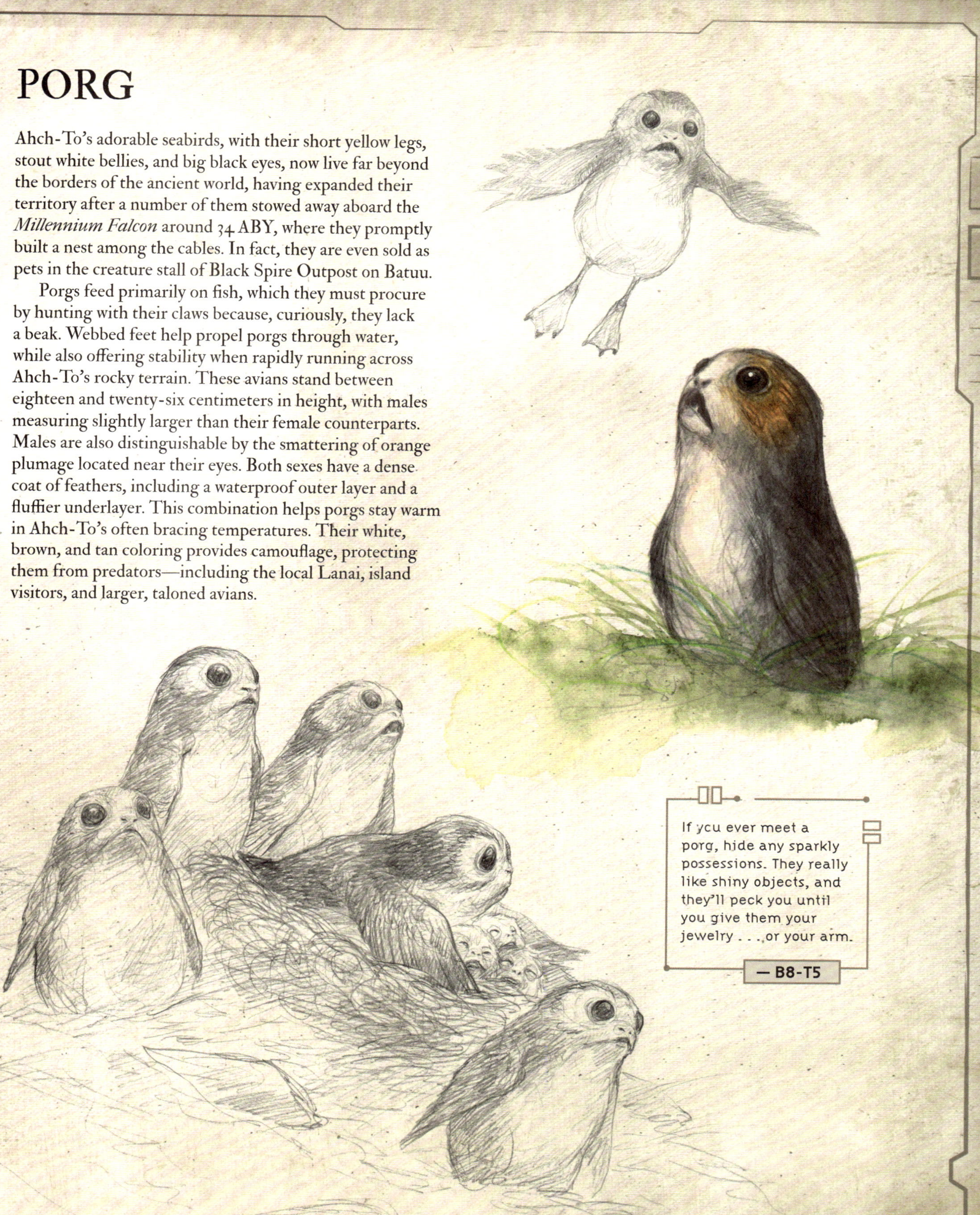

If you ever meet a porg, hide any sparkly possessions. They really like shiny objects, and they'll peck you until you give them your jewelry . . . or your arm.

— B8-T5

Porgs possess telescopic eyes that enable them to locate fish from the air. After procuring their meal by performing a controlled dive into the sea, they consume it in one large gulp. Porgs live in large groups known as murders and mate for life. Bonded pairs use grass, hair, and other fibrous materials to build their nests along the cliffs of Ahch-To and then decorate them with shiny objects. The parents work together to raise porglets by taking turns retrieving fish and crustaceans that they feed to their young.

These seafaring creatures are innately curious. They love to play, whether in water or even just with newcomers they encounter in their now-varied habitats. When approached by sentient beings, they exhibit highly social tendencies, often jumping onto the visitor's lap and angling their heads so as to be petted behind the ears. When they feel threatened, however, the oft-friendly porgs grow intensely shy and retreat from their perceived assailant.

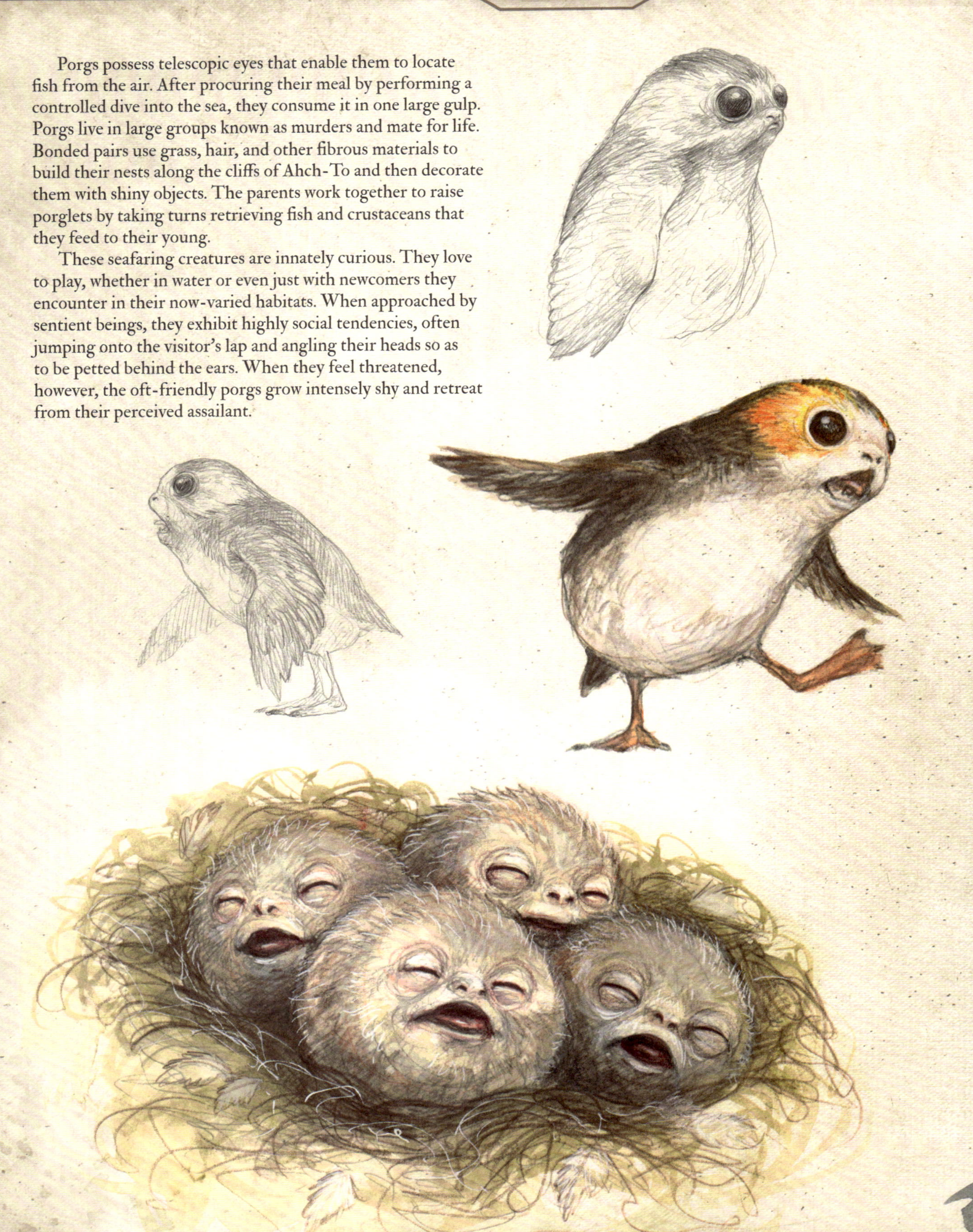

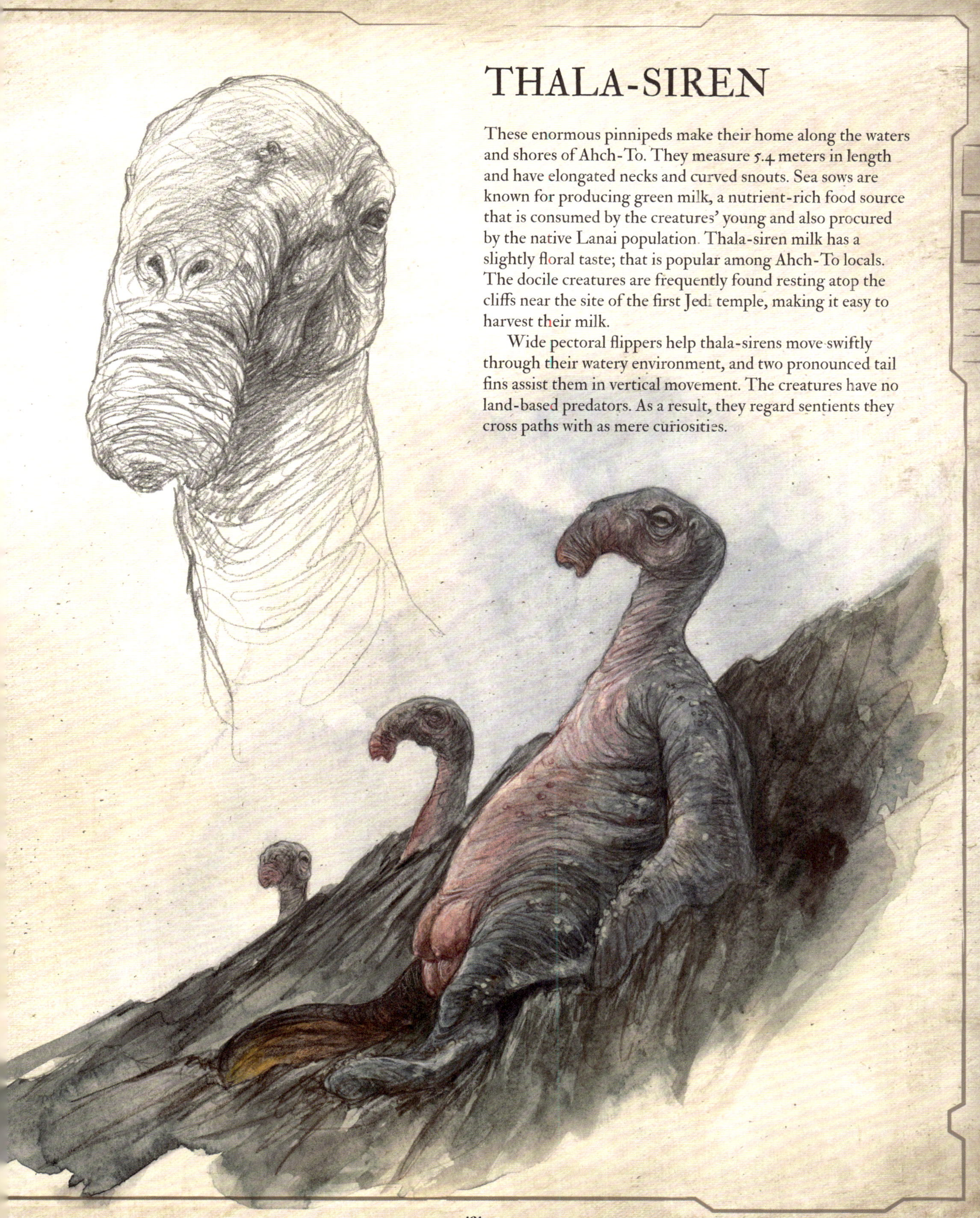

THALA-SIREN

These enormous pinnipeds make their home along the waters and shores of Ahch-To. They measure 5.4 meters in length and have elongated necks and curved snouts. Sea sows are known for producing green milk, a nutrient-rich food source that is consumed by the creatures' young and also procured by the native Lanai population. Thala-siren milk has a slightly floral taste; that is popular among Ahch-To locals. The docile creatures are frequently found resting atop the cliffs near the site of the first Jedi temple, making it easy to harvest their milk.

Wide pectoral flippers help thala-sirens move swiftly through their watery environment, and two pronounced tail fins assist them in vertical movement. The creatures have no land-based predators. As a result, they regard sentients they cross paths with as mere curiosities.

FRESHWATER LAKES, RIVERS, AND FROZEN WATER CREATURES

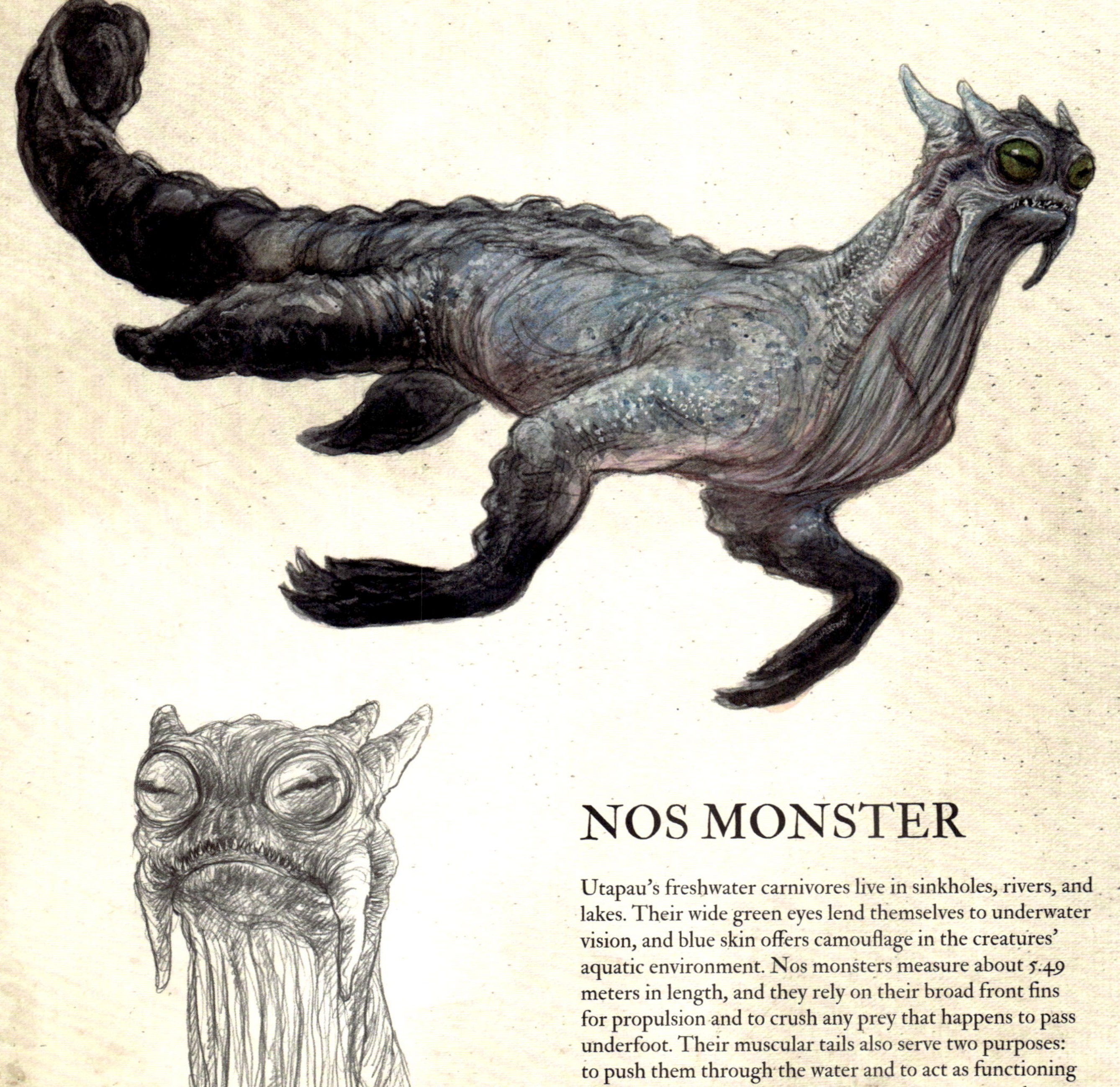

NOS MONSTER

Utapau's freshwater carnivores live in sinkholes, rivers, and lakes. Their wide green eyes lend themselves to underwater vision, and blue skin offers camouflage in the creatures' aquatic environment. Nos monsters measure about 5.49 meters in length, and they rely on their broad front fins for propulsion and to crush any prey that happens to pass underfoot. Their muscular tails also serve two purposes: to push them through the water and to act as functioning weapons, which they use to swing at any creatures that are unwise enough to attack.

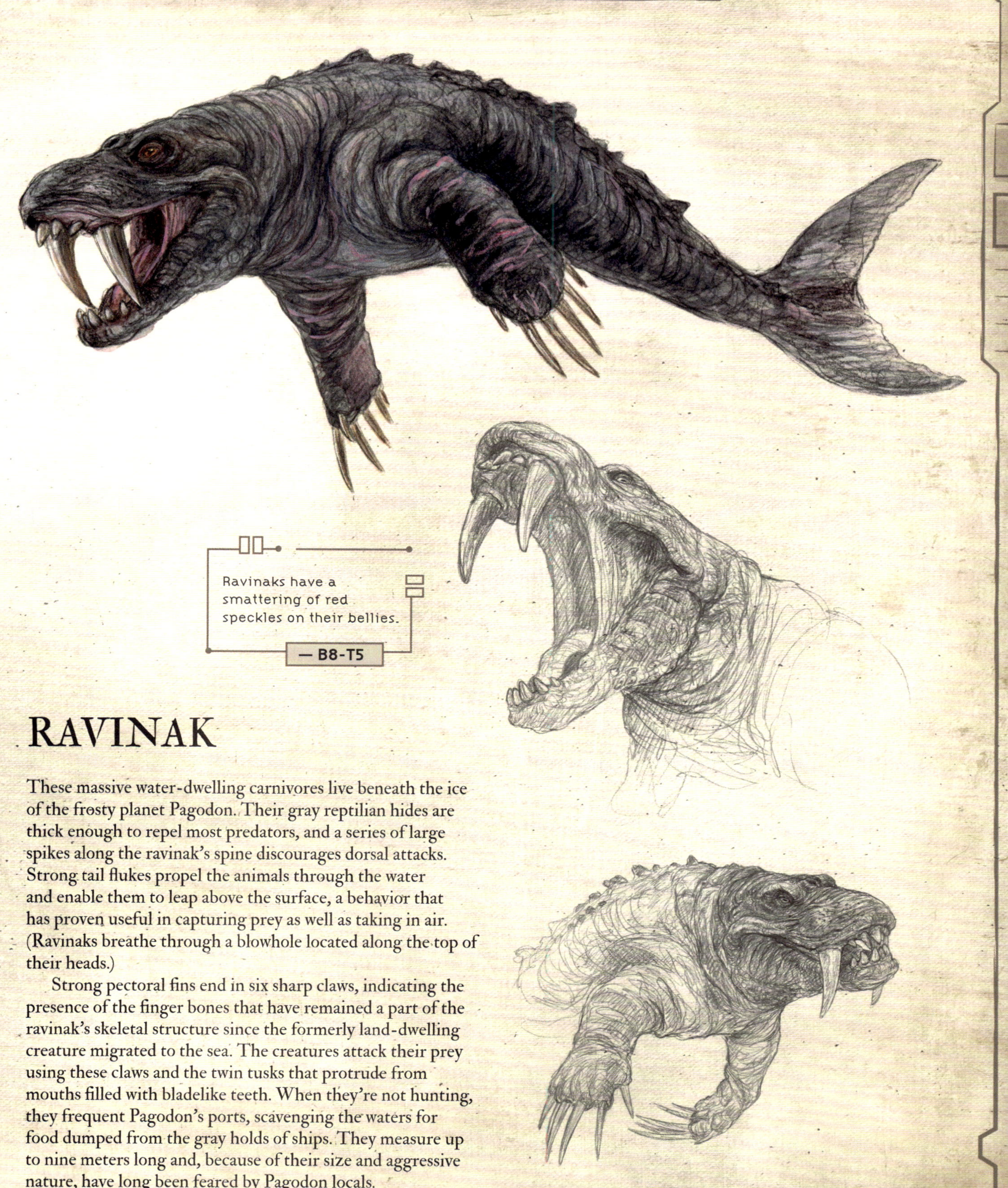

RAVINAK

These massive water-dwelling carnivores live beneath the ice of the frosty planet Pagodon. Their gray reptilian hides are thick enough to repel most predators, and a series of large spikes along the ravinak's spine discourages dorsal attacks. Strong tail flukes propel the animals through the water and enable them to leap above the surface, a behavior that has proven useful in capturing prey as well as taking in air. (Ravinaks breathe through a blowhole located along the top of their heads.)

Strong pectoral fins end in six sharp claws, indicating the presence of the finger bones that have remained a part of the ravinak's skeletal structure since the formerly land-dwelling creature migrated to the sea. The creatures attack their prey using these claws and the twin tusks that protrude from mouths filled with bladelike teeth. When they're not hunting, they frequent Pagodon's ports, scavenging the waters for food dumped from the gray holds of ships. They measure up to nine meters long and, because of their size and aggressive nature, have long been feared by Pagodon locals.

OCEAN AND SEA CREATURES

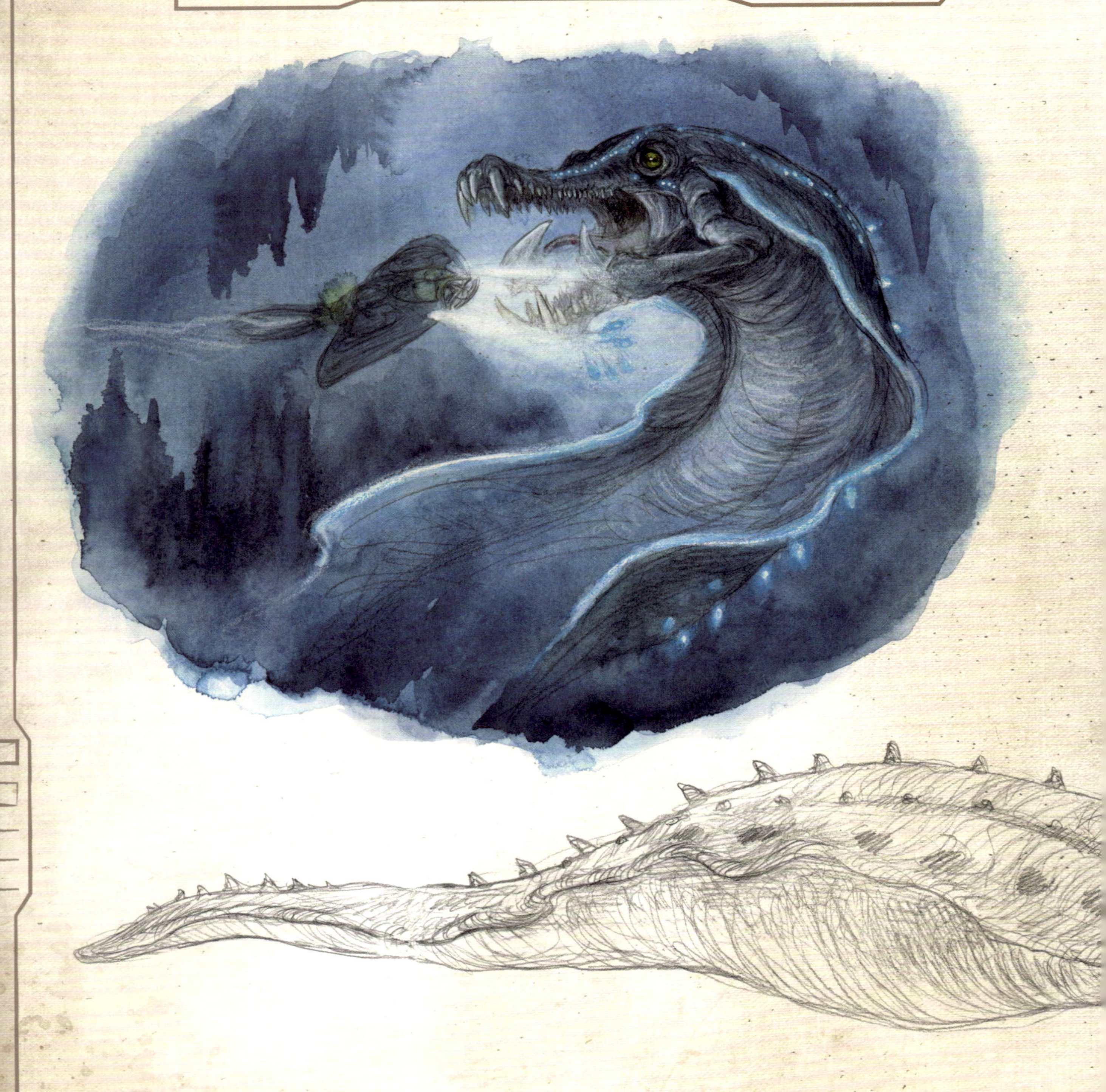

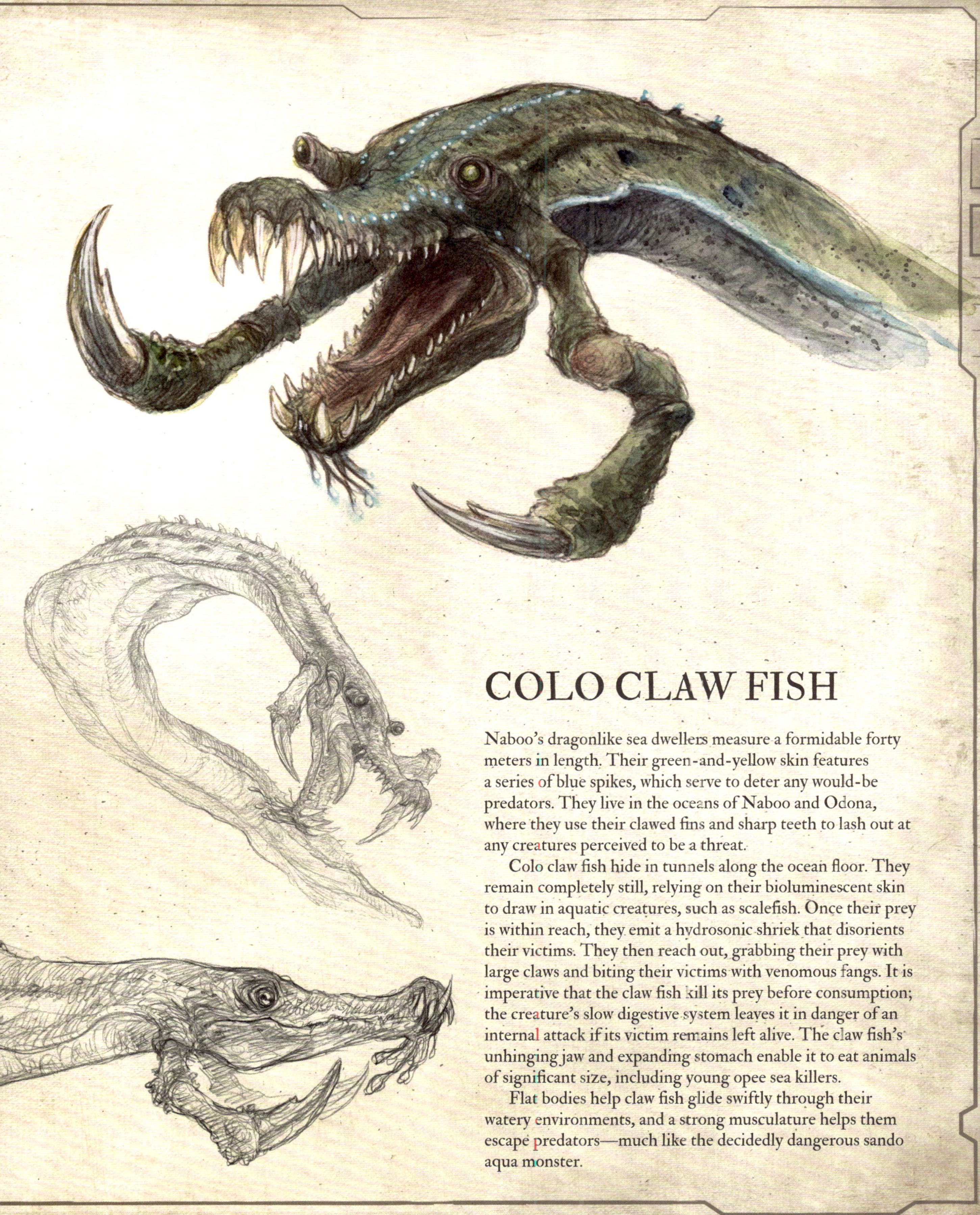

COLO CLAW FISH

Naboo's dragonlike sea dwellers measure a formidable forty meters in length. Their green-and-yellow skin features a series of blue spikes, which serve to deter any would-be predators. They live in the oceans of Naboo and Odona, where they use their clawed fins and sharp teeth to lash out at any creatures perceived to be a threat.

Colo claw fish hide in tunnels along the ocean floor. They remain completely still, relying on their bioluminescent skin to draw in aquatic creatures, such as scalefish. Once their prey is within reach, they emit a hydrosonic shriek that disorients their victims. They then reach out, grabbing their prey with large claws and biting their victims with venomous fangs. It is imperative that the claw fish kill its prey before consumption; the creature's slow digestive system leaves it in danger of an internal attack if its victim remains left alive. The claw fish's unhinging jaw and expanding stomach enable it to eat animals of significant size, including young opee sea killers.

Flat bodies help claw fish glide swiftly through their watery environments, and a strong musculature helps them escape predators—much like the decidedly dangerous sando aqua monster.

KAMORADON

These large aquatic reptiles are also known as kamoradon sea dragons. They live in the waters of Kamino, where they troll the sea near Tipoca City in search of food. Their long, pointed snouts are filled with rows of sharp teeth that they sink into their prey, from smaller sea creatures to ill-begotten sentients. Three sets of flippers propel them through the water, and long tails serve as both stabilizer and weapon. The kamoradon's smooth shell and blue-and-green camouflage coloring offer protection from predators, although few creatures are foolhardy enough to attack them. These massive sea creatures measure up to one hundred twenty meters long and weigh approximately a thousand kilograms.

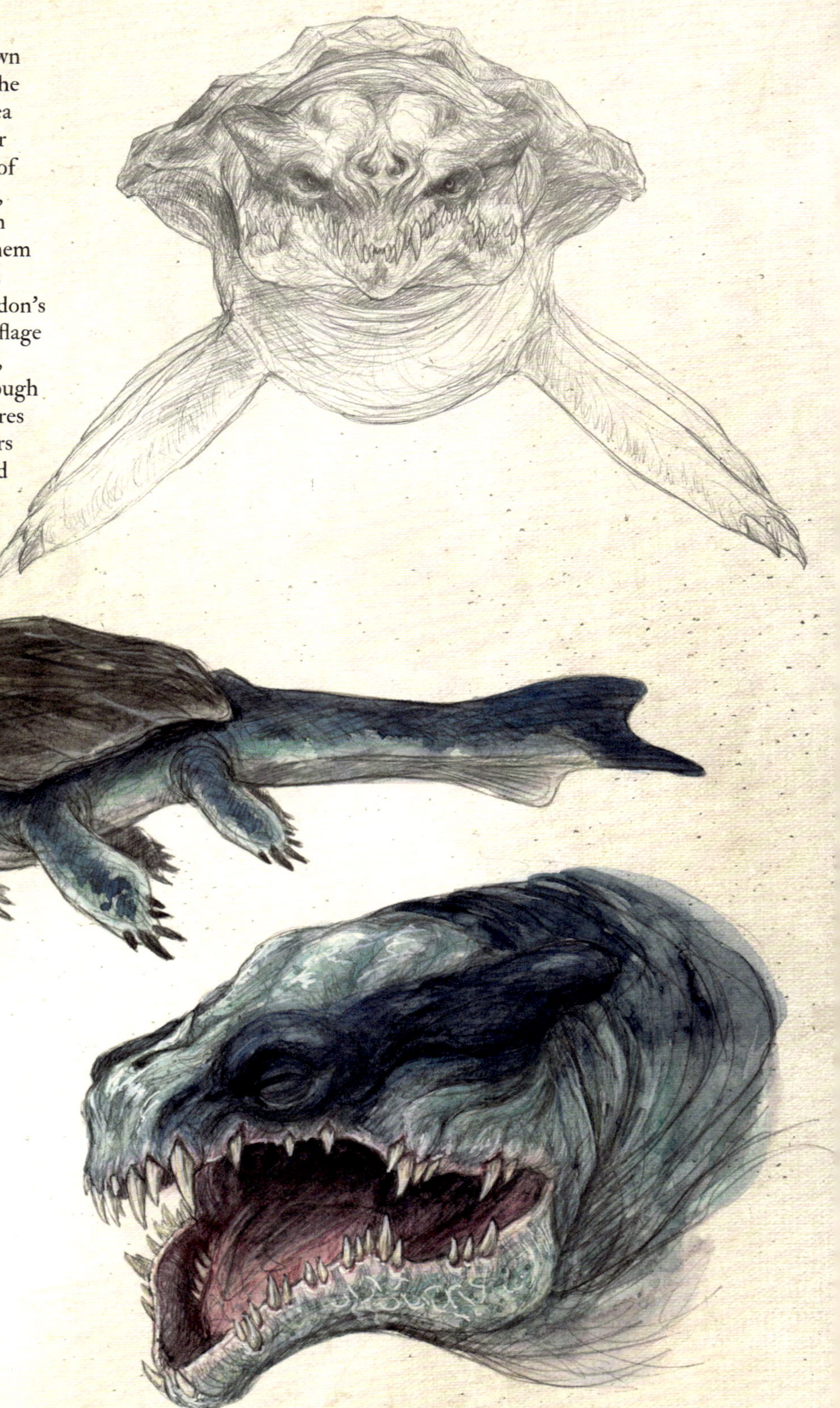

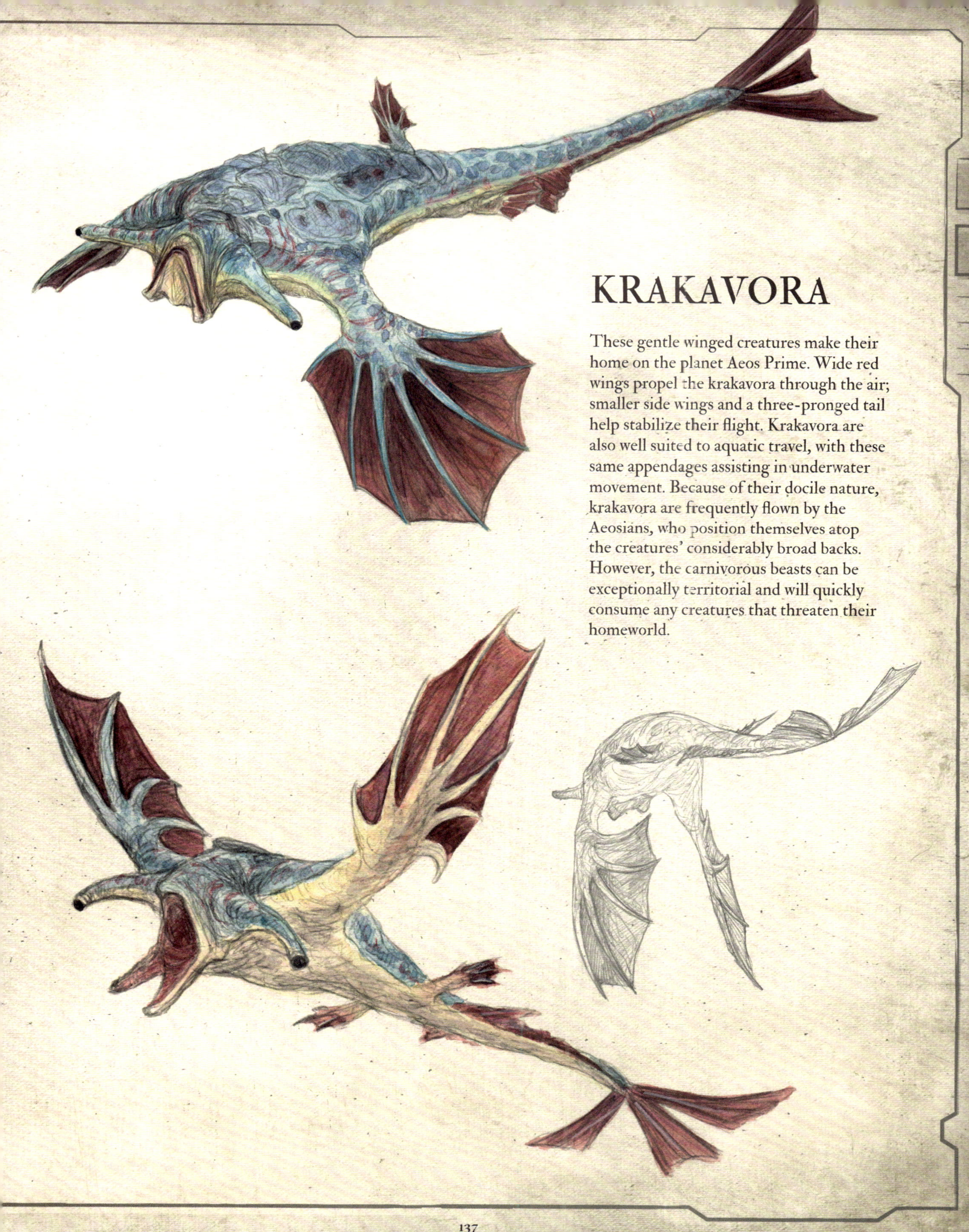

KRAKAVORA

These gentle winged creatures make their home on the planet Aeos Prime. Wide red wings propel the krakavora through the air; smaller side wings and a three-pronged tail help stabilize their flight. Krakavora are also well suited to aquatic travel, with these same appendages assisting in underwater movement. Because of their docile nature, krakavora are frequently flown by the Aeosians, who position themselves atop the creatures' considerably broad backs. However, the carnivorous beasts can be exceptionally territorial and will quickly consume any creatures that threaten their homeworld.

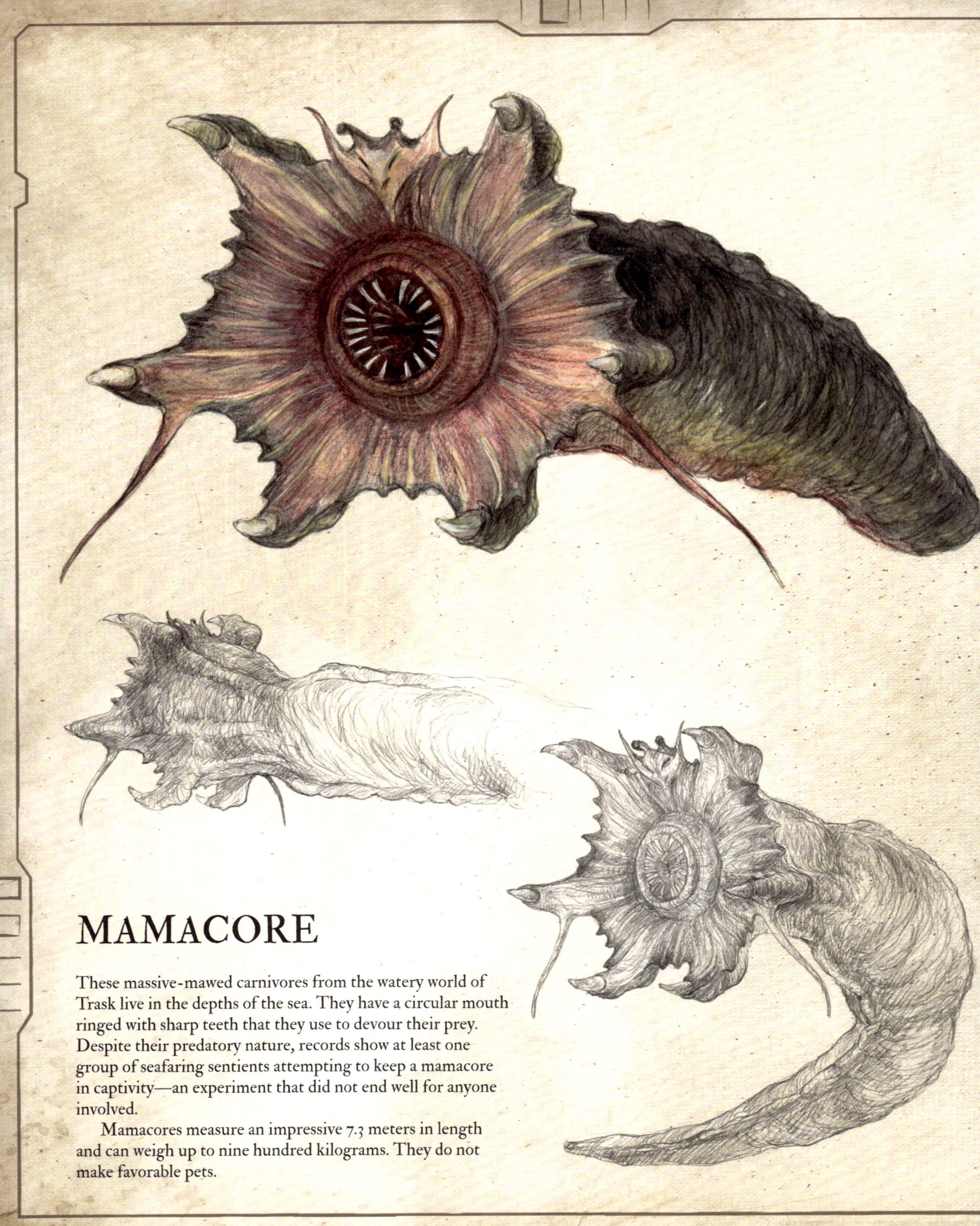

MAMACORE

These massive-mawed carnivores from the watery world of Trask live in the depths of the sea. They have a circular mouth ringed with sharp teeth that they use to devour their prey. Despite their predatory nature, records show at least one group of seafaring sentients attempting to keep a mamacore in captivity—an experiment that did not end well for anyone involved.

Mamacores measure an impressive 7.3 meters in length and can weigh up to nine hundred kilograms. They do not make favorable pets.

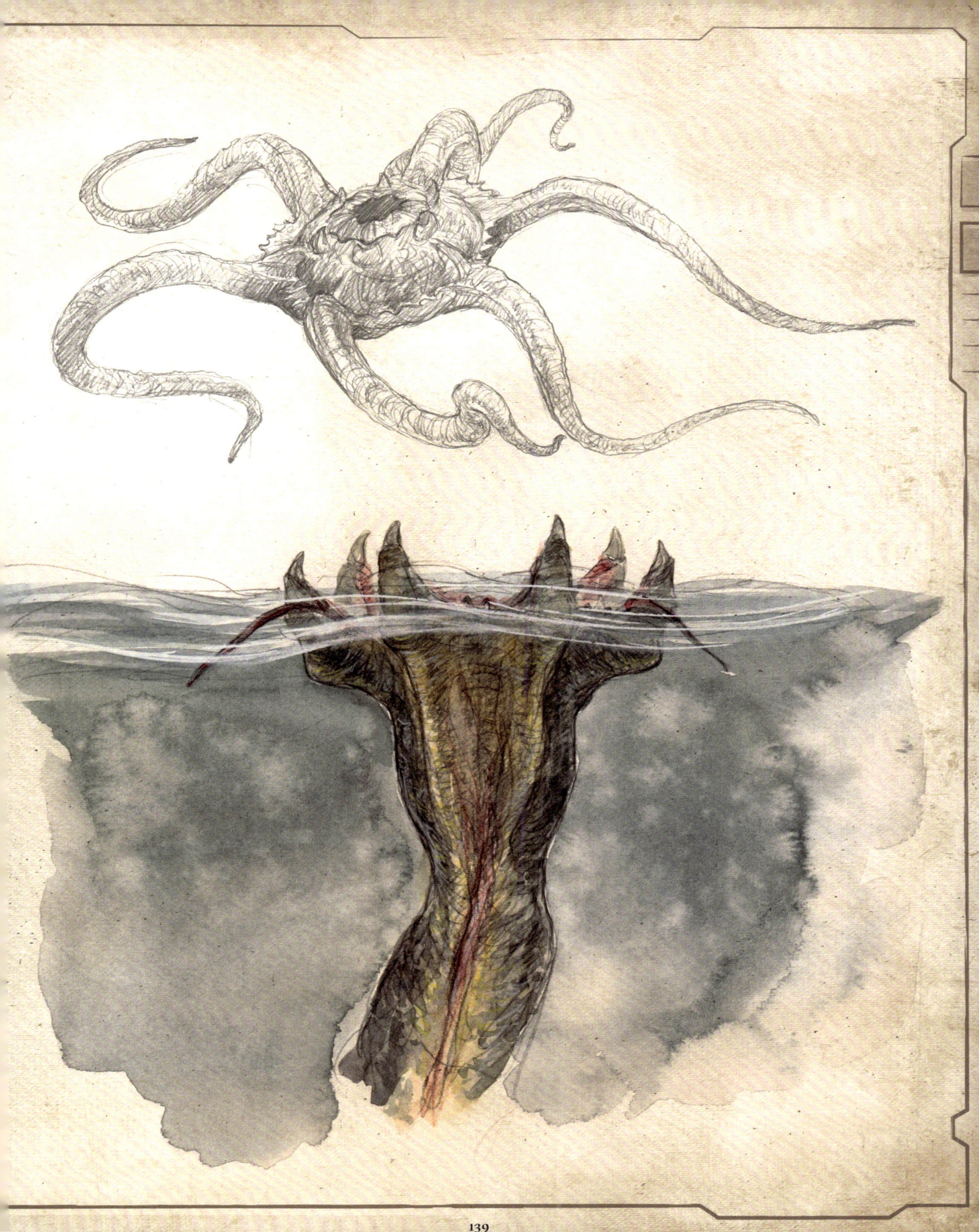

OPEE SEA KILLER

These twenty-meter-long predatory crustaceans spark fear in the hearts of many seafarers. Native to Naboo and Strokill Prime, the sea killers possess a veritable variety of evolutionary traits belonging to other ocean dwellers, from armor-coated shells to twin rows of teeth. These predators use their two antennae to entice prey before attacking from a distance—swimming just close enough to eject a purple prehensile tongue that grabs a victim and forces it into its mouth.

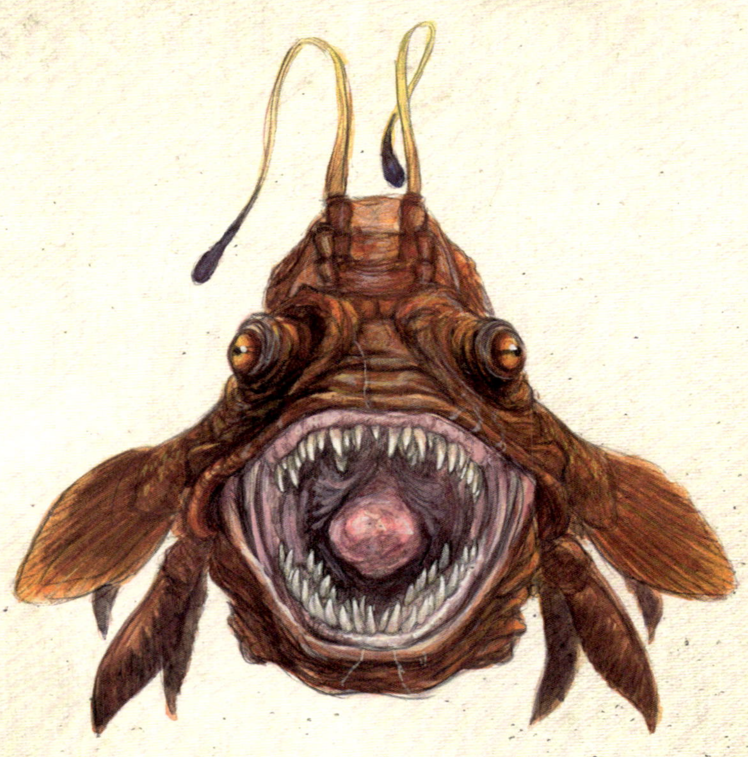

Opee sea killers have a rather unconventional method of movement. Instead of relying on their fins to push them across their oceanic habitat, they draw water into their mouths and expel it through a series of pores at the back of their bodies. This propels the creatures forward, often at great speeds, making them difficult to both evade *and* pursue. Their aggressive nature leaves them unintimidated by predators, although they are known to be hunted by sando aqua monsters.

Males of the species play a key role in the species' propagation. Fathers spend three months carrying eggs within their mouths, forgoing all food until their young have safely hatched.

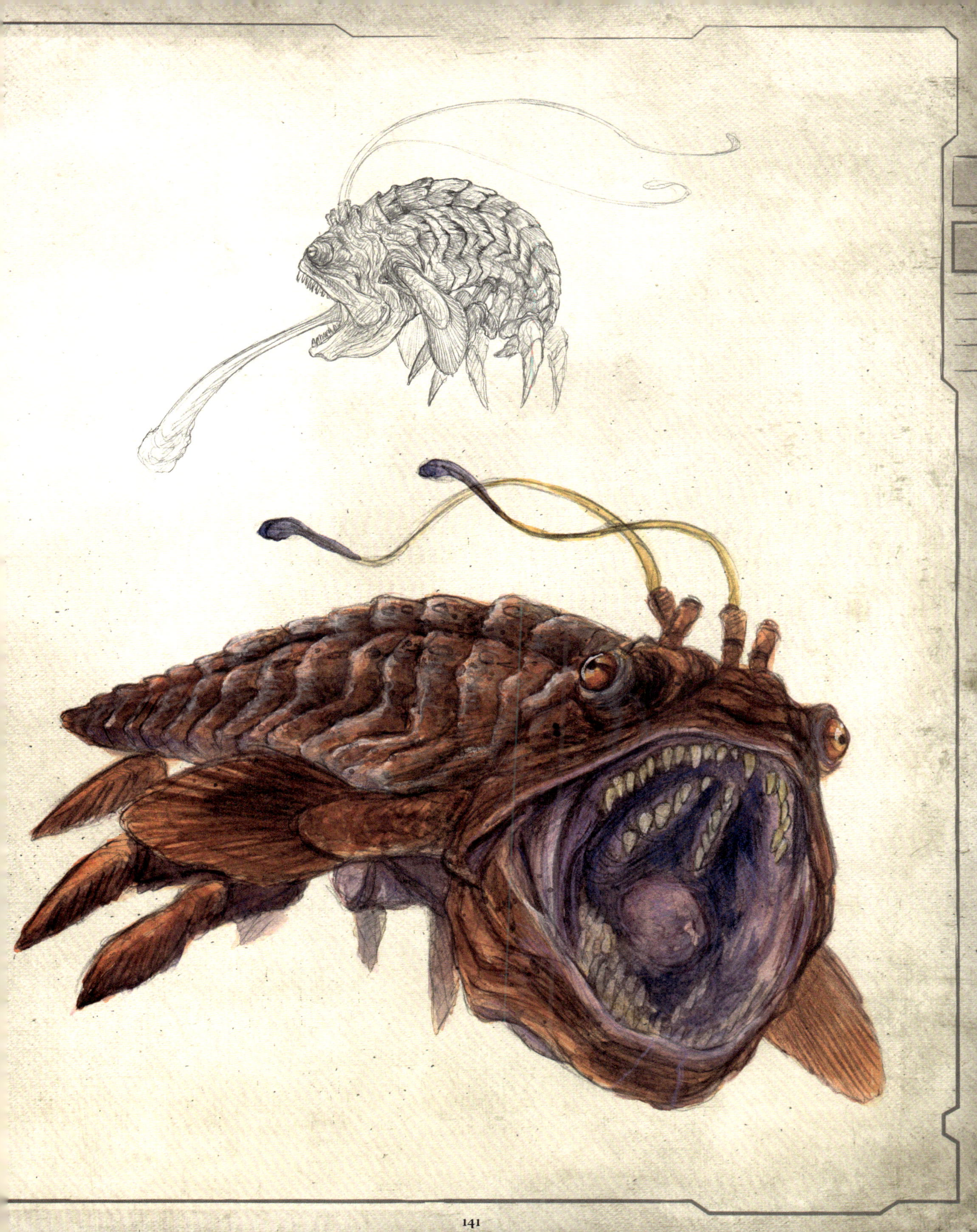

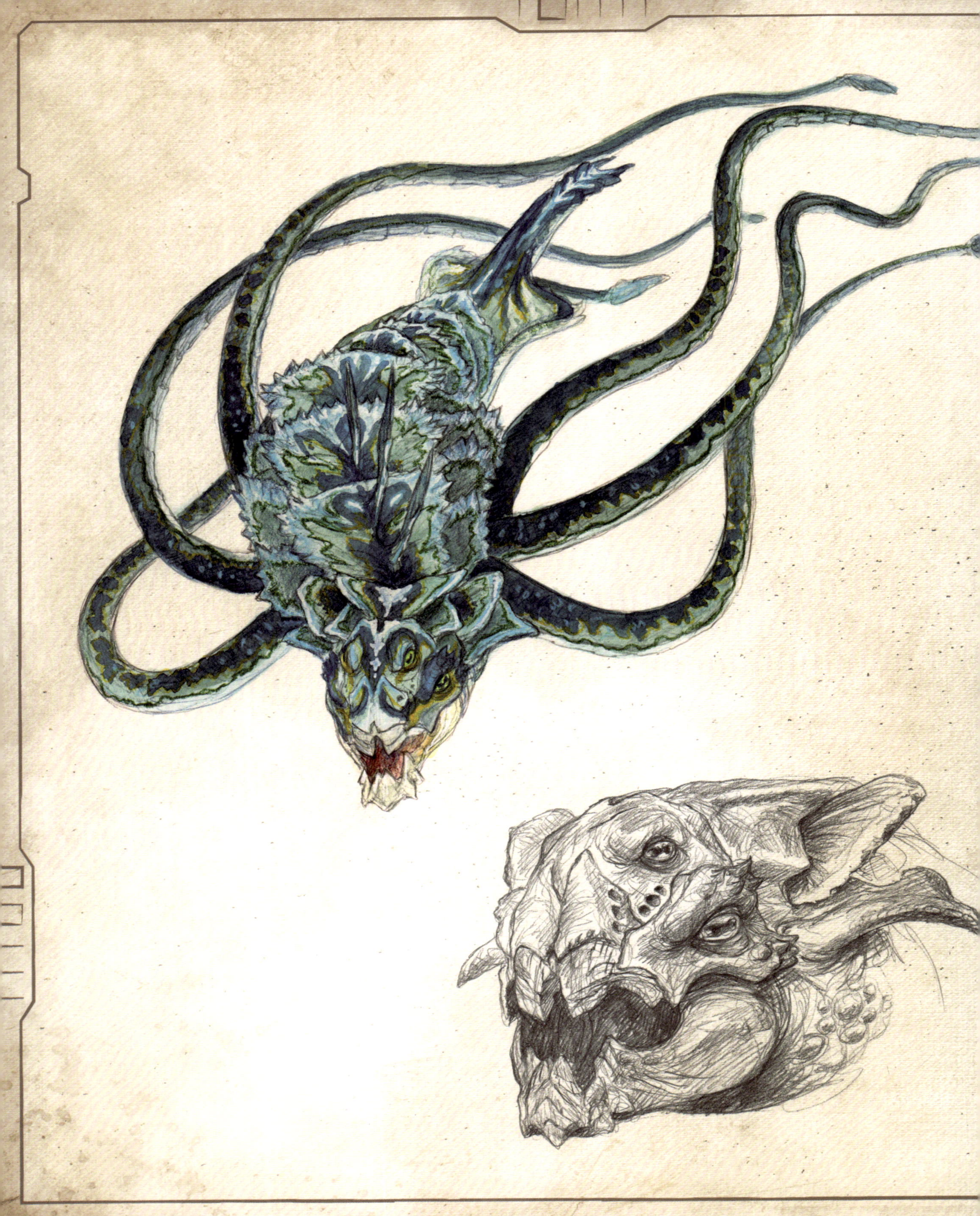

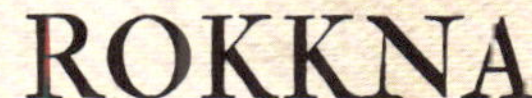

ROKKNA

The enormous tentacled rokkna lives in the ocean of the planet Castilon. It stretches a full two hundred twenty meters long, although its green-and-blue coloring helps it blend into its watery environment. Rokkna have four green-and-black eyes that house curious, hourglass-shaped pupils. They emit a strong odor to attract mates while simultaneously repelling predators. They have six long tentacles that they use to attack their prey, and a fully grown adult is capable of destroying an entire refueling station platform.

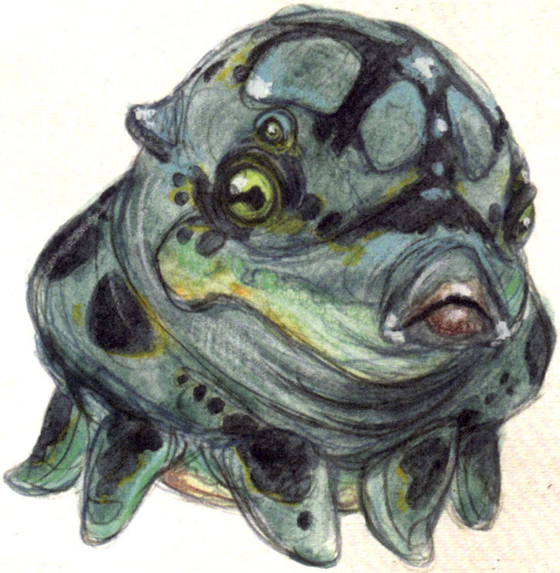

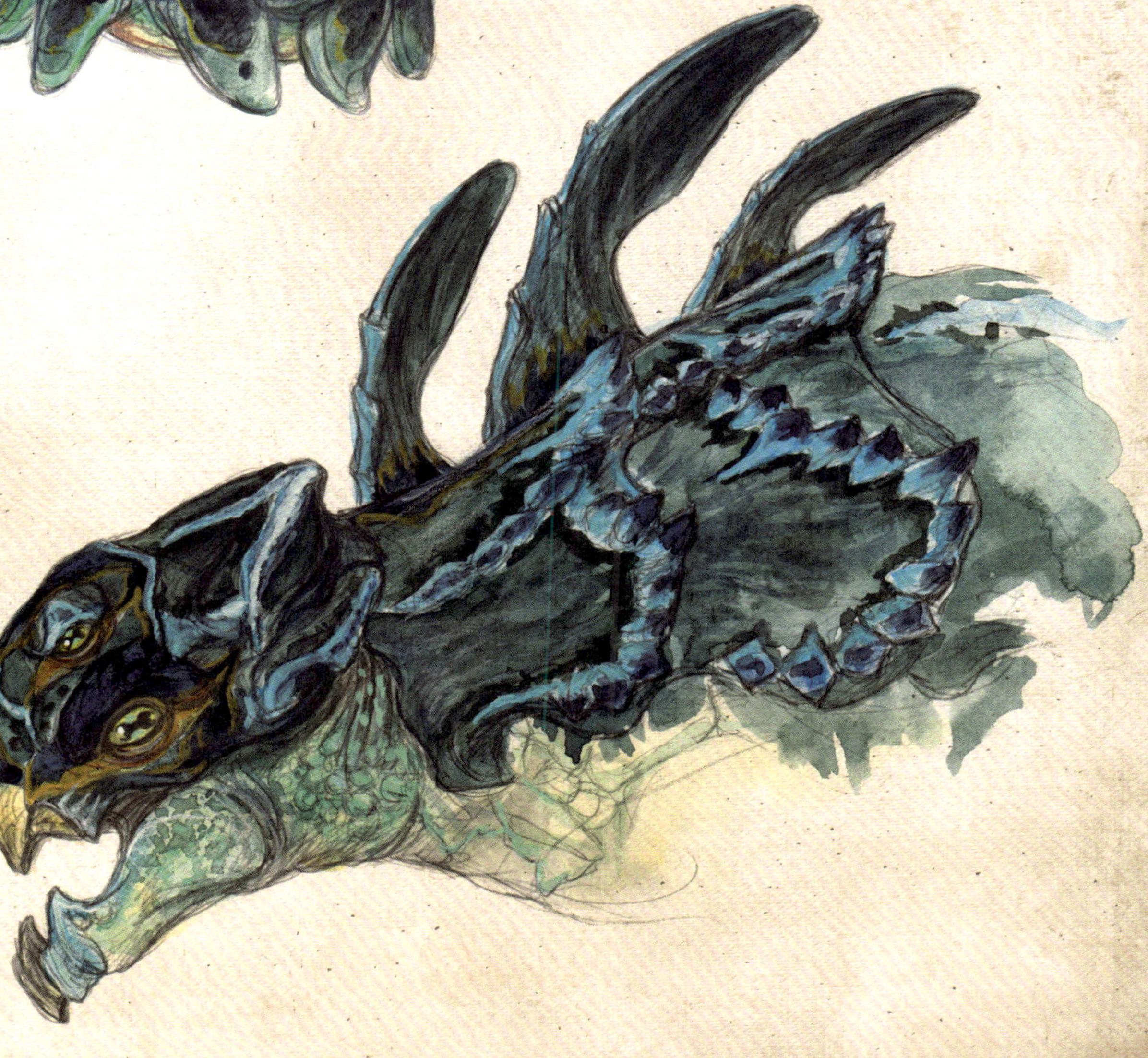

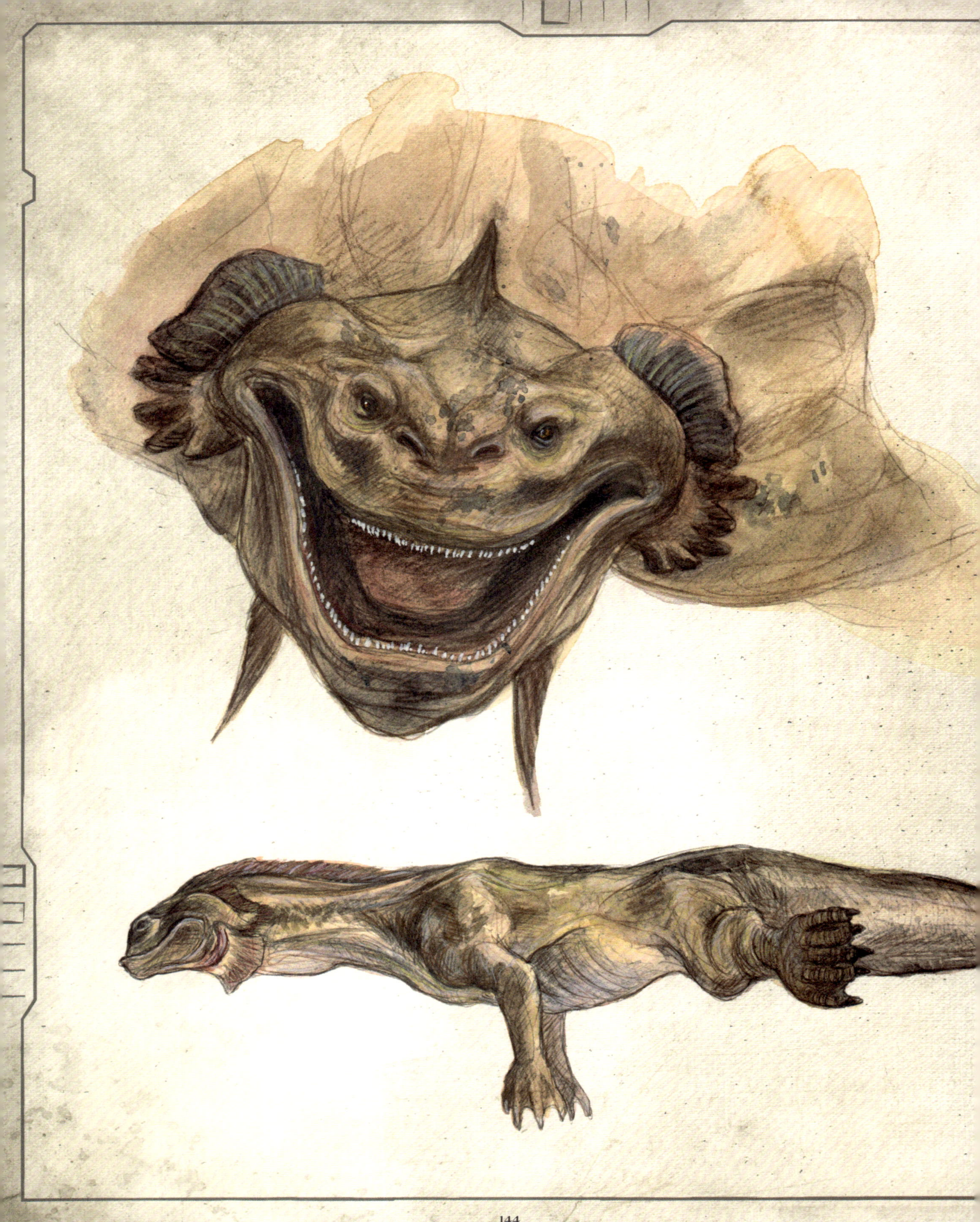

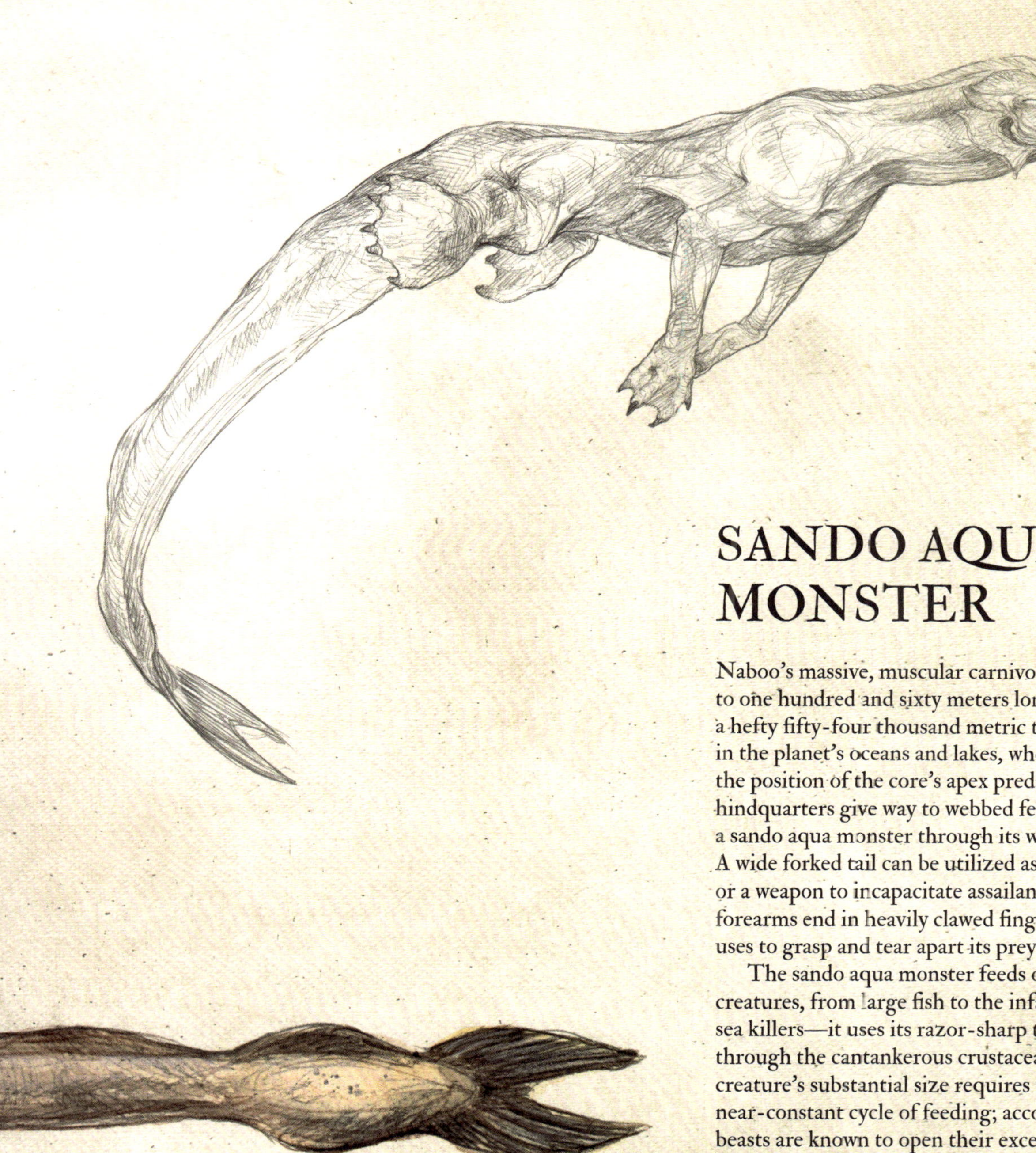

SANDO AQUA MONSTER

Naboo's massive, muscular carnivores measure up to one hundred and sixty meters long and weigh a hefty fifty-four thousand metric tons. They live in the planet's oceans and lakes, where they hold the position of the core's apex predator. Broad hindquarters give way to webbed feet, which propel a sando aqua monster through its watery world. A wide forked tail can be utilized as a stabilizer or a weapon to incapacitate assailants. Its strong forearms end in heavily clawed fingers, which it uses to grasp and tear apart its prey.

The sando aqua monster feeds on a variety of creatures, from large fish to the infamous opee sea killers—it uses its razor-sharp teeth to bite through the cantankerous crustacean's shell. The creature's substantial size requires that it be in a near-constant cycle of feeding; accordingly, the beasts are known to open their exceedingly wide mouths to consume an entire school of fish.

The creatures live an average of one hundred years—although the holonet states that the specimen killed by the Sith Lord Darth Vader lived to be 932. They have an exceptionally slow life cycle and a very minimal population, necessitating conservation of the species.

SHARVO FISH

Castilon's carnivorous natives dwell in the waters that surround the former location of the planet's *Colossus* platform. Their dark blue skin is marked by twin rows of bioluminescent spots. Sharvos have two protruding dorsal fins, along with a series of pectoral flippers. They live in large groups known as schools.

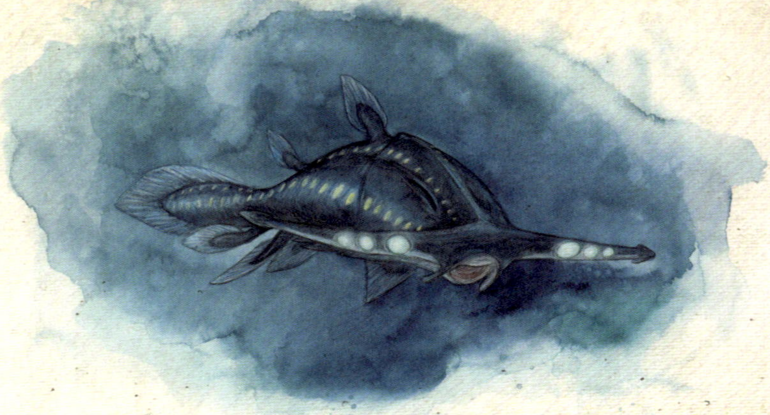

Doo, faa, laa, mee, see, and tee tend to stick together in their watery environments—a very melodic sounding bunch.

— B8-T5

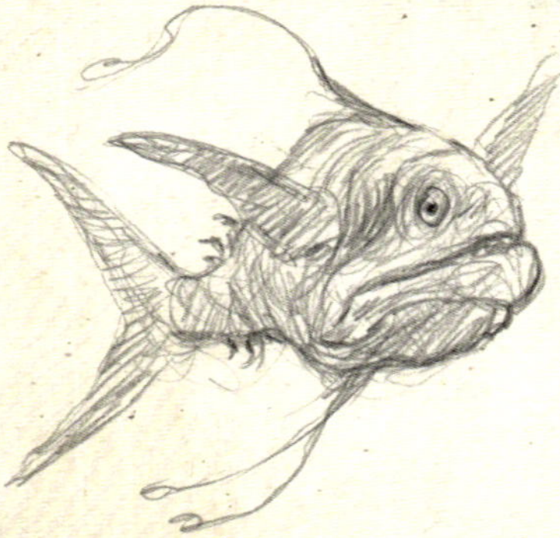

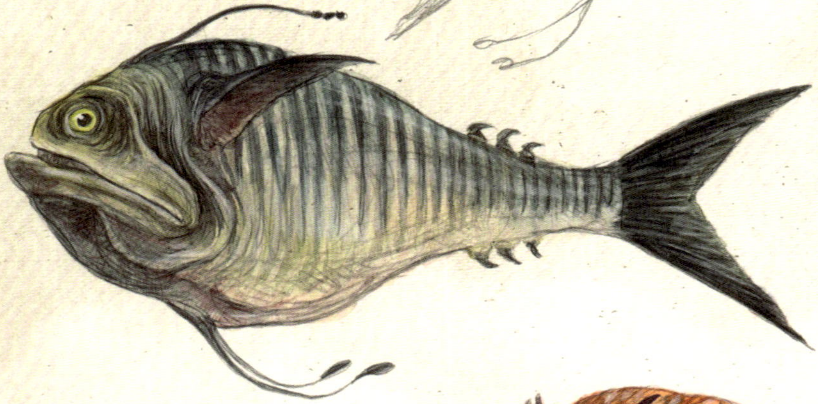

DOO

These yellow-and-gray scalefish are one of six species that live together in Naboo's famed Lake Paonga. They have large jaws and black eyes, and they feed on yobshrimp—small creatures known to live in the gills of other fish. Vertical blue stripes aid in camouflage, and small organs on the underside of their bodies help detect movement and function as an early alarm to alert the doo to approaching predators.

Doo are also found in the Abyss, where they are constantly in danger of consumption by the predatory colo claw fish and the opee sea killer.

FAA

The second of the Lake Paonga scalefish has a wide, flat head; a narrow, elongated midsection; and a wide, paddlelike tail. Tiny pectoral fins flutter at its sides, which have a graduated orange hue. Jagged blue stripes stretch vertically from the faa's spine, and its puffy, bulbous eyes sit prominently at the front of its head. Like its brethren, faa are also found in the Naboo Abyss, where they are preyed upon by colo claw fish and opee sea killers. However, unlike the doo, laa, mee, see, and tee, the faa is a ferocious carnivore that readily feeds on smaller sea creatures.

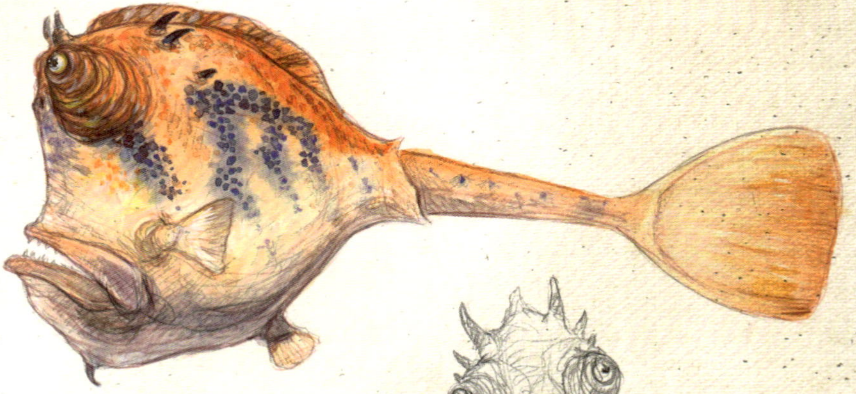

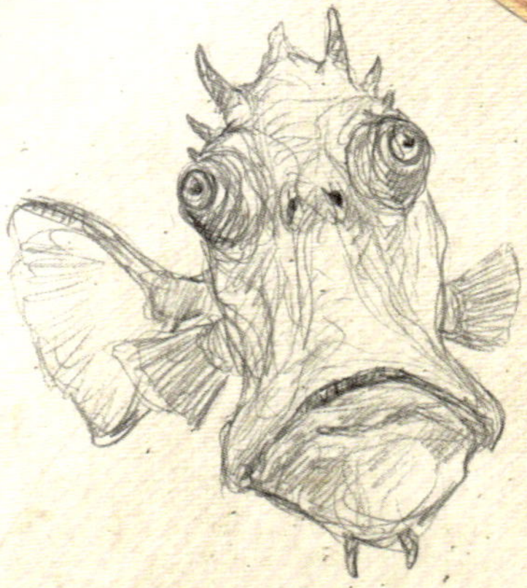

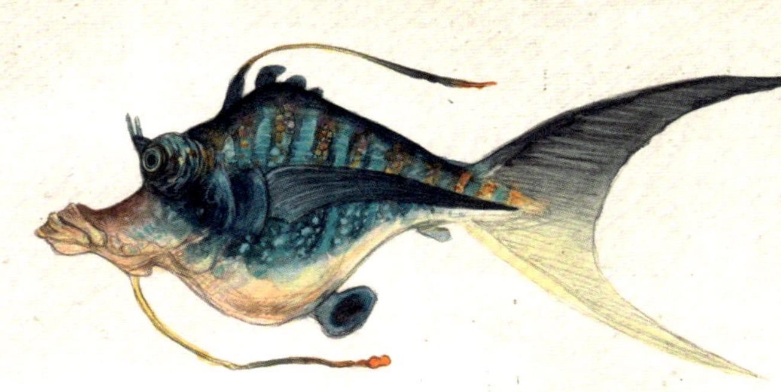

LAA

These blue-green scalefish with orange and peach gradations have elongated snouts and wide, tapering pectoral fins. Two antennaelike appendages stretch from between yellow eyes, and curved tails propel the fish through Lake Paonga at high speeds. Like their counterparts, the laa feed on yobshrimp, which they remove from the gills of their fellow scalefish, the tee. They are also found in the Naboo Abyss.

MEE

Of the six Lake Paonga scalefish, the mee pose the greatest danger to passersby because of a poisonous spine that sits atop their yellow back. Vertical brown charlike stripes stretch the width of their bodies, and whiskerlike flaps trail from their cheeks. The herbivorous mee makes its homes in swamps and oceans, from the lake to the Naboo Abyss.

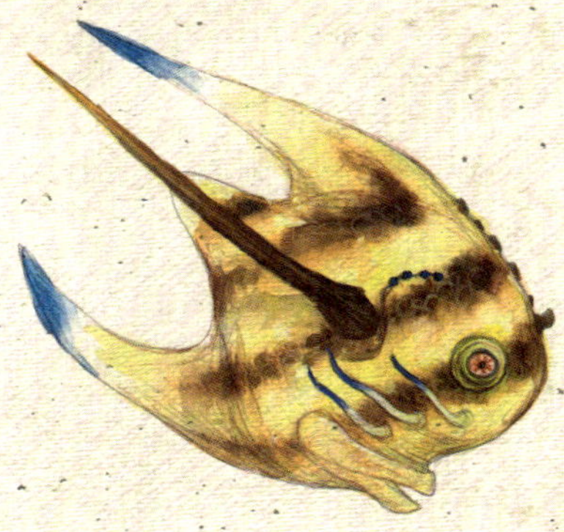

SEE

See are the fifth of the Lake Paonga scalefish that can also be found in the Abyss. The see, however, is notable for its stouter proportions and wide, oarlike pectoral fins. It has a green-and-orange checked pattern along its back, simulating the appearance of shadows when viewed from above. Its bulbous blue eyes help it see through murky waters, an evolutionary adaptation that has enabled it to thrive in Naboo's swampy environs.

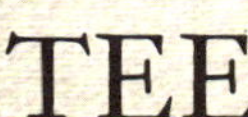

TEE

The most colorful of the six fish displays a brilliant coat of impossible-to-miss red scales, alongside a plethora of low-hanging feelers. Wide lips sheathe a jaw that absolutely brims with sharp teeth. Its gills are home to the tiny yobshrimp, the species most commonly consumed by the tee and its scalefish relations.

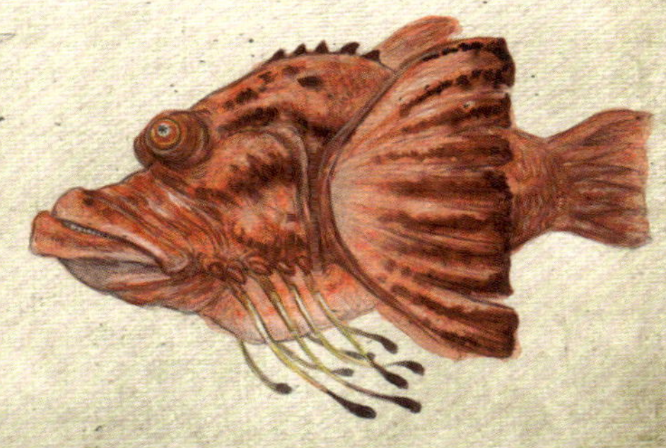

SWAMP AND LAGOON CREATURES

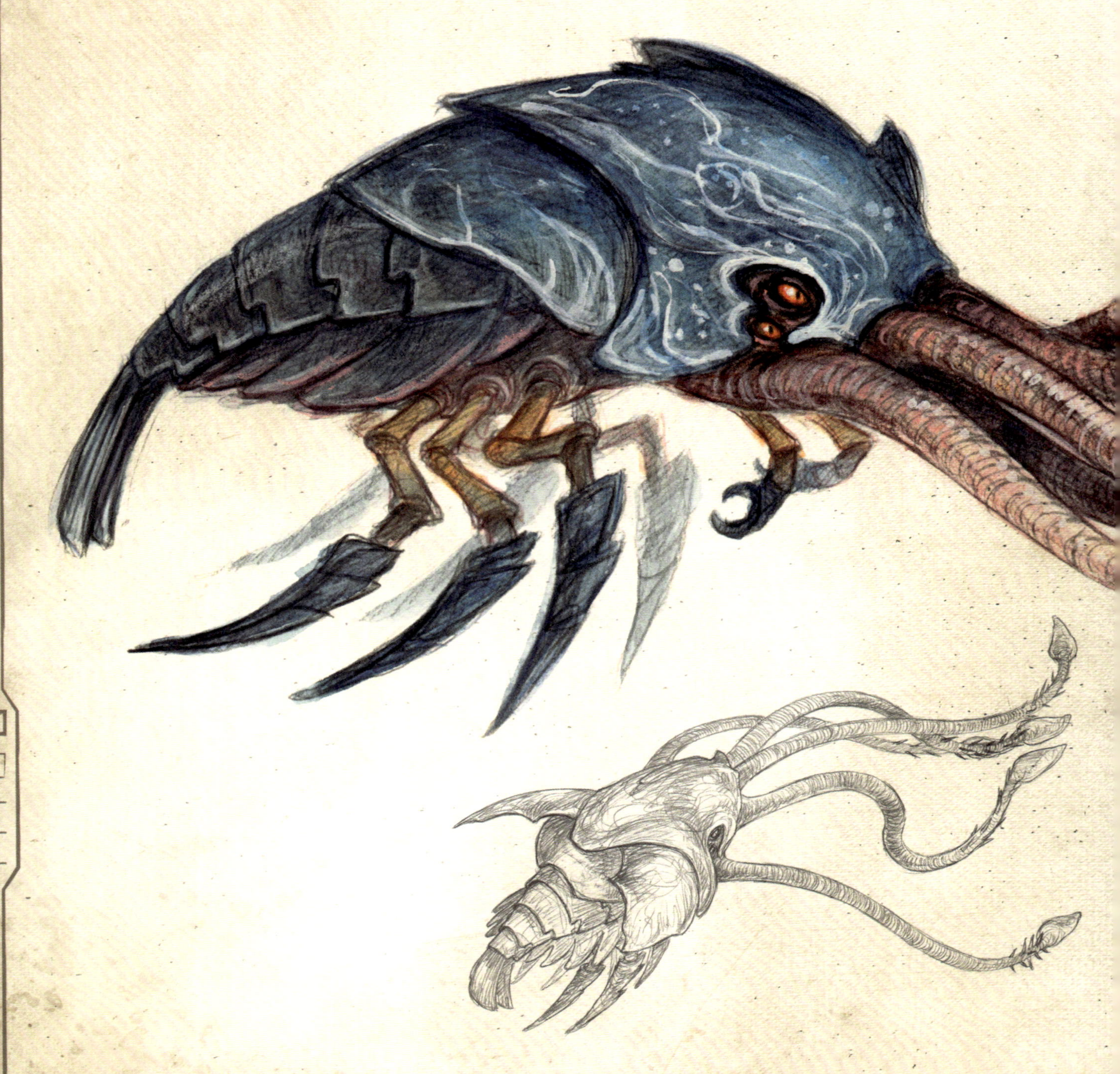

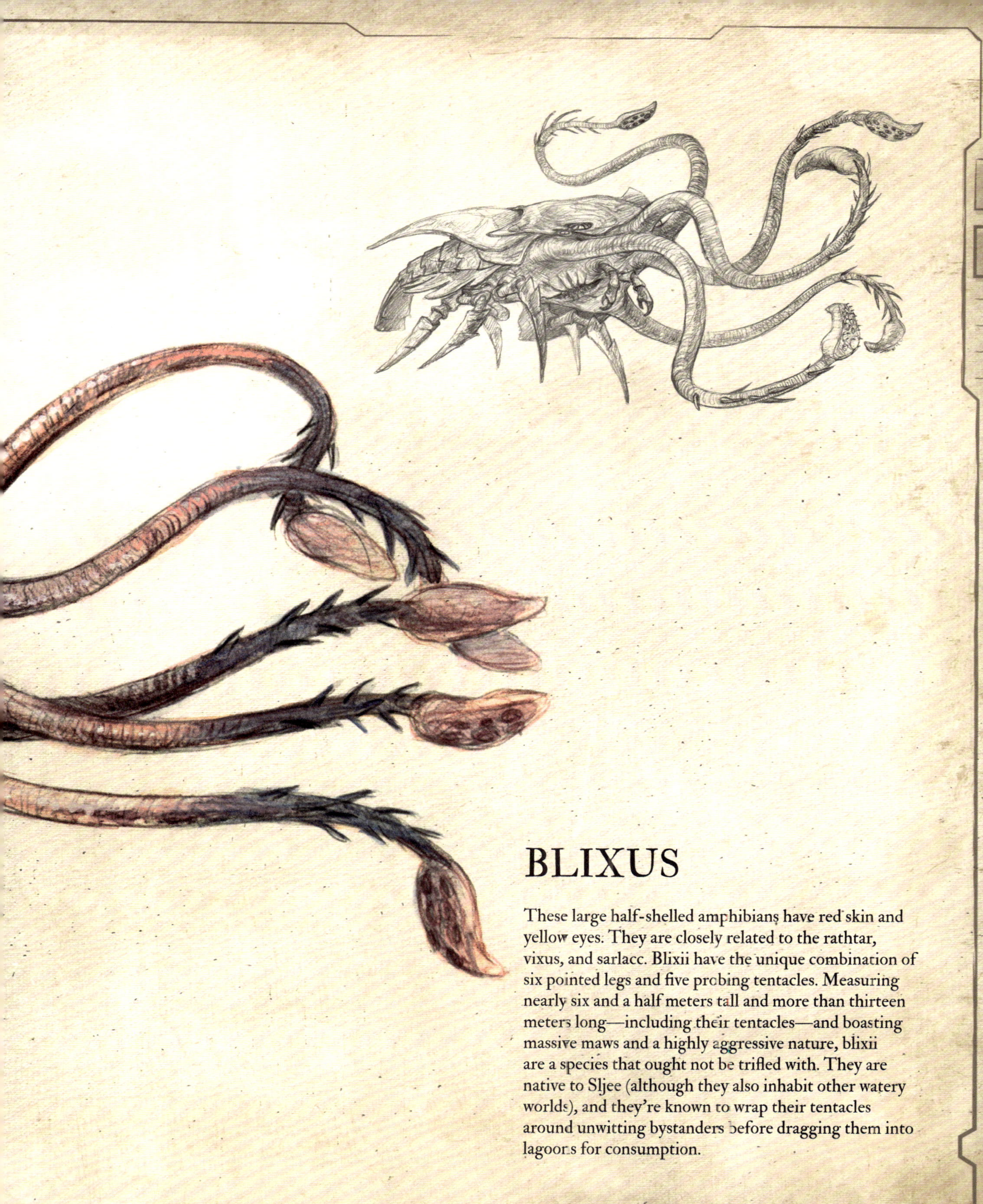

BLIXUS

These large half-shelled amphibians have red skin and yellow eyes. They are closely related to the rathtar, vixus, and sarlacc. Blixii have the unique combination of six pointed legs and five probing tentacles. Measuring nearly six and a half meters tall and more than thirteen meters long—including their tentacles—and boasting massive maws and a highly aggressive nature, blixii are a species that ought not be trifled with. They are native to Sljee (although they also inhabit other watery worlds), and they're known to wrap their tentacles around unwitting bystanders before dragging them into lagoons for consumption.

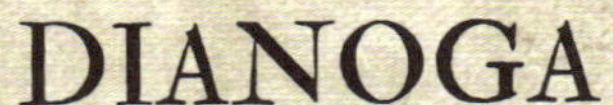

DIANOGA

These dark purple cephalopods measure an average of seven meters in length, and weigh up to ninety-five kilograms. They have seven tentacles, each carrying an array of suckers that help the creatures cling to surfaces as well as prey. Their regenerative capabilities enable them to regrow lost limbs, and their ability to change color allows them to camouflage in nearly any environment—some specimens have developed the ability to turn transparent! Dianogas live in swamps, sewers, and junkyards of their native Vodran; over time, they have also been exported to other worlds.

A dianoga has multiple hearts, with blue blood pumping ferociously through each one. Its long neck gives way to a singular eye stalk that it can raise above the water to assess threats. However, dianogas must limit their eye stalks' time away from aquatic environs because their bodies will dry out if removed from their natural habitat for too long. The creatures are developmentally advanced, living together in primitive tribal communities and communicating among their species using a series of hums. Their language carries a great distance across the water, leading to the unfortunate effect of frightening off prey.

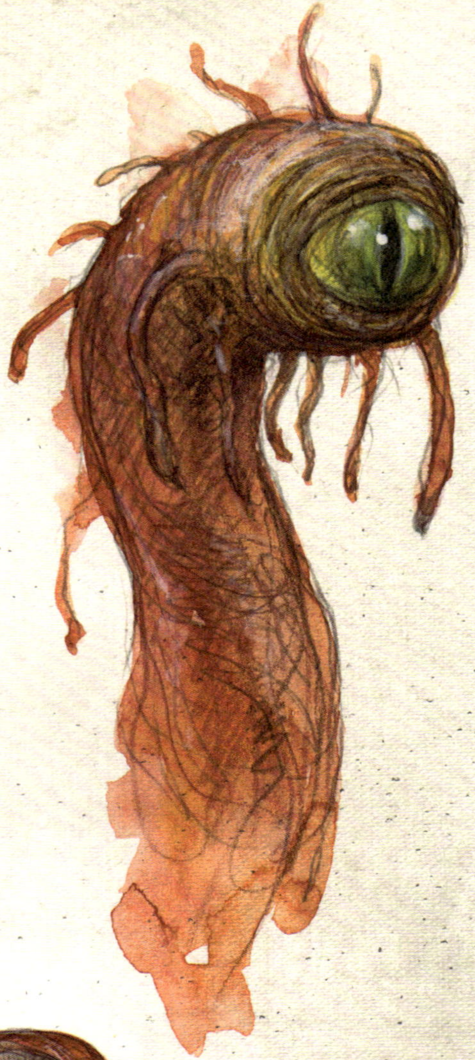

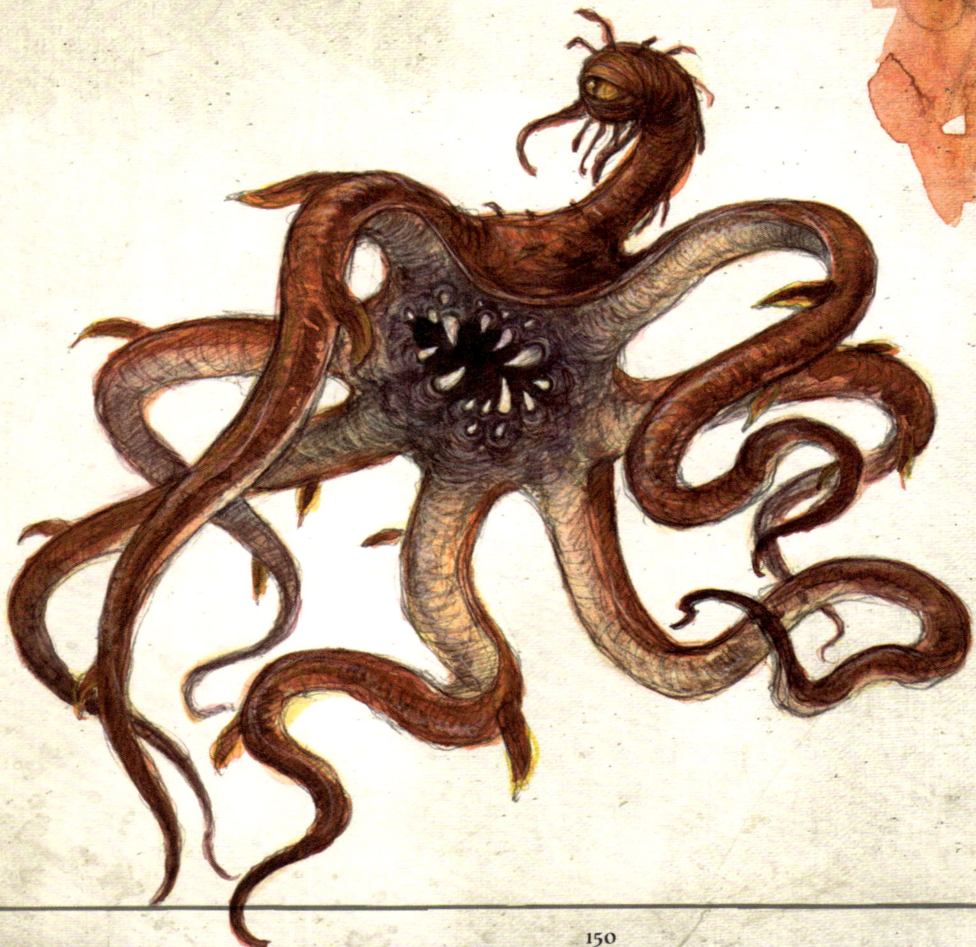

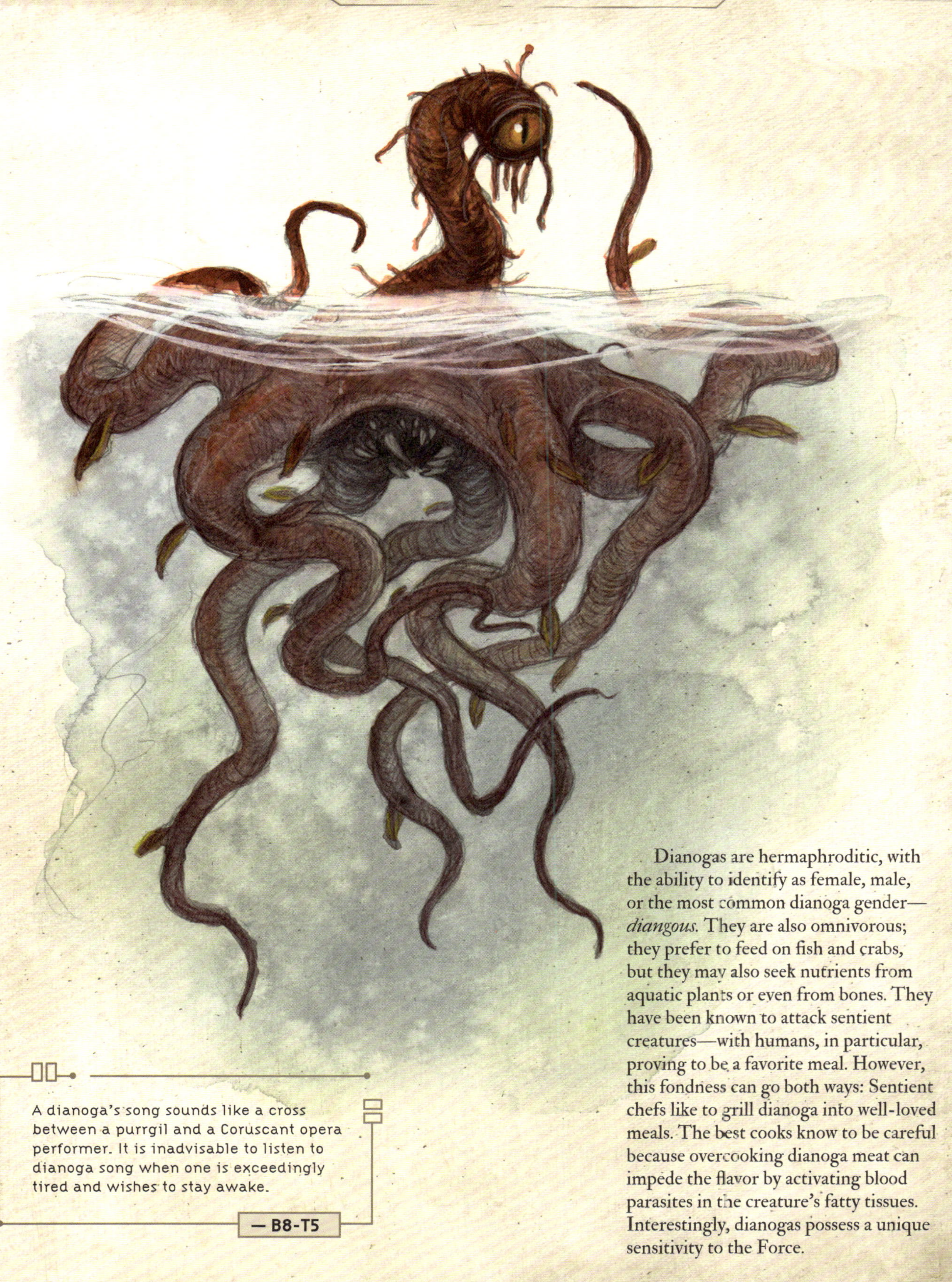

A dianoga's song sounds like a cross between a purrgil and a Coruscant opera performer. It is inadvisable to listen to dianoga song when one is exceedingly tired and wishes to stay awake.

— B8-T5

Dianogas are hermaphroditic, with the ability to identify as female, male, or the most common dianoga gender—*diangous.* They are also omnivorous; they prefer to feed on fish and crabs, but they may also seek nutrients from aquatic plants or even from bones. They have been known to attack sentient creatures—with humans, in particular, proving to be a favorite meal. However, this fondness can go both ways: Sentient chefs like to grill dianoga into well-loved meals. The best cooks know to be careful because overcooking dianoga meat can impede the flavor by activating blood parasites in the creature's fatty tissues. Interestingly, dianogas possess a unique sensitivity to the Force.

DRAGONSNAKE

These carnivorous reptiles live in swamps throughout the galaxy—from Nal Hutta to Dagobah. Although their appearances can vary, they generally measure approximately seven meters long and can weigh up to two hundred kilograms. They feed on a variety of aquatic and avian creatures, hiding beneath the muddy waters of their environment and holding themselves still until their prey draws near enough to attack. The dragonsnake then sinks its bladelike teeth into its victims before dragging them underwater for consumption. The creatures are feared throughout their natural habitats and are said to be both vicious hunters and untamable beasts.

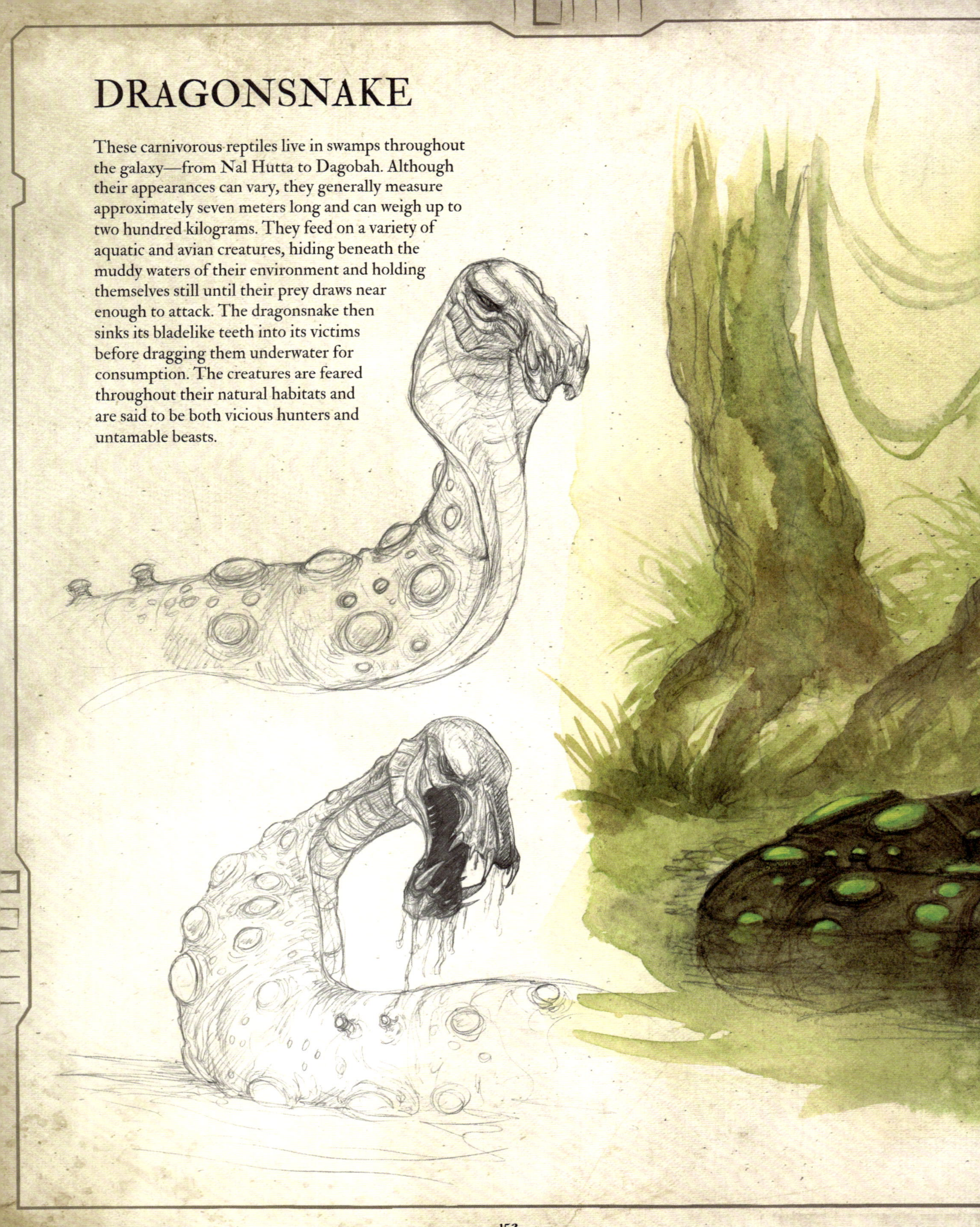

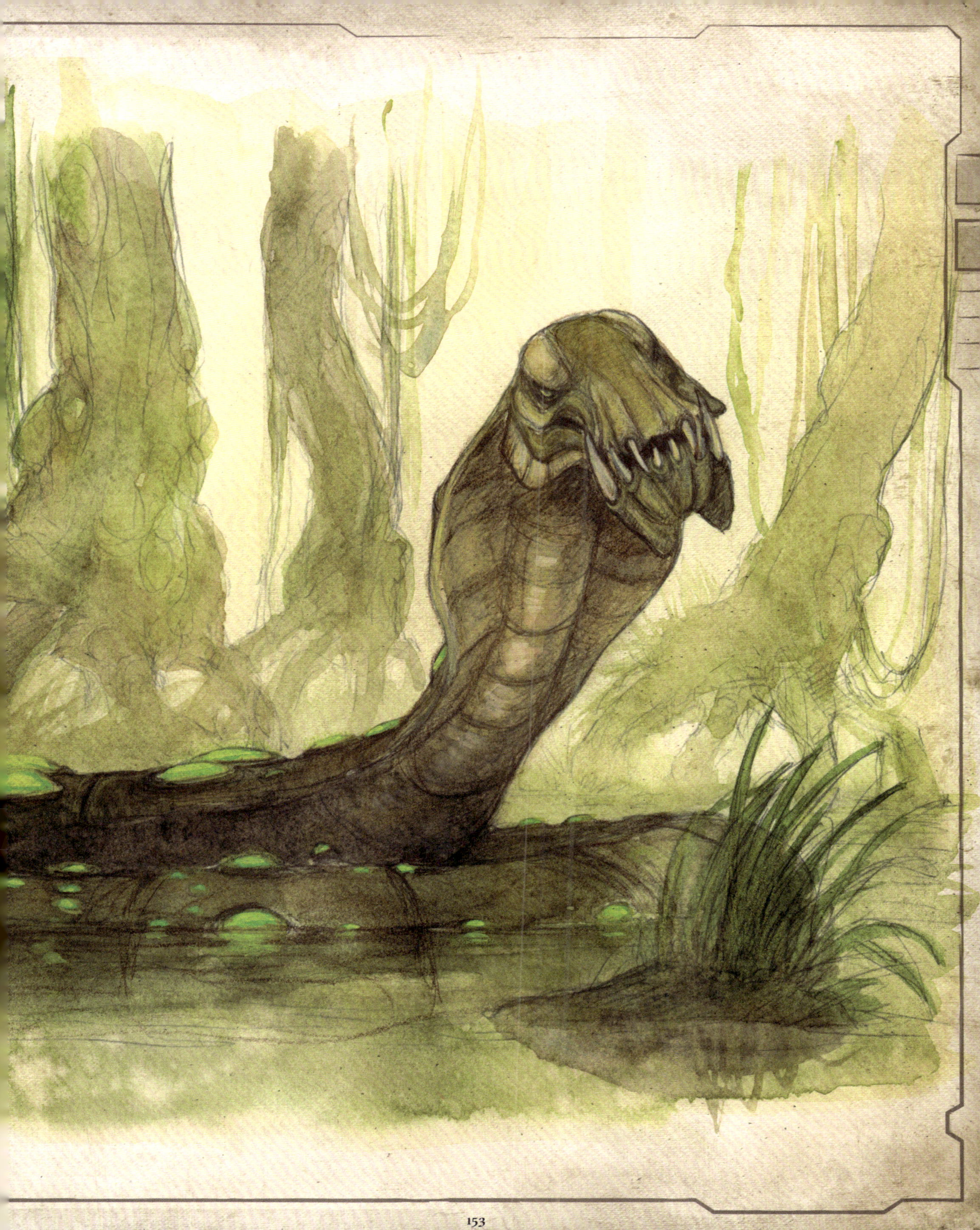

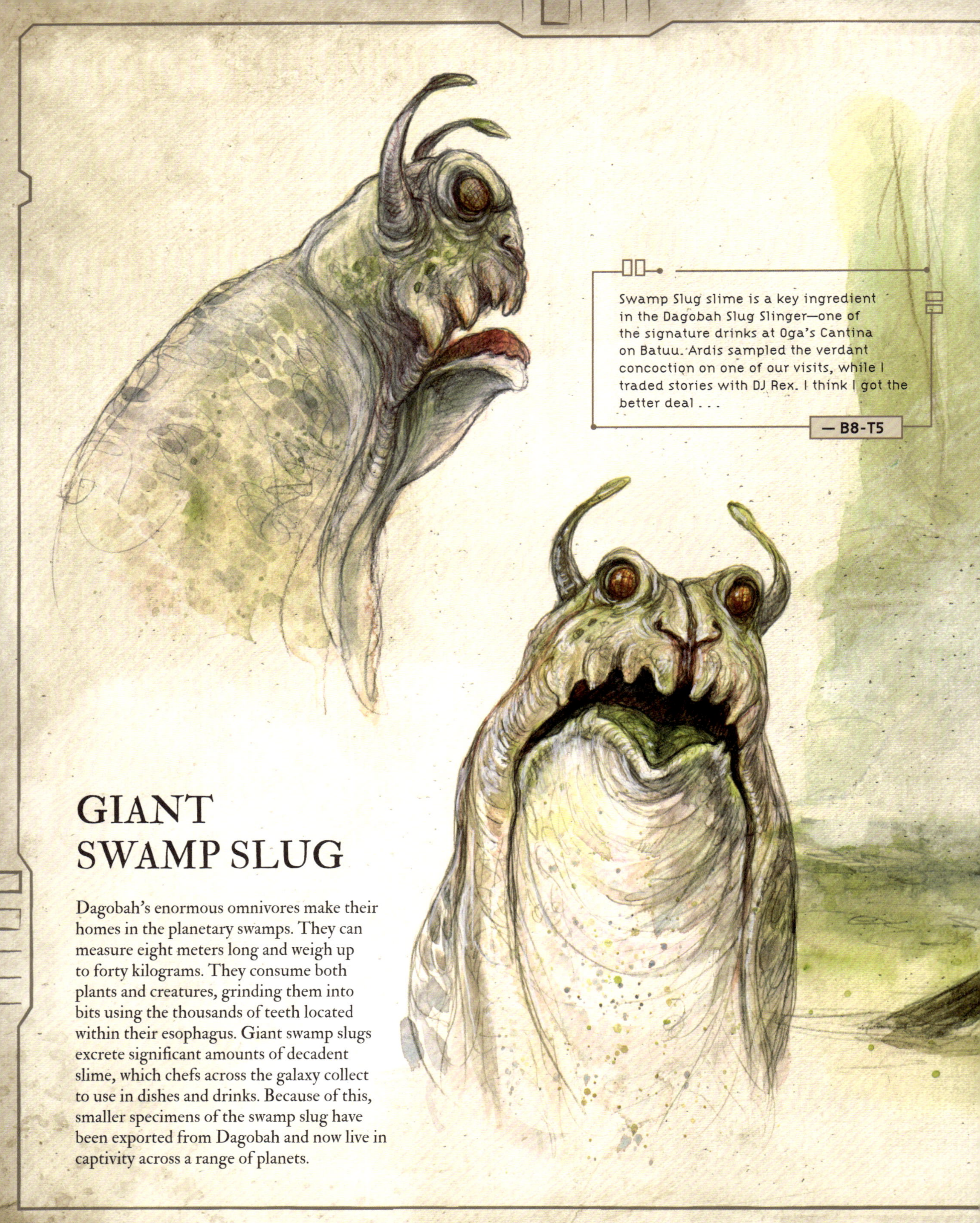

Swamp Slug slime is a key ingredient in the Dagobah Slug Slinger—one of the signature drinks at Oga's Cantina on Batuu. Ardis sampled the verdant concoction on one of our visits, while I traded stories with DJ Rex. I think I got the better deal . . .

— B8-T5

GIANT SWAMP SLUG

Dagobah's enormous omnivores make their homes in the planetary swamps. They can measure eight meters long and weigh up to forty kilograms. They consume both plants and creatures, grinding them into bits using the thousands of teeth located within their esophagus. Giant swamp slugs excrete significant amounts of decadent slime, which chefs across the galaxy collect to use in dishes and drinks. Because of this, smaller specimens of the swamp slug have been exported from Dagobah and now live in captivity across a range of planets.

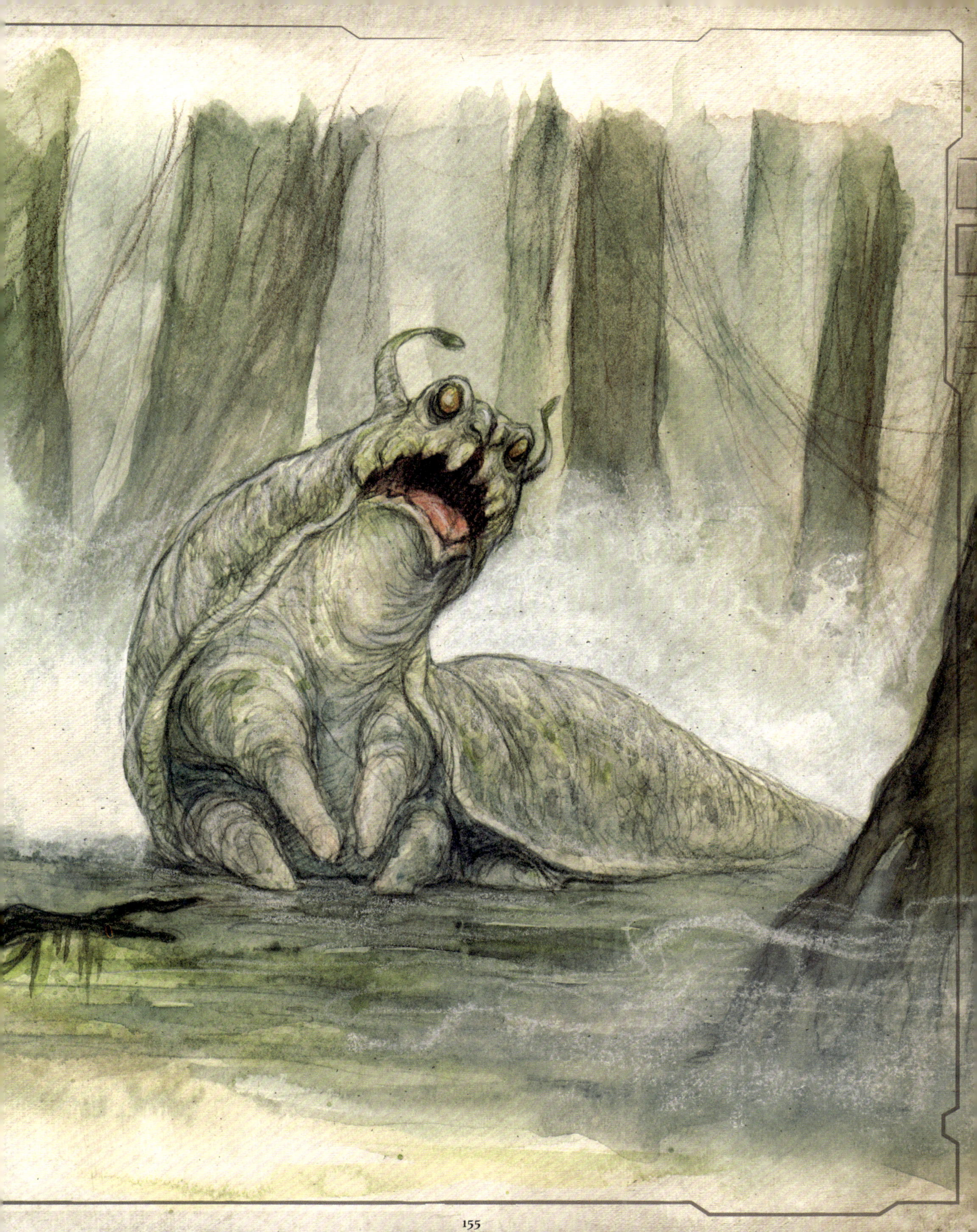

HRUMPH

Naboo's broad-backed herbivores stand about three to four meters at their shoulders and can weigh more than thirty kilograms. Their lightly tanned skin is interrupted by a smattering of purple dots across their stomach, increasing in concentration as they make their way toward the spine. There, these dots morph into a series of cartilaginous indigo spikes. Hrumphs have four long horns and highly sensitive ears, which they use to scout for and evade predators.

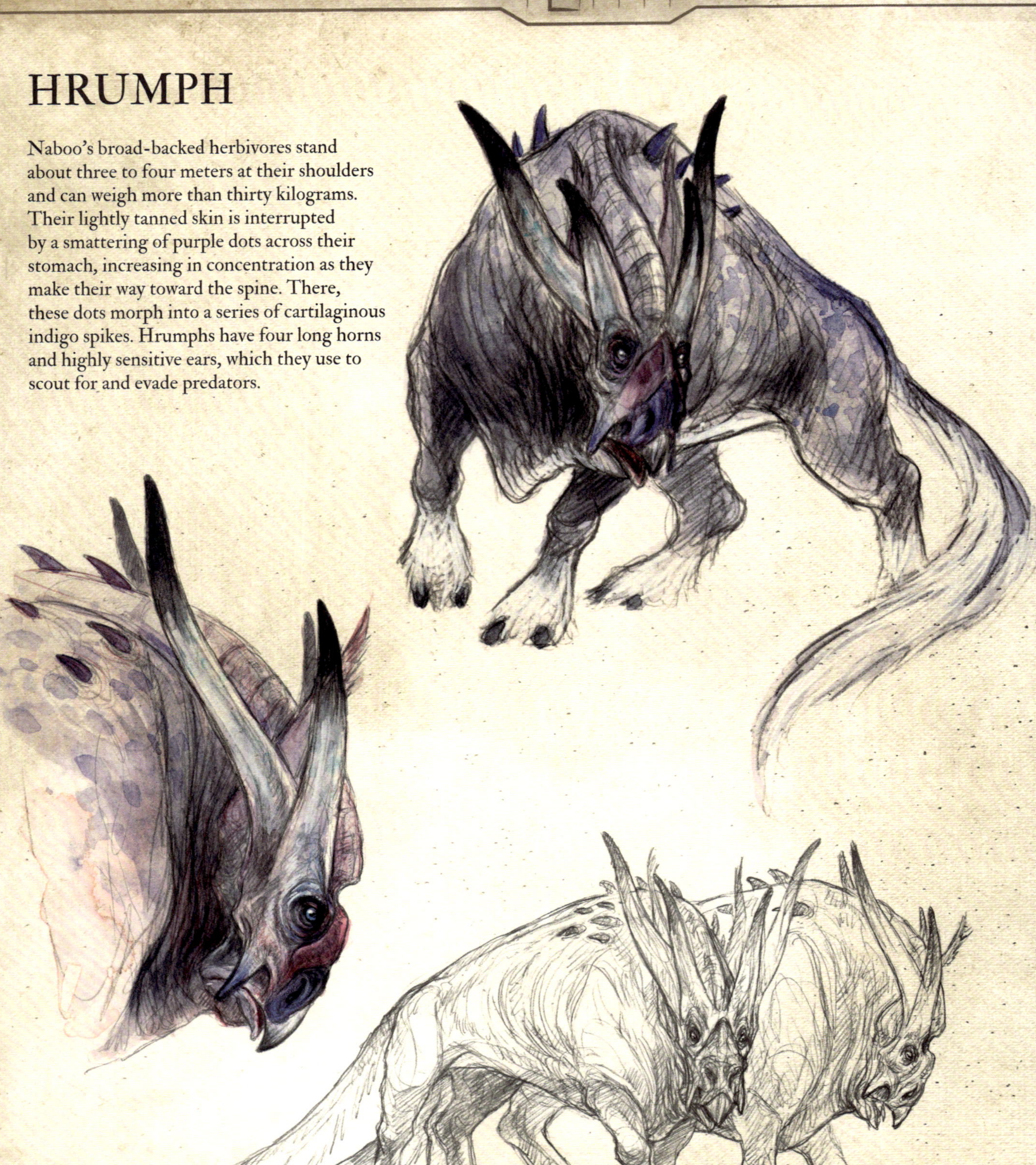

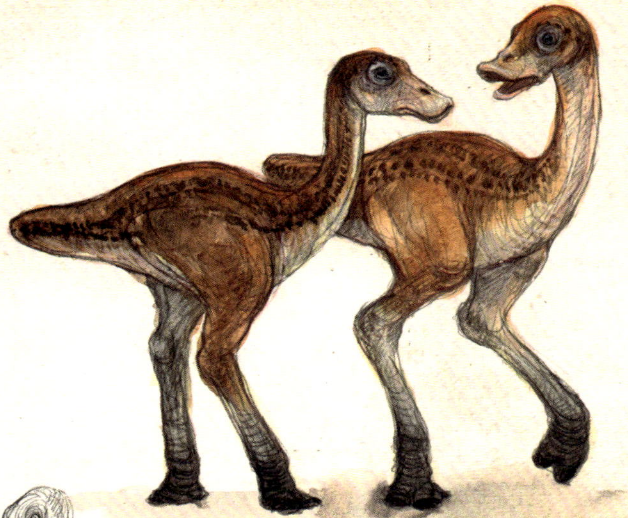

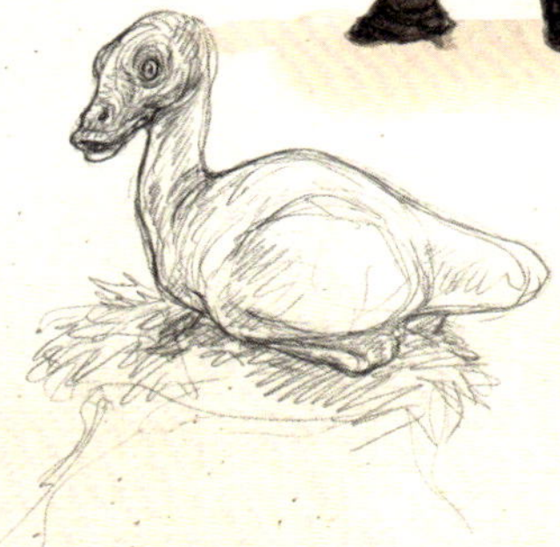

KAADU

Naboo's native reptavians stand more than two meters tall and weigh approximately thirty-five kilograms. They make their homes in the Gungan swamps, where their long legs help them traverse their ecosystem. Although they live mostly on land, kaadu are also capable of breathing underwater, a trait that enables them to hunt for aquatic food sources when land-dwelling prey is scarce.

Kaadu have a strong sense of smell and excellent hearing, both features that help them avoid predation. They live in flocks comprised exclusively of either males *or* females, with numbers topping out at 100 members. Mothers lay anywhere from six to eight eggs in one reproductive cycle.

The creatures' significant strength and impressive endurance make them excellent mounts for the Gungans, who decorate their kaadu with feathers and employ them as patrol beasts. They are also raised as livestock, with smoked kaadu ribs among the more popular dishes at restaurants across the galaxy—including Black Spire Outpost's Docking Bay 7.

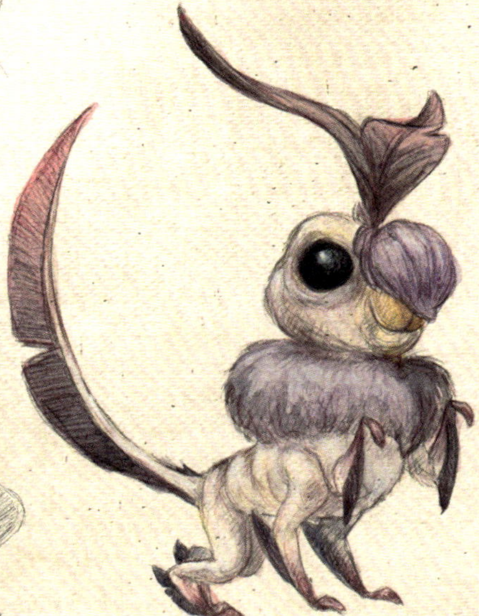

KIBBIN

The purple-and-gray kibbins are native to the planet Tenoo. Their large black eyes enable them to see at great distances, and four lithe legs help them run at speeds of up to twenty kilometers per hour. Kibbins make popular house pets because of their small size, soft fur, and fondness for being carried. They feed on channelfish and eagerly lap up other treats doled out by their owners. Their curious nature makes them a favorite among children, who enjoy playing catch and cuddling up with the easygoing creatures.

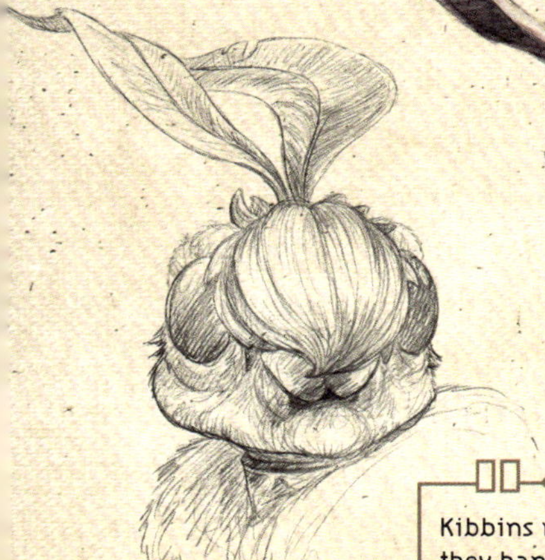

Kibbins really love feathers. If they happen to spot you with one the kibbin will chase you all the way back to your ship.

— B8-T5

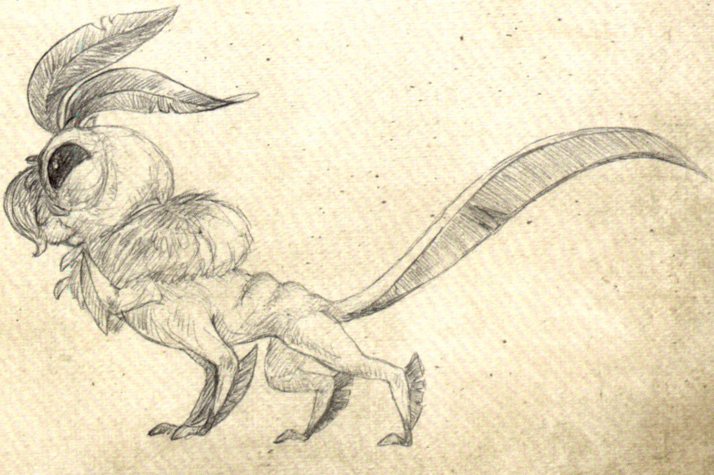

KWAZEL MAW

These large aquatic slugs make their homes in the swamps of Rodia, although they are also capable of living on land. Their torsos have a series of appendages that they use (along with their huge tails) to maneuver along their swampy environment. Wide, elongated bodies are covered in a dense, resilient skin—which is more than capable of deflecting blaster bolts! The kwazel maw also displays a layer of bioluminescence, helping the creatures to see within the muddied swamps. The maws are highly predatory—their mouths can open wide enough to consume a fully grown humanoid!

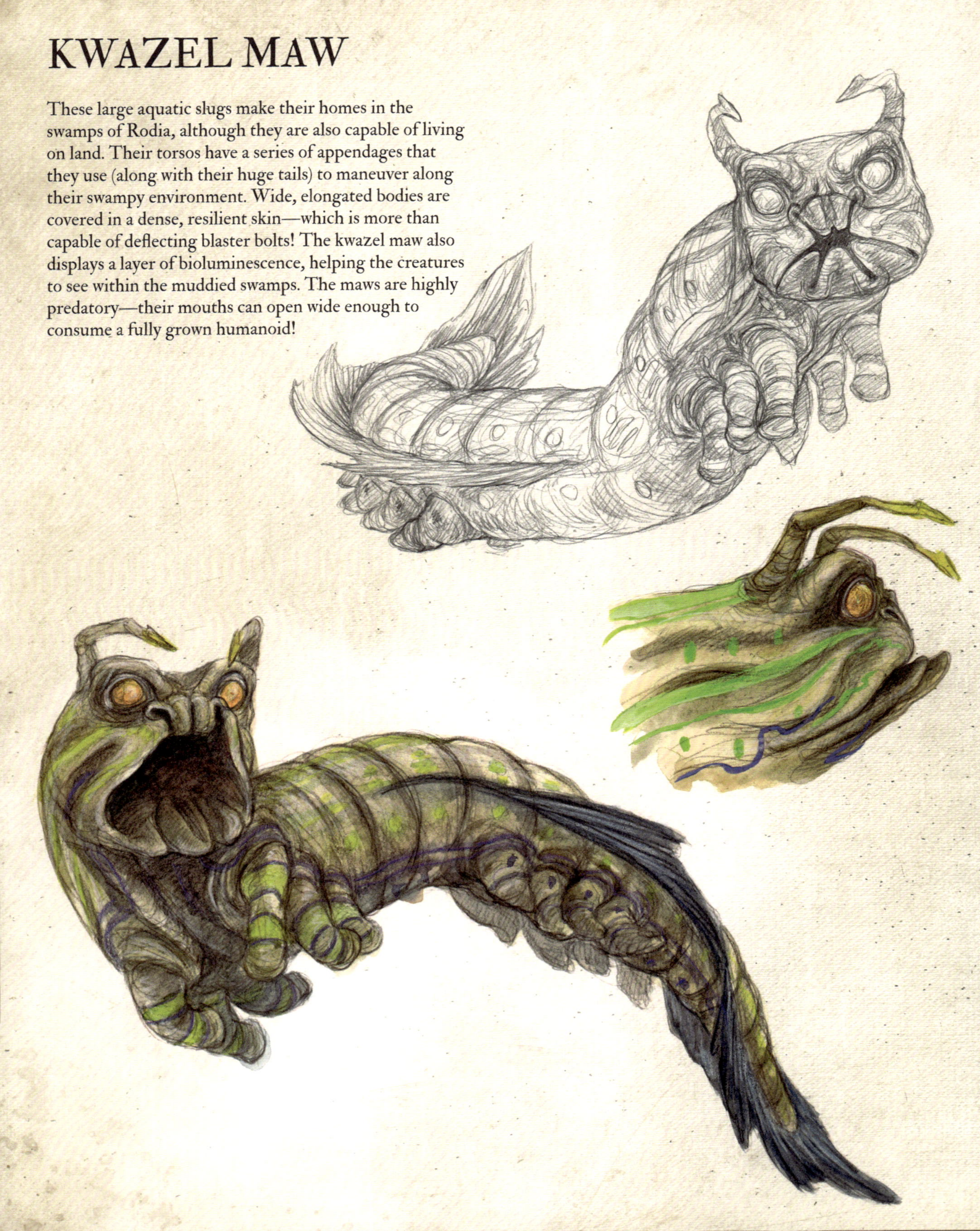

MOTT

Naboo's native herbivores make their home among the planet's swamps. They use their broad snouts and wide facial horn to root in the mud, digging up vegetation that they then gnaw with wide, flat teeth. Motts stand approximately 1.1 meters at the shoulders and weigh in at roughly 100 kilograms. They are known for fits of aggression, and they use their horns to resolve mating disputes and defend against attack. Females bear large litters, with an average of fifteen young produced in a single breeding cycle.

Mott calves are frequently hungry and spend more than half of their time eating. I estimate that young motts consume approximately thirty liters of milk each day.

— B8-T5

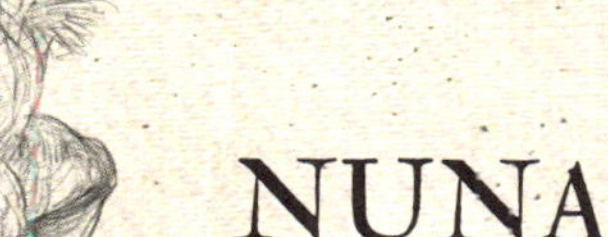

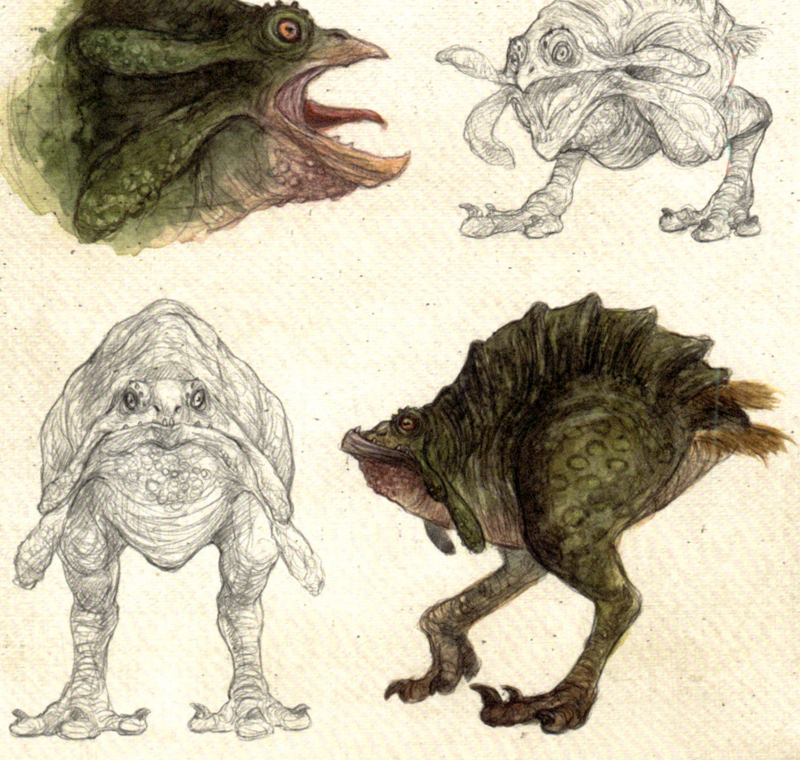

NUNA

These bipedal avians live in Naboo's swamps, where they feed on plants and fish. They stand approximately seventy-five meters tall and weigh just under four kilograms. The average creature provides enough meat to feed a family of four human-size sentients. These "swamp turkeys" are generally considered to be a rather unintelligent species. However, their adaptable nature, minimal care requirements, and rapid production of eggs make them a popular livestock animal. When agitated, nunas inflate to nearly twice their size. Although they are normally green in hue, they are also able to grow blue and red feathers—despite not being able to fly. They are perhaps best known for becoming a variety of food products, from nuna turkey jerky to roast nuna.

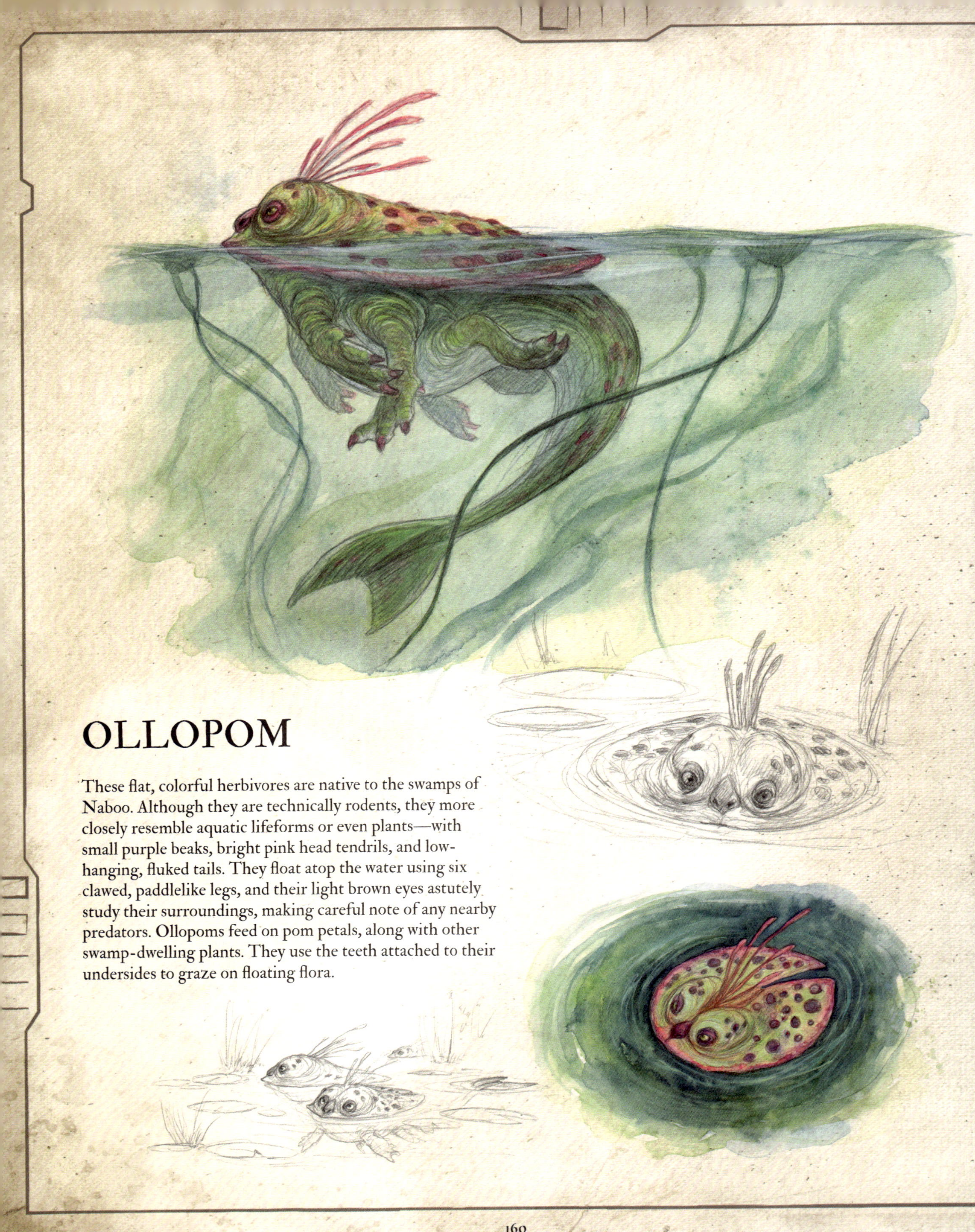

OLLOPOM

These flat, colorful herbivores are native to the swamps of Naboo. Although they are technically rodents, they more closely resemble aquatic lifeforms or even plants—with small purple beaks, bright pink head tendrils, and low-hanging, fluked tails. They float atop the water using six clawed, paddlelike legs, and their light brown eyes astutely study their surroundings, making careful note of any nearby predators. Ollopoms feed on pom petals, along with other swamp-dwelling plants. They use the teeth attached to their undersides to graze on floating flora.

PEKO-PEKO

Naboo's elegant avians have brilliant blue plumage and a long, feathered tail. Their wings end in sharp claws, and they use their upturned beaks to peel fruits and pry nuts from their shells. They live in flocks, with pairs mating for life and producing up to two chicks in any given breeding cycle. Considered the birds of royalty, a peko-peko appears in a painting with the late Queen Padmé Amidala—a work of art that remains in a place of prominence within the Theed Royal Palace.

Not only can pikobis walk and swim immediately after hatching, but they can do both of those things **really fast**. Given that, it is inadvisable to attempt to record a pikobi birth at close range.

— B8-T5

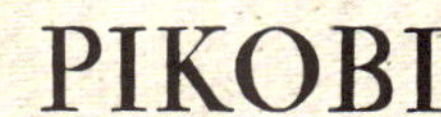

PIKOBI

These carnivorous reptavians originated on Naboo, although they have since migrated to Coruscant, Lothal, Onderon, and Dagobah. They possess above-average intelligence and are able to both walk and swim immediately after hatching. These quick-moving creatures travel in packs of up to six members, and they feed on smaller creatures. When attacked, they can shed their tails, which regenerate in due time. Occasionally, a forked appendage is produced in place of the original—an adaptation that often results in the creature developing an enhanced sense of balance!

RATHTAR

Another sizable cephalopod, the rathtar measures up to 1.74 meters in height and 6.09 meters long (including its tentacles). It weighs a whopping six hundred fifty kilograms, with the bulk of this weight situated in its bulbous midsection. With its blood-red skin and a series of orange, boil-like sensor orbs resting atop its back, the rathtar communicates its dangerous nature in every way it knows how. The creature's wide, circular maw is ringed with rows of sharp teeth, and its many tentacles are primed with suckers to cling to prey. Wide, paddlelike appendages grow from the ends of the creature's two frontmost tentacles. Although they possess a plethora of optical spheres, their eyesight is extremely poor—in fact, the creatures are nearly blind!

The primary species of rathtar is native to the planet Twon Ketee. However, the subspecies known as the dwarf rathtar calls Trillia home. The carnivorous creatures live in groups called remorses. They hunt throughout the planet's swamps, reaching out to grasp a victim and then drag it into its massive maw.

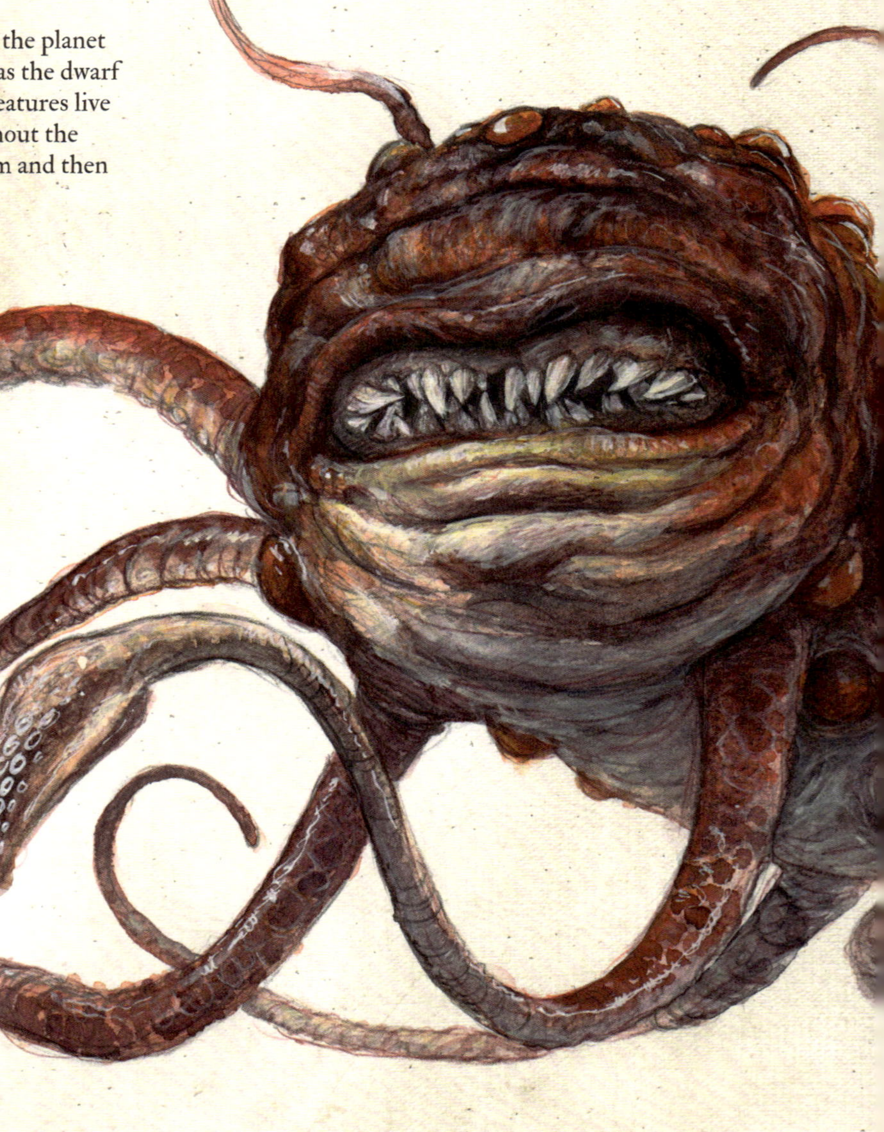

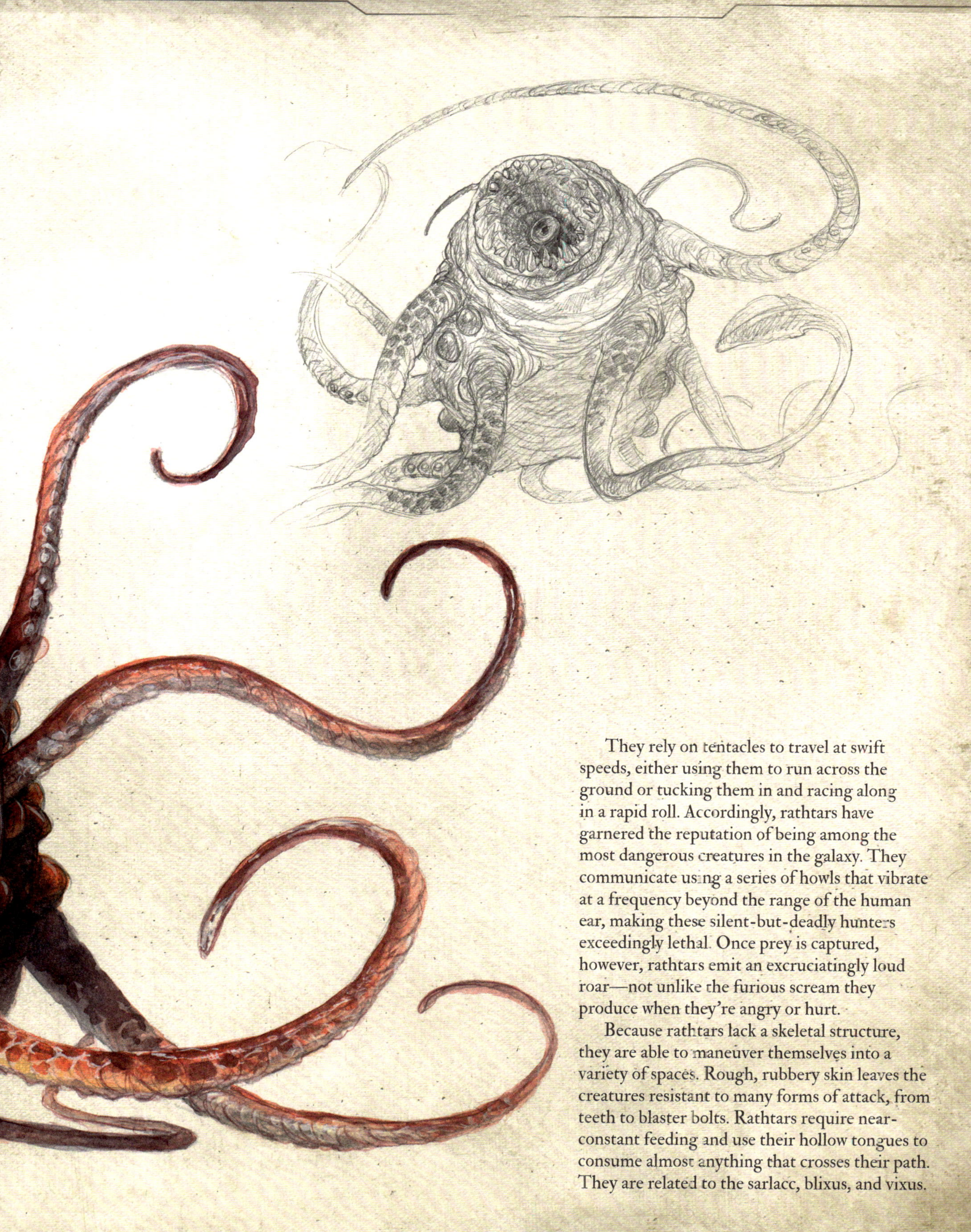

They rely on tentacles to travel at swift speeds, either using them to run across the ground or tucking them in and racing along in a rapid roll. Accordingly, rathtars have garnered the reputation of being among the most dangerous creatures in the galaxy. They communicate using a series of howls that vibrate at a frequency beyond the range of the human ear, making these silent-but-deadly hunters exceedingly lethal. Once prey is captured, however, rathtars emit an excruciatingly loud roar—not unlike the furious scream they produce when they're angry or hurt.

Because rathtars lack a skeletal structure, they are able to maneuver themselves into a variety of spaces. Rough, rubbery skin leaves the creatures resistant to many forms of attack, from teeth to blaster bolts. Rathtars require near-constant feeding and use their hollow tongues to consume almost anything that crosses their path. They are related to the sarlacc, blixus, and vixus.

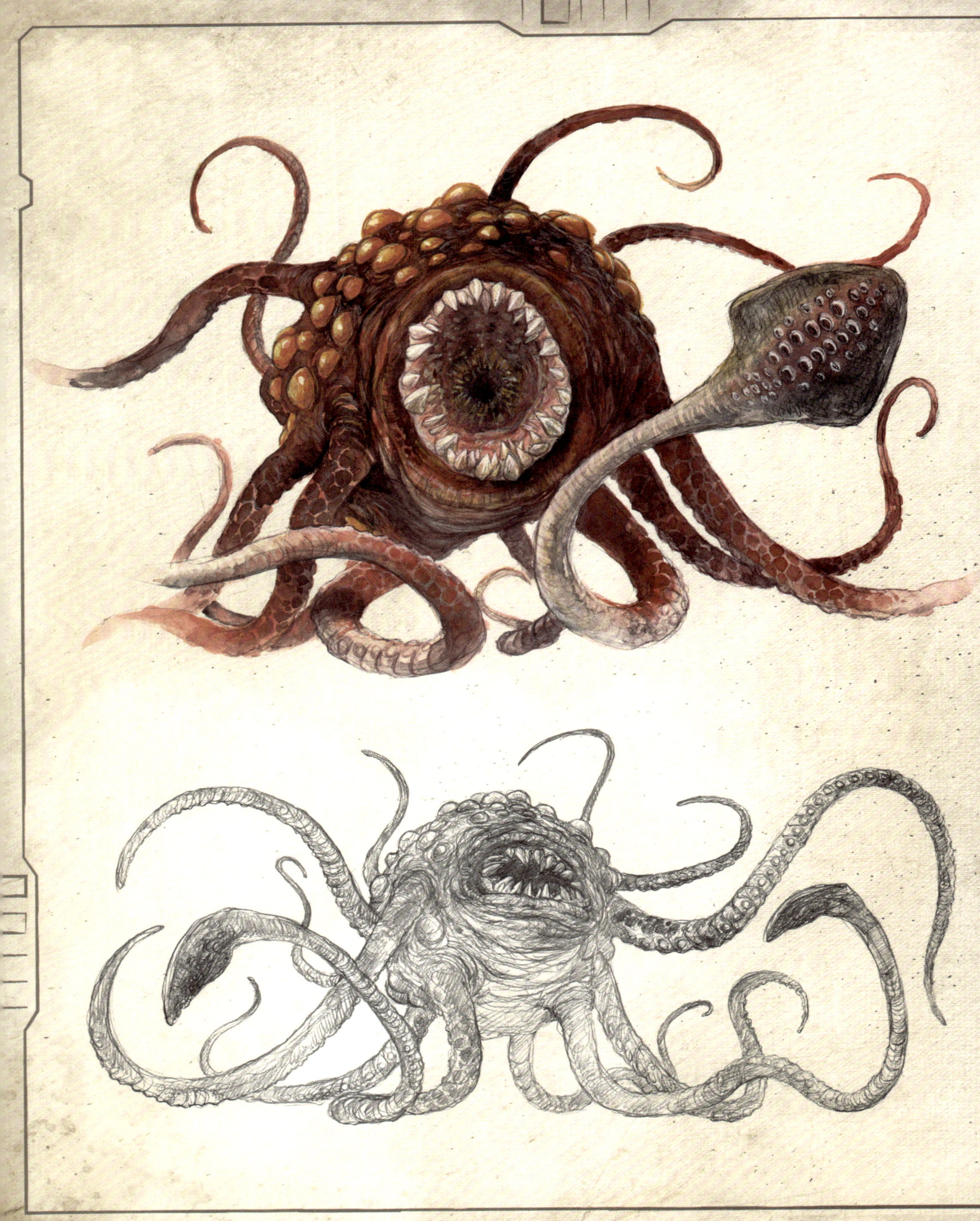

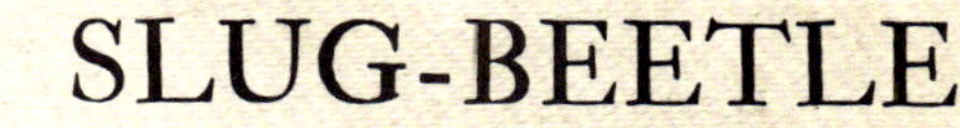

SLUG-BEETLE

These winged blue beetles are native to both Tatooine and Naboo. On the swampy planet, they make their homes in the roots of Naboo's perlote tree, which grows only in the eastern regions. These insects make for a popular snack, with Gungans preferring to consume the creatures in one bite.

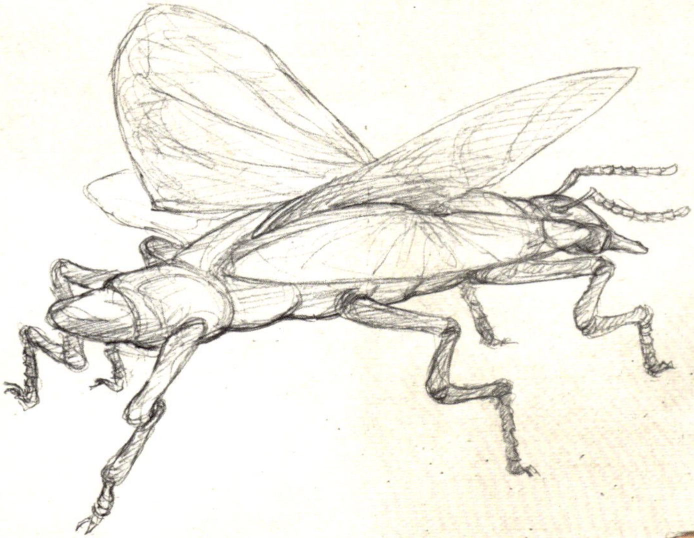

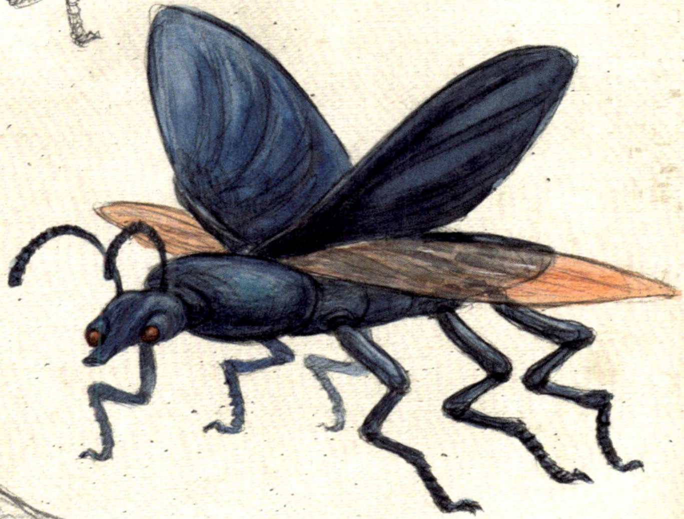

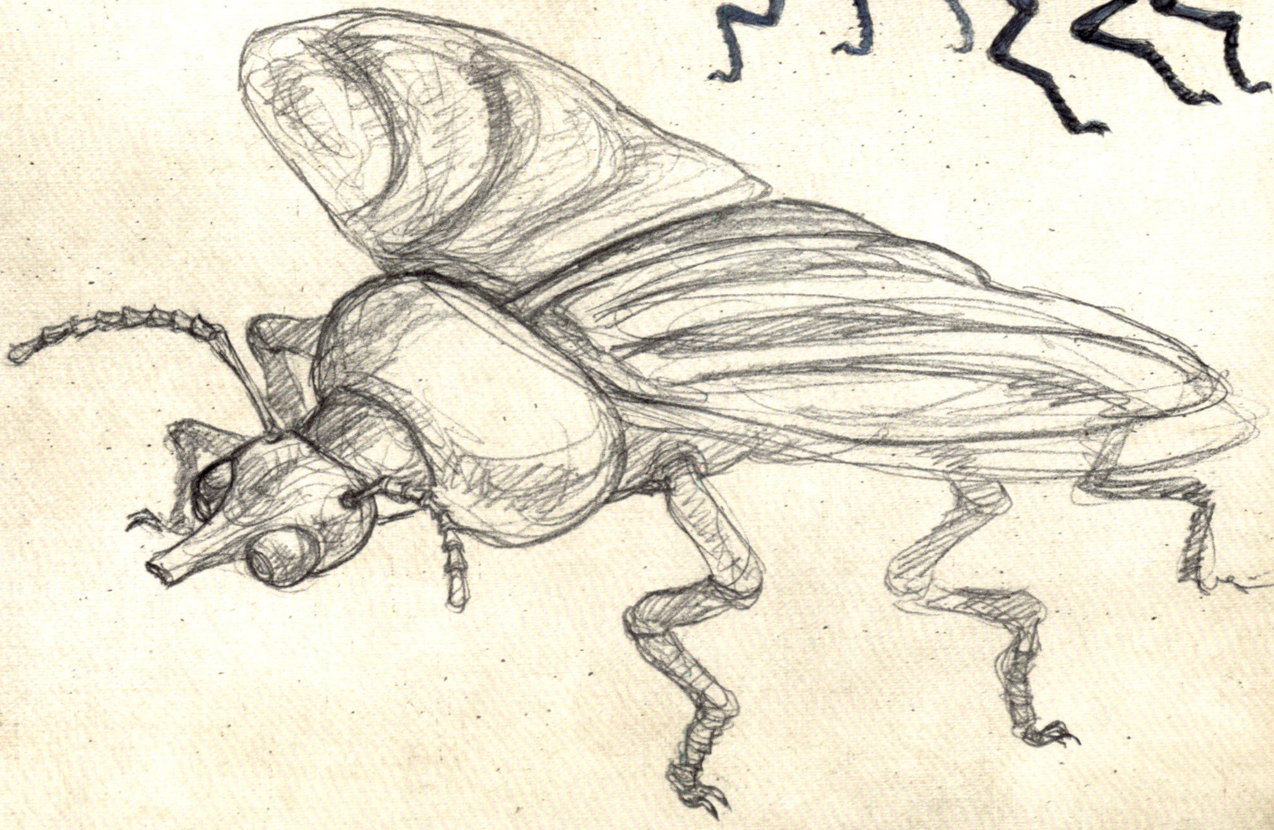

SUBTERRANEAN CREATURES

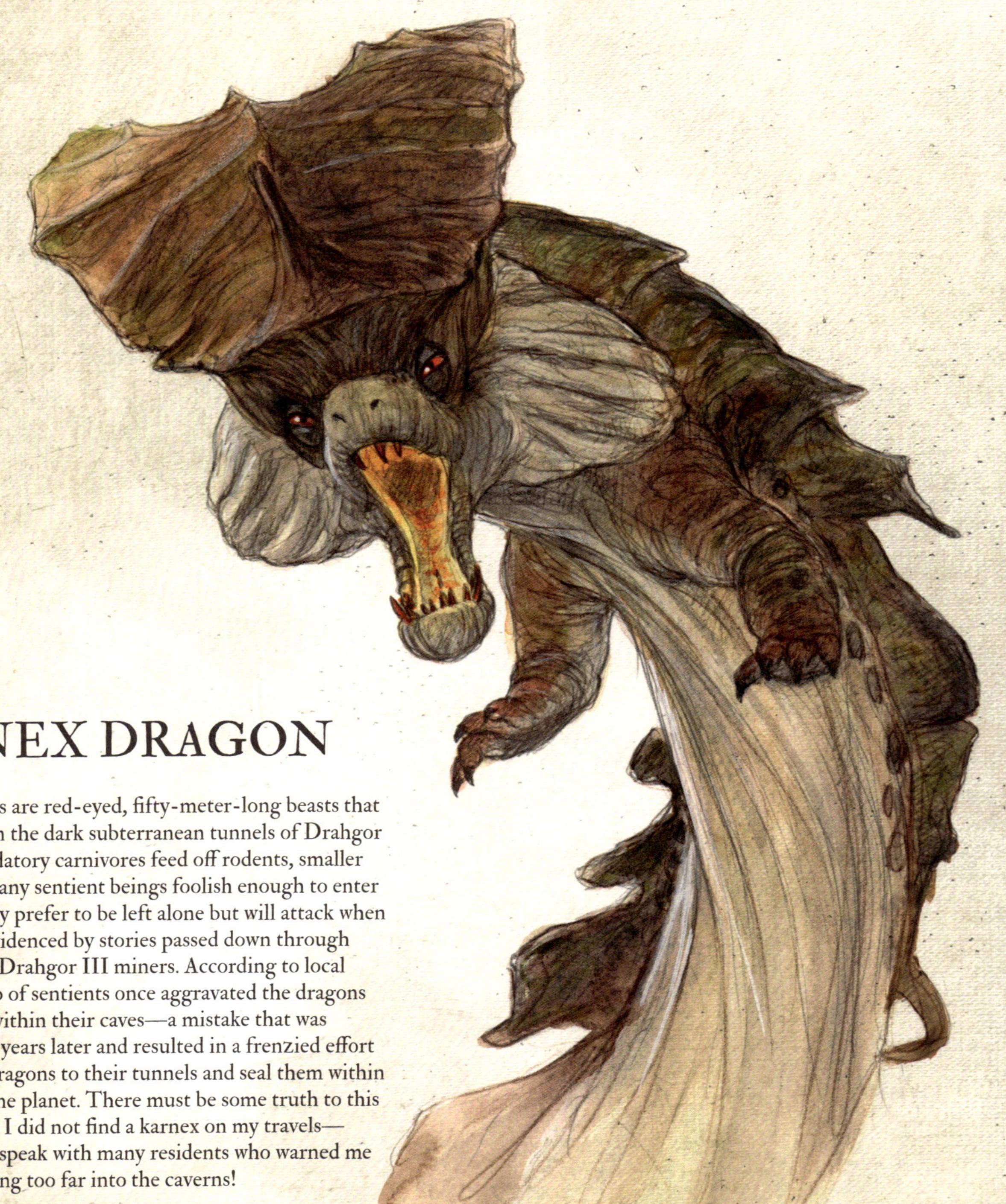

KARNEX DRAGON

Karnex dragons are red-eyed, fifty-meter-long beasts that live deep within the dark subterranean tunnels of Drahgor III. These predatory carnivores feed off rodents, smaller mammals, and any sentient beings foolish enough to enter their lairs. They prefer to be left alone but will attack when provoked, as evidenced by stories passed down through generations of Drahgor III miners. According to local legend, a group of sentients once aggravated the dragons while drilling within their caves—a mistake that was repeated many years later and resulted in a frenzied effort to return the dragons to their tunnels and seal them within the depths of the planet. There must be some truth to this legend because I did not find a karnex on my travels—although I did speak with many residents who warned me against venturing too far into the caverns!

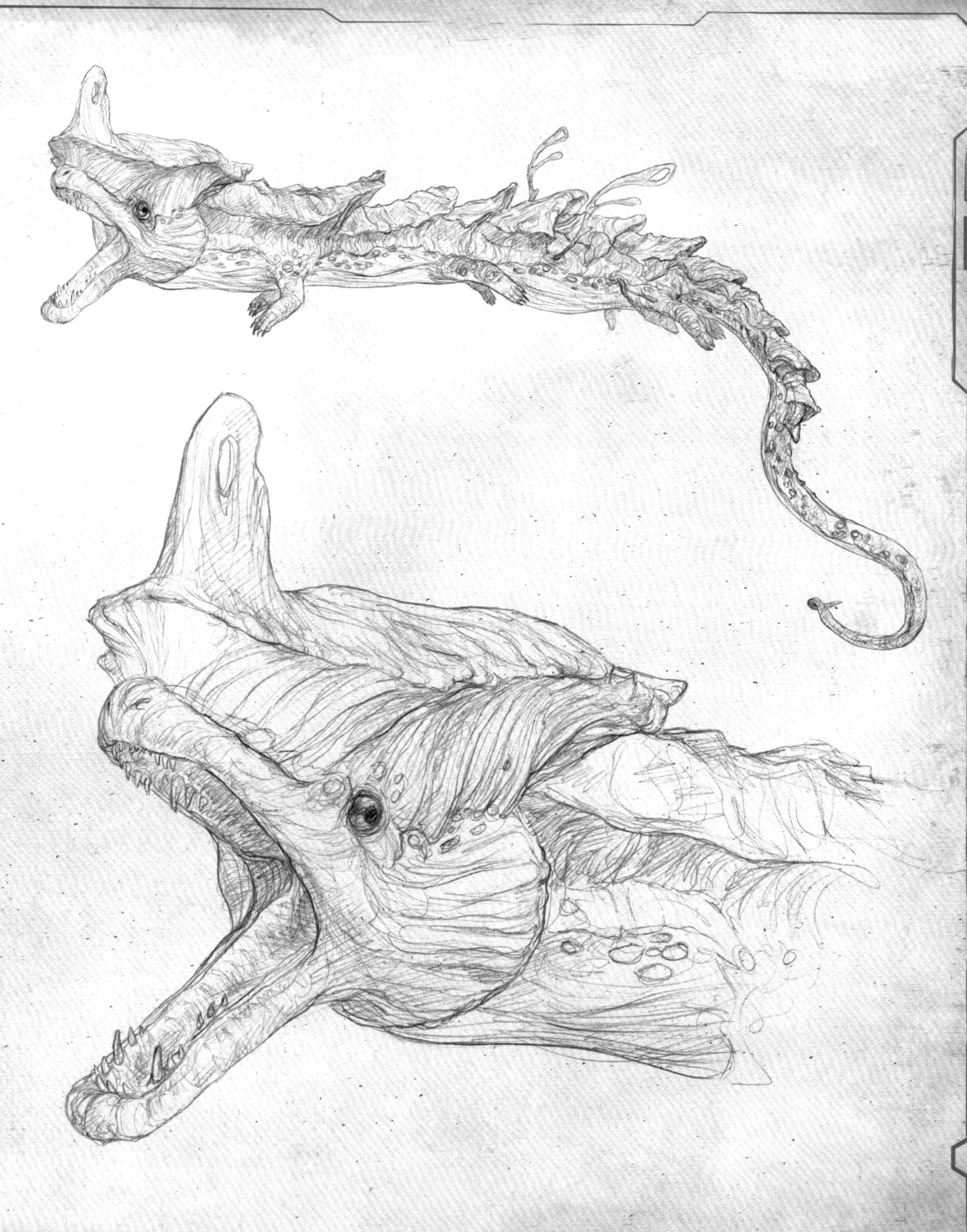

MYTHOSAUR

These massive, not-so-mythical creatures are said to have once ruled Mandalore. According to legend, the mythosaurs were tamed by Mandalore the Great and were ridden by ancient Mandalorians. To commemorate this feat, the Mandalorians adopted the creature's skull as the symbol of their civilization. Today many clans place the signet in prominent places within their dwellings and atop their armor. Following the rise of the planet's sentient beings, the mythosaurs ceded their position as Mandalore's apex predator.

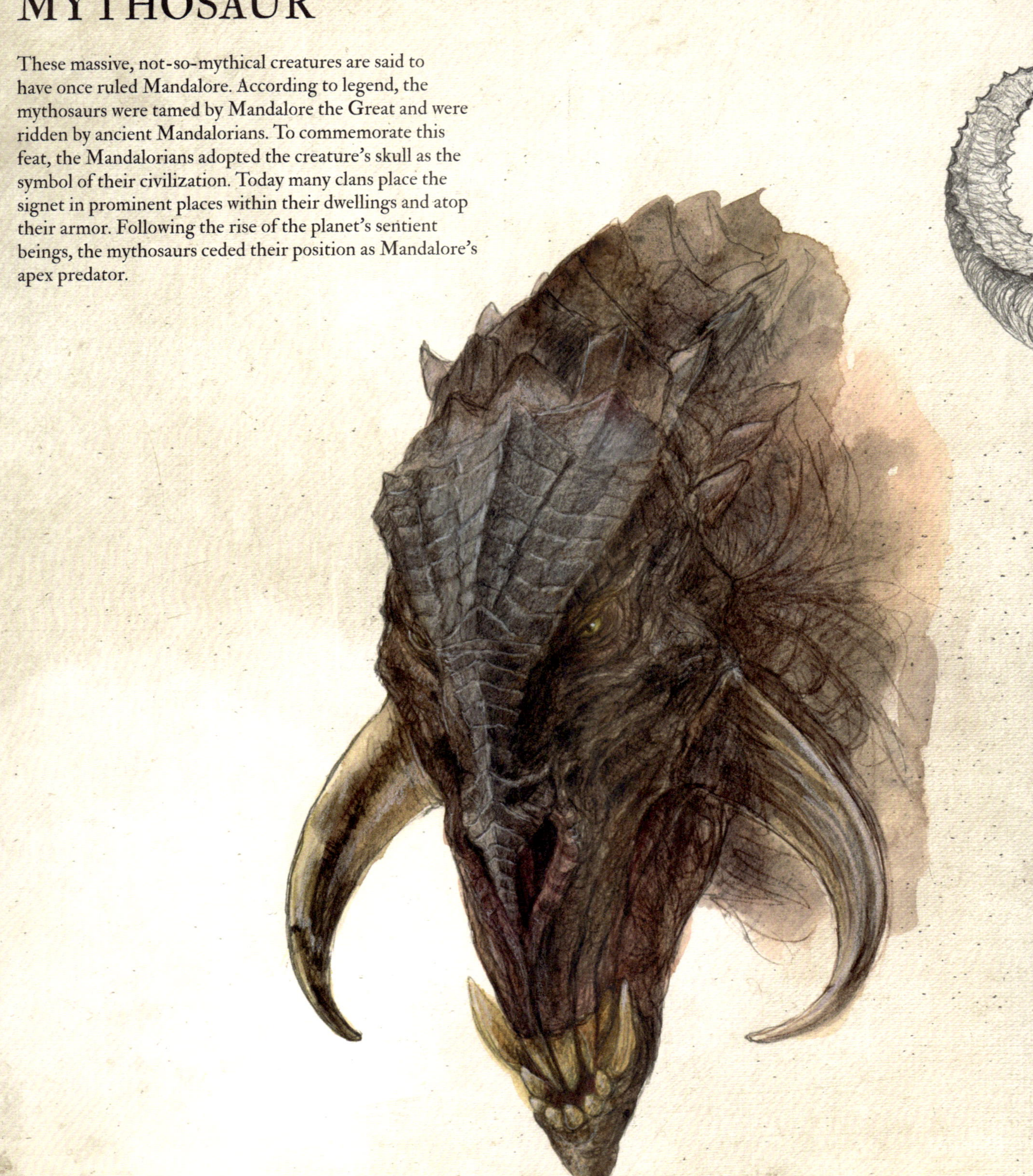

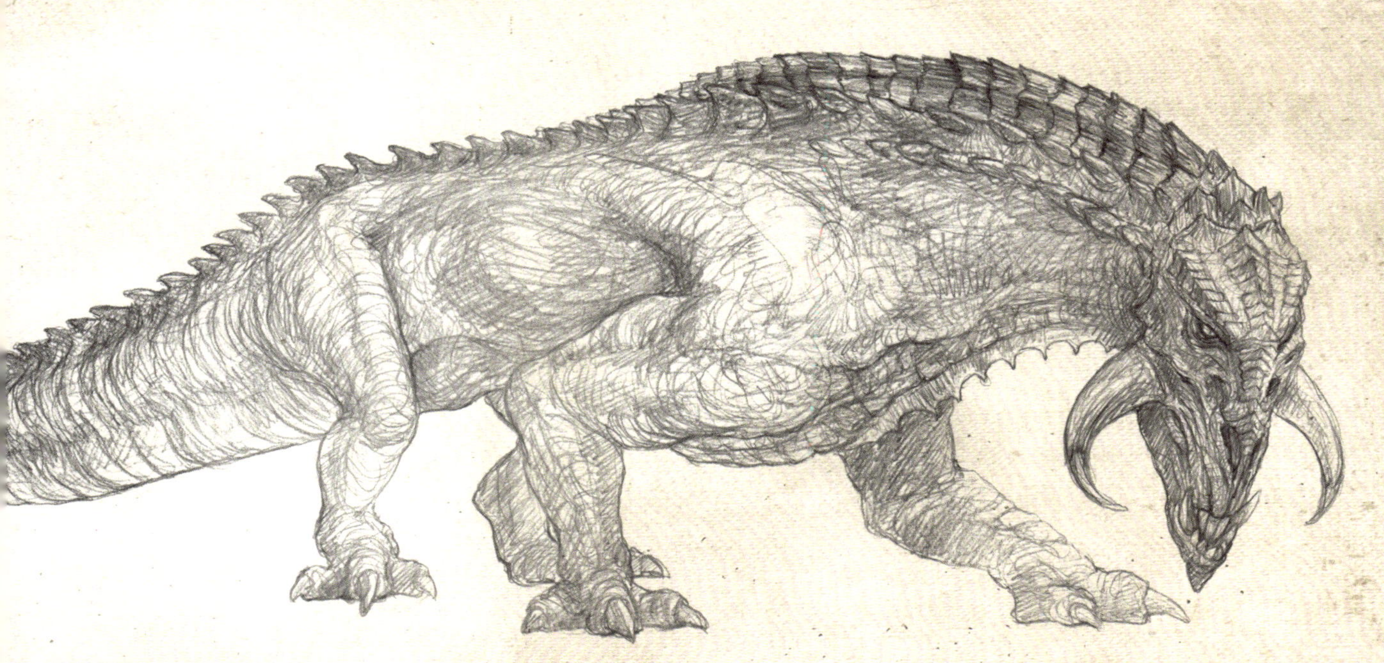

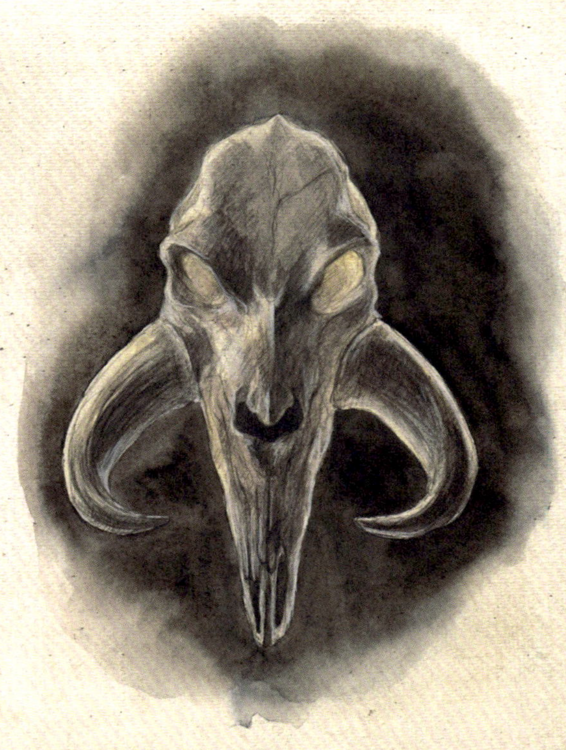

Mythosaurs have twin tusks and elongated faces, and their exact specifications remain unknown. These beasts have scaly yellow skin and black eyes. They are capable of residing on land as well as within the Living Waters of Mandalore, although they are believed to be more comfortable in their aquatic environment. They use their tusks to hunt, fight, and forage for food, with their meals ranging from fauna to large fish, to crustaceans. Mythosaurs were long believed to be extinct, but at least one member of the species survived the destruction of its homeworld: Its existence was reported by the Mandalorian warrior Lady Bo-Katan Kryze in the Mines of Mandalore. Mandalorians believe that mythosaurs will one day rise up to usher in a new age for their people.

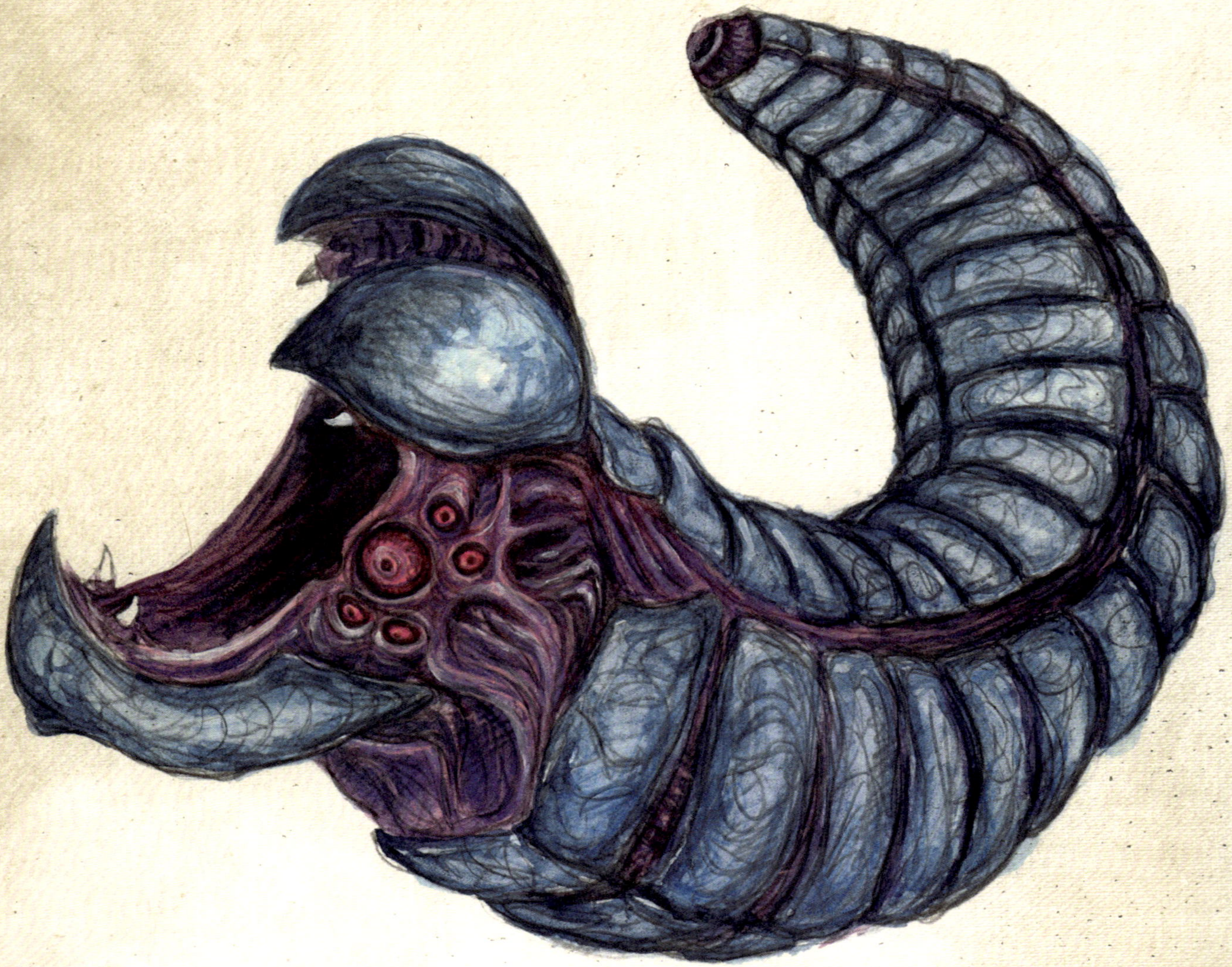

RISHI EEL

These elongated predators make their homes on the Rishi Moon. Their blue-and-green skin provides camouflage, and sharp mandibles and carnivorous palates make them deadly adversaries. Rishi eels are capable of slaughtering—and consuming—a fully grown human. They live in tunnels beneath the surface of the moon and are known to bleed blue blood.

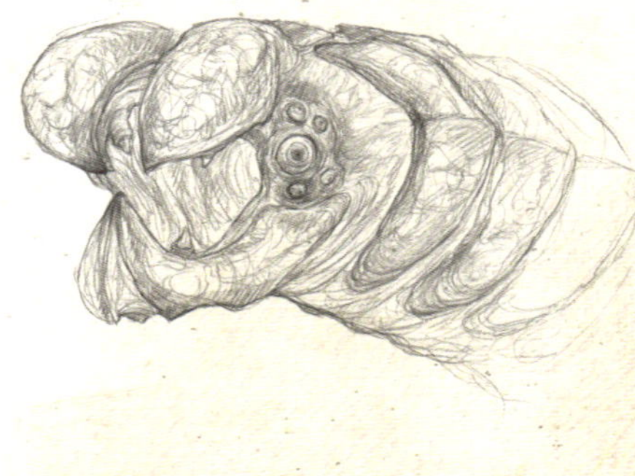

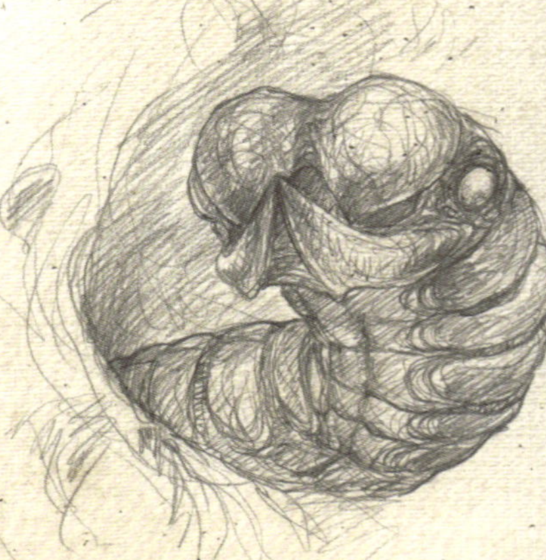

VARACTYL

With their elegant back feathers and green-and-blue crests, varactyls are absolutely breathtaking beasts. Utapau's reptavian herbivores stand four meters at the shoulders and can measure up to fifteen meters in length. Their long, muscular bodies have been reported to weigh up to 1,150 kilograms. The creatures are known for their loyalty, and their willingness to obey their riders has made them a popular mount. They possess above-average intelligence, and they can easily navigate the perilous cliffs and crevices of their homeworld with their lithe limbs and wide wingspans.

The Pijal varactyl, a subspecies of the creature, was imported by the Iltan clan and bred to be more aerodynamic than its counterparts. These creatures are easily identifiable by their brilliant plumage of crimson feathers.

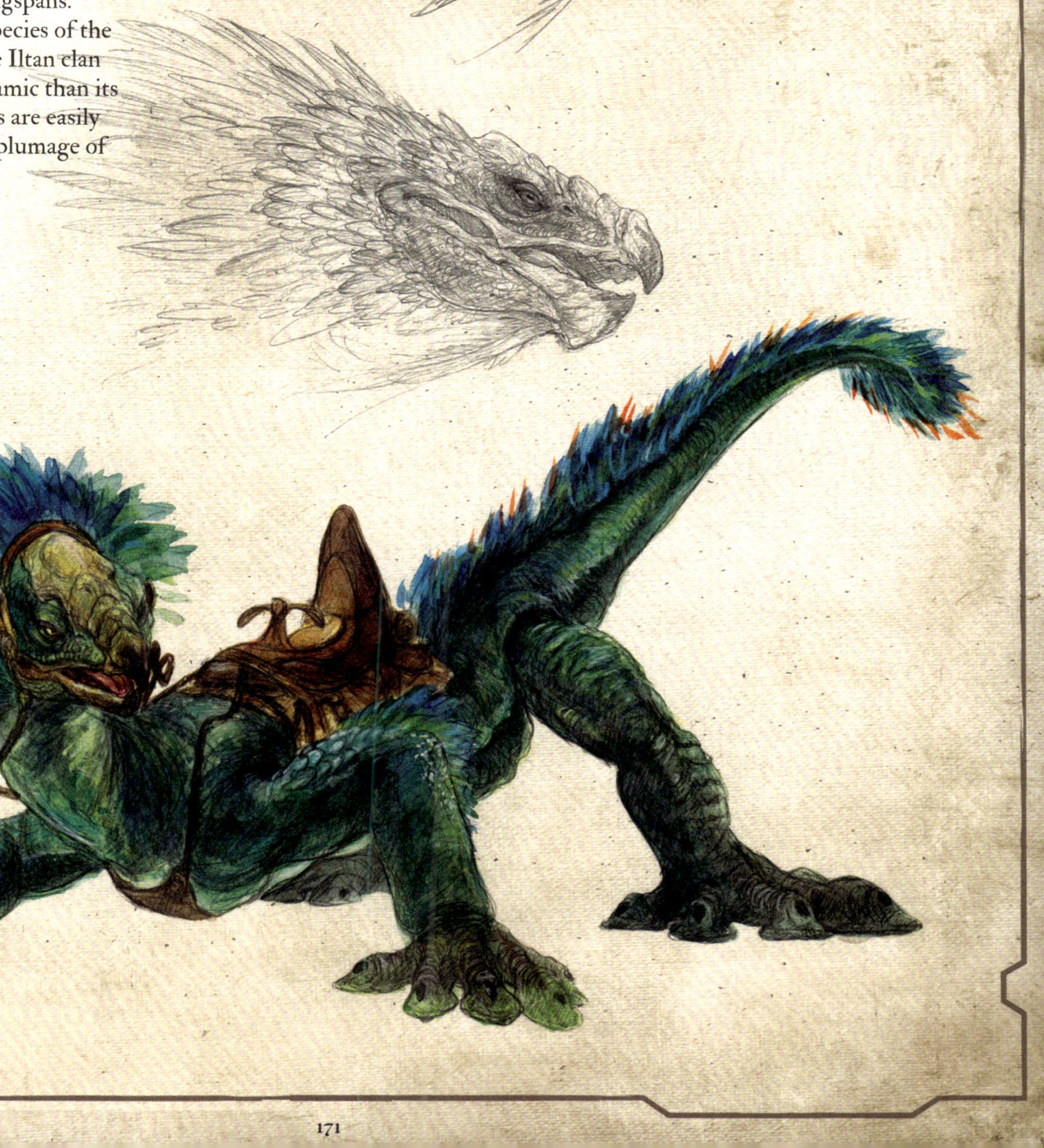

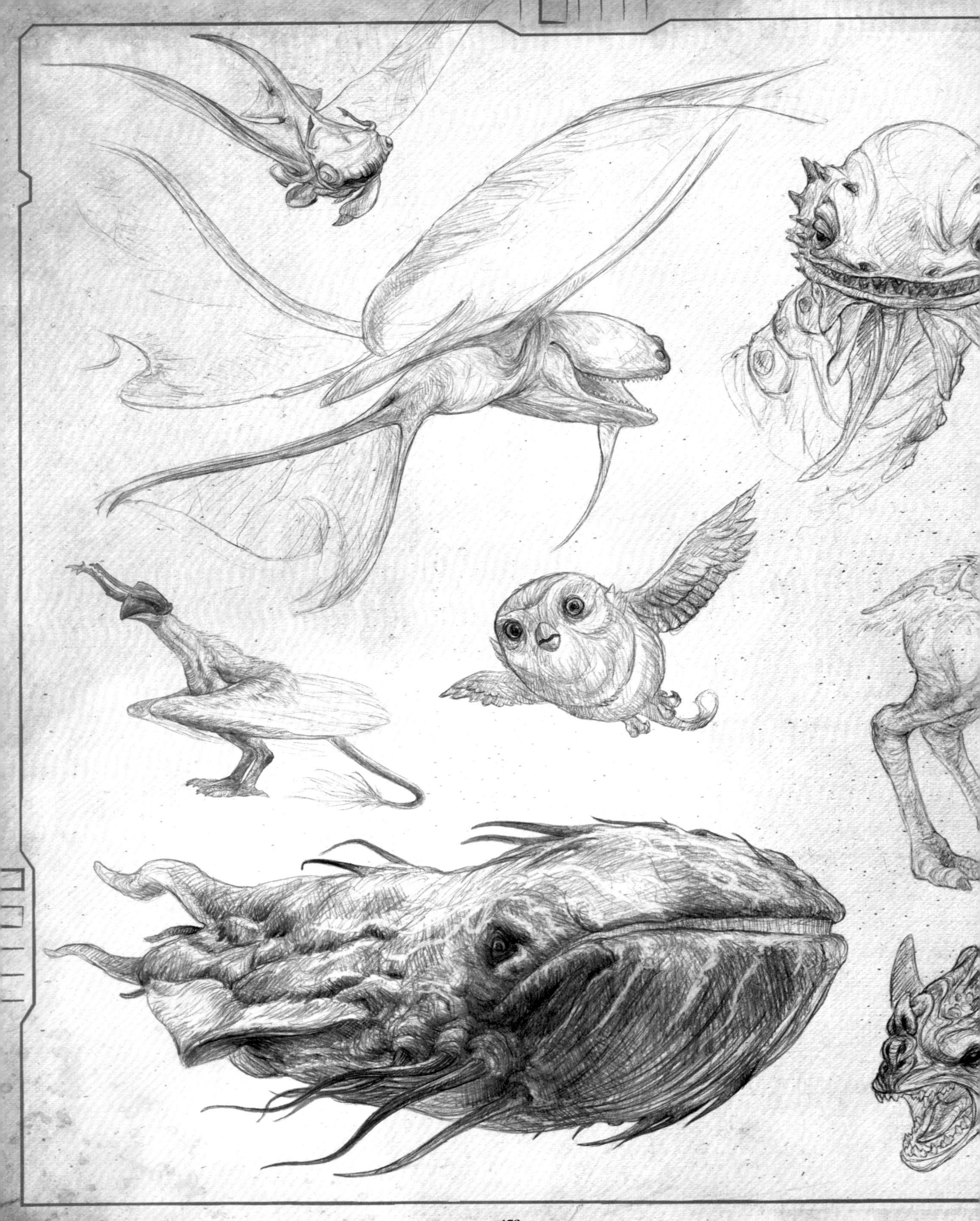

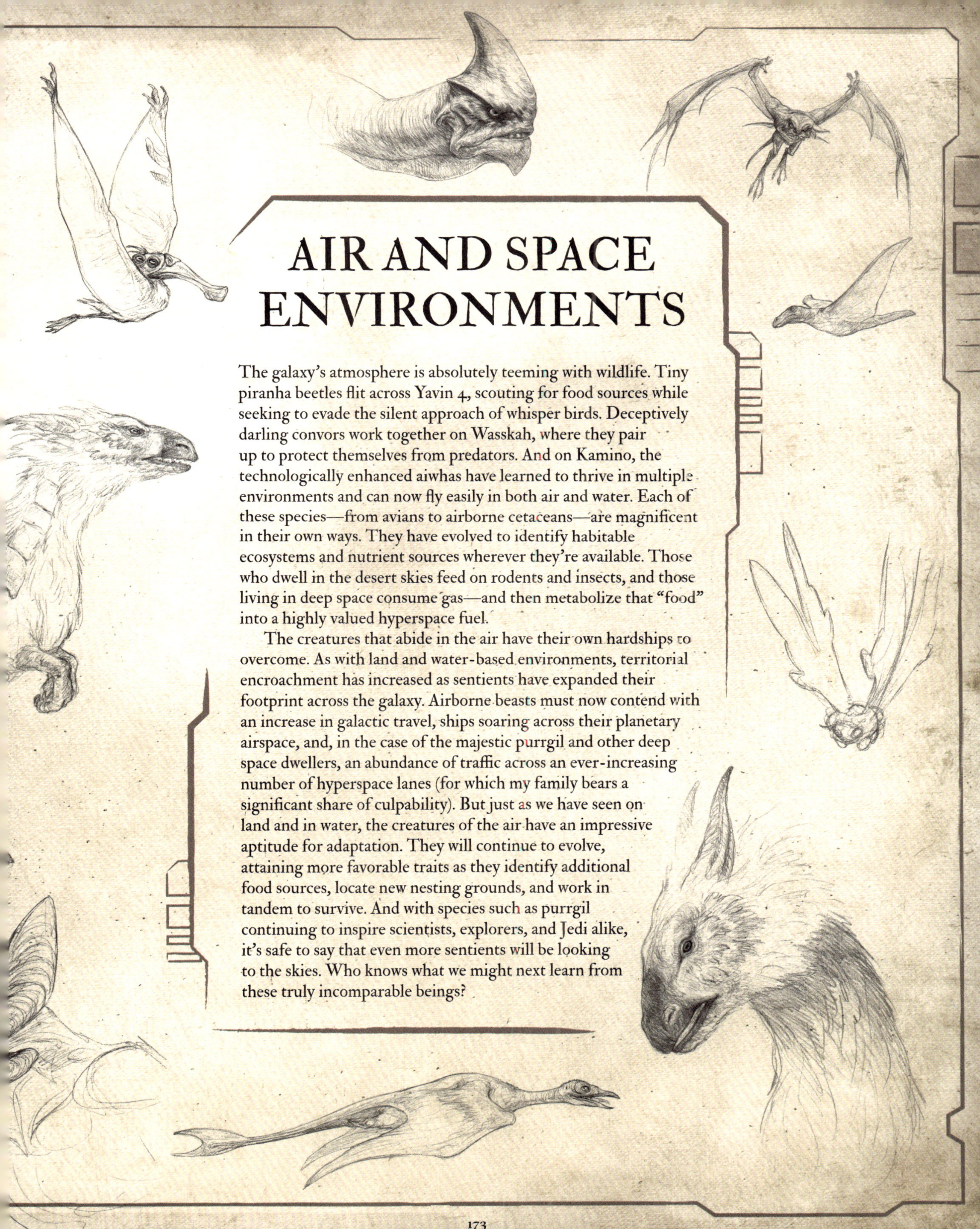

AIR AND SPACE ENVIRONMENTS

The galaxy's atmosphere is absolutely teeming with wildlife. Tiny piranha beetles flit across Yavin 4, scouting for food sources while seeking to evade the silent approach of whisper birds. Deceptively darling convors work together on Wasskah, where they pair up to protect themselves from predators. And on Kamino, the technologically enhanced aiwhas have learned to thrive in multiple environments and can now fly easily in both air and water. Each of these species—from avians to airborne cetaceans—are magnificent in their own ways. They have evolved to identify habitable ecosystems and nutrient sources wherever they're available. Those who dwell in the desert skies feed on rodents and insects, and those living in deep space consume gas—and then metabolize that "food" into a highly valued hyperspace fuel.

The creatures that abide in the air have their own hardships to overcome. As with land and water-based environments, territorial encroachment has increased as sentients have expanded their footprint across the galaxy. Airborne beasts must now contend with an increase in galactic travel, ships soaring across their planetary airspace, and, in the case of the majestic purrgil and other deep space dwellers, an abundance of traffic across an ever-increasing number of hyperspace lanes (for which my family bears a significant share of culpability). But just as we have seen on land and in water, the creatures of the air have an impressive aptitude for adaptation. They will continue to evolve, attaining more favorable traits as they identify additional food sources, locate new nesting grounds, and work in tandem to survive. And with species such as purrgil continuing to inspire scientists, explorers, and Jedi alike, it's safe to say that even more sentients will be looking to the skies. Who knows what we might next learn from these truly incomparable beings?

AIR CREATURES

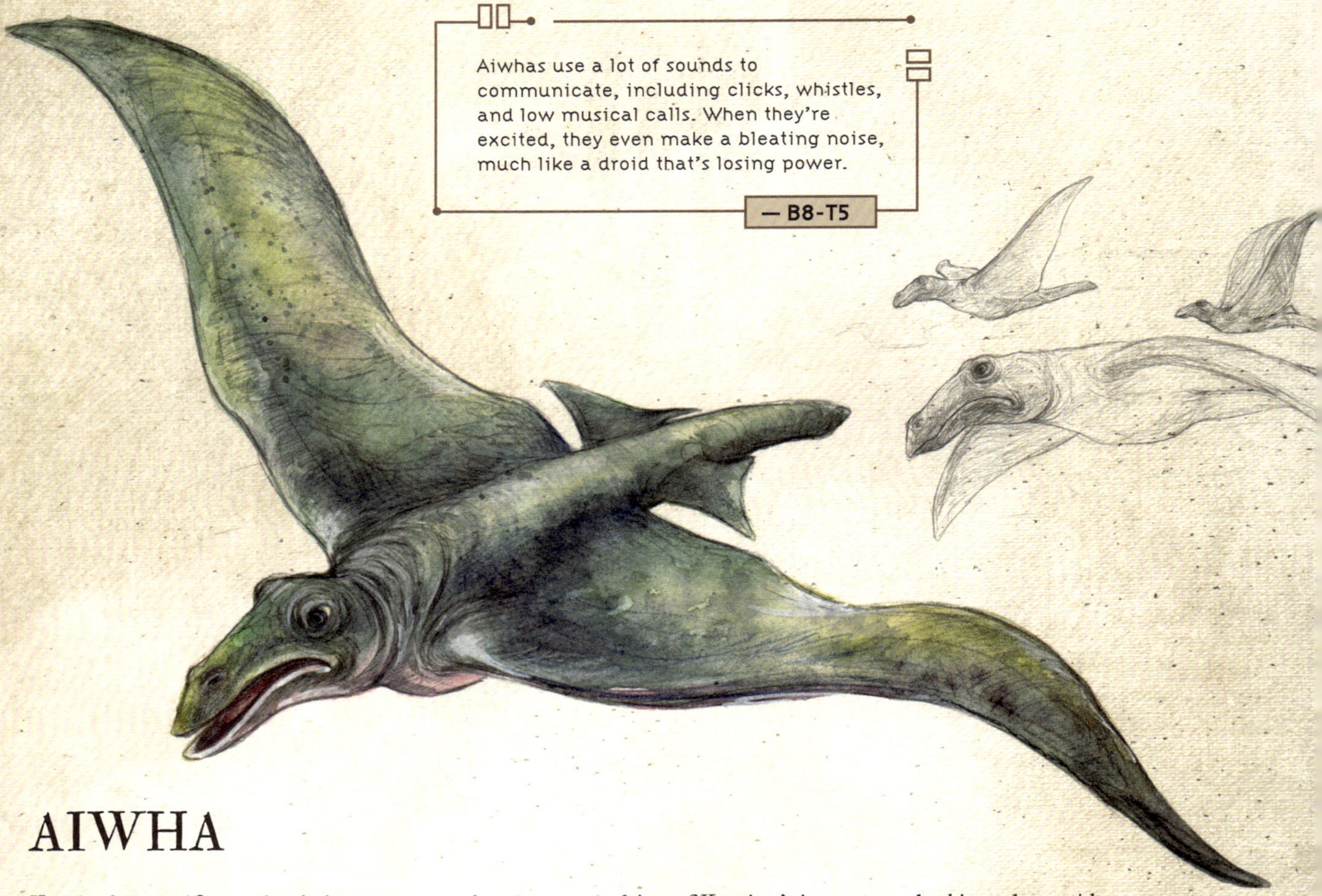

Aiwhas use a lot of sounds to communicate, including clicks, whistles, and low musical calls. When they're excited, they even make a bleating noise, much like a droid that's losing power.

— B8-T5

AIWHA

Kamino's magnificent air whales are among the relatively few recorded species of flying cetaceans. Their wingspans can measure up to 11 meters wide, and the largest specimens weigh up to 1,200 kilograms. Aiwhas feed on oceanic krill, utilizing dense strands of baleen to filter the tiny creatures from the seawater. Their enormous size requires that they exist in a near-constant state of consumption; they are often spotted swimming through Kamino's oceans with their mouths open, ensuring a near-constant intake of nutrients.

Aiwhas are a peaceful species whose gentle nature led the sentient Kaminoans to utilize them as mounts. The two developed a symbiotic relationship after the melting of Kamino's icecaps resulted in a planetwide flood. When the Kaminoans realized the air whales were struggling to survive the watery shifts brought on by climate change, they drew upon their intricate cloning technology to help the creatures adapt. These enhancements enabled aiwhas to use their wings to propel across both air and sea, ensuring their survival above *and* below the water. This technologically assisted adaptation saved the aiwha from a climate-induced catastrophe—and gave the Kaminoans a multipurpose mount. Following the adaptation, the two species were frequently seen flying across their homeworld—traveling through the air in clear skies and diving underwater in the event of electrical storms.

BELDON

Bespin owes much of its economic vitality to the tenacious, tendrilled beldon. These floating creatures use their enormous tentacles to collect chemicals and atmospheric plankton, which they ingest before metabolizing them into Bespin's primary resource, tibanna gas. Beldons have rich purple exteriors and orange gas bladders, the latter of which enables them to float across the atmosphere. They measure between eight hundred meters and ten kilometers long, and they live among large herds. They rely on pectoral fins to push themselves through the air—although their slow rate of movement means that they frequently fall victim to the predatory velkers and scavenging crab gliders.

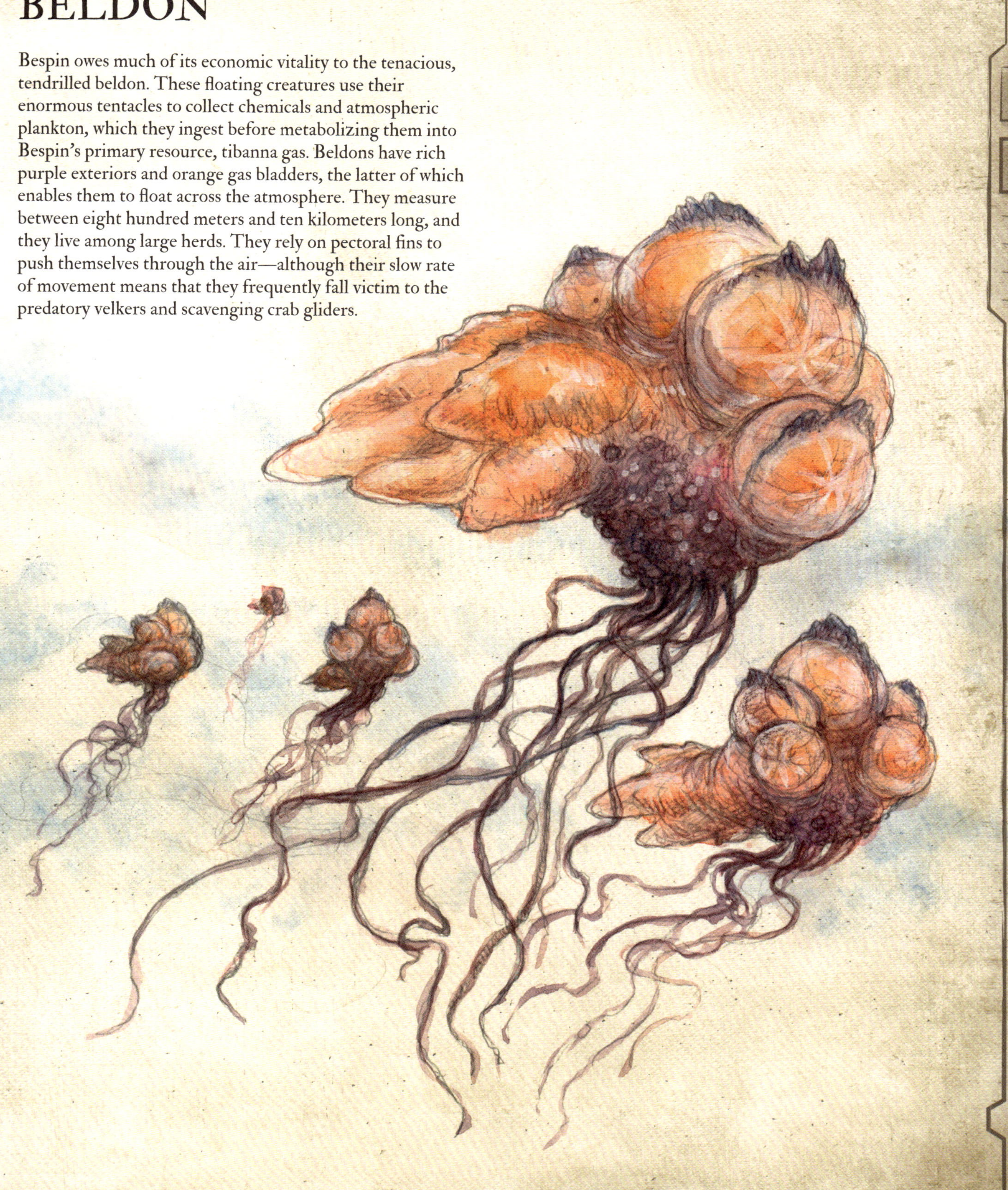

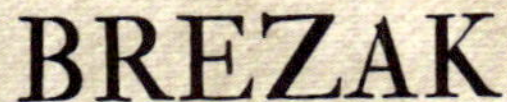

BREZAK

These carnivorous, reptavian lizards are native to the planet Zygerria. They glide easily through the air, thanks to their lightweight skeletal structure and long arms laced with sturdy skin flaps. They use their tails as rudders, shifting the appendages for directional assistance during flight.

Brezak average six meters wide and ten meters long. They are excellent climbers that can scale cliffs and mountains with relative ease, and they can move seamlessly through the air. Accordingly, they were the transport of choice for their homeworld's military, the Zygerrian Royal Guards.

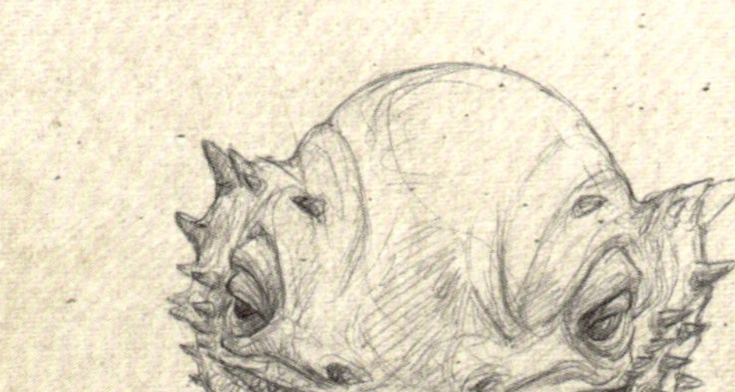

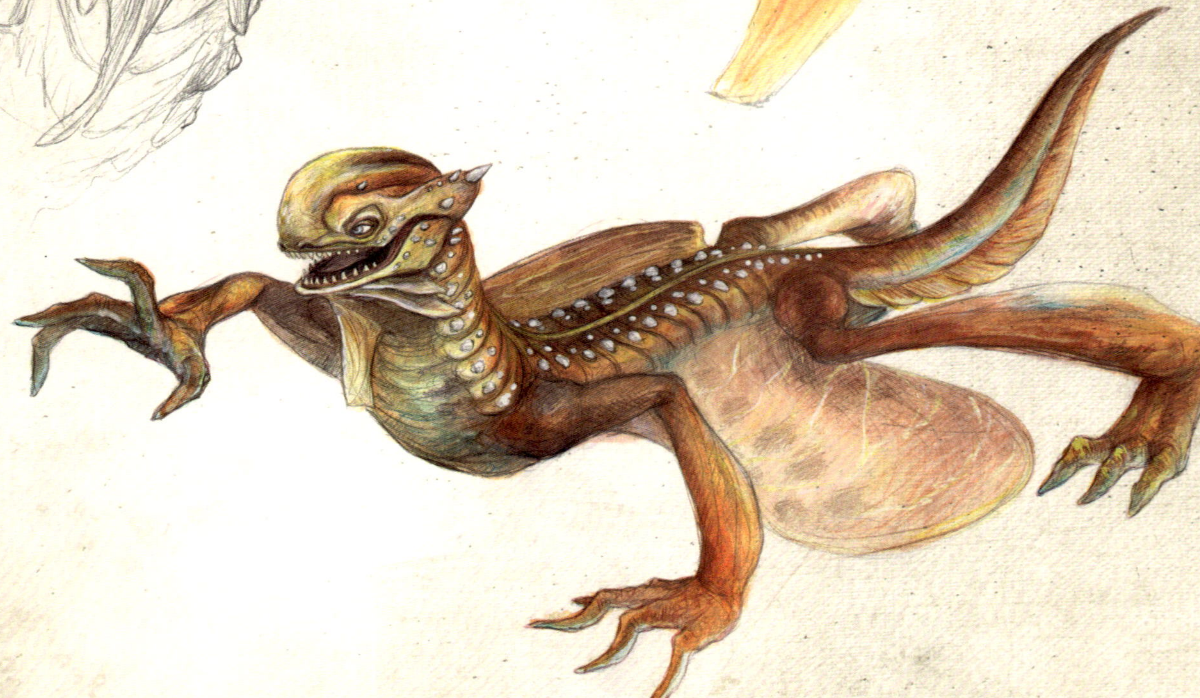

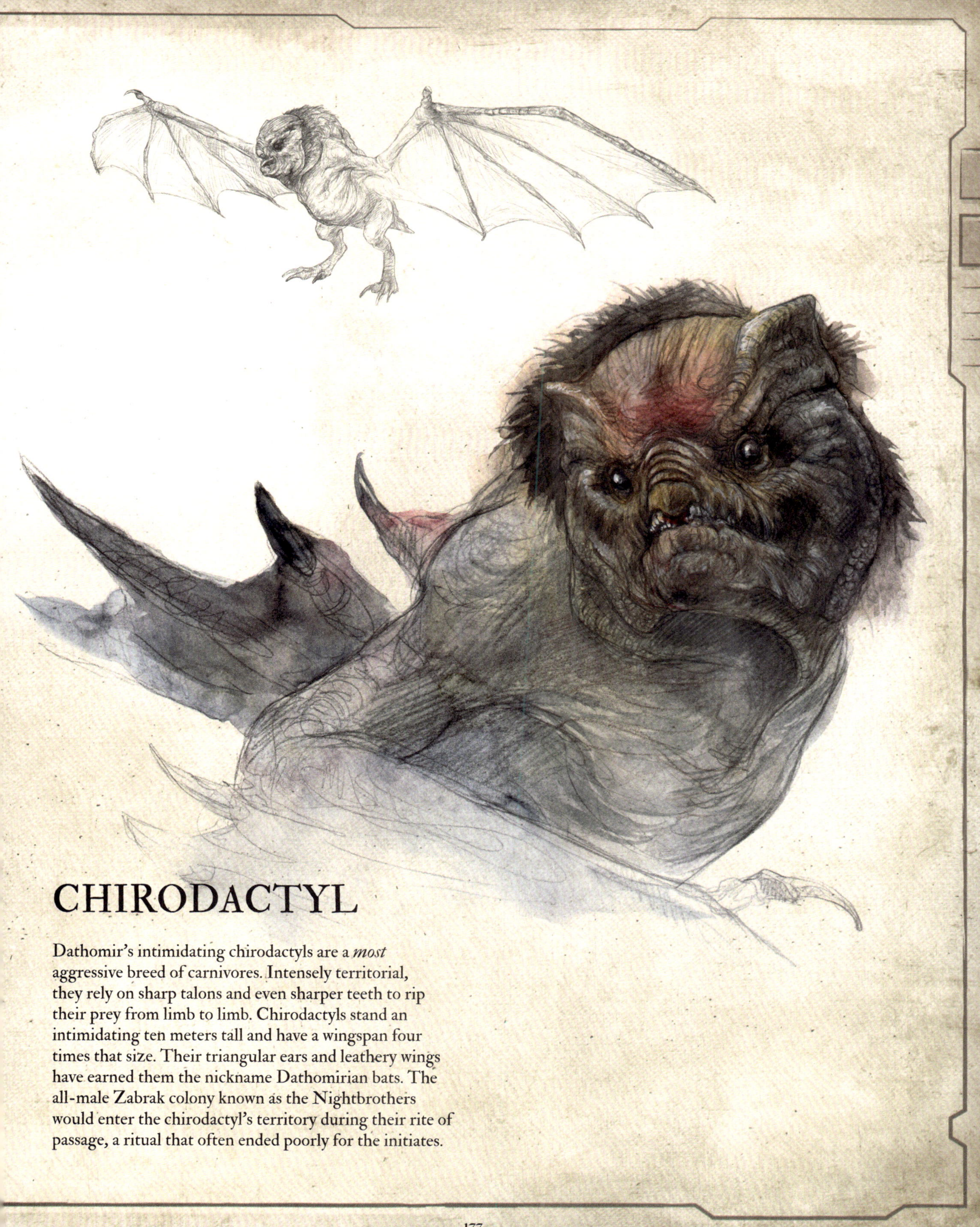

CHIRODACTYL

Dathomir's intimidating chirodactyls are a *most* aggressive breed of carnivores. Intensely territorial, they rely on sharp talons and even sharper teeth to rip their prey from limb to limb. Chirodactyls stand an intimidating ten meters tall and have a wingspan four times that size. Their triangular ears and leathery wings have earned them the nickname Dathomirian bats. The all-male Zabrak colony known as the Nightbrothers would enter the chirodactyl's territory during their rite of passage, a ritual that often ended poorly for the initiates.

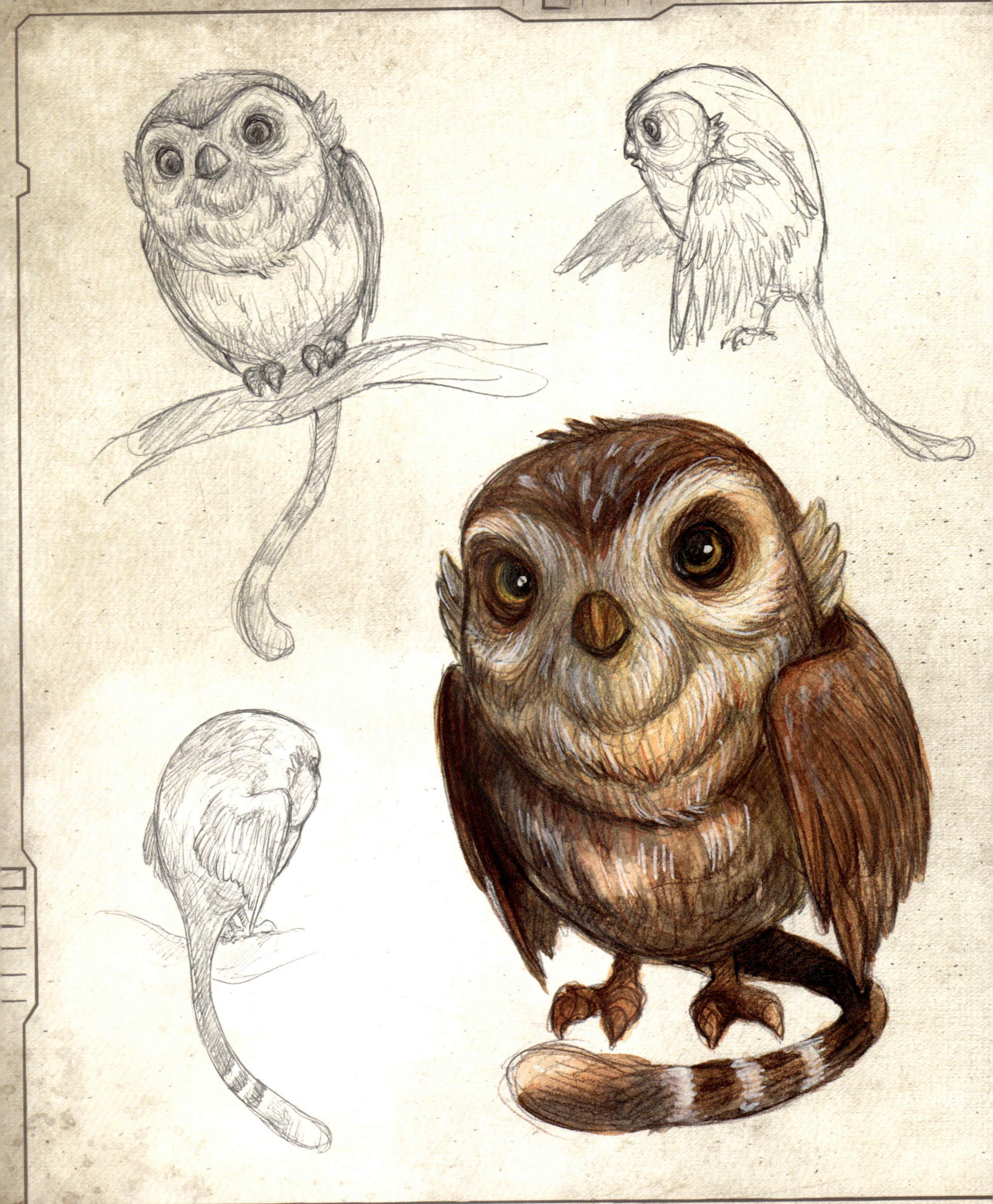

CONVOR

Wasskah's carnivorous avians stand a mere twenty centimeters tall and weigh just less than two kilograms. They make for popular pets, with their compact size and wide, trusting eyes. Convor are traded across the galaxy, with specimens showing up everywhere from Atollon to Malachor and even Takodana. They're most closely related to owls, although their cheerful gold-and-brown feathers are rather reminiscent of porgs.

Convor make their homes in the uppermost branches of trees, where their prehensile tails help them maintain a steady hold. They feed on small rodents and insects, and they travel across Wasskah in pairs, working together to protect themselves from predators. When attacked, a pair of convors grabs the assailant in their talons, ascends into the air, and drops the creature from an unsurvivable height. It's a brilliant example of nature's interconnectivity and proof that size truly matters not—thanks to determination and teamwork.

Convor are perhaps most well known for having a strong connection to the Force, with the species showing a particular fondness for the famed Togruta Ahsoka Tano.

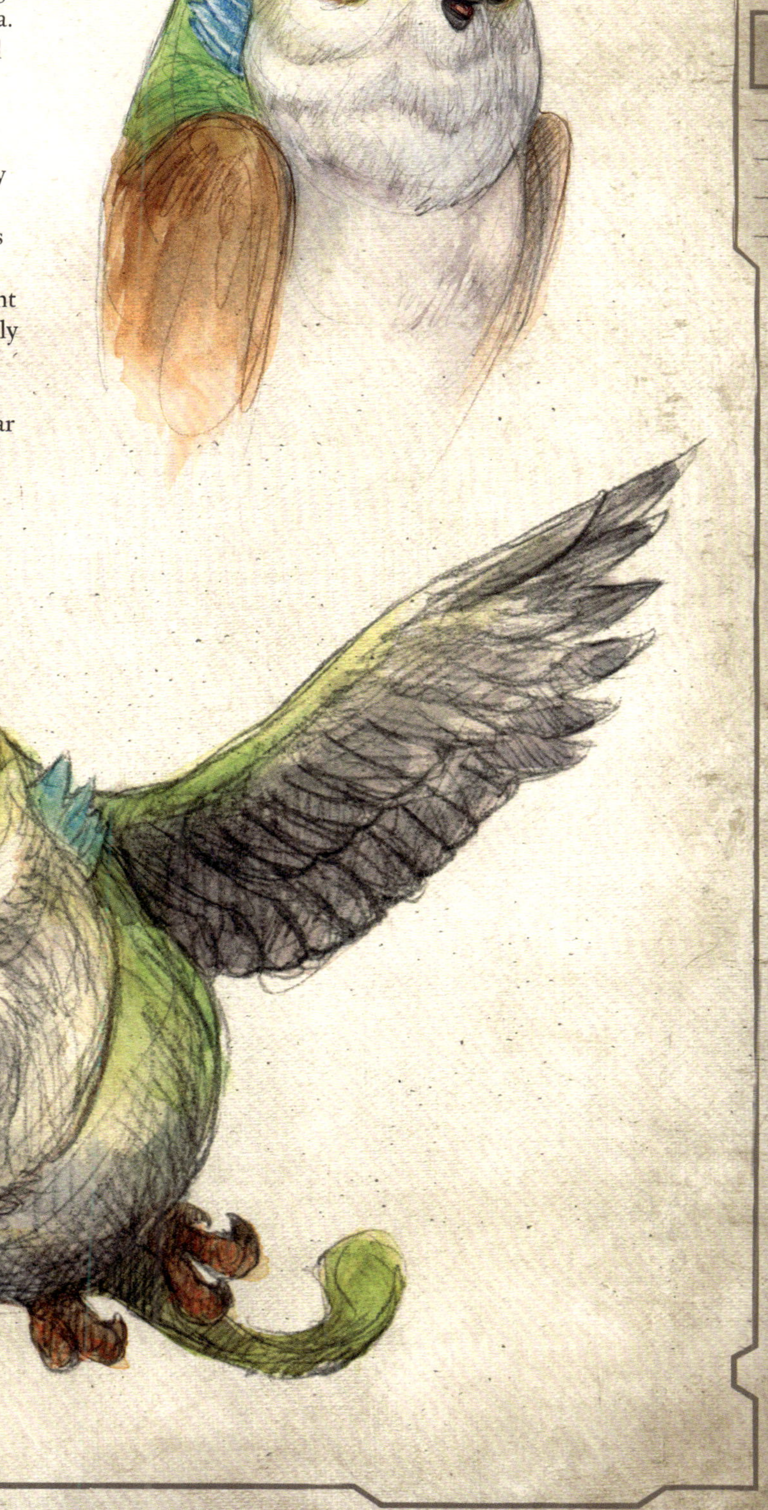

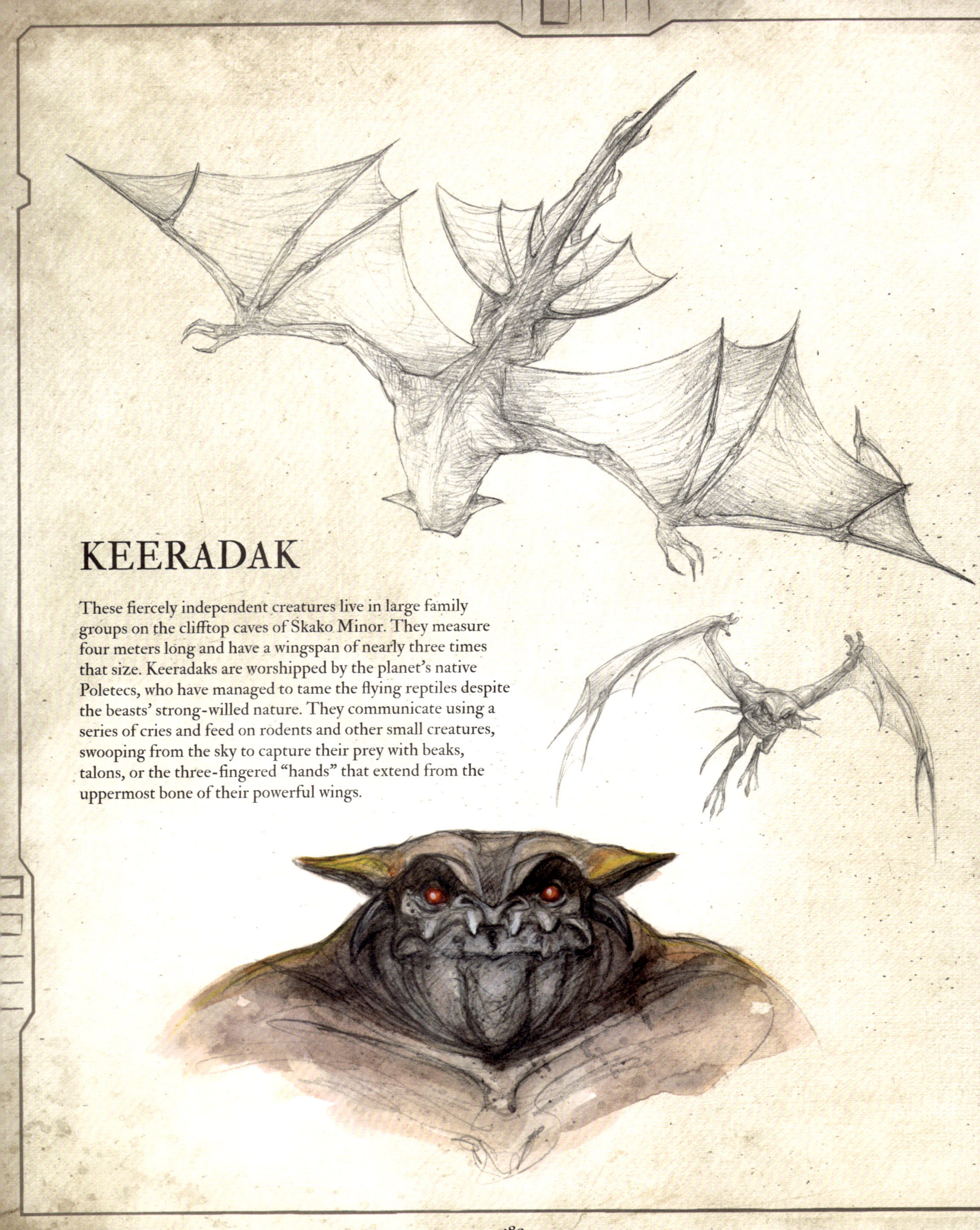

KEERADAK

These fiercely independent creatures live in large family groups on the clifftop caves of Skako Minor. They measure four meters long and have a wingspan of nearly three times that size. Keeradaks are worshipped by the planet's native Poletecs, who have managed to tame the flying reptiles despite the beasts' strong-willed nature. They communicate using a series of cries and feed on rodents and other small creatures, swooping from the sky to capture their prey with beaks, talons, or the three-fingered "hands" that extend from the uppermost bone of their powerful wings.

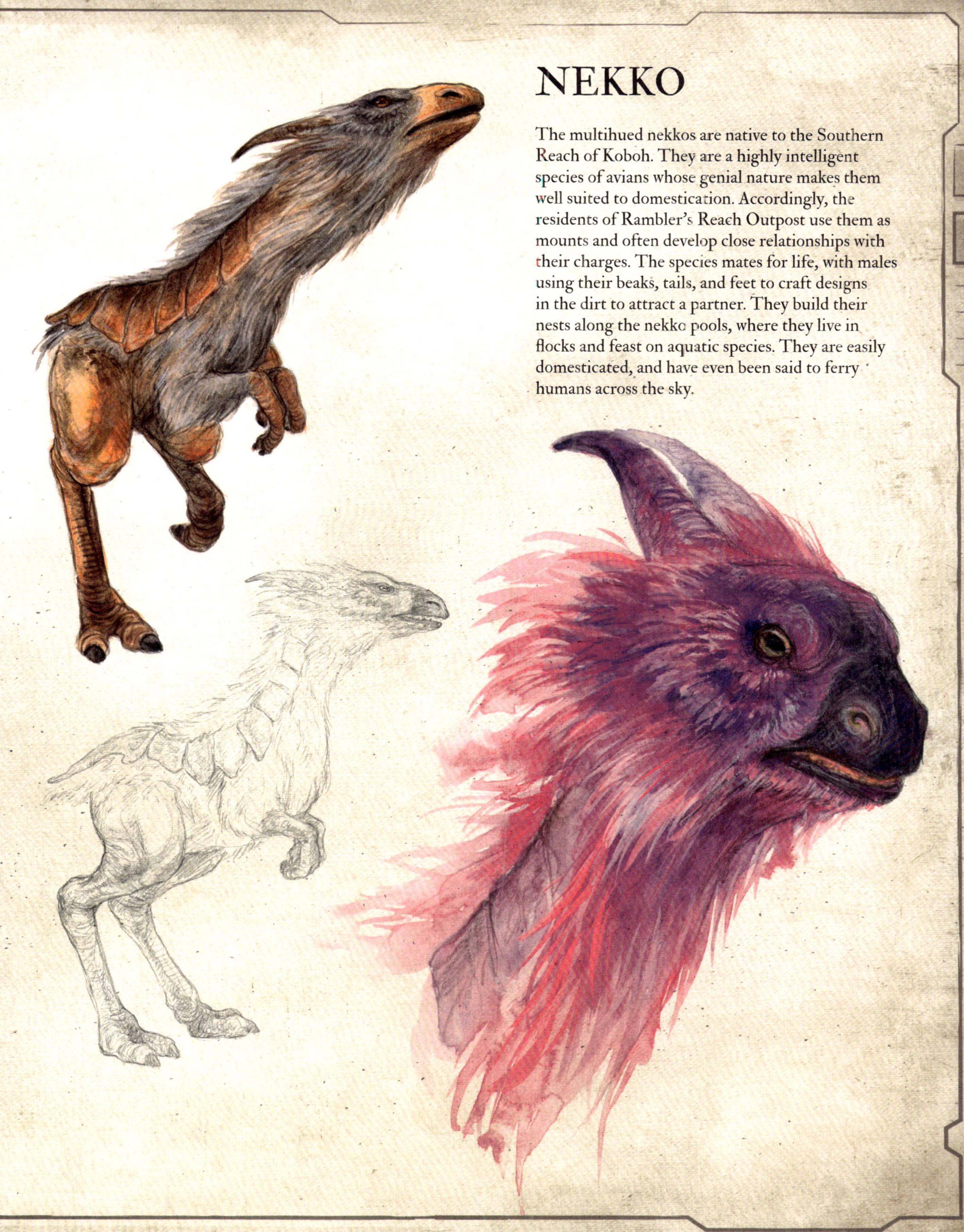

NEKKO

The multihued nekkos are native to the Southern Reach of Koboh. They are a highly intelligent species of avians whose genial nature makes them well suited to domestication. Accordingly, the residents of Rambler's Reach Outpost use them as mounts and often develop close relationships with their charges. The species mates for life, with males using their beaks, tails, and feet to craft designs in the dirt to attract a partner. They build their nests along the nekko pools, where they live in flocks and feast on aquatic species. They are easily domesticated, and have even been said to ferry humans across the sky.

LOTH-BAT

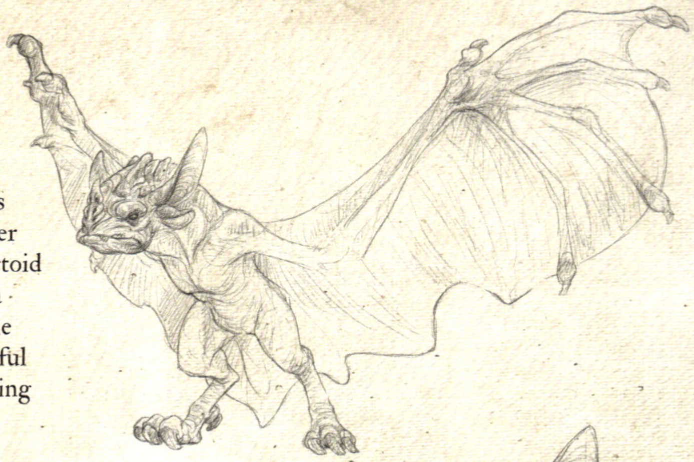

Lothal's giant, five-meter wing span Loth-bats make their home beneath building eaves. They travel in packs, gliding easily over long distances and communicating through a series of high-pitched squeals. Loth-bats hibernate during the colder months, conserving their energy while their heat-loving insectoid food sources remain scarce. Upon awakening, they feed with a vengeance, descending on fruit trees and crops and earning the ire of Lothal's farmers. These flying mammalians have powerful wings that enable them to fly at great speeds, with some reaching speeds of more than one hundred fifty kilometers per hour.

Loth-bats respond to droid sounds. I was able to lure an entire colony out on our "bat night" using my standard frequency. Up close, I saw that they have pink ears, noses, and feet. Loth-bats are color blind, so they see best by using echolocation—they send a sound wave from their forehead to an object, receive the vibration back in their jaw, and translate it to an image in their brain.

— B8-T5

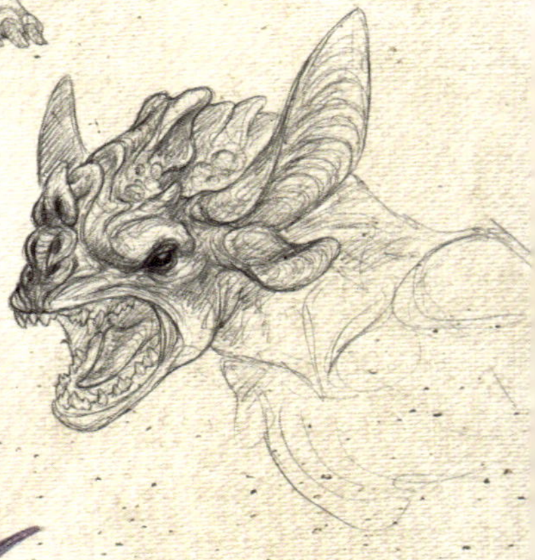

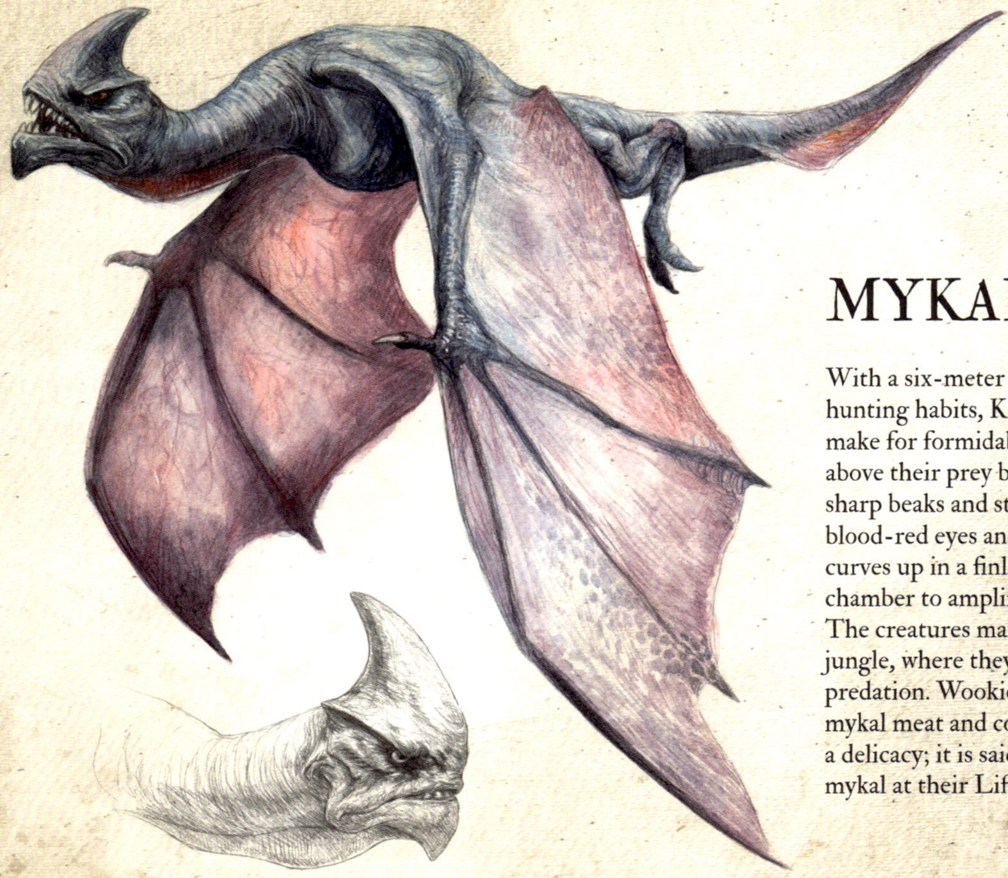

MYKAL

With a six-meter wingspan and well-practiced hunting habits, Kashyyyk's airborne carnivores make for formidable foes. They soar silently above their prey before diving to attack with sharp beaks and strong talons. The mykal has blood-red eyes and gray-blue skin, and its head curves up in a finlike crest, serving as an echo chamber to amplify its intimidating screeches. The creatures make their homes in the jungle, where they build treetop nests to avoid predation. Wookiees are particularly fond of mykal meat and consider the creatures to be a delicacy; it is said they often serve roasted mykal at their Life Day feasts.

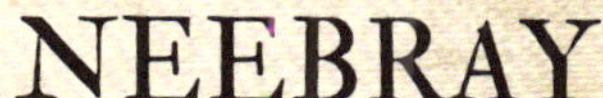

NEEBRAY

The red-and-gray neebray mantas can be found across the galaxy, including the Rishi Moon, Tatooine, and the Kaliida Nebula. These gentle creatures are related to mynocks and tibidees, although their 1,674-meter wingspan makes them significantly larger than either. They feed off space gasses and have four enormous yellow eyes that allow them to spot predators at great distances. Young neebray are born with solid red or gray skin. As they age, they develop dark spots along their wings and torsos.

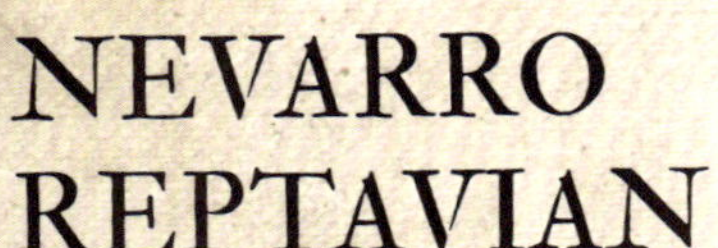

NEVARRO REPTAVIAN

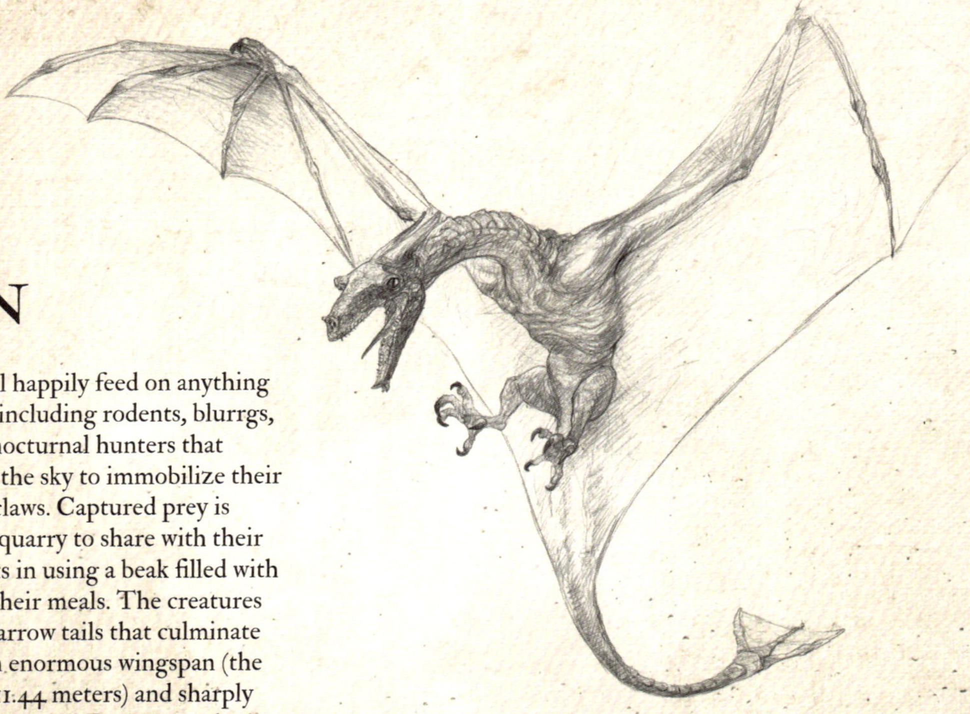

These predatory carnivores will happily feed on anything they can sink their talons into, including rodents, blurrgs, and sentient beings. They are nocturnal hunters that travel in flocks, dropping from the sky to immobilize their victims with sharp, venomous claws. Captured prey is brought back to the creatures' quarry to share with their young, who mimic their parents in using a beak filled with razor-sharp teeth to tear into their meals. The creatures have scaly gray skin and long narrow tails that culminate in a cetaceanlike fluke. With an enormous wingspan (the average reptavian measures at 11.44 meters) and sharply taloned toes, Nevarro reptavians are difficult to evade—and are best observed from a safe distance.

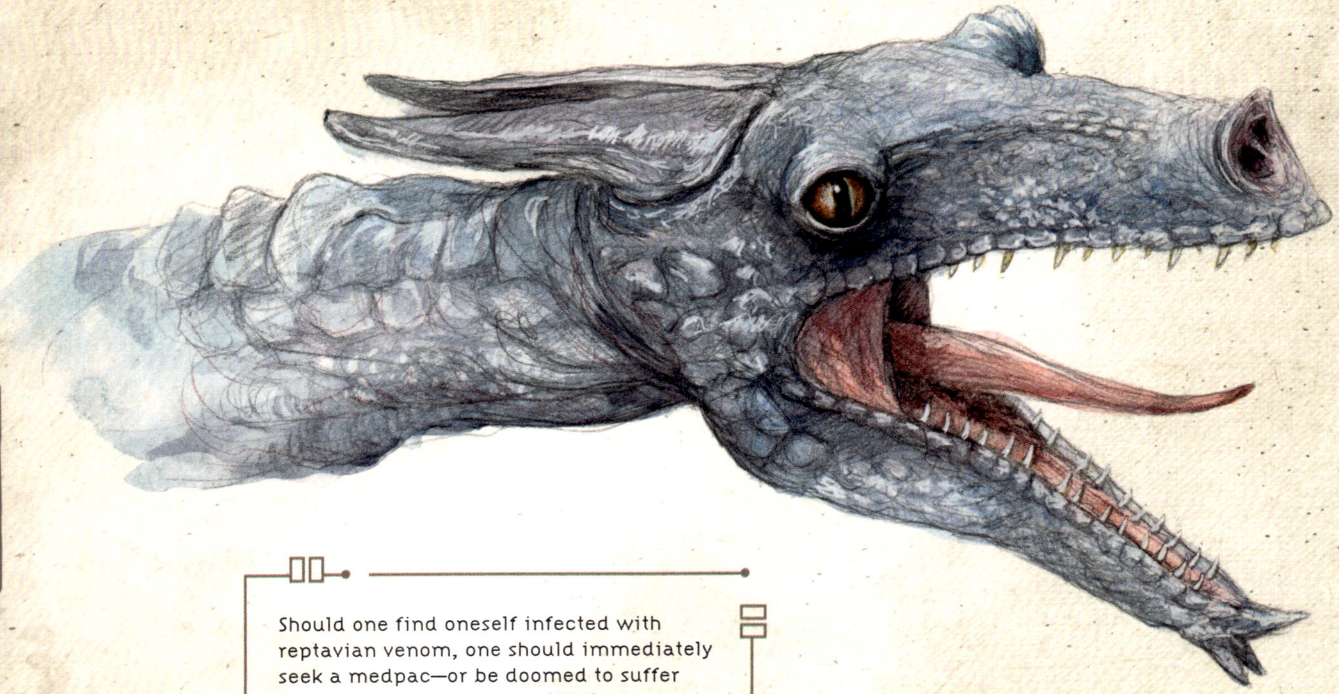

Should one find oneself infected with reptavian venom, one should immediately seek a medpac—or be doomed to suffer disastrous symptoms ranging from organ shutdown to cardiac arrest.

— B8-T5

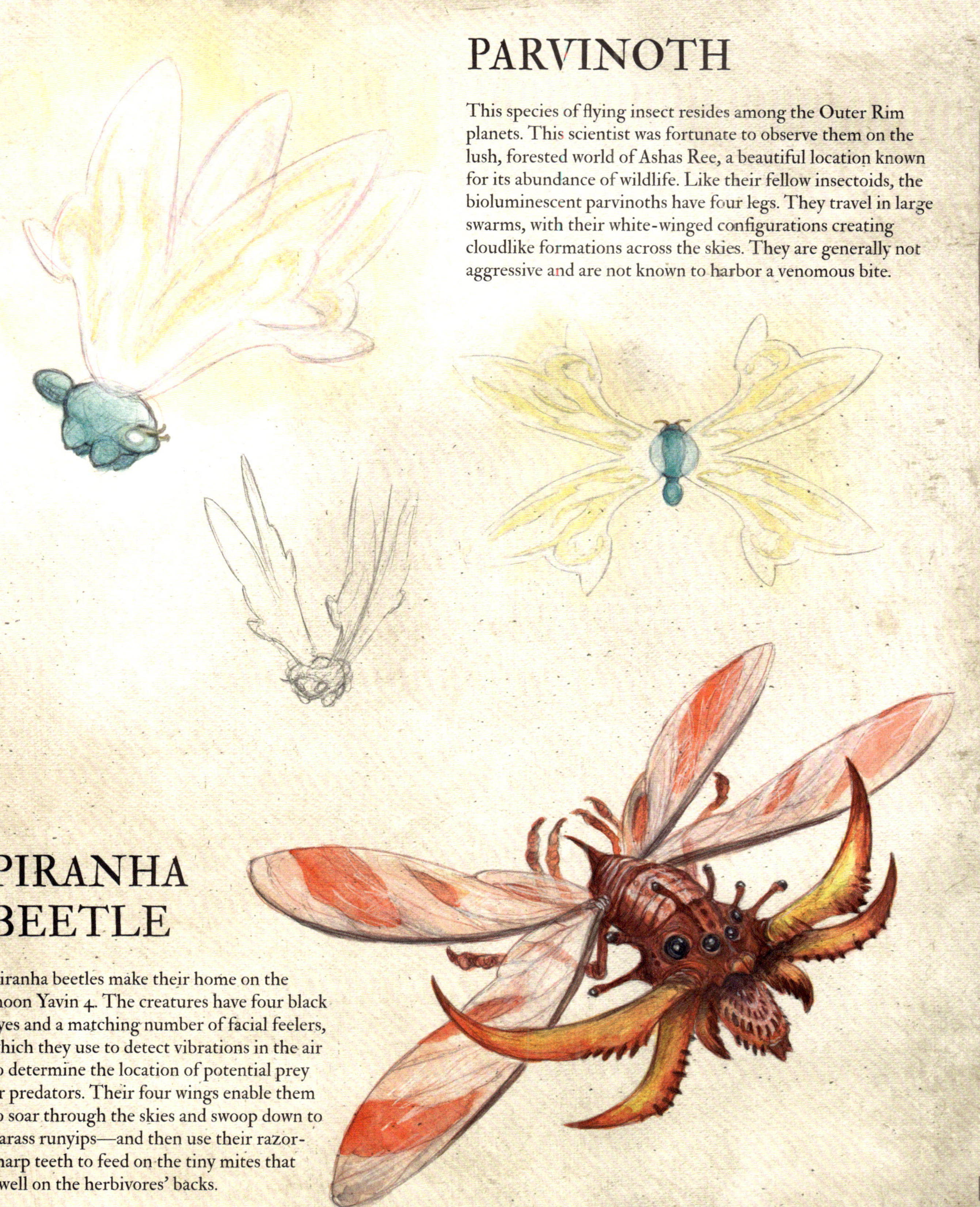

PARVINOTH

This species of flying insect resides among the Outer Rim planets. This scientist was fortunate to observe them on the lush, forested world of Ashas Ree, a beautiful location known for its abundance of wildlife. Like their fellow insectoids, the bioluminescent parvinoths have four legs. They travel in large swarms, with their white-winged configurations creating cloudlike formations across the skies. They are generally not aggressive and are not known to harbor a venomous bite.

PIRANHA BEETLE

Piranha beetles make their home on the moon Yavin 4. The creatures have four black eyes and a matching number of facial feelers, which they use to detect vibrations in the air to determine the location of potential prey or predators. Their four wings enable them to soar through the skies and swoop down to harass runyips—and then use their razor-sharp teeth to feed on the tiny mites that dwell on the herbivores' backs.

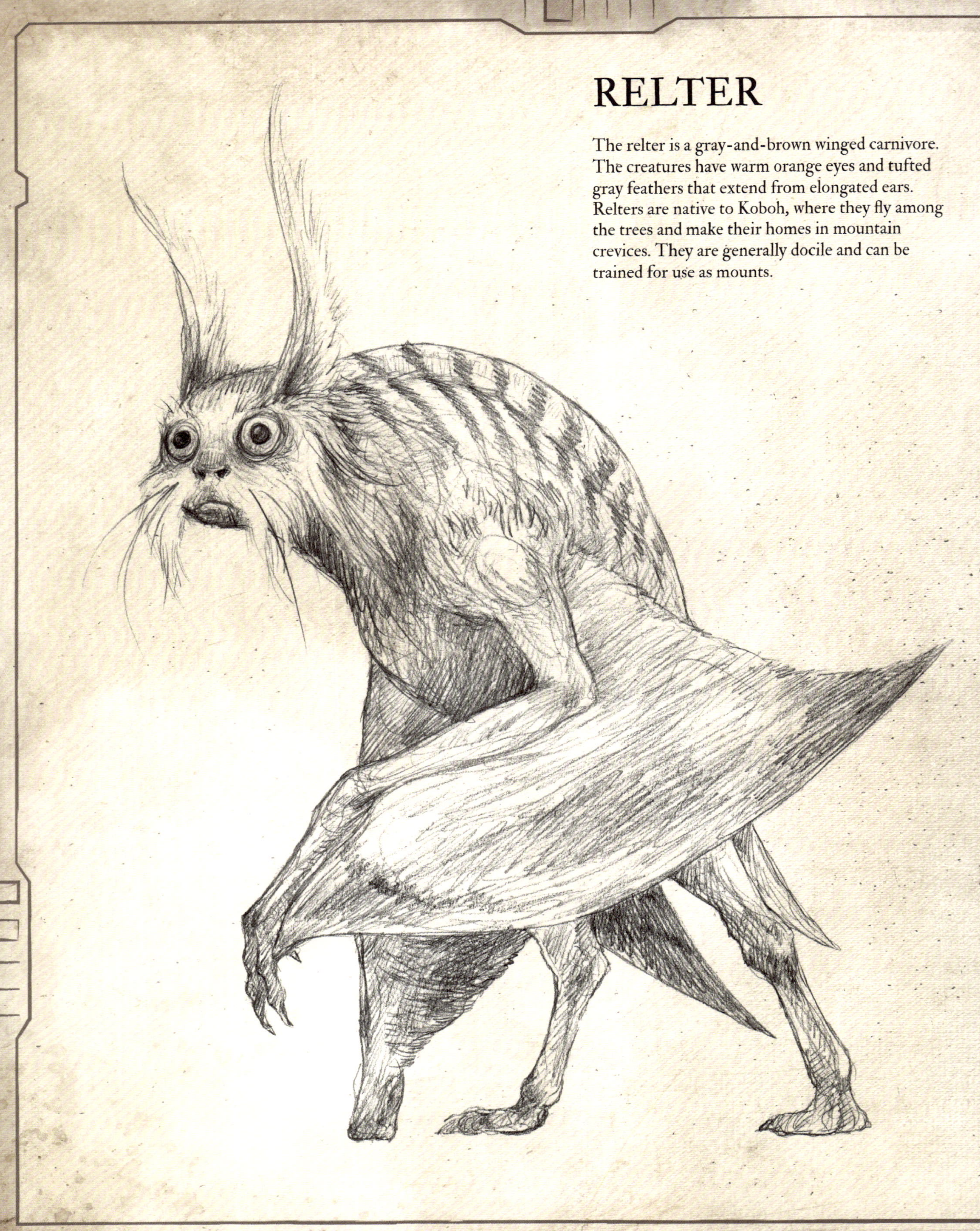

RELTER

The relter is a gray-and-brown winged carnivore. The creatures have warm orange eyes and tufted gray feathers that extend from elongated ears. Relters are native to Koboh, where they fly among the trees and make their homes in mountain crevices. They are generally docile and can be trained for use as mounts.

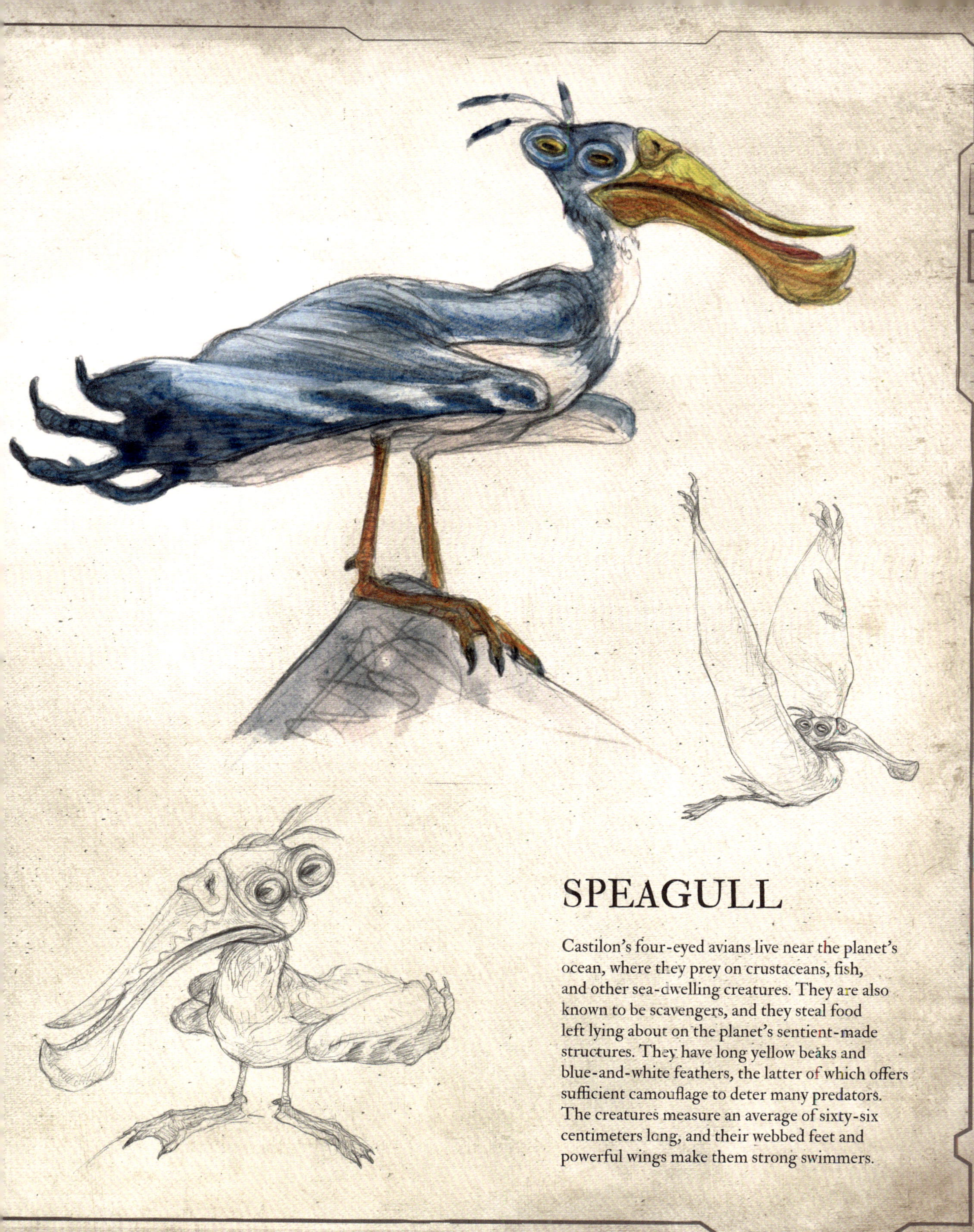

SPEAGULL

Castilon's four-eyed avians live near the planet's ocean, where they prey on crustaceans, fish, and other sea-dwelling creatures. They are also known to be scavengers, and they steal food left lying about on the planet's sentient-made structures. They have long yellow beaks and blue-and-white feathers, the latter of which offers sufficient camouflage to deter many predators. The creatures measure an average of sixty-six centimeters long, and their webbed feet and powerful wings make them strong swimmers.

SHYYYO BIRD

Kashyyyk's elegant shyyyo birds are so rarely seen that their existence was long believed to be a myth. This scientist hardly dared hope to spot one in the wild, but after days of waiting, a specimen *finally* passed overhead. Its five-meter wingspan and brilliant white feathers made it impossible to miss, and its intimidating horns and long, taloned toes made it clear that this carnivorous avian is best left undisturbed—at least, by beings who value their lives! The shyyyo bird has a long tail that helps stabilize its flight, and its aerodynamic form enables it to glide great distances with minimal effort. The creatures make their homes deep in the forests of Kashyyyk, where they live in nests among the planet's giant trees. Although these homebodies spend most of their time in their nests, they make weekly hunting excursions to hunt for their favorite meals, slyyygs and wyyyschokks.

Shyyyo birds are revered on Kashyyyk as the protectors of the Wookiees and the native wroshyr tree.

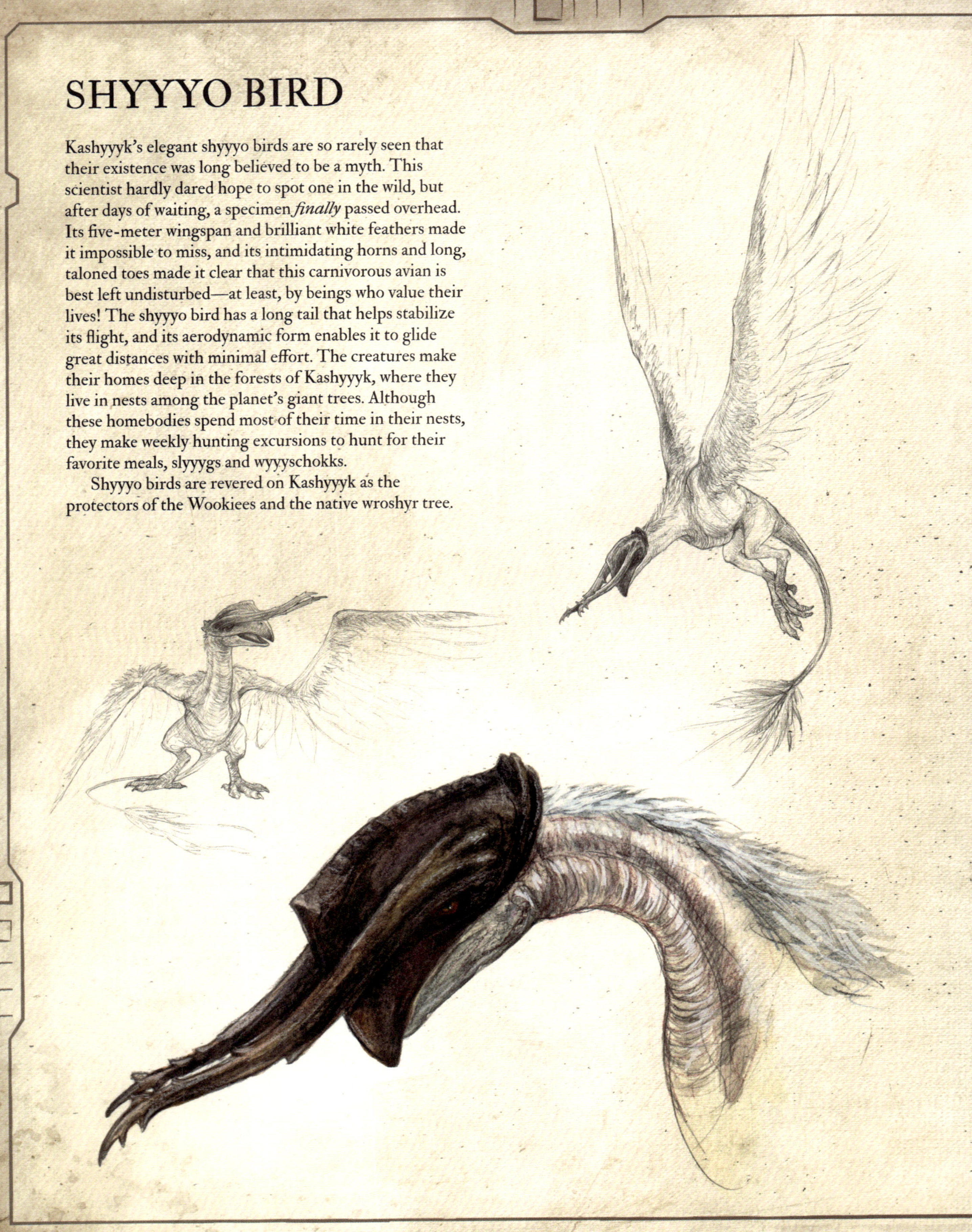

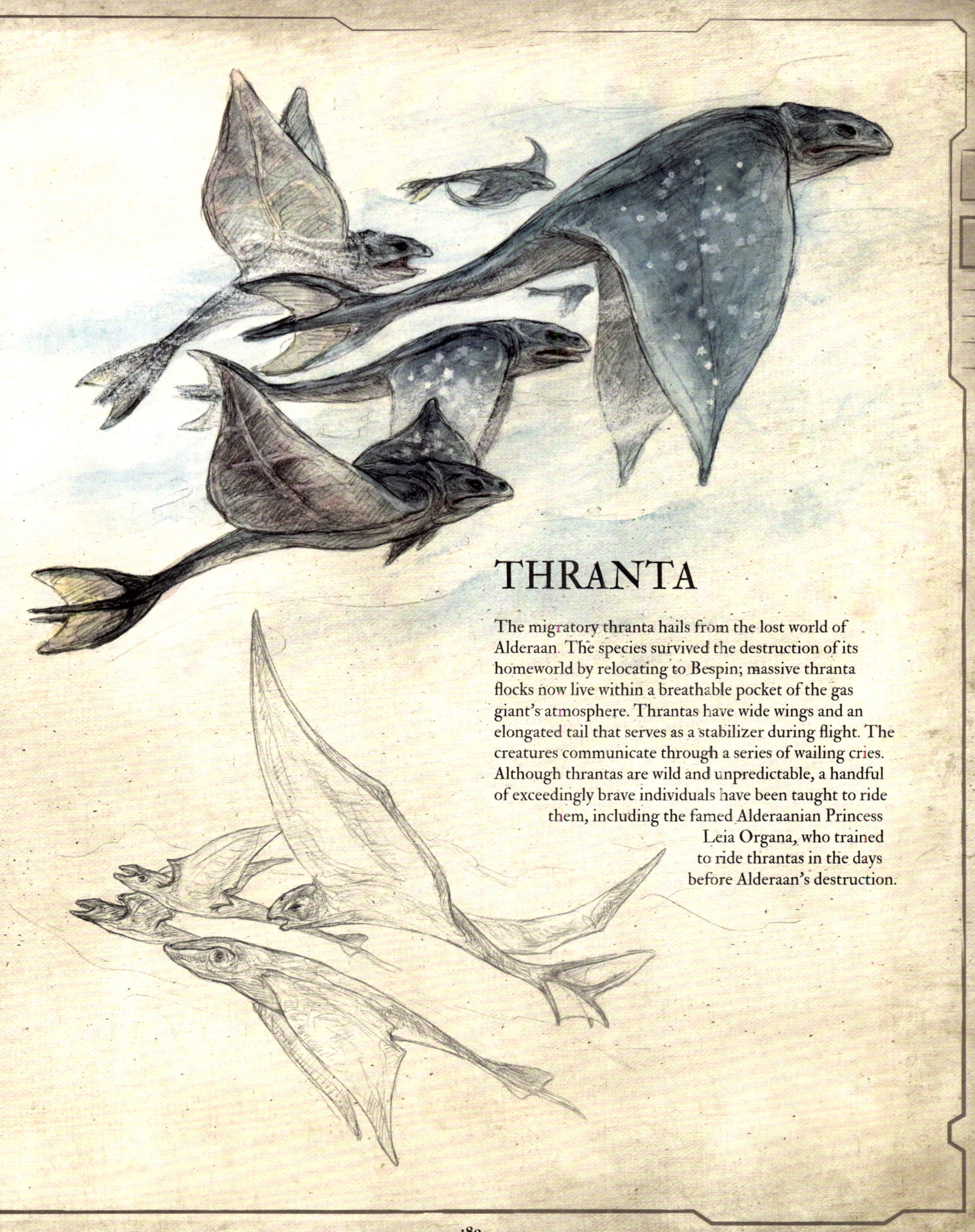

THRANTA

The migratory thranta hails from the lost world of Alderaan. The species survived the destruction of its homeworld by relocating to Bespin; massive thranta flocks now live within a breathable pocket of the gas giant's atmosphere. Thrantas have wide wings and an elongated tail that serves as a stabilizer during flight. The creatures communicate through a series of wailing cries. Although thrantas are wild and unpredictable, a handful of exceedingly brave individuals have been taught to ride them, including the famed Alderaanian Princess Leia Organa, who trained to ride thrantas in the days before Alderaan's destruction.

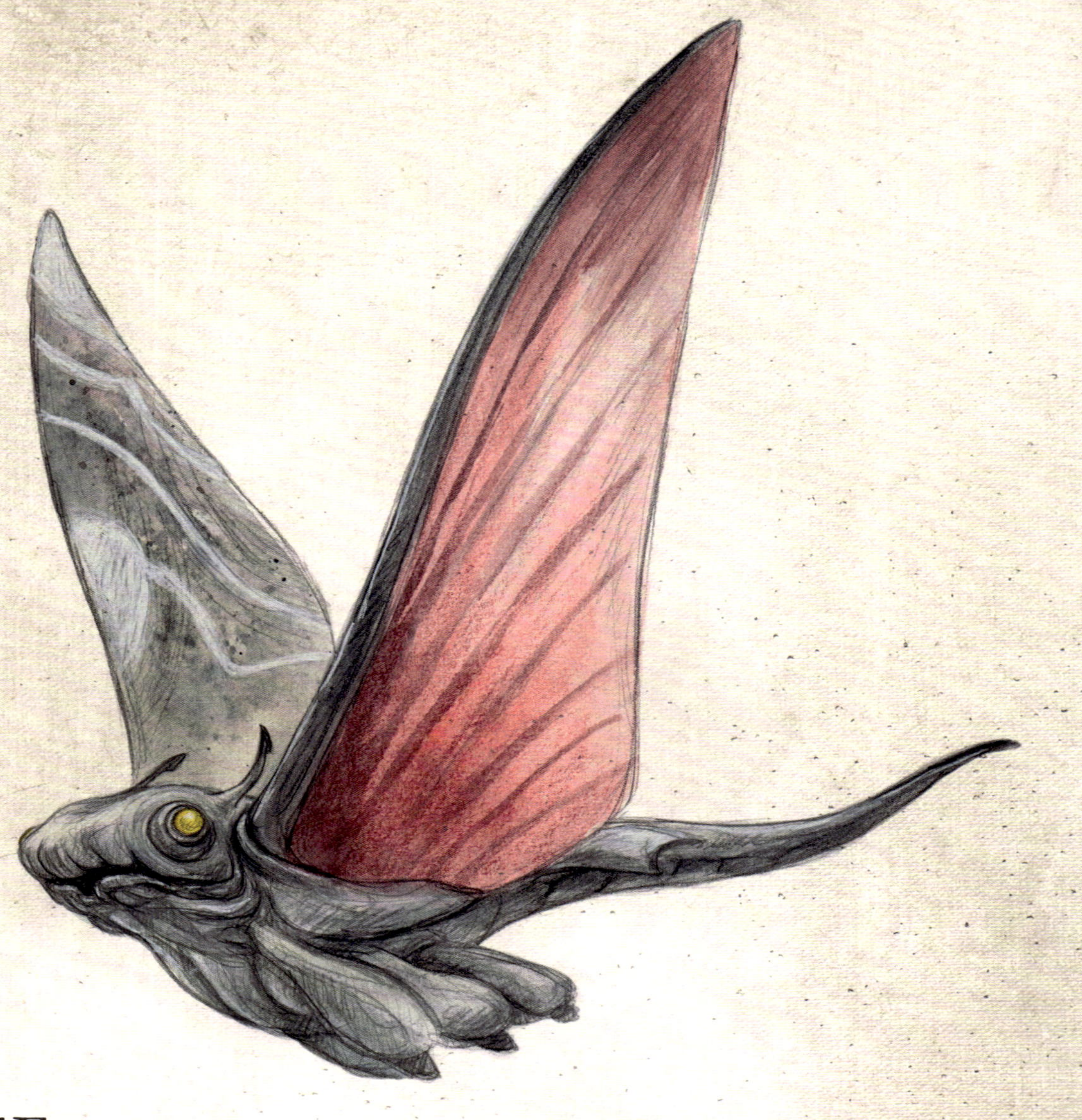

TIBIDEE

The massive airborne tibidees are distant relatives of the mynock and the neebray. They measure 16.17 meters long and weigh up to 750 kilograms. Despite their substantial size, tibidees are elegant fliers. They use internal gas bags and long, flat wings to soar through the mountain ranges of their homeworlds, Stygeon Prime and Oosalon. Their long tails offer stability, and their emerald green eyes offer keen vision, enabling the creatures to spot potential prey at significant distances. Tibidees are known to be attracted to the communication frequencies of sentients because these devices vibrate at a similar resonance to the beast's mating calls. This has resulted in multiple space vessels being attacked by the confounded creatures—including the revered rebel ship the *Phantom*.

WHISPER BIRD

The densely feathered, long-tailed whisper bird lives in the rainforests of Yavin 4, although specimens have also been found on Null and Coruscant. These omnivorous creatures feed on weeds and fish, swooping into rivers and lakes to snatch up prey with their sharply taloned feet. Their name comes from their ability to soar silently across the sky, an adaptation that makes the species among the most efficient of the planet's hunters. However, whisper birds also find themselves on the other end of the food chain: They make their homes high in the Massassi trees in order to avoid predation by Yavin 4's stintaril rodents.

Whisper birds communicate with one another using a series of low-pitched calls. They have a thick coat of golden-hued feathers, and they travel in flocks of multigenerational family groups.

The famous cartographer Auric Graf named his ship the *Whisper Bird* because it looked just like the creature. Our ship bears a resemblance to the shyyyo bird, but we didn't want to call it that, so we named it after our favorite podracer, Gasgano.

— B8-T5

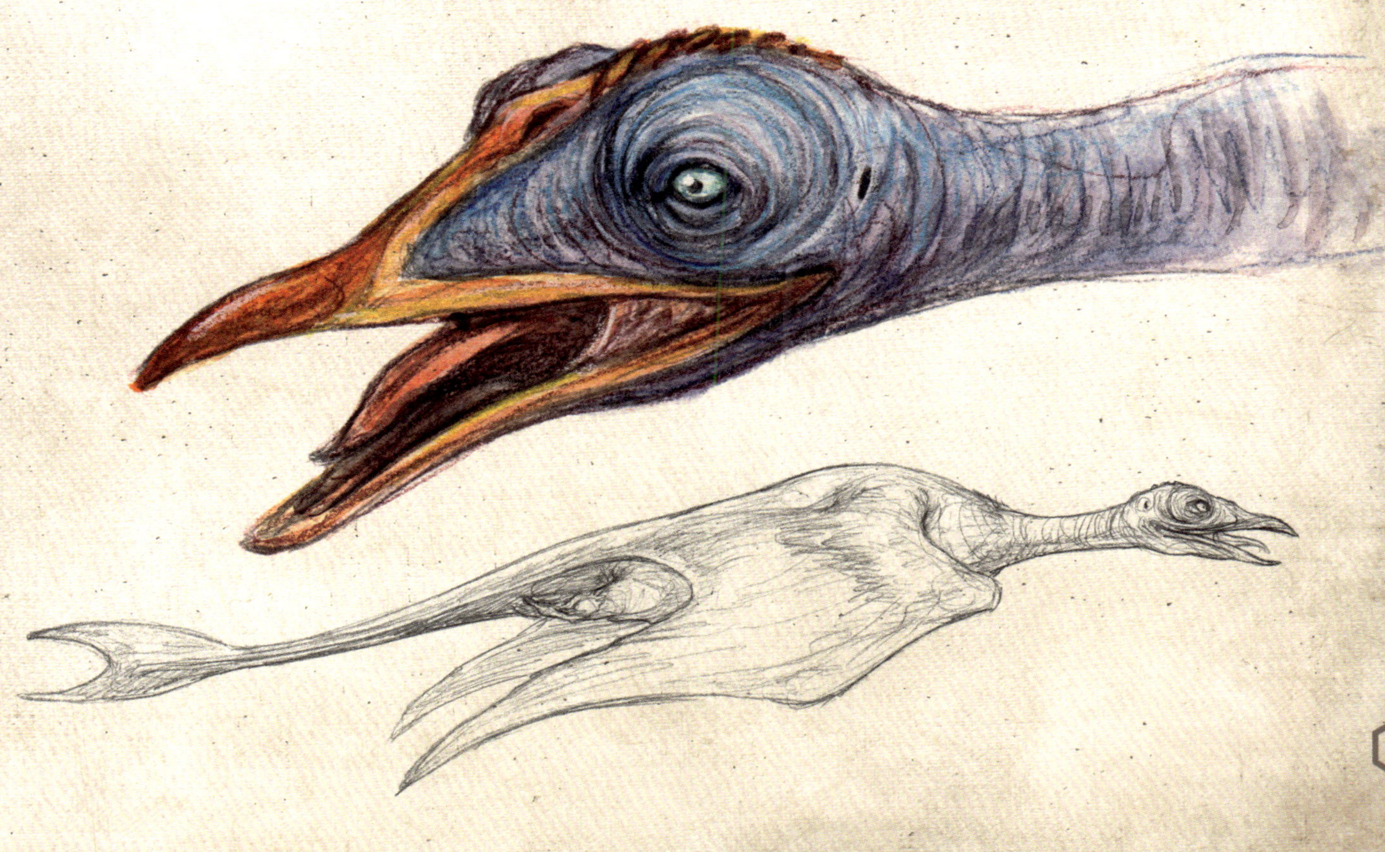

SPACE CREATURES

EXOGORTH (SPACE SLUG)

The enormous exogorths make their homes in the hollows of asteroids. Because of their considerable size, these creatures remain mostly dormant. To feed, they hold their jaws open atop an asteroid's cratered surface and remain perfectly still, in hopes of trapping unsuspecting prey. If a surface-traveling meal does not present itself, exogorths will push through the asteroid, launching themselves high in the air in order to capture their victims. After such a surge, these space slugs will grow sluggish and remain unable to exert themselves for a substantial time period.

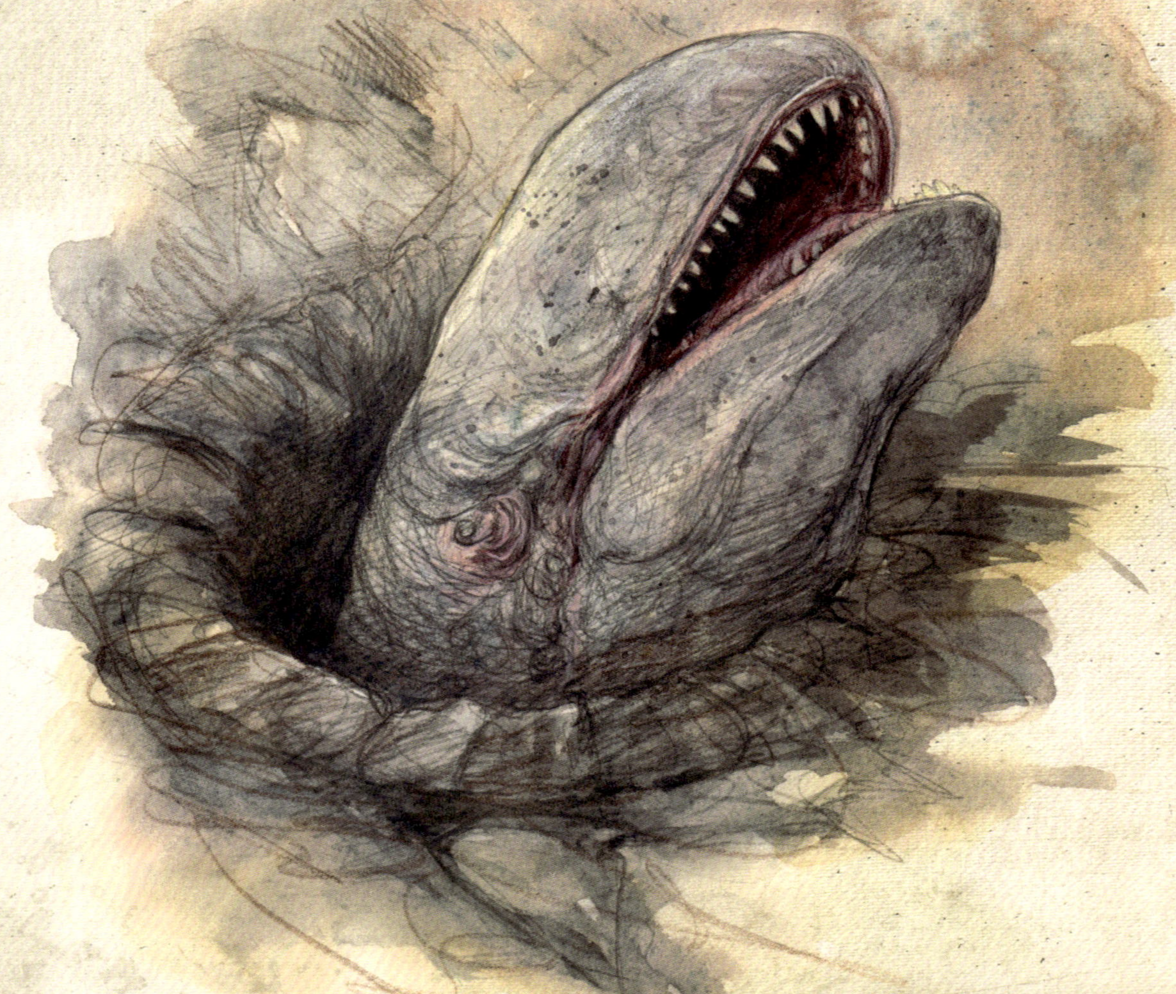

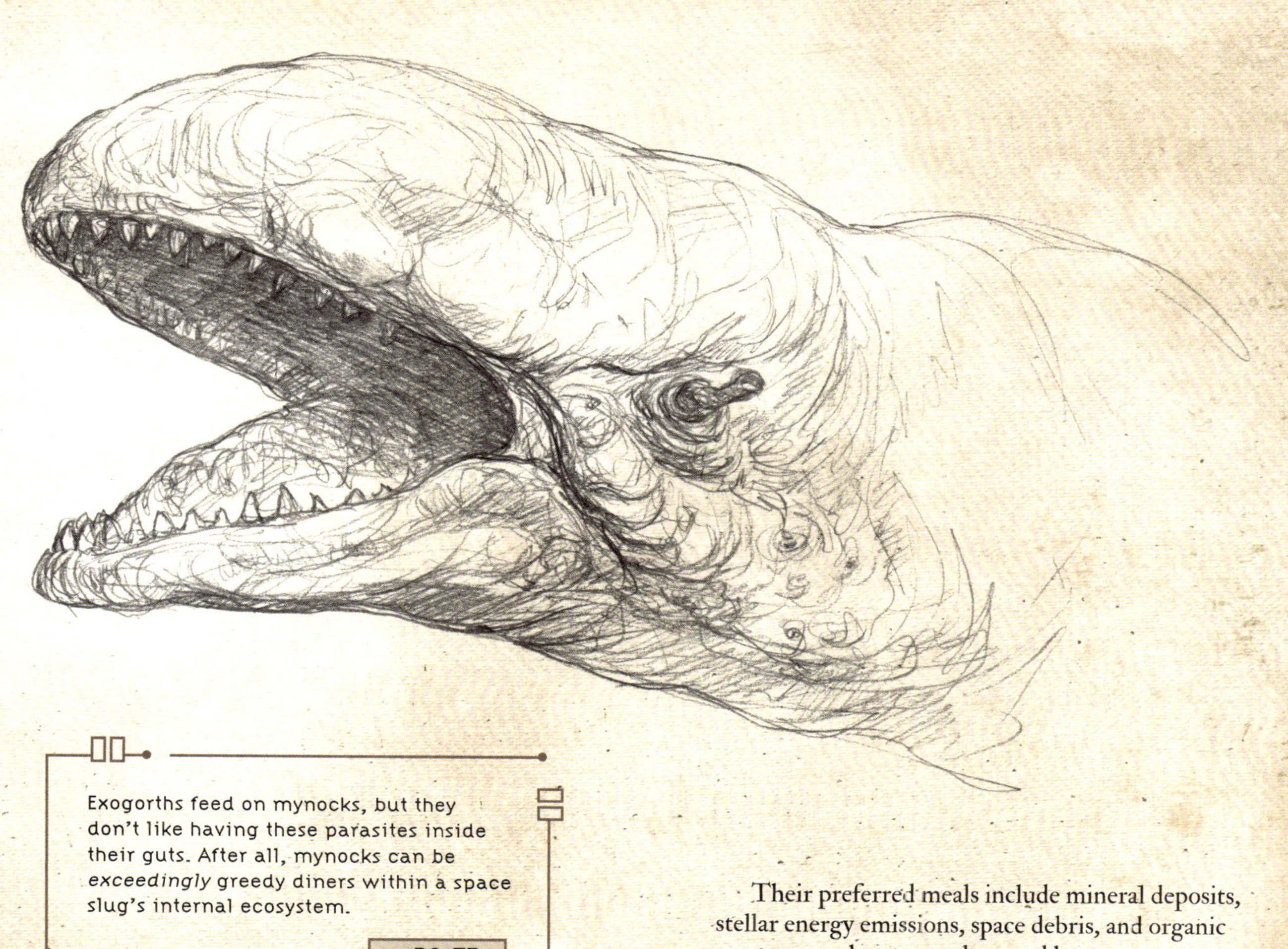

Exogorths feed on mynocks, but they don't like having these parasites inside their guts. After all, mynocks can be *exceedingly* greedy diners within a space slug's internal ecosystem.

—B8-T5

Their preferred meals include mineral deposits, stellar energy emissions, space debris, and organic creatures such as mynocks—and humans.

Exogorths can live for more than a billion years. They reach maturity when they grow ten meters long, at which point they usually split themselves into two separate bodies. If this reproduction fails to occur, the space slug will continue to grow until it reaches the enormous size of nine hundred meters. Slugs of this size have been known to consume entire starships!

The creatures have red-and-gray skin, forty-five silvery teeth, and green saliva. They take pride in providing stable ecosystems to the multitude of species that can dwell within their bodies. Specimens that host a more varied internal ecology are held in high esteem among their peers, whereas exogorths that host only a handful of lifeforms are looked down upon. For this reason, starships are among an exogorth's most treasured meals: Such a bounty allows the creature to increase the diversity of its internal ecology by adding the abundance of species that happen to occupy the consumed vessel.

MYNOCK

Ord Mynock's parasitic natives are a silicon-based breed of airborne creatures. Loosely related to tibidees and grallocs, they have three-fingered leathery wings and long, narrow tails that enable them to travel great distances. Some members of the species leave their homeworld and journey to nearby asteroids and planetoids. Mynocks have a wingspan of up to two meters and can weigh up to eight kilograms. They have the ability to thrive in multiple environments, including within planetary atmospheres and also within vacuums. This makes the mynock one of the rare creatures that can live on planets or moons *and* in space. One particular flock even lived inside the stomach of an exogorth!

Mynocks feed off energy, using wide, suckerlike mouths and sharp teeth to chew the power cables of starships and other energetic sources. This action causes significant damage and often renders ships unflyable. Mynocks also feed off their host creatures and consume residual sustenance from their host bodies. Much like the Endorian chickens, they are prone to overfeeding. When they consume more than their fill, they enter an inebriated state known as spark dunk.

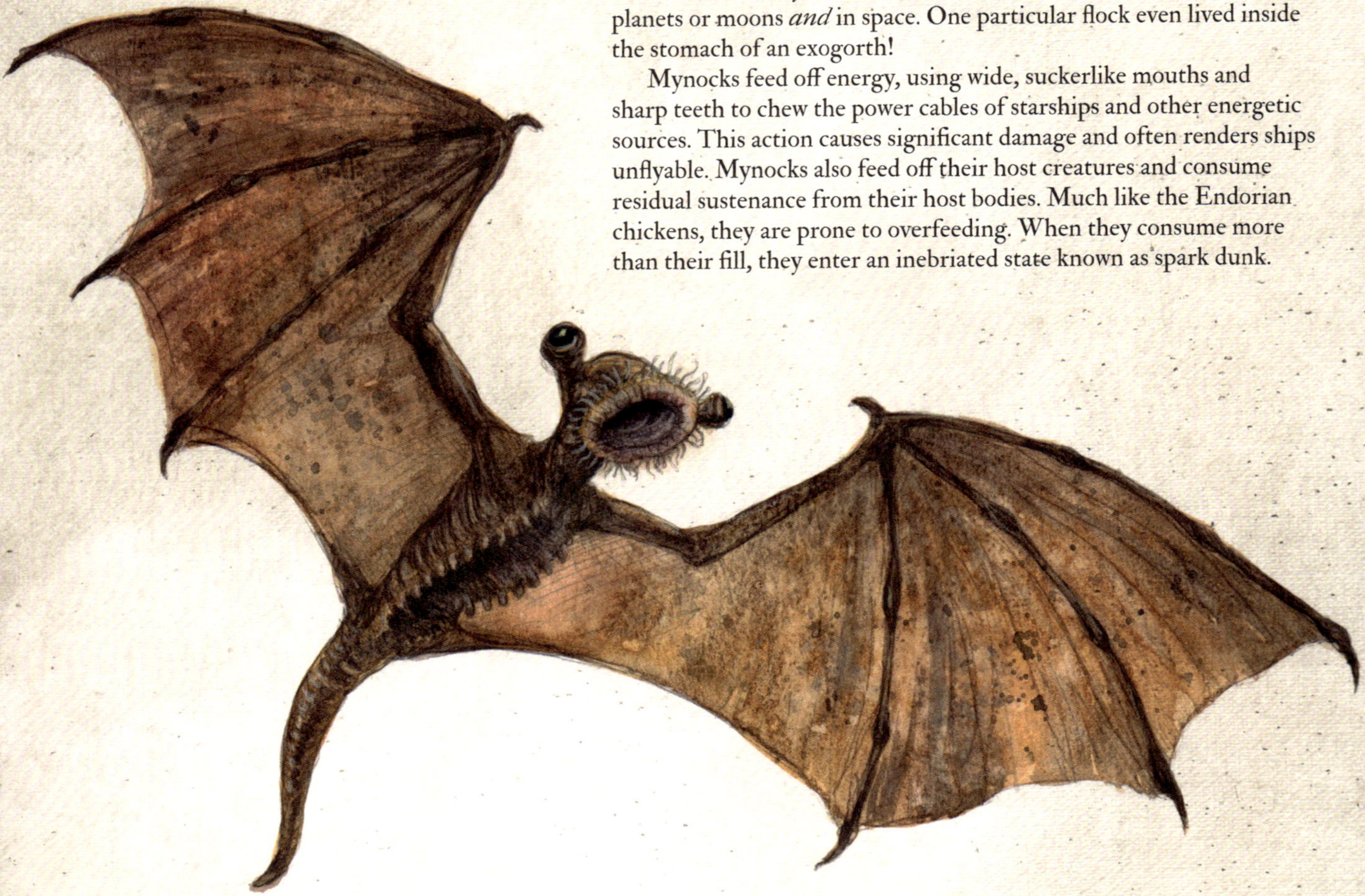

Mynocks have a unique reproductive process. Instead of giving birth or laying eggs, they split themselves in two and regenerate, growing comprehensive creatures from each fractured half. They are hunted by sentients, who consider their meat to be a delicacy. Mynock roasts are a popular form of entertainment on planets such as Ardennia, and Twi'leks craft spice-based dishes such as Mynock Cloud City and Mynock Coronet City. Across the galaxy, cantina proprietors use pickled mynock as a flavorful addition to their beverages. This scientist enjoyed one such libation at Oga's Cantina on Batuu!

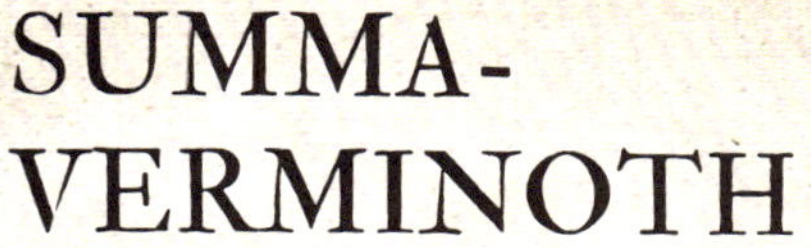

SUMMA-VERMINOTH

Considered by some to be the galaxy's greatest predator, the summa-verminoth is certainly one of the grandest! The beasts measure up to 7,432 meters long and can weigh up to 2,000 kilograms. This massive space dweller makes its primary home in Kessel's Akkadese Maelstrom, although specimens have also been found around the Si'Klaata Cluster.

Summa-verminoth have gray skin and multiple glowing blue eyes that they use to scout potential food sources. Once they spot food, the creatures rely on an intimidating series of suckers and electrically charged tentacles and stingers to capture their prey. They feed frequently, readily consuming any matter they come across—although they prefer organic beings to minerals or starships.

A subspecies of summa-verminoth lives within the Red Honeycomb Zone, a passage through the Galactic Barrier that leads to unknown regions. This specimen has black skin and one enormous yellow eye. When threatened, it executes a psychic attack on its assailant. Accordingly, it is highly inadvisable to approach *any* species of summa-verminoth.

PURRGIL

The elegant space whales are among the species I have most hoped to encounter on my travels. As a child, I would watch for them as I ventured across the galaxy. Once one kept pace with my family's hyperspace lane, and I have searched for another ever since. Running into a new specimen en route to the Outer Rim was among my favorite moments as a creature cartographer—and one I took tremendous joy in documenting.

Purrgil measure 5.5 meters high and up to 30 meters long, with some growing substantially larger. They have four long tentacles, along with two pectoral fins and solitary dorsal, anal, *and* ventral fins—all of which stabilize the species during high-speed travel. They make their home in deep space, traveling the galaxy in immense groups. Purrgil have two blue eyes positioned on either side of their heads, egg-shaped teeth, and two long organs that dangle beneath their mouths. Purrgil pods (which are also referred to as flocks or swarms) are led by a large male member known as the Purrgil King. When threatened, the creatures emit a sorrowful cry.

These enormous airborne creatures are unique in their ability to create simu-tunnels, the hyperspace channels through which they cross the galaxy at great speeds. To create these tunnels, a purrgil must first ingest a substantial amount of their food source, Clouzon-36, a green gas that allows the creature to breathe. The substance also provides the purrgil with its purple-and-yellow coloring; specimens deficient in Clouzon-36 turn a grayish-brown. Purrgil that consume an abundance of the gas metabolize the substance into hypermatter fuel. When this occurs, the creatures' tentacles glow, their bodies vibrate, and they make the jump to hyperspace. They then travel through a simu-tunnel in pods that can number in the dozens, with entire family groups migrating together between star systems.

Purrgil have played a substantial role in a series of scientific and Force-specific discoveries. Study of the creature's simu-tunnels led scientists to seek out means to pursue sentient hyperspace travel, ultimately bringing about the development of coaxium fuel for this very purpose. Further research into the purrgil's migration patterns and use of Clouzon-36 then led to the discovery of coaxium reservoirs throughout the galaxy. Examination of a deceased purrgil's brain and carcass also led both Jedi and Sith to develop wayfinders, a navigational tool that enabled Force wielders to make their way across the stars.

These behemoths register their surroundings using their eyes and echolocation, similar to Loth-bats. Purrgil are playful creatures—if you toss a space rock to them, they'll swat it back at you with their tentacles.

— B8-T5

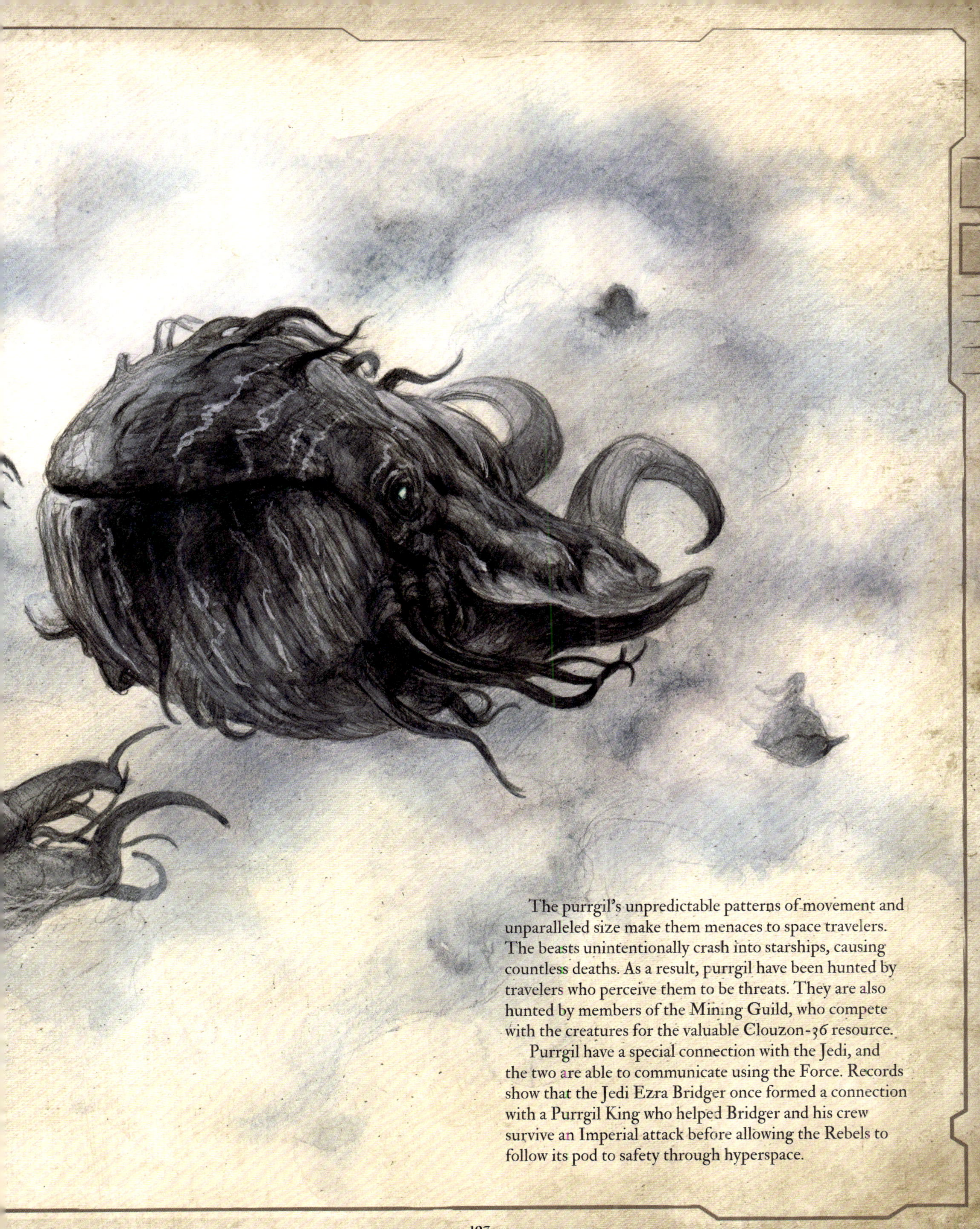

The purrgil's unpredictable patterns of movement and unparalleled size make them menaces to space travelers. The beasts unintentionally crash into starships, causing countless deaths. As a result, purrgil have been hunted by travelers who perceive them to be threats. They are also hunted by members of the Mining Guild, who compete with the creatures for the valuable Clouzon-36 resource.

Purrgil have a special connection with the Jedi, and the two are able to communicate using the Force. Records show that the Jedi Ezra Bridger once formed a connection with a Purrgil King who helped Bridger and his crew survive an Imperial attack before allowing the Rebels to follow its pod to safety through hyperspace.

CONCLUSION

Over the years, I have studied a great many species. From the tiniest beetle to the enormous purrgil, each of these creatures has left a bantha-sized imprint on my heart, my consciousness, and my awareness of the interconnected nature of all living things. Countless lessons can be learned from our natural world, and infinite paths to wisdom can be discovered by studying the magnificent beasts that dwell atop the land, swim within the waters, and soar through the air. To begin:

1. Adaptation is the key to survival. Migratory patterns continue to shift over time, with some creatures even altering their environment-of-origin. The technologically enhanced aiwhas are now able to claim both air and sea as their home. A handful of formerly land-dwelling creatures also left their dirt-packed abodes in search of more abundant resources, making a permanent migration to the seas—a fact confirmed by the existence of skeletal finger bones beneath these species' pectoral fins. Like these ever-evolving creatures, we, too, may find ourselves in a frequent state of adjustment. It is imperative that we adapt in a manner befitting the greatest good of the great multitude of species.

2. Nearly anything can be accomplished through hard work and collaboration. On their own, the tiny convor stands little chance of survival against an army of alarmingly aggressive predators. Yet the birds work in pairs to lift their attackers high into the sky before dropping the assailants to their death—a feat no solitary convor could accomplish on its own. Like these plucky avians, all species, sentient or otherwise, stand to benefit from the cumulative effects of teamwork. Through the amalgamation of pooled resources, strengths, and willpower, nothing is truly impossible.

3. To paraphrase an illustrious Jedi—one who was revered for his appreciation of the natural world—size truly matters not. The mighty sarlaccs rely on the tiny urusai to clean their teeth, an act that rids their bodies of bacteria before disease can take root while simultaneously providing a much-needed food source to creatures that would otherwise struggle to survive in the barren desert. Similar examples of symbiosis abound in the physical world and ought to be emulated by all who bear witness to them. Each of us has the ability to contribute something substantial, regardless of our physical strength, and, yes, our size.

My experiences as a creature cartographer have been among the most rewarding and most joyful of my life. I have been honored to witness firsthand the births of pikobis, the migration of banthas, and (twice now) the appearance of the illustrious purrgil. It is up to all of us to ensure that the creatures of the land, air, and sea can thrive so that future generations can appreciate the bounty of beasts that grace our galaxy. After all, isn't that what coexistence is truly about?

ACKNOWLEDGMENTS

S.T. BENDE

Treats galore to Snuggles, whose steady paw and encouraging chuffs bolstered me through *all the drafts*. You are the loveliest little lava meerkat a writer could hope for. Much gratitude to the Lucasfilm Animation team, for creating the airborne cetaceans that captured my heart in *Rebels*. (And brought back fond memories of my favorite flippered friends!) Warm hugs to Sammy Holland for her grace, patience, and infinite organization, and to the incomparable Iris Compiet, whose inspired visions of these amazing creatures literally bowled me over every time I opened a file. I am so grateful for your friendship, and so happy we got to create this world together! A hearty *hello there* to Chris Prince, who welcomed me into this menagerie, and to Emma Merwin who always goes above and beyond. *Tusen takk* to my grandma and to Mormorma, whose artistry and sense of adventure combined to create a Creature Cartographer. And as always, I *thank the maker* for my husband, and my boys - whose love, kindness, and special brand of pixie dust inspire me every day. (And whose craftiness inspired a certain sassy droid!) Truly, the Force is strong with you.

IRIS COMPIET

A big thanks to Chris Prince, Sammy Holland, and of course the wonderful S.T. Bende, the Force is definitely strong in each of you. I'd also like to acknowledge all the amazing artists who have been part of the Star Wars legacy, creating unforgettable creatures and characters that have had an impact on me as an artist. My husband and our own little Ewok, Hella for cheering me on and finally I'd like to say thank you to my father, who introduced me to Star Wars as a kid, he will forever be Yoda in my memories.

PO Box 3088
San Rafael, CA 94912
www.insighteditions.com

Find us on Facebook: www.facebook.com/InsightEditions
Follow us on Instagram: @insighteditions

ISBN: 979-8-88663-098-5

Publisher: Raoul Goff
SVP, Group Publisher: Vanessa Lopez
VP, Creative: Chrissy Kwasnik
VP, Manufacturing: Alix Nicholaeff
Editorial Director: Lia Brown
Art Director: Matt Girard
Designer: Leah Bloise Lauer
Senior Editor: Samantha Holland
Assistant Editor: Emma Merwin
Executive Project Editor: Maria Spano
Senior Production Editor: Katie Rokakis
Senior Production Managers: Joshua Smith and Greg Steffen
Senior Production Manager, Subsidiary Rights: Lina s Palma-Temena

Illustrations by Iris Compiet

FOR LUCASFILM
Senior Editor: Brett Rector
Editor: Jennifer Pooley
Creative Director: Michael Siglain
Art Director: Troy Alders
Story Group: Leland Chee, Kate Izquierdo, Matt Martin, Emily Shkoukani, Kelsey Sharpee
Creative Art Manager: Phil Szostak
Lucasfilm Asset Management: Shahana Alam, Chris Argyropoulos, Elinor De La Torre, Gabrielle Levenson, Micaela McCauley, Michael Trobiani, and Sarah Williams

REPLANTED PAPER

Insight Editions, in association with Roots of Peace, will plant two trees for each tree used in the manufacturing of this book. Roots of Peace is an internationally renowned humanitarian organization dedicated to eradicating land mines worldwide and converting war-torn lands into productive farms and wildlife habitats. Roots of Peace will plant two million fruit and nut trees in Afghanistan and provide farmers there with the skills and support necessary for sustainable land use.

Manufactured in China

10 9 8 7 6 5 4 3

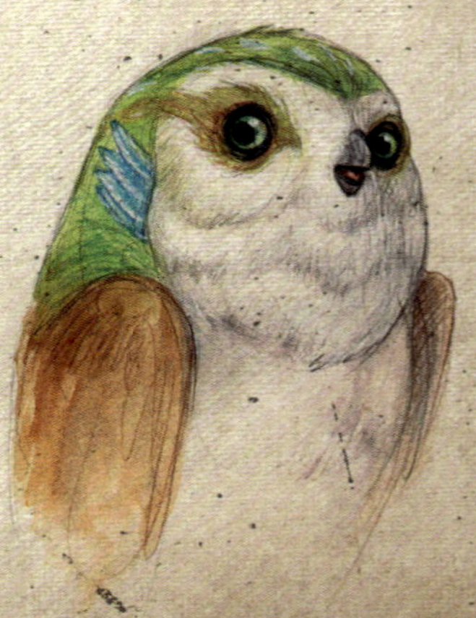

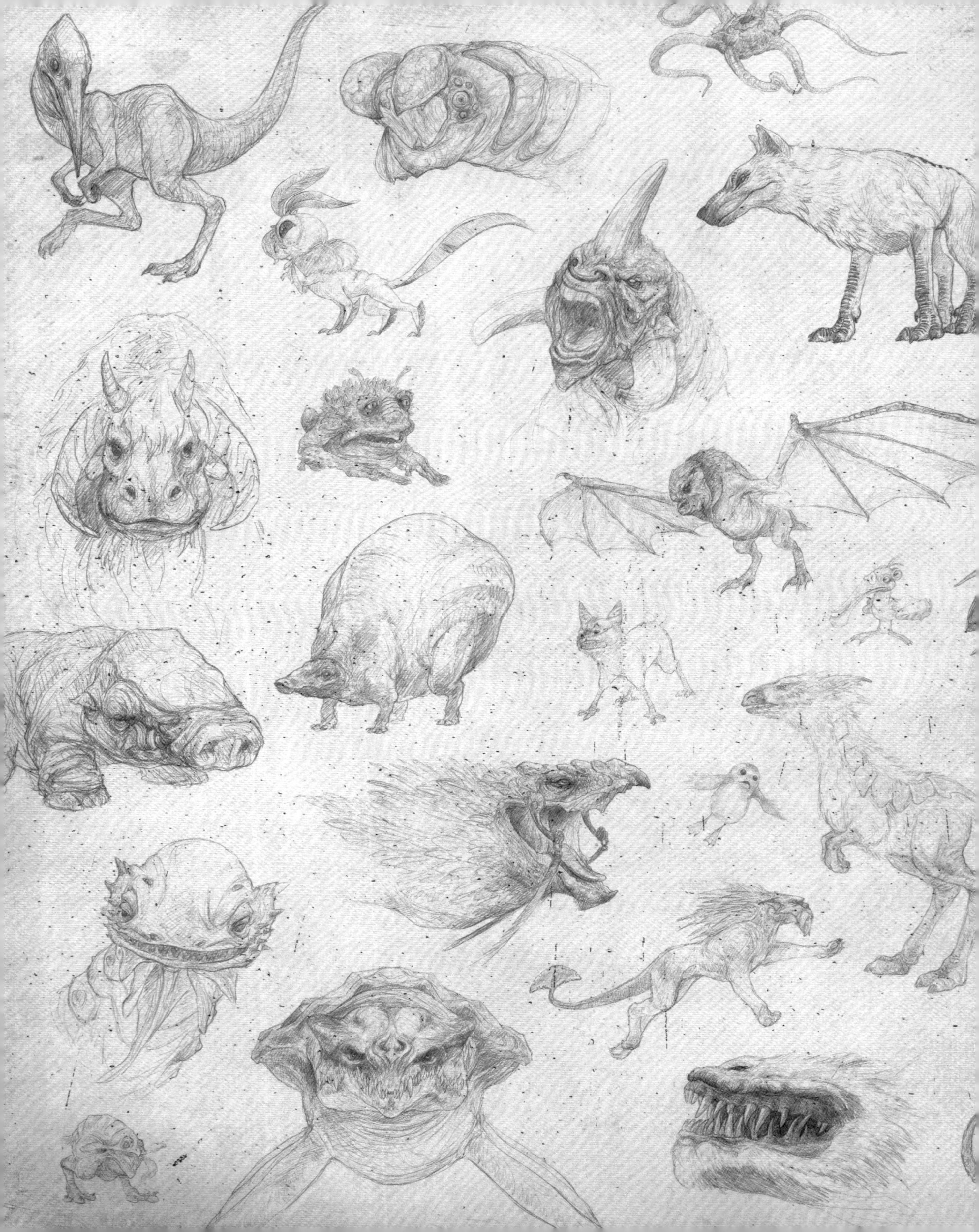